George Dickson, Graeme Mercer Adam

A History of Upper Canada College

1829-1892

George Dickson, Graeme Mercer Adam

A History of Upper Canada College
1829-1892

ISBN/EAN: 9783337187545

Printed in Europe, USA, Canada, Australia, Japan

Cover: Foto ©ninafisch / pixelio.de

More available books at **www.hansebooks.com**

THE NEW COLLEGE, DEER PARK.

A HISTORY

OF

UPPER CANADA COLLEGE,

1829 — 1892.

WITH CONTRIBUTIONS BY

Old Upper Canada College Boys,

LISTS OF HEAD-BOYS, EXHIBITIONERS, UNIVERSITY
SCHOLARS AND MEDALLISTS, AND A
ROLL OF THE SCHOOL.

COMPILED AND EDITED BY

GEORGE DICKSON, M.A.,

AND

G. MERCER ADAM.

ILLUSTRATED.

TORONTO:
ROWSELL & HUTCHISON.

1893.

ENTERED according to the Act of Parliament of Canada, in the year of our Lord one thousand eight hundred and ninety-three, by MR. GEORGE DICKSON, in the Office of the Minister of Agriculture.

ROWSELL AND HUTCHISON, PRINTERS, TORONTO.

PREFACE.

A HISTORY of Upper Canada College needs no introduction to the class to whom this book especially appeals, except for the opportunity it offers of thanking many of them for the kind assistance the editors have received in its preparation.

The object has been to produce a history of the College, written for the most part by Old College Boys themselves. Among those, besides the Editors, who have contributed to the volume or furnished materials for it, are:

The REV. HENRY SCADDING, D.D., who entered the College in 1829; HON. JOHN BEVERLEY ROBINSON, 1830; WILLIAM WALLBRIDGE, SR., 1833; WILLIAM WEDD, M.A., 1837; W. THOMSON, ESQ., 1837; C. J. RYKERT, Q.C., 1846; N. O. WALKER, M.A., M.D., 1847; J. ROSS ROBERTSON, ESQ., 1850; RUPERT E. KINGSFORD, M.A., LL.B., 1859; REV. T. F. FOTHERINGHAM, M.A., 1863; D. R. KEYS, M.A., 1868; W. N. PONTON, M.A., 1870; G. G. S. LINDSEY, M.A., 1871; REV. J. STREET MACKLEM, M.A., 1874; A. H. YOUNG, M.A., 1878; A. A. MACDONALD, M.A., 1879; S. B. LEACOCK, B.A., 1881; J. E. HALL, Secretary of the Canadian Cricket Association.

The chapters are classified, and the story told under the régimes of the Head Masters, beginning with that of the Rev. Joseph Harris, D.D., the first to hold the position.

It is impossible within reasonable limits to be at the same time comprehensive and exhaustive. It has not been the aim to make the work biographical. The lives of Old College Boys, however prominent, have not been dwelt on save in so far as was necessary to illustrate their connection with the College.

Lists of Head-Boys, Exhibitioners, University Scholars and Medallists, together with the Roll of the School from 1829 to 1892, and the Cricket teams during the same period are appended. The histories of the College organizations, such as the Cricket Club, Rifle Company, etc., are written by those who had taken an active part as members of these school institutions. Reminiscent chapters also deal with life at the Boarding House, and the several Janitors of the College, with an account of College Journalism, and other early and late features of school life, and its scholastic and recreative annals.

A list with its columns of even bare names is full of pleasant memories. Conning such, one may recall a more or less distinct vision of every one in his own part of the school, his appearance, character, and nick-name. But the chief interest, perhaps, is to be found in the fact that the names that occur, more especially in the early part of the roll, may be recognized as those belonging to the families who have taken an active part in the public affairs of the Province and the Dominion. "How peculiarly Upper Canada College," aptly observes one of its masters, "has fulfilled this function of the training of leaders for public life may be realized by a glance at a few of the names of her alumni. They abound in every sphere of life. In the army we have the names of General Charles Robinson, commander of the forces in the Mauritius; General Samuel Jarvis; General Sir Francis Colborne; General Ingall, of Chester; Colonels Dunn and Wells, who charged with the Six Hundred at Balaclava; Lieut. Maule, who also distinguished himself in the Crimea, and was killed there; Col. McLeod; Lieut.-Col. Williams; Messrs. Mewburn, Tempest, and many others who fought for Canada within her own borders; Col. Fred. C. Denison, C.M.G., M.P., who commanded the Canadian contingent in Africa; Col. G. T. Denison, who won, against the military experts of the world, the Czar's great prize for the best history of Cavalry Tactics; and many others. Prominent among those who have entered the world of politics is the Hon. Edward Blake, member of the Imperial Parliament; and in the present Dominion House of Commons there are seven old college boys; in the Senate there are three, while in the Provincial Legislatures the school is proportionately represented. In the legal profession the college claims six chief justices and fourteen other judges, over fifty Q. C.'s, and more than one hundred barristers and attorneys now in practice. In the academic world it can point to over thirty former pupils holding professorial chairs and lectureships, while the President of Toronto

University is a former head-boy. The President and two ex-Presidents of the Ontario Medical Council, the Surgeon-General of the Militia of Canada, Dr. Bergen, the Secretary of the Provincial Board of Health, and others, all received their education at the college, and show by their standing that, in this sphere, too, the old college boy holds his own. With such a record to look back upon, Upper Canada College can surely claim, with justice, to be an institution for the training of leaders."

The memory of the early pioneers of the higher education amongst us is in danger of being wholly lost, and it is most desirable that the mass of interesting information to be obtained from the lips of living witnesses should be preserved. Impressed by this idea, the Editors have striven to glean what they could for the literary enrichment of the volume. For its pictorial enrichment, they are indebted to the skill and taste of Mr. W. J. Thomson, late of *The Globe* art staff, artist and engraver, who has been happy in reproducing and preserving many of the familiar faces and haunts of the College.

The assistance received from Old College Boys in the preparation of this—the first History of the College—has been most helpful, and without which many errors and omissions would have to be recorded. Notwithstanding this aid, it is feared, however, that not a few such will still be found in the following pages.

THE PRINCIPAL'S LIBRARY, NEW COLLEGE.

TABLE OF CONTENTS.

		PAGE
I.	INTRODUCTORY .... *The Editors*	9
II.	THE COLLEGE AND THE ERA OF 1830............................. *The Editors*	12
III.	THE FIRST MASTERS............................. *Rev. Henry Scadding, D.D.*	23
IV.	THE COLLEGE AND ITS ENDOWMENT .... *R. E. Kingsford, M.A., LL.B.*	44
V.	THE RÉGIME OF REV. JOSEPH H. HARRIS, D.D., 1829-38........... *The Editors*	50
VI.	THE COLLEGE AND THE REBELLION OF 1837 .... *W. Thomson*	66
VII.	THE RÉGIME OF REV. JOHN MCCAUL, LL.D., 1839-43..... *William Wedd, M.A.*	76
VIII.	THE RÉGIME OF F. W. BARRON, M.A., 1843-56 .... *N. O. Walker, M.A., M.D.*	87
IX.	THE RÉGIME OF REV. WALTER STENNETT, M.A., 1857-61 .... *"Head-Boy"*	97
X.	THE COLLEGE RIFLE COMPANY.................. *Rev. T. F. Fotheringham, M.A.*	103
XI.	THE RÉGIME OF G. R. R. COCKBURN, M.A., 1861-81 .... *D. R. Keys, M.A.*	113
XII.	"THROUGH UPPER CANADA COLLEGE"............................ *(Contributed)*	127
XIII.	RÉGIME OF JOHN MILNE BUCHAN, M.A., 1881-85............ *A. H. Young, M.A.*	136
XIV.	A TRANSITION PERIOD.. *G. Mercer Adam*	156
XV.	THE OLD BLUE SCHOOL .... *J. Ross Robertson*	177
XVI.	THE JANITORS OF THE COLLEGE .... *J. Ross Robertson*	200
XVII.	LIFE AT THE BOARDING HOUSE........................ *J. Ross Robertson*	218
XVIII.	COLLEGE JOURNALISM.................................. *"An Old College Boy"*	232
XIX.	COLLEGE CRICKET .... *G. G. S. Lindsey*	263
XX.	OTHER COLLEGE SPORTS .... *A. A. Macdonald*	271
XXI.	CRICKET CLUB—"THE ELEVENS," 1836-92........................ *J. E. Hall*	275
XXII.	APPENDIX I.—HONOUR BOARDS	279
XXIII.	APPENDIX II.—LIST OF EXHIBITIONERS, 1853-91.............................	290
XXIV.	APPENDIX III.—ROLL, 1829-1892	295
XXV.	APPENDIX IV.—ON THE AFFAIRS OF THE COLLEGE, 1852	326

ILLUSTRATIONS.

	PAGE
1. The New College, Deer Park	Frontispiece
2. The Principal's Library, New College	6
3. Field-Marshal, Lord Seaton (Sir John Colborne)	9
4. The Three Eras of the College	12
5. Five Members of the College Board at different periods	17
6. The Seven Principals	24
7. Six of the College Masters	32
8. Upper Canada College in 1829, from a sketch by J. G. Howard	40
9. The Countess of Elgin and Lady Lambton receiving Bouquets and the Crest of the College, October 20th, 1847, copied from an old engraving	57
10. Dinner at the College on the occasion of Laying the Corner Stone of Old King's College, Queen's Park	73
11. Upper Canada College, 1877-1891	89
12. The Public Hall, 1877-1891	97
13. The Old Prayer Hall, 1829-1877	113
14. Upper Canada College—View from Adelaide Street	128
15. The Three Janitors—the two Alderdices and Frost	144
16. Monuments erected to the memory of the late Principal Buchan and to the Alderdices	160
17. The Old Blue School, and the College Clock (the time-keeper for over sixty years)	177
18. The New Public Hall, taken May, 1891	192
19. Principal's House, Janitor's Cottage, and old Draw Well	209
20. The Quadrangle, Old Belfry, and Belfry Ladder	225
21. Upper Hall-way, the Long Study, etc.	240
22. The Gymnasium, as renovated in 1888, and the Play Ground, viewed from the fence on John Street	256
23. The Principal's Private Room, Old College	273
24. The School Study and Old Dining Hall	288
25. Views of the Old College from the Quadrangle and from "No. 2"	304
26. Entrance Hall, Principal's House, and Principal's Garden	320
27. View of the Old College from Government House, King Street, and the Old College Bell	324

FIELD-MARSHAL, LORD SEATON (SIR JOHN COLBORNE).

Upper Canada College Memorial Volume.

INTRODUCTORY.

UPPER CANADA COLLEGE, it will readily be admitted, occupies a unique place among the educational institutions of Ontario. Within its walls have been educated the flower of Canadian youth, and for the long period of sixty years it has been associated with all that is best in the professional, industrial, and social life of the Province. From Upper Canada College has gone forth the young life of the country that has found occupation either in the ranks of those who have been engaged in the task of building up our young Canadian nation, or have been privileged to take part in the illustrious service of the Motherland, in the wider and grander interests of the Empire. To both these classes the history and traditions of Upper Canada College are presumably dear. Dear also, it is thought, to the same minds must be the records of the Institution, with its proud tale of academic successes, and all the fortune, with not a little of vicissitude, that have followed it since its foundation by the gallant soldier-Governor in what may be termed the medieval era of the Province. Not without interest, either, must be the mere annals of administration and the personal incidents in the lives of those who, either as Head Masters or Assistant Masters, have successively taught in the Institution, and have been more or less instrumental in fashioning the young life that has passed from it into the world.

With these and other matters of general and special interest connected with Upper Canada College, in the sixty years of its work, during the formative period of the country's history, it is proposed in the following pages to deal. In setting out on their task, the Editors are encouraged in the belief that no meagre amount of interest must centre in the records of an educational institution which can claim, comparatively speaking, so ancient and honourable a descent as can Upper

Canada College, and whose history is closely identified with the early manhood of many of the best and most distinguished of Canadians. It is true that the College, in an Old World sense, can boast of no great antiquity. Compared with the great Public Schools of England, many of whose endowments date back to the reigns of Edward VI. and Elizabeth, Upper Canada College is but an infant of days. Yet, as age goes in the New World, it has a venerable, we might almost say, a hoary, past; and were we to boast of its ancient flogging *régime*—for flogging as an educational corrective of youthful idleness or indiscretion was still in its undimmed glory when the College was founded—it is old enough to say that but few of its early pupils are now alive who within its walls first felt the smart of the rod. But this, doubtless, is a painful subject to raise in the memory of old College boys, and with due apologies to old as well as modern sensitiveness, we shall make haste to leave it. All we meant by the reference was to illustrate, in some faint but graphic manner, the comparative antiquity of Upper Canada College; and the flogging reminds one that, not only has this so-called device of incompetent rulers now largely passed away, but that the beginnings of the College are antecedent to the beginnings of some notable schools in England which have come into existence in the post-flogging era. Upper Canada College, for instance, is older than Marlborough College, in England, of whose pupils it is said, that it is as difficult to meet with a flogged Marlburian as, according to tradition, it is difficult to find an unflogged Etonian. The rarity of the latter may well be proverbial, for history narrates that during a mutinous period in the annals of Eton, a headmaster, single-handed, flogged eighty boys in one night! It is proper to say to the readers of this volume that its Editors have no such delirious incident here to recount. Still less is it theirs to boast, that of the seven thousand pupils who in the sixty years of its existence have passed from the Institution, a larger proportion than the average has had an exceptionally brilliant career. In the case of Upper Canada College, the average, however, has been high. We may not be able, for example, with veracious chroniclers of Westminster School, to boast, that a headmaster could once number among his pupils sixteen bishops on the bench, or that out of eight field-marshals in the British army, five had been educated during his *régime* at school. This is a record that, admittedly, it would be difficult to beat. But if its Canadian counterpart cannot approach this position of full-orbed glory, it may shine with a lustre of its own,—with the reflected light of Old World scholarship, and the aid of such local suns as have given it vitality, and gilded it with the glow of the west. Upper Canada College can at least assert for itself this position—that it has been the fruitful mother of such talent as a great lusty Province can claim as the source and stimulus of half-a-century's prosperity and honour. Much indeed of what the Dominion of Canada is to-day is due to the educational status of the College and the intellectual labour of her sons. In the mental outfit of life in the New World much is required, and that in a brief space of time, for the tasks that lie before the toiling brain and the brawny arm of man. That outfit the College has efficiently and generously given, and as generously, and with loyal enthusiasm, has the gift been owned.

Of various events in the early annals of the College, and of whatever is deemed interesting in its internal history, we propose here to speak briefly, then to make way for those who shall deal with the successive periods in its after-career. In recounting its history, the Editors must obviously rely on the indulgence of those readers especially who have themselves been actors on the scene. The materials for anything like a detailed chronological history can hardly be said to exist. Not many of the first pupils of the College now survive, or can readily be got at in taking down the story from living lips. Nor, where early pupils have been found, is memory always responsive. Much, therefore, of interest has been lost, or, from other and unavoidable causes, could not be gathered. Such as the story is, however, those who are responsible for the following pages diffidently submit it. As was originally announced, the work will primarily appeal to those who retain their interest in the historic institution in which they received their early training, and who no doubt love to trace the roots of their lives back to old College days, enriched with the memories of friendships and academic associations which the volume may be expected pleasantly to revive. It will also appeal, it is hoped, however, to all who take an interest in education and feel a natural pride in the history of an institution which perhaps more than any other in the country has been instrumental, not only in training the mind and moulding the characters, but in sensibly influencing the manners, of generations of public men in Canada in almost every path of life.

From the task they have here undertaken the Editors would naturally have shrunk, had they not been kindly promised the ready assistance and encouragement of former and present Masters of the College, of members of the Board of Management, and of a number of active and zealous "Old Boys" and friends of the Institution. The extent of this aid has very materially lightened their task, and, as will be seen, has given increased interest to the book and added to it the charm of variety. The assistance the Editors have received in other ways need not here be detailed. Elsewhere the attempt has been made to acknowledge it. But they can hardly proceed without here confessing how valuable an incentive it has been in overcoming difficulties and in illuminating the path of their work.

THE COLLEGE AND THE ERA OF 1830.

BY THE EDITORS.

THE PUBLIC SCHOOL SYSTEM of Upper Canada (or, as we should now properly write, Ontario,) practically dates from the year 1844, when the Rev. Dr. Egerton Ryerson was appointed Chief Superintendent. Before that date, however, the Legislature had thoughtfully made provision for education, and the subject was one which from an early period had engaged the attention of an Educational Committee of the House of Assembly. But, strange as it may seem, the natural order was in Canada, as in England, reversed, and provision was first made by the Government for the higher, rather than for the commoner, educational wants of the people. It was University training and what we now term secondary, and not elementary, education that first enlisted the interest of the authorities. In 1797, when the Province was but a wilderness, over half-a-million acres of public land were set apart for the endowment of a University and four Royal Grammar Schools. This inversion of the order on which education in a colony might be expected to proceed was, under the circumstances of the country, probably attended by no great loss to the Province, though time somewhat modified the first proposals. A system of popular education, even if the subject had so early aroused attention, was not possible in sparse and isolated communities. Nor at that early period, when the public domain had little market value, was there much revenue to be looked for from the land appropriation of the Government. Years were to pass before education could benefit from such a provision of the Legislature; and when some income was reached there were Radicals even then to contest the purposes of the appropriation. From the first, there was a cry that the money should be devoted to elementary, and not to higher, education. It was the need of the many, and not of the few, that contended for the expenditure. Nor was Dissent silent when the denominational complexion of the Executive and its Board of Education impressed itself on the mind of the restive but powerless electorate. Much the same religious controversy was about to be fought out in the Motherland, and for a time to retard the dawn of education for the masses. In England, as yet, there was no State

provision for elementary education, though the National Church and other religious societies had done much for popular enlightenment. The ancient endowed schools were not adapted to meet the wants of the poor; and England had, as yet, nothing corresponding to the parish schools of Scotland—a boon which, as is well known, the latter kingdom owed to the Reformation. Already, however, the machinery of the National Society and the British and Foreign School Society was actively at work, though great tracts of the country were still in ignorance and unprovided with schools. At last, Government awoke to its duties and responsibilities, and in 1833 a Committee of Council on Education was appointed, and a grant of £20,000 a year, soon to be increased, was made from the Treasury. This new departure met from the outset with fierce opposition, for the Church of England was then hostile to State or secular education, disliked the idea of Government training schools, and could ill brook, though it had no reason to fear, Government inspection.

There is no need to follow the successive steps which led England to adopt and finally to develop a national system of education. Nor would it be fair, nor have we the least desire, to say a word in deprecation of the system or the organization of Church Schools. The voluntary system did yeoman service in its day, and the efforts of the Church of England clergy in behalf of education, before the intervention of the State, are beyond praise. Even Matthew Arnold, who cannot be accused of being over-favourable to the Church, has put himself on record on this subject. "In truth," he says, "if there is a class in English society whose record in regard to popular education is honourable, it is the clergy. Every inquiry has brought this out."

While England was yet groping its way in the endeavour to found a system of national education, Upper Canada, as we have seen, was not unmindful of the country's higher needs. At the opening of the century even private enterprise was active in behalf of education, for we find Classical Schools established and in operation at various centres in the as yet thinly-settled Province. Of these private schools, we learn that one was opened at Cataraqui (Kingston), by the Rev. Dr. Okill Stuart, in 1785; one in Newark (Niagara), by the Rev. Mr. Addison, in 1792; one at the same place, in 1794, by the Rev. Mr. Burns, and another in 1796, by Mr. Richard Cockrell; one at York (Toronto), in 1802, by Dr. Baldwin; and one at Cornwall, in 1804, by the Rev. Dr. Strachan, who afterwards took charge for a time of the School at York. In 1806, the Government itself, however, seriously took up the question of education. Acts were passed establishing eight Grammar Schools, one in each of the several districts into which

Upper Canada was then divided. Each headmaster was given annually £100. Ten years later, the Legislature made provision for elementary instruction. An Act was passed establishing Common Schools, and an appropriation of £6,000 was made for their maintenance. In 1822, a Board of Education was created for educational purposes, and for the management of the University and School lands which the Crown, twenty-five years previously, had set aside.

The Crown lands were now beginning, though as yet slowly, to yield a revenue. Those reserved for the purposes of education were not in all cases wisely chosen. The situation of some of them was so remote that for the uses of the trust not a little of the land had to be exchanged for other portions of the Crown Reserves. The original appropriation, in 1798, was 549,217 acres. Of this land grant, 190,573 acres were turned over to the General Board of Education; while it was further diminished by grants to facilitate settlement in the districts where the lands were situated. These grants amounted in all to 109,786 acres, and were conveyed to various individuals for the construction of roads and other objects. The lands held for the founding of a University, after these reductions were made, still amounted to 248,858 acres. Authority was given by the Home Government to make an exchange of the undesirable or unproductive lands for such of the Crown Reserves as were available for the purposes of the trust. After this was done, there yet remained of the original land grant for the endowment of a University, 225,944 acres. These 225,944 acres were formally made over, on the 28th of February, 1828, by the Legislature of Upper Canada to the University of King's College. In May of the previous year, Sir Peregrine Maitland, then Lieutenant-Governor of the Province, had granted the College a Charter. This instrument, however, did not escape criticism, for the Legislature was divided, first as to the desirability, just yet, of having a University; and secondly, if it was to go into operation, as to how far it should be under the control of the clergy and laity of the Anglican Church.

The Executive Council of the Province, if not the majority in the House of Assembly, were, it is hardly necessary to say, members of the dominant Church. Even at this early period, there was a decided want of harmony in both branches of the Legislature. The differences between them found ready expression on the subject of education. The popular cry was for primary schools, or, at the most, for a preparatory or "minor" College. The state of general education among the people was alleged to be deplorable. The whole colony at the time was said to be totally uneducated. The chairman of a Committee of the House on Education reported, in a memorial to the Lieutenant-Governor, that "the little instruction given to the children under the name of education has no influence over their morals—does nothing to open or expand their intellectual faculties, much less to direct them in their conduct through life. English reading, imperfectly taught ; something of writing, and the first five rules of arithmetic, which the teachers we employ are seldom able to explain, make up the meagre sum total of what the rising generation learn at our Common Schools." This picture, coming as it does from a minority in the House of Assembly, may be, and possibly was, exaggerated and overdrawn. But make what allowance we may on this score, there is little reason to doubt that elementary education in Upper Canada, about the year 1830, was not, whatever it afterwards became, a subject to boast of. At the time, the lower classes, it is to be feared, were greatly neglected, for education then was a mark of caste, and the fast-consolidating "Family Compact" were not anxious to see the rise of an educated and influential middle class. We may say this to-day without derogating from the honour due to its members, or being accused of holding revolutionary opinions.

Just then came upon the scene a new Lieutenant-Governor. In 1829, Sir John Colborne was appointed by the Home Government to administer the affairs of the Province. The ruling party in the country was still full of the idea of a University, and the sympathies of the Lieutenant-Governor himself was with higher education. One of the most strenuous and persistent advocates of an institution of superior learning was the Rev. Dr. John Strachan,—the first bishop to be appointed by the Crown in Upper Canada. Dr. Strachan had originally come to the colony under the promise of the Principalship of a Government College. With no doubt the best motives, he made repeated appeals on behalf of a Provincial University, and had already spent a number of years in the country in educating the sons of the governing families. His ambition was the training of opulence for the administrative offices and positions of public trust. As a member of the Executive Council, we naturally find him urging the claims of a seminary of higher learning. But the people and a large number of their representatives in the Legislature were unwilling to hasten the founding of a University. It was as yet, they thought, premature, and in advance of the wants of the country. If more was required in the way of higher education than the District Grammar Schools furnished, they were willing to sanction in Toronto a "minor" College. Sir John Colborne himself saw that this was all that at present was needed. The time would come, he assured himself, that King's College—as the proposed University had come to be called—would be required ; but the immediate want was for an institution that would be a stepping-stone and ultimate feeder to the University.

Sir John Colborne, though a military man, was not unfitted for initiating and carrying out the scheme which he had determined upon, namely, the founding and endowing of a College in the Provincial Capital on the lines of the great Public Schools in England. His immediate model seems to have been Elizabeth College, Guernsey. He had come to Canada directly from the field of his administration in the Channel Islands, and fresh from the task of re-founding and modernizing an old Elizabethan College in Guernsey, which had fallen into decay. As an old and gallant soldier, he was a man of action and full of resource. His experience in the Peninsular War, where he had his shoulder half shot away, and his right arm partly disabled at the storming of Ciudad Rodrigo, lent a fearlessness to his character, and taught him to brook no opposition. But though a man of much force of character, he was eminently just; and he had the special merit of being at once stern and conciliatory. No sooner had he arrived at his new post in Canada than a serious tax was placed upon his good nature. From the moment of his arrival at York (Toronto), he was beset with political grievances, and had dinned into his ears the story of the struggle for popular rights. Among the dissensions of the time was the educational imbroglio and the clamour for and against a native University. In his accession to office Sir John Colborne was in no hurry to commit himself prematurely to action. He took time to review the situation and carefully to study the wants of the young country. His decision was not to push too hastily the organization of King's College. It was a preparatory institution he saw that was wanted. Arriving at this conclusion, he placed himself in communication with the Home Government, and obtained permission to call into existence what has since been known as Upper Canada College.

In 1829, tenders for the erection of buildings for this now historic institution were called for, and the enterprise was immediately put under way. Almost concurrently two other notable buildings were proceeded with in York, viz., the Parliament Buildings, which, like those of the College, are now about to come into disuse; and the buildings long known as Lawyers' (now Osgoode) Hall, the home of the lately incorporated Law Society of Upper Canada. Pending the completion of the new buildings, in what was at the time known as Russell Square, the College opened the first page of its history in the Home District School, one of the original Royal Grammar Schools which was now, for a time at least, merged into Upper Canada College. These Grammar Schools, which had increased to eleven in 1830, were maintained by Government, aided by local fees. At this period their combined cost to the Province for maintenance was some $17,000 a year.

THE COLLEGE AND THE ERA OF 1830.

Not until 1839, was the principle acted upon of aiding the secondary schools by a municipal grant.

In January, 1831, the staff and pupils of Upper Canada College moved into the new buildings. In December of the same year, the Lieutenant-Governor, acting on the authority received from England, endowed the College with a land grant of 66,000 acres. The Legislature made some difficulty about this appropriation, evidently deeming it within its exclusive province to make over and settle on the College the sources of its maintenance. After sundry communications between the House and the Governor, and the reference of the matter to England, the Legislature, by an Act passed in 1833, finally concurred in the land appropriation, and ratified the College's incorporation and endowment.

Quite disturbing controversies have at various times arisen on the subject of Upper Canada College endowment. By some it was alleged that Block D., in the city of Toronto, in the school buildings on which the College first began its operations, was not part of the property conveyed to the College, but was despoiled from the District Grammar School, and hence part of the General Education Fund of the new Province. Others, again, put forward the more serious statement that the College endowment was diverted unfairly from the lands appropriated for the founding of Toronto University. So much credence had been given to this latter assertion that, at a recent session of the Ontario Legislature, the Upper Canada College endowment was confiscated, and, at the bidding of sectional prejudice, the Institution was deprived of its historic site, and is about to be removed out of the city, and put on a new financial basis. This is not the place here to discuss this act of spoliation (it will be dealt with at a later stage); but the Editors may be permitted to call the reader's attention to the chapter on the College Endowment, contributed by Mr. R. E. Kingsford, M.A., in which erroneous views of the endowment are clearly and effectively combated, and the rights of the College to its lands are maintained. Hardly a greater service could be done by an *alumnus* of the College than has been rendered by Mr. Kingsford, in setting forth, in clear legal fashion, the successive incidents in the founding and endowing of his traduced but now vindicated *Alma Mater*.

Before leaving this subject for the present, there are one or two points which Mr. Kingsford's carefully-prepared paper brings out, in valid defence of the position all along assumed by well-informed friends of the College. They are these. That Sir John Colborne, in founding Upper Canada College, was not carrying out despotically a mere fad of his own. He took the step in concert with his constitutional advisers, the Executive Council of the Province; after consultation and in harmony with the views of the Home Government; and at the express instigation, and with the approval and indorsement, of the Legislative Assembly. Equally emphatic must be our judgment, and that of the reader, on the question of land usurpation. The College was founded and endowed on its own lands, and on its own lands, until recently despoiled of them, has it subsisted and been maintained. It robbed the University of no lands, and trenched in no way on those set apart for the Provincial Grammar Schools. Only malice or reckless misrepresentation could cloud or distort these facts. The facts were brought forward, in 1869, by Principal Cockburn in his "Statement" on the affairs of the College to a Committee of the Legislature on Education. They were advanced during the discussion in the Ontario Legislature, when the fate of the College hung in the balance, and the Executive and the House committed themselves to the new order of things. They are now repeated and embodied in this volume, as matters of history, and in justification of the views held and acted upon by many friends and well-wishers of the College. In a memorable message of Sir John Colborne to the House of Assembly, in 1830, he made use of these words: "Before I leave the Province, I shall endeavour to procure for the institution (Upper Canada College) such protection as may enable it to counteract the influence of local jealousies, or of the ignorance, or vice, to which in a new country it may sometimes be naturally exposed." The Lieutenant-Governor's designs were honourable and were carried out in good faith. Unfortunately, he did not foresee a time, "sixty years' afterwards," when the sinister influences he speaks of, instead of vanishing in the clear sunshine of a better day, were still active enough to set historic association, patriotism, and even material interest aside, and allow a blow to be dealt at Education and the College!

But let us, for a while, turn to pleasanter things. We shall in time arrive at the later stages of the College's career: at present, we are but at the birth of its academic life. We have seen that it owes its parentage to Sir John Colborne. We have not yet seen who were its foster-fathers —those whom the Lieutenant-Governor had brought out and was to leave behind him, to nurture its youth, and in the training process to develop both wind and limb. These the next chapter will bring before the reader. Happy are the Editors that they can introduce these first masters through one who knew them in the flesh, and who was himself distinguished as the first head-boy in the College. Dr. Scadding's contribution will be eagerly read by pupils of the Institution, both young and old. By "Old Boys" it will be read for the associations that increase in charm and interest as Time lays its mellowing touch on the fading memories of the past. By the later pupils it will be read with that pardonable pride with which one scans the family pedigree and traces the line of honourable descent from some doughty ancestor. If pride of birth has any justification it lies in this, that one may have the grace to emulate the virtues, re-enact the good deeds, and hand down with increased honour the memory, of an unsullied name. Nor will either class of readers forget, that not only was the writer of the chapter the first head-boy, but that for the long period of five-and-twenty years he was a master in the College. Very charming is the picture he has given us of those who were his professional colleagues, and, in the early years of the Institution, his own first masters. Elsewhere we learn of a curious contemporary criticism passed on these early imported masters of the College. A certain Dr. Dunlop, a well-known, early Canadian *littérateur*, of pronounced Tory views, found fault with them because they were all Cantabs. "It would have been more advisable," said he, "had they been selected from the more orthodox and gentlemanly University." In the remark, observes Dr. Scadding, our authority for the story, "we have the record of a foolish prejudice on the part of Dr. Dunlop, derived, possibly, from his long association with writers in *Blackwood* and *Fraser*, among whom the fixed notion prevailed that Cambridge was innately Whiggish, and therefore, not gentlemanly." But, Whig or Tory, it cannot be said that they were wanting in the qualities of a gentleman; still less, that they were indifferent teachers, or deficient in learning or scholarship. The pupils they turned out and the high repute of the Institution testify to the contrary. We shall see more of them later on, as well as of newer masters and pupils, who were soon to add to the increasing honour and fame of the College.

We have referred to some contemporary criticism of the first masters; let us make a brief allusion to what was said at the period about the design and methods of the College. From the founding of the Province, Upper Canada had been almost entirely ruled by an oligarchy, composed of men of education and good positions in life. Incidentally these men, as self-interest drew them together in close alliance, came to have matters pretty much their own way. They not only monopolized the public offices, but shaped the administration of the Province in accordance with their own wishes and in the class interest of their Order. This was particularly shown in the matter of education. In the Old World the age was still largely tinctured with classical ideas; the era of popular science and common schools was yet in the womb of time. In Upper Canada, what educational facilities existed were in the main for the sons of the rich. From the earliest period, we have seen, that even the private schools were seminaries of the higher learning. The first Governm schools, opened in 1806, were Grammar or Classical Schools ; and not till ten years later was any provision made for elementary instruction. Even in Simcoe's day the main purpose of the appropriation of Crown lands was to found a University. The whole pother in Sir Peregrine Maitland's *régime* was as to whether or not they should call King's College into existence. Even at that time the cost of civil government ate largely into the substance of the people. There was plenty of money to be had for the purposes of legislation, but very little for the purposes of education. This is seen from a report of the Education Committee presented in the Session of 1832 to the House of Assembly. Says the report : "Your Committee most earnestly draw the attention of your honourable House to the astounding fact that less is granted by the Provincial Legislature for educating the youth of 300,000 people than is required to defray the *contingent* expenses of one Session of Parliament!" Much, we know, has been unfairly laid at the door of the Family Compact; but it is a Tory educational authority who tells us that the chief obstructive in school matters, in pre-Rebellion times, was the Legislative Council. It was almost impossible, we are told, to get that body to concur in the legislation of the Lower House when it proposed levying rates for the support of Common Schools. In the minds of all but the governing families it may be doubted whether, at that era, this was deemed to be the best of all possible worlds.

Under the social conditions of the time, with the prevailing disregard of the weal of the people, we can quite understand the opposition to Government expenditure on seminaries of higher learning. The people had not their rights. A better day was to come with Responsible Government and its enlightened measures of popular education; but that day had not yet dawned on the young colony. Not unreasonable, therefore, was the cry against the premature founding of the University. Hardly less unreasonable was public impatience with the design that Sir John Colborne's scheme of a College should be incorporated with the University and its management placed under its control. Happily part of the difficulty was got over by importing its first masters from England, and the opposition for the time disappeared in the pride felt at the success of the Institution.

Of course, then, as now, the impossible thing was to please all. Now and then rumblings of discontent were heard as to the disproportionate sums spent on primary and higher education. Without impugning the motives of those who administered the affairs of the Province, it may be questioned whether, considering the youth of the country, a more generous expenditure on schools for the people would not have been wisdom. It may also be questioned whether Dr. Strachan was either wise or politic in so baldly disclosing his object in pressing for a University and urging the extension of the machinery of Classical Schools. Here is a quotation from one of his appeals : " It is indeed quite evident that the consequences of a University • • possessing in itself sufficient recommendations to attract to it the sons of the most opulent families, would soon be visible in the greater intelligence and more confirmed principles of loyalty of those who would be called to various public duties required in the country—*i. e.*, the governing classes." We might well doubt whether the avowal of such motives would help his cause. They too plainly declare what must at the time have been most offensive, that education was a class distinction, and that loyalty could not be on the side of the lowly born. Happily, the good bishop lived, we know, to change his mind.

Hardly serious could have been the objection to the College and the District Grammar Schools because they devoted so much time to the study of the Classics. So far as the College is concerned, if "Tiger" Dunlop's gibe about the masters being all Cantabs was warranted, the charge would lie as much against Mathematics. The objection can be understood only in the light of the general indictment. The Schools, it must be acknowledged, were for a class, and the goal of that class was the public service, or one or other of the professions. Hence the prominence given to the Classics. Here, as in the Motherland at the period, there may have been too much homage paid at the shrine of Latin verse. If the specimens from Gray and Ben Jonson, from an old Upper Canada College boy, which we meet with in the *College Times* for June, 1872, are to be taken as average examples, the Latin verse was undoubtedly however of a high order. Yet considering the practical wants of the country, perhaps less flowery studies would have been more useful, and proved as good a mental discipline. But we are not of those who deride the Classics and would cram a boy with a smattering of universal knowledge. Nor does the result prove that the College was wrong in its methods. Classics, it will be admitted, however, should hardly be the pivot on which the whole machine turns. "The real problem of a large school," observes a writer, "is not to teach this or that subject, but to promote, at once, every form of development, so as to give the chances to the largest variety of natural gifts and dispositions." As yet, the old systems held their ground and the era of "moderns" had not dawned. But this was clearly no drawback to the pupils of the College, for of those annually turned out of the Institution, not only many were distinguished, but the education of all may be said to be both general and sound. Nor must we forget that the College was founded to provide not a common or narrow, but a liberal, education. Double and almost incompatible functions were at the time required of it. It was a University and a Preparatory

College in one. If at the outset its cost was great to the Province, and there was more or less warrant for criticism, this is the defence that must be made for it.

In Education, and its appliances, a long road has been travelled since the era of 1830. In Classics, we still, to some extent, endeavour to compete with the Roman poets in the manufacture of Latin verse. But in the study of the ancient, as well as in the modern languages, the student of to-day does not now grind in the old mill. Our systems have been revolutionized by the science of history. Comparative philology has given a new charm to the study of the languages. What used to be largely a mechanical task is now an instructive and absorbing study. The curriculum too, as well as the school methods, have been widened and broadened, and a new world and new fields of thought have been opened by Science. In other respects, a wonderful change has come over education in the last half-century. To realize this one has only to compare the school-books of to-day with those in use when the College was founded. In nothing perhaps has there been a greater advance than in the subject matter and literary form of the school text-books. But with all the drawbacks which the student of 1830 had to contend with, the after-career of the average "old College boy" proves that they were no detriment to his success in life.

Looking back from the standpoint of to-day, it is with no little pride that one sees how great has been the success of the College. It had its origin at a period in the Provincial history seemingly little favourable to its taking vigorous root. No sooner was it founded than it had to encounter the twin-perils of pestilence and rebellion. In 1832, Toronto was ravaged by Asiatic Cholera, and five years later political dissension threatened the overthrow of the social fabric. If neither of these sinister forces seriously affected its fortunes, they disturbed the calm of the time favourable to intellectual labour, and for a while diverted public interest from educational work. Still bravely did the College hold on its way, and in renewed successes compelled the return to it of public favour and support. The passing years, while they added to its trials and vicissitudes, brought also the prestige and moral force to overcome them. Upper Canada College has had its day of exultation, and its day of depression; but through both it has done the duty of the hour and deeply rooted itself in the growing life of the young nation.

THE COLLEGE, ITS INCEPTION, AND FIRST MASTERS.

BY THE REV. DR. SCADDING.

A MONUMENT of the era of Sir John Colborne, afterwards Lord Seaton, still exists amongst us, in the institution known as Upper Canada College. This great Public School was brought into complete operation through the instrumentality of Sir John Colborne, in 1830. Tenders for the erection of the buildings were advertised for in the *Loyalist* of May 2nd, in the preceding year, in these words ; " Minor College.—Sealed Tenders for erecting a school-house and four dwelling houses, will be received on the first Monday of June next. Plans, elevations, and specifications may be seen after the 12th instant, on application to the Hon. George Markland, from whom further information may be received. York, 1st May, 1829."

In Sir John Colborne's opening speech, on the 8th of January, 1829, after the remark—" the public schools are generally increasing, but their present organization seems susceptible of improvement"—there occurs this passage ; " Measures will be adopted, I hope, to reform the Royal Grammar School, and to incorporate it with the University recently endowed by His Majesty, and to introduce a system in that seminary that will open to the youth of the Province the means of receiving a liberal and extensive course of instruction. Unceasing exertion should be made to attract able masters to this country, where the population bears no proportion to the number of offices and employments that must necessarily be held by men of education and acquirements, disposed to support the laws and your free institutions."

In the general form given to the echo of this portion of the Speech on the Address from the Commons, there is a good deal of meaning. " We will direct our anxious attention to the state of the Public Schools," the House of Assembly said, " and consider what improvements in the present imperfect and unsatisfactory system are best calculated to open to the youth of this Province the means of receiving a liberal and extensive course of instruction ; and we are fully sensible of the vast importance of unceasing exertions to attract able masters to the country, where the population and wealth bear no proportion to the number of offices and employments, which ought to be held by men of education and acquirements disposed to support the laws, and, what we are highly gratified to find so favourably mentioned by your Excellency, the free institutions of our country." Satire possibly lurked in the expression "*ought* to be held."

When Sir John Colborne arrived in Upper Canada, he came straight from Guernsey, and fresh from a task of educational reform accomplished by him in that island. He had rendered his administration there memorable by the successful renovation and modernization of Elizabeth College, a foundation of the times of Queen Elizabeth, but fallen to decay. In Upper Canada, a formal University, after the model of the English Universities, had been from the beginning an element in the polity of the country ; but actually to set up and put in motion such a piece of learned machinery seemed hitherto premature. On his settlement at York, Sir John Colborne soon made up his mind not to push forward into immediate existence, as by some he was urged to do, the larger establishment, but to found a preliminary and preparatory institution, which should meet the immediate educational wants of the community. He obtained the sanction of the home authorities; and the substance of a despatch from headquarters on the subject was communicated to the House in the following terms, which shew a certain indefiniteness, as yet, in regard to the organization and exact aim of the proposed establishment : " The advantages that will result from an institution conducted by nine or ten able masters, under whose tuition the youth of the Province could be prepared for any profession are indisputable ; and if such a school were permanently established, and the Charter (of King's College) so modified that any professor shall be eligible for the Council, and that the students of the College shall have liberty and faculty of taking degrees in the manner that shall hereafter be directed by the statutes and ordinances framed by His Majesty's government, the University must flourish, and prove highly beneficial to the colony."

By adopting this line of action, Sir John Colborne lost the favour of some of the customary advisers of Lieutenant-Governors in Upper Canada, as seeming to postpone the establishment of the University proper to a very distant day ; but he gained the gratitude of many throughout the country.

With necessary modifications, Elizabeth College, Guernsey, was reproduced at York, in the institution which soon became famous as Upper

Canada College. Among some it was long familiarly spoken of as the Minor College, with allusion to the University which was to be; and this was the title placed, as we have seen, at the head of the original advertisement for tenders. The *Loyalist* newspaper refers to the institution, while yet in embryo, as Colborne College, as if to suggest that name for it.

The Rev. Dr. Harris, with a staff of masters, for the most part selected in England, was nominated as the head of the new institution, and entrusted with the task of its actual organization. Dr. Harris himself had been highly distinguished at the University of Cambridge, where he had been a Fellow of Clare Hall. Dr. Phillips, the Vice-Principal, was also a Cambridge man, long since graduated at Queen's College. He was already in the country, at the head of the District or Royal Grammar School at York. Mr. Dade, the mathematical master, was, at the time of his appointment, a Fellow of Caius College, and continued for a number of years still to retain that honourable distinction. Mr. Mathews, the first classical master, was a graduate of Pembroke College, a brilliant classical scholar, and a proficient in Hebrew, having won the Tyrwhitt Hebrew Scholarship of the University; and Mr. Boulton, the second classical master, a son of Mr. Justice Boulton, of York, was a graduate of Queen's College, Oxford, and for some time engaged in tuition in the old endowed Blundell's School, at Tiverton, Devon. Each of these gentlemen was an acquisition to the community at York. They were all of them instrumental in inaugurating and fostering in Upper Canada a sterling scholarship peculiarly English. "The jar long retains the odour of the wine with which, when new, it was first filled." In minds here and there in Upper and Lower Canada and elsewhere there lingers yet the aroma of Horatian, Virgilian, and other classic tinctures, dropped into them years ago by Harris and his worthy colleagues.

Another gentleman attached to Upper Canada College by Sir John Colborne was Mr. Drewry, an artist of no ordinary skill, whose paintings in oil of scenery about the Falls of Niagara and in the White Mountains were held by judges to be remarkable for their great excellence. Mr. Drewry did a good deal in the way of cultivating art and artistic matters at York. The same may be said of Mr. J. G. Howard, afterwards the eminent architect at York, who, although not brought out expressly to undertake duties in Upper Canada College, was attached to that institution very soon by Sir John Colborne. The French master was Mr. J. P. de la Haye, of St. Malo, who had had much experience in schools in England.

The plot of ground on which the College buildings were erected had previously been known as Russell Square. While these were being prepared, the work of the College began in the old District or Royal Grammar School, situate, at the time, at the southern corner of March and Nelson Streets (now known as Lombard and Jarvis Streets), but previously placed in the middle of the school block defined by Church, Adelaide, Jarvis, and Richmond Streets, a building itself already memorable to many in Upper Canada as the scene of their boyish training in the *literæ humaniores*. For the purposes of the new College, the interior of the old school was divided into rooms by panelled partitions, which reached not quite to the ceiling, one room being assigned to each master. The rooms of the Principal and Mathematical Master were upstairs, as was also the Assembling or Prayer Hall. In 1831 teaching began in the new building, and there the first examination and distribution of prizes took place.

ADDITIONAL NOTE ON THE REV. DR. HARRIS.

Not long after his retirement from the Principalship of Upper Canada College, and his return to England, Dr. Harris was presented with the living of Tor Mohun, in Devonshire. He died at his house, named Sorèl, at Torquay, in 1881, in his 81st year, greatly respected and beloved.

In his spare and wiry figure, as well as in the aquiline outline of his features, the first Principal bore a considerable resemblance to the "Iron Duke," a resemblance also to be traced in the personal qualities of a strong dislike for verbiage and display, and the possession of great firmness, decision, and energy.

Not having at hand any literary relic of Dr. Harris of a general character, I transcribe a few passages from a pamphlet of his on the subject of Upper Canada College. He is endeavouring to make the members of the Opposition in the Local House and others to see the economic value of a superior education, whilst at the same time he gives some interesting particulars connected with the history of education in England:

"As to the 'public expense' at which the College is upheld," Dr. Harris writes, "I would submit that allowing it to be, in itself, apparently great, two considerations present themselves with respect to the benefits purchased at this expense which arise with regard to any purchasable commodity, first, can the commodity be procured in every respect of equal goodness at a less price? and secondly, if it be necessarily an expensive article, is it worth the price to the purchaser?

"Now, to the first question, it is a certain fact that a liberal and comprehensive education cannot be provided but at a considerable expense to be borne somewhere. The people in general, in a new country, cannot bear it from their private means, and it must, therefore, if provided for at all, be borne from the public. Even in the old countries of Europe, and particularly in England, all the leading seminaries are supported by endowments ; and limited indeed in comparison with what they actually are, would be the means of education in Great Britain, had not Royal and individual munificence founded schools and colleges for the promotion of learning, and made such permanent provision for the maintenance of tutors and masters, as leaves little comparative expense to be defrayed by many parents, whose sons must otherwise have wanted that which has proved to them more valuable than the richest inheritance.

"To this patriotic and generous regard of our forefathers for the interests of learning it is to be ascribed that in England so many men of humble origin have been enabled to raise themselves to proud distinction as statesmen, and scholars, and philosophers. Looking particularly at the profession of the law, how many of our most considerable families and of our nobility are indebted to the facilities which happily existed for the education of that ancestor whose superior talents first raised himself and his name from humble obscurity? This allusion reminds me of the recommendation which was made at a popular meeting in this place, some few years since, that the Home Government should send out Judges to Canada from the English Bar, till the improved state of education in the Province should render such a course unnecessary.

"Now in one point of view I should certainly not have adverted to this circumstance as making for my present argument, for to nothing could a stronger appeal be made in proof of the insufficiency of the existing means of education in than to the actual discharge of the judicial functions in Upper Canada; but I may fairly be allowed to infer from the fact that such an opinion having been expressed that it was not generally considered that the then available means of education were adequate to the requirements of the Colony ; and that, therefore, an Institution which is every year sending out youths not inferior in classical knowledge to the greater part of those who leave our public schools in England for the Universities, and with the addition of many useful attainments which the latter do not generally possess, is not conferring unimportant advantages on the Province at large, and could not be dispensed with, but at the certainty of still keeping the standard of education below that point which is correspondent with the general advancement and exigencies of the community.

"But to return from this longer discussion than I had intended. If in so old, and populous, and wealthy a country as England, liberal education has been maintained at an expense so much greater than is covered by the mere payment made by individual parents for the instruction of their children, it is not to be expected that the case should be otherwise here; but rather that the expense of a higher order of education should, for some time to come, appear more disproportionate to the extent of good effected than where society has been increasing and advancing for ages.

" This is a consequence necessarily resulting from the nature of the case, and for the same reasons, the disproportion between the expense and the amount of the advantage diffused through the Province would be still more apparent with regard to a University, the expenditure of which must be manifold greater than that on an introductory seminary, whilst the number of individuals who would probably avail themselves of the advantages of the former, could not for many years be at all equal to the number of pupils receiving their education at the latter. And yet I never heard any objection of this nature to the University as though its endowment were too great, &c., as though the Province in general were likely to derive very little advantage from it; for besides the fact that the expense of education beyond a certain grade increases in a rapid ratio as the standard rises it must be obvious with respect to the higher pursuits of learning and science that the taste and demand for them, in a new community, must not only be encouraged but in a great measure created; and this is to be done not by a tardy supply of facilities and assistance, only afforded when the necessity can no longer be denied, but by providing opportunities in advance, which may elicit latent genius, and lead the way to the loftier paths of knowledge. To delay, therefore, the commencement of the University till a much larger number of students actually present themselves to enter its walls, would be to postpone the cultivation of a field till a few spontaneous ears had multiplied themselves to a full crop; forgetting the danger that the seeds thus left to themselves may perish, whereas, if carefully collected and cultivated, they would probably in a few seasons produce an abundant increase.

"The above desultory remarks may perhaps suffice to show that education of a superior kind, is, to a certain extent, necessarily an expensive commodity. I proceed to the question whether it is worth the cost to the purchaser, *i.e.*, to the Province; or, in other words to reply to the opinions that " the Province generally derives very little advantage from the College, and that it might be dispensed with." I infer from the expression " the Province generally" that it is implied that the advantages of the College are chiefly confined to the immediate vicinity of Toronto; and it is certainly the case that the greater part of the pupils has always been from this city and neighbourhood. The number of boys from the country (and some from very distant parts), has generally been rather more than a third of the entire number; and when it is considered how many circumstances, besides the expense, may concur to make it convenient to parents to send their sons far from home, this is perhaps nearly as large a proportion as could be expected. But the benefits to the Province at large are not to be solely estimated by the comparative number of pupils who are sent to the College from districts more or less remote from its vicinity. The beneficial effects of talents which are drawn forth and cultivated by a systematic course of education are not confined to the locality, either of the school or of the home, of the talented individual; the talents thus matured are the property and advantage, no less than the ornament, of the country at large.

"No one thinks of inquiring whether a Bacon or a Newton, a Johnson or an Addison, received his education in his native town or at a distant school; the whole nation enjoys the fruits of their talents, and glories in their fame wherever they were educated.

"It may, indeed, be a source of honest pride to particular schools to have educated such luminaries, as it may be to their native places to have produced them, but the distinction thus enjoyed by the one or the other, does not in the least diminish the public advantage and the public honours derived from their abilities. But to meet more directly the question of advantages derived by the Province generally from the founding of Upper Canada College we must remember that it is too soon to judge of the fruit of a tree before the period of its maturity is arrived; and that it is equally unreasonable to expect that a place of education for youth should have produced any demonstrable present influence on the community, in the course of six years from its foundation."

To the Rev. Dr. Harris is due the now well-known selection from Horace (Carm. iv. 4, ll. 33-36), which is appended to the labels inserted in the prize books annually given at Upper Canada College:

> "Doctrina sed vim promovet insitam,
> Rectique cultus pectora roborant;
>   Utcumque defecere mores,
>   Dedecorant bene nata culpae."

> "Yet training quickens power inborn,
> And culture nerves the soul for fame,
> But he must live a life of scorn
>   Who bears a noble name,
> Yet blurs it with the soil of infamy and shame.

"Still training speeds the inborn vigour's growth,
Sound culture is the armour of the breast,
Where fails the moral lore,
Vice disennobles even the noblest born."

Lord Lytton's Translation.

ADDITIONAL NOTE ON THE REV. DR. PHILLIPS.

The Rev. Dr. Phillips resigned the Vice-Principalship in 1834. The title was not continued. The Master next in rank after the Principal was now styled First Classical Master. Dr. Phillips became Rector of Weston on the Humber, about ten miles from Toronto. I remember seeing the inscription *Deus nobis haec otia fecit* over a rustic seat in the grove overlooking the river not far from the Church, placed there by the Doctor. He died in the year 1849, aged 68. The text-books, grammars, and so on used in the old District or Royal Grammar School, presided over by Dr. Phillips, prior to the establishment of Upper Canada College, were those of Eton, including even the old untranslated Greek Grammar. At noon every day, it was the duty of the censor, or head-boy of the highest class to proclaim the hour *Duodecima hora est*, to which was added *Pueri, armorum scholasticorum reminiscimini:* implying that the lads were to carefully gather up their books, papers, and so on, and deposit them in their proper places. Any one who may happen to recall a portrait of Dr. Hawtrey, formerly Head Master of Eton, which appeared a few years since in the London Illustrated papers, will have before his mind's eye a rather faithful "counterfeit presentment" of Dr. Phillip's contour of head and expression of countenance. Dr. Phillips did what he could to prepare the minds of his young friends for the new era about to dawn upon them. The subject proposed by Dr. Phillips for a short poem in 1829, was: *Viris doctissimis varia facultate docendi institutis Regiae Scholae Grammaticae Eboracensi laeta dies aderit, i. e.:* "Happy will be the day for the Royal Grammar School at York when well-learned men shall be appointed for it in the several departments of instruction." As a literary memorial of Dr. Phillips I give some lines written by him and recited by one of his pupils on the last prize day of the old school. It is a review in verse of the ups and downs of the Institution with a hopeful onward glance at its future:

"As when the vessel laden with her store,
Quits distant climes, and seeks the long left shore;
Now cuts the foaming wave of boist'rous seas,
And crowds her swelling canvas for the breeze;

"But while for home each sailor's bosom burns,
  And hope and fear, perplexing, reign by turns;
  The kindly blowing gales at once subside,
  And leave the ship on sullen deeps to ride.

"Behold the burden on the ocean stands,
  Longing in vain to reach far distant lands;
  A deadly quiet overspreads the main,
  Nor vivid lightnings flash, nor falls the rain;

"Yet courage animates the sailor's heart,
  And undismayed he nobly plays his part;
  For tho' a transient calm his voyage stay,
  Still to his native land his wishes stray.

"Again the wind their spreading canvas swells,
  And the swift vessel on its course impels;
  Till ev'ry danger, ev'ry terror past,
  The wished for haven they regain at last.

"So man, as thro' life's short'ning track he goes,
  Feels ev'ry varying gale that round him blows;
  One while, his sails propitious zephyrs fill,
  Another, on the deep his barque stands still;

"So, we too, once a well-matched crew came here,
  And in ourselves a host, had naught to fear;
  We cut the ocean with undaunted force,
  And brisker gales propell'd us on our course.

"But tho' our canvas feel a gentler breeze,
  We still with patience plough pacific seas;
  And tho' with lessen'd force we now turn out,
  Again anticipate enliv'ning shout;

"For say, why should we from these Boards withdraw,
  And cease our humble efforts here to shew?
  Who give up tamely in the fight for fame,
  Nor make one effort to support our name?

"No! let us rather all our efforts raise,
  And put forth all our powers to gain your praise,
  Cling to the vessel while a plank remains,
  Nor quit our anchor, Hope! for all our pains.

"This happy day, our hearts with pleasure hail,
This day, thro' ev'ry bosom joys prevail ;
Each toil, each labour, in the day is crown'd
Our pride content, our highest wishes bound.

"Our dearest friends around us here to meet,
Our long known, long tried friends again to greet,
For this, O welcome, all the School boy's care !
O welcome, e'en for this, the School boy's fear !

"For competition is a noble thing,
It gives our flagging genius a wing ;
Puts ev'ry latent power of mind to test,
And makes us labour to perform our best.

"Then listen with good-will ; our cause befriend ;
Withhold your judgment till you see the end ;
Take all in all, our greatest faults pass by,
And view each error with benignant eye.

"Well pleased, if from this Royal School you go,
What happiness within our breast will flow !
For, be assured, we all have this at heart ;
To strive with zeal, who best can act his part."

These lines are preceded in the copy which I possess of them by the following quotation from Horace :—

Lib. I. Ode xxxiv. ll. 12-16.

" .... Valet ima summis
Mutare et insignem attenuat Deus,
Obscura promens. Hinc apicem rapax
 Fortuna cum stridore acuto
  Sustulit, hic posuisse gaudet."

Lord Lytton's Translation, page 112.

" .... A God reigns,
Potent the high with low to interchange,
Bid bright orbs wane, and those obscure come forth;
Shrill sounding, Fortune swoops—
Here snatches, then exultant drops, a crown."

ADDITIONAL NOTE ON THE REV. C. DADE.

The Rev. Charles Dade died May 2nd, 1872, at his residence in Georgetown, Esquesing, in his 70th year, having been born at Yarmouth in Norfolk, June 4th, 1802. He resigned the Mathematical Mastership in 1838.

Mr. Dade was a man of unusual attainments in science and general learning. At the University of Cambridge he obtained the high wrangler's degree in the Mathematical Tripos, distinguishing himself also at the same time, in a marked manner, in the examination for Classical Honours. Immediately after obtaining his degree, Mr. Dade was elected a fellow of Gonville and Caius College, where, as the lists show, several of his own name had preceded him in that honourable position. His memory will continue to be to the early *alumni* of Upper Canada College in the future, what in every review of the past it has already been, one of their valued recollections. Again and again have they discovered by experience that the foundations of science laid in their minds by the first master in mathematics, were solid and trustworthy. Again and again, in their intercourse with men, have they felt the abiding effect for good upon themselves, of the sterling honesty and blunt straightforwardness which so conspicuously characterized their former guide and friend. Perhaps in the severe temperature of " the mathematical master's room," in the olden time, kept as little above freezing as possible, some of our eminent engineers and explorers tested for the first time that power of endurance and that capacity for solving problems under difficulties which have contributed to their success ; a power and a capacity brought prominently out, perhaps also for the first time, in some one or other of the memorable tramps laboriously undertaken on the ice of Toronto Bay, and elsewhere, in company with their iron-sinewed teacher, whilst being shown by him practically how to run base lines and take angles, and measure the altitude of the sun and other objects.

Besides being a vigorous and accurate thinker, Mr. Dade was, to the close of his career, an indefatigable and very literal manual worker. On his farm near Oakville, to which he withdrew when he resigned his mastership in Upper Canada College, some very remarkable trenches and dykes for drainage purposes excavated by the might of his own arm will be re-called.

Whilst at Cambridge, in 1826, he gained what is called the Member's Prize, a distinction greatly desired at Cambridge, and attained only by first-rate scholars. It is one of four annual prizes given by the representatives in Parliament of the University for dissertations in Latin Prose, which are read publicly by the prizemen in the Senate-House on a day.

appointed near the Commencement. Mr. Dade's Essay was afterwards printed in full in the *Classical Journal* for March and June, 1827, published by A. J. Valpy, London. The prize dissertation fills sixteen closely printed octavo pages in the *Classical Journal*.

It is an admirably sustained discussion, in pure easy flowing Latin, of the most striking points in which modern men have the advantage of their predecessors in the by-gone ages.

"*Quibusnam praecipue artibus recentiores antiquos exsuperant*"?

It is thrown into the form of a conversation between the author and a friend, after the manner of Cicero.

Papers of permanent value by Mr. Dade, on the Law of Storms, and on the Cholera Seasons of 1832 and 1834, are preserved in Volumes 5 and 7 respectively, of the second series of the *Canadian Journal*.

A note by him on some Indian remains in the township of Beverley, in volume one of the first series of the same Journal, is characteristic for its brevity and directness. A valuable contribution on the Meteorology of Toronto and its vicinity, by the same hand, was also communicated to the Canadian Institute. Mr. Dade's Tables of Observations on our local physical phenomena, carefully made from 1831, downwards, are held by the authorities at the Toronto Observatory to be of special importance as appertaining to a period of which no other records of the kind are extant.

A few years since a monument was erected to the memory of the Rev. Mr. Dade, in the Churchyard, at Georgetown, by a number of his former pupils. It consists of a handsome obelisk of stone bearing a simple and suitable inscription. Towards the top of one side of the obelisk is carved as a kind of memorial hieroglyphic, the well-known figure employed in the demonstration of the 47th proposition of the first book of Euclid.

ADDITIONAL NOTE ON THE REV. CHARLES MATHEWS.

In the year 1867, the Rev. Charles Mathews, formerly a master of Upper Canada College, published in London a poetical translation of the Odes, Epodes, and Carmen Saeculare of Horace, marked by much originality. Usually concise and close, it is now and then curiously but always gracefully paraphrastic, whilst the metre and language often reminds one of quaint George Herbert. I give two extracts for the purpose of showing how much the writer's experience of Canadian life helped him to a graphic reproduction of some of Horace's descriptions.

The first is from Book III., Ode xxiv., ll. 36-39.

> If not that part of the sphere
>   Included to the tropic ray,
> Nor that side o' the round
>   Confine to Boreas, where the broad
> Snows hardened to the ground
>   Are all the metal to the road.

>   si neque fervidis
> Pars inclusa caloribus
>   Mundi nec Boreae finitimum latus,
> Durataeque solo nives
>   Mercatorem abigunt?

Would such an expression as "all the metal to the road," as here used, be ever thought of by a translator of Horace unacquainted with a Canadian highway, with its two or three feet of snow well beaten down and compacted together by the careering to and fro over it of innumerable sleighs?

The second extract is from the 16th Epode, ll. 43-48:

> "Where corn is reaped from earth's unlaboured bosom,
>   And vines undressed eternal blossom,
> And dusky figs mature on their own wood,
>   And olives unassisted bud,
> Where the primæval hollow trunk of tree
>   Drips with the labour of the bee,
> And the sound forest stems and prairied reed,
>   Autumnal tapped or vernal, bleed
> With syrups! where tall mountains stretch and from
>   Their tabled summits sounding come—
> Not rills, by tempests into volume fed,
>   But rivers deep and ample spread.

> Reddit ubi Cererem tellus inarata quotannis,
>   Et imputata floret usque vinea,
> Germinat et nunquam fallentis termes olivae,
>   Suamque pulla ficus ornat arborem,
> Mella cava manant ex ilice, montibus altis
>   Levis crepante lympha desilit pede.

In this translation or rather paraphrase of the words of Horace, we have plainly reminiscences of the first tillage of virgin soil, as witnessed in

Canada of the ancient hollow pine tree, met with every now and then, the haunt and hoarding-place of the wild bee ; of the stout stems of tall maples tapped every spring for the sake of their sugar-yielding sap ; and of the wild Canadian grape vines with their flagrant efflorescence.

In the "rivers deep and ample spread," descending from "their tabled summits," we have surely Niagara itself. In the "prairied reed" we are plainly carried south of Canada into the region of the sugar-cane.

Two briefer expressions are added, coloured possibly by Canadian experience.

> "The Meads their icy coating doff,
> And roars the river rolling off
> His plethora of snow."

A spring freshet in the Nottawasaga or the Grand River was here plainly in the mind of the translator.

The Latin represented is the following :—

> "*Jam nec prata rigent nec fluvii strepunt
> Hiberna nive turgide.*" Lib. IV., Ode. xii., ll. 3-4.

> "The white tracts snow-spread
> Of Thrace, far vestiged by barbarian tread."

The Horatian language is :—"*Nive candidam Thracen, ac pede barbaro Lustratam Rhodopen.*" Lib. III. Ode. xxv., ll. 10-12.

Have we not here in "vestiged" for *lustratam* the *vestigia* or prints of snowshoe and moccasin marking out afresh, after every snow fall, the line of an Indian trail?

Mr. Mathews' own ideas of the proper qualifications of a translator of Horace in general, and of his own qualifications in particular, may be gathered from a letter of his. His correspondent had observed in regard to his poetical version of Horace, "You certainly understand your author,"— the reply was, "You think I understand my original (thank you), but if it be not like-natured, like-minded also, I cannot attain to him, with or without metempsychosis.

May not nature repeat herself in a distant generation for utterance in another language?

Without understanding him certainly, without resembling him also, I believe certainly whoever attempts to transmute him, had better leave him alone, *recalcitrat undique tutus.*"

Intimate relations seem to have subsisted between the family of Mr. Mathews and that of Lord Byron; he possessed a magnificent copy of the complete works of the poet presented to him by Lady Augusta Leigh, Lord Byron's sister. (The name Byron, it may be noticed, was always pronounced 'Birron' by Mr. Mathews, a peculiarity at one time affected, I believe, by Byron himself.)

Mr. Mathews was one of those who had the power of inspiring in pupils a strong love of study and a true taste in regard to nice points in the Greek, Latin, and English Classics. He was a man of quick humour and wit; he was never at a loss for a merry rejoinder. I have often found useful a little precept of his, formulated on the spur of the moment and delivered with a laugh, to the effect that people should map their minds as well as mind their maps. This was said in connection with some attempt to realize the circumstances of some ancient battle involving the necessity of a clear recollection of the relative positions of hill and plain, of river and morass. Finely cut Graecian features, dark sallow complexion, and an abundance of raven black hair were faithful indications of mind and temperament in the case of the accomplished scholar whose memory we have endeavoured to recall. After his retirement from Upper Canada College, in 1843, Mr. Mathews resided in the Island of Guernsey, where he died in 1877.

Mr. Mathews had accidentally found in Ausonius a passage much resembling Wordsworth's "And 'tis my faith that every flower enjoys the air it breathes," [NOTE.—"Lines Written in Early Spring," Wordsworth, p. 341, edition, Boston, 1839,] and had communicated the circumstance to the poet. The result was the following characteristic note, which was given to me by Mr. Mathews, and preserved as an interesting autographic memorial in my collection of such things:

THE POET WORDSWORTH'S LETTER TO THE REV. CHARLES MATHEWS.

DEAR SIR,—

I was not acquainted with the passage of Ausonius to which you alluded, nor with any part of his writing at the time, nearly fifty years since, when I composed the lines which you quote. I perfectly remember the very moment when the Poem in which they occur fell from my lips. I do not say my pen, for I had none with me. The passage in Ausonius does not put the case so strongly as mine, as the mere word "gaudere," is not perhaps much more than a strong expression for "thrive."

The interest you take in this little matter is gratifying to me as a proof of sympathy between us, and emboldens me to subscribe myself

Sincerely, your much obliged

WM. WORDSWORTH.

RYDAL MOUNT, December 29, 1836.

FROM AUSONIUS.

Ed. J. Stoer, 1588.

AUSONII ROSAE. IDYLL XIV.

" Ver erat ; et blando mordentia frigora sensu
　Spirabat croceo mane revecta dies.
Strictior Eoos praecesserat aura jugales,
　Aestiferum suadens anticipare diem.
Errabam riguis per quadrua compita in hortis,
　Maturo cupiens me vegetare die.
Vidi concretas per gramina flexa pruinas
　Pendere, aut olerum stare cacuminibus
Caulibus et patulis teretes colludere guttas
　Et coelestis aquae pondere tunc gravidas.
Vidi Paestano gaudere rosaria cultu
　Exoriente novo roscida Lucifero."

Mr. Mathews received his primary education at the well-known Blue-coat School in London. On the 21st of September, 1829, he was selected as the preacher at the Annual Commemoration of that institution, held at Christ Church, Newgate. His discourse on that occasion on Psalm 122, 6-9, was published at the time in London. In it he alludes to his recent appointment to an educational post in Canada. The new school to which he is going is spoken of as " King's College, York," Upper Canada.

I leave to other contributors to this volume to give notices of the remaining first masters of the College. The faithful and much-enduring first janitor of the College, Samuel Alderdice, will also probably not be overlooked. The bent and somewhat aged form of Alderdice—his strongly-marked, longish, Druid-like visage, his deep-set, watchful and withal kindly eyes, his iron-grey hair spread out over the collar of the coat, and in front smoothed modestly down on the forehead, were long remembered by all early pupils of the College ; as also was that peremptory " Open the doo-er !" which (uttered in high-keyed, hollow-sounding tone and strong Celtic accent,) occasionally startled the ear of the young day scholar, who, living perhaps at a distance, was glad to ensconce himself along with a class-mate in one of the master's rooms during the noontide recess, contrary to the regulations. In a lithograph representing the masters of the College assembled in the Prayer-room, a likeness on a small scale of Alderdice is preserved. He stands there, as he used to be seen standing every morning, mute and motionless by the side of the Principal's chair awaiting orders, or by the chair of one of the masters, while names of absentees were being taken down.

ADDITIONAL NOTE ON ELIZABETH COLLEGE, GUERNSEY.

Elizabeth College, Guernsey, as restored and modernized by Sir John Colborne, in 1829, furnished the model on which Upper Canada College was organized both in respect to its curriculum and its methods. We have in Brayley's "Graphic and Historical Illustrator," published in 1834, an account of the Institution in Guernsey, referred to. We there learn that it was founded in Queen Elizabeth's reign, 1563, for the benefit of the youth of the Island. It was divided into six classes; books and exercises were appointed respectively for each, the scholars to be admitted being required "to read perfectly, and to recite an approved Catechism of the Christian Religion by heart." In all the six classes the Latin and Greek languages were the primary objects of instruction; but the statutes permitted the Master at his discretion "to add something of his own," and even to concede something for writing, singing, arithmetic, and a "little play." The school had fallen greatly into decay, when in 1823, Sir John Colborne, governor of the Island, determined to re-establish it; and in 1829, he had the satisfaction of seeing the Institution once more in complete operation in a handsome building, with an attendance of one hundred and twenty pupils.

Its staff of instructors consisted of a Principal, Vice-Principal, a First and Second Classical Master, a Mathematical Master, a Master and Assistant of the Lower School, a Commercial Master, and two French Masters and an Assistant, a Master of Drawing and Surveying, besides extra Masters for the German, Italian, and Spanish languages, and for Music, Drawing, and Fencing. The course included instruction in "Divinity, History, Geography, Hebrew, Greek, Latin, French, English, Mathematics, Arithmetic, and Writing."

It is evident that, in the main, Upper Canada College was modelled after the pattern of Elizabeth College, Guernsey, its curriculum of studies, however, being somewhat less comprehensive, and its staff of instructors not so numerous.

The Upper Canada College building of 1830, was a plain, substantial roomy edifice of red brick without any architectural pretentions. The internal fittings and finish were of the most solid and unadorned character The benches for the classes were placed round the rooms against the wall; they were movable, narrow, and constructed of thick planks in a very primitive fashion, as also were certain narrow tables. Each room was provided with a very large wood box set near the capacious fireplace, to hold the huge masses of hard maple, beech, and hickory used for fuel; there was also a plain, strong, movable lock-up closet for the reception of loose books, maps, and papers. The masters' desks were of heavy black walnut, the legs of each fastened by clamps to a small platform of its own which might be shifted about with ease on the floor. The wainscotting throughout the building was composed of stout boards of irregular width hand-planed, and nailed on longitudinally, all painted of a uniform drab colour. Rough usage was everywhere challenged, and rough usage speedily came. Benches, tables, and desks soon began to wear a very battered appearance. The wainscotting of the passages and other portions of the building was soon disfigured by initials, and sometimes names, carved at full length in accordance with a rude custom prevailing aforetime in English public schools,—a custom more honoured in the breach than in the observance.

It is safe to say that no pupil pursuing his studies in the renovated and enlarged Upper Canada College of the present day would feel any pleasure in seeing the walls around him decorated in this peculiar manner. A similar change for the better has come over the feelings and tastes of the scholars frequenting all our public schools and other places of education. It cannot be doubted that next to the companionship of refined teachers a refined environment has the most happy effect on the young. *Emollit mores nec sinit esse feros.* The experiment has now been in progress amongst us for some time with satisfactory results. The establishment of beautiful boulevards in our streets and the more or less complete throwing open of parks and other ornamental grounds, have produced a like effect on the general population of our cities and towns. With a youth trained to admire and prefer neat surroundings in their places of education, and an adult population habituated to respect and enjoy the beautiful adornment of places of public resort, the present generation may well congratulate itself on the point of civilization to which it has attained in this respect.

Let this condition of things be maintained through a series of years; let peace with our neighbours continue, and love and good fellowship prevail among ourselves; let plentiful appliances for a real education still be rendered easily accessible to all, and made use of by all; whilst, simultaneously, innumerable influences for good are kept steadily in operation through the usual beneficent agencies. What is there to prevent very many of the high hopes entertained by the optimist in regard to the human race from being, in due time, realized in the people of the Canadian Dominion?

H. S.

UPPER CANADA COLLEGE IN 1829.
(From a sketch by J. G. Howard).

NOTE ON THE COLLEGE MOTTO.

Palmam qui Meruit Ferat as a Motto.

It has been customary of late years in Upper Canada College to make use of the words *Palmam qui meruit ferat* as a kind of general motto for the Institution. The adoption of such a motto may seem to a stranger to imply a good deal of self-appreciation ; but the suffrages of a very large portion of the community will, it is believed, at the present time fully bear the College out in its procedure. Like *Dieu et mon droit* appended to the arms of England, *Palmam qui meruit ferat* may now without serious challenge be inscribed beneath the escutcheon of the College. And here it is pertinent to ask, how is it that the College has no escutcheon ? As a Royal Grammar School it ought to have one. Such badges do much to create and maintain an *esprit de corps*. What *alumnus* of Eton, let him be ever so advanced in years, can look without a certain pleasurable emotion on the "three lilies slipped and leaved," and other heraldic symbols on the shield of his college ? Could not the device on the old seal of the Province of Upper Canada be utilized for this purpose, emblazoned on a shield with an open book or two "in its chief" to indicate the educational character of the Institution thus presented ?

The words, *Palmam qui meruit ferat*, were, in the first instance, employed at Upper Canada College, not as a general motto for itself, but simply as an inscription stamped upon its prize books, indicative of the impartiality with which the Institution dispensed its rewards and honours. The words having thus become so much associated with the College, it was a matter of some interest to discover its source.

It was early observed that they formed the motto appended to the arms of Lord Nelson ; but this, of course, did not determine the writer from whom they were quoted. Having addressed an inquiry on this subject to the well-known London *Notes and Queries*, I was informed that the words in question occurred in a Latin poem, by Dr. J. Jortin.

The poem itself was not given, but I was told it might be found in a volume of Jortin's, entitled "*Lusus Poetici*." A friend in London kindly undertook to search out this work of Jortin's in the British Museum, and I have received from him a fair transcript of the Latin poem containing the words referred to. [*Vide* "Tracts, Philological, Critical, and Miscellaneous." By the late Rev. John Jortin, D.D., in two volumes. 8vo. London, 1790, vol. i., p. 17.] It is an Ode to the Winds, and reads as follows :

AD VENTOS.

ANTE A.D., MDCCXXVII.

Vatis Threicii nunc citharam velim
Vocisque illecebras blanda furentibus
  Dantis jura procellis ;
    Mulcentis pelagi minas.

Venti, tam rapido turbine conciti,
Quâ vos cunque vagus detulerit furor,
  Classis vela Britannæ
    Transite innocui, precor.

Ultores scelerum classis habet deos,
Et pubem haud timidam pro patriâ mori.
  En ut lintea circum,
    Virtus excubias agit.

Et nobis faciles parcite et hostibus,
Concurrant pariter cum ratibus rates ;
  Spectent Numina ponti, et
    Palmam qui meruit, ferat.

TO THE WINDS.

Would now that I had the lyre of the Thracian bard [Orpheus] and the blandishments of his voice, giving gentle laws to the raging storms, soothing the threats of the deep.

O ye winds, when stirred up by ever so furious a hurricane, whithersoever its errant rage shall bear you, pass harmless, I pray, over the sails of the British fleet.

That fleet hath in it divinities, avengers of evil deeds, and young crews not afraid to die for their country. See how around the canvas-crowded masts Valour keeps ceaseless watch.

Lenient to us and to our foes spare both. In battle fair let our ships engage. Let the Powers that rule the deep look on ; and whoever in their eyes hath deserved it let him bear off the palm.

Judging from the memorandum [Ante A.D. MDCCXXVII.] prefixed to Jortin's Ode, it would seem that the reference is either to the fleet under Sir John Jennings, despatched to the Baltic in 1726, or to that under Sir John Jennings, despatched to the coast of Spain in the same year, both intended to check sinister machinations against England, on the part of Catharine, of Russia, and the Spanish Court, in favour of the Old Pretender. The true inwardness of the sentiment possibly is—If the Stuart cause be pleasing to Heaven let it win ; if the Hanoverian, let the victory be given to it !

As to the metre of Jortin's stanzas, it is precisely that of the famous ode of Horace, addressed "*Ad Rempublicam*," and beginning, *O Navis* [bk. I, xiv.], whence probably has come the English expression. "Ship of State," meaning the nation with its Ministry or Government. Pitt, "the pilot who weathered the storm," as he was popularly styled, would naturally admire this ode of Horace. Jortin's stanzas accordingly plainly inspired, as I think, by the same ode, in subject as well as metre, would also be to his taste, and when a motto was wanted for the shield of the naval hero, Nelson, he, with much felicity, selected for that purpose their closing words, "*Palmam qui meruit ferat.*"

The phrase thus acquired a world-wide celebrity. To find that it does not date back to the age of Augustus continues to be a matter of surprise with many. It must be remembered, however, that Jortin flourished in the era of Vincent Bourne, who in England, about the year 1745, wrote Latin verse held by the poet Cowper almost to rival that of Tibullus and Ovid.

In the elaborate armorial bearings granted to Nelson the palm appears repeatedly. In the chief of the shield a palm tree rises out of waves. The dexter supporter, a sailor, bears a palm branch in his left hand, and the sinister supporter, a lion rampant, has a palm branch in his right paw. The palm tree rising from waves recalls the famous anagram *Honor est a Nilo*, formed from the words Horatio Nelson.

The two palm branches encircling the name of the College and fastened together by a riband bearing the College motto first appeared on the sides of the College prize books about the year 1833. The money laid out by the College authorities for the purchase of prize books was a wise expenditure. These volumes were always of the most solid and sterling character. They consisted of standard English works, and first class editions of the Greek and Latin Classics. They were ordered directly from London, where also they were handsomely full bound in library style previous to exportation. The influence of these books upon the literary tastes of the country was without doubt considerable. They encouraged studies of a superior kind, and created a fondness for handsomely bound works. They also did much to foster a spirit of loyalty towards the Institution. They made their way into families and houses, where, sixty years ago at all events, books of this description would rarely be seen in Canada. In many households, clerical and lay, the prize books acquired by the younger members of the family became the foundation afterwards of extensive and very valuable collections.

H. S.

THE COLLEGE AND ITS ENDOWMENT.

BY RUPERT E. KINGSFORD, M.A., LL.B.

IT has been deemed advisable in this paper to present an account, in chronological order, of the steps taken to found the College. References are made to the original sources of information, so that verification, if desired, will be simple.

In Sessional Papers, old Province of Upper Canada, 1831, at p. 105, will be found a despatch from the Duke of Portland to Mr. President Russell, dated 4th November, 1797. This despatch recites an address from the Legislative Council and Legislative Assembly of the Province of Upper Canada praying that "His Majesty be graciously pleased to direct his Government to appropriate a certain portion of the waste lands of the Crown as a fund for the establishment and support of a respectable Grammar School in each district, and also of a College or University for the instruction of youth in the different branches of liberal knowledge."

The despatch then states that the King has granted the prayer of the petition, firstly, the establishment of Free Grammar Schools in those districts in which they are called for; and in due process of time, by establishing other seminaries of a larger and more comprehensive nature for the promotion of religious and moral learning, and the study of the arts and sciences.

On the 6th November, 1798, Honourable President Russell communicated with Chief Justice Elmsley, and asked that the Council recommend how the objects contemplated in the despatch should be carried out. On the 1st December, 1798, the recommendations were made (1) that 500,000 acres should be set apart for the establishment and maintenance on the royal foundation of four Grammar Schools and a University in the Province of Upper Canada. (2) That the provision for the establishment and maintenance of the University be at least equal to the endowment of the four schools taken together.

THE COLLEGE AND ITS ENDOWMENT. 45

The above letter and the recommendations will be found in Sessional Papers, 1831, pp. 106-107.

It is stated, Sessional Papers, 1831, p. 108, and it is probably the fact, that no answer was made to these recommendations, nor was there any further confirmation of them. They have been accepted as the basis on which all subsequent grants were made.

District Grammar Schools were founded, but were not endowed with land, though the masters were paid in accordance with another recommendation.

On 7th January, 1819, the Executive Council communicated with Sir Peregrine Maitland, Lieut.-Governor of the Province, on the subject. They requested (Sessional Papers, 1831, p. 109) formal sanction to sell, lease, grant and dispose of 500,000 acres above referred to for the purpose of establishing a University. They stated that the District Schools were not required, and asked for a Commission to manage the lands and for a Royal Charter for the University. Communications then took place between Sir Peregrine and the Home Government, and in a despatch written in 1822 (Sessional Papers, 1831, p. 108) Sir P. Maitland suggests that: "Much good might be effected by the organization of a general system of education; an object to which might be applied the proceeds of the sale of some portion of the lands set aside under the title of "School Reserves," consisting of twelve townships, or 740,000 acres, still however reserving a certain portion for the future endowment of a University, should such an establishment not be considered advisable at present."

On the 12th October, 1823, Lord Bathurst wrote as follows (Sessional Papers, 1831, p. 106): "I am happy to have it in my power to convey to you His Majesty's consent that you appropriate a portion of the Reserves set aside for the establishment of a University for the support of schools on the national plan of education. In 1823, the General Board of Education was established (Sessional Papers, 1831, p. 106). On the 19th December, 1825, Sir Peregrine Maitland wrote again to Lord Bathurst recommending the establishment of the University, and stated that 450,000 acres of land reserved for education and set apart were not very available, and asked that an equal quantity of these lands be exchanged for that portion of Crown Reserves still belonging to the Government. (Sessional Papers, 1851, Appendix E. E. E.)

On the 10th March, 1826, the Legislative Council reported as follows: "In 1798, 549,000 acres were set apart for purposes of education and endowment of schools. Of these, 190,573 acres were assigned to the General

Board of Education, leaving for the endowment of a University, 358,427 acres, or about seven townships. It is proposed to exchange four of these townships for Crown Reserves. The advantage would be reciprocal, as the Government would have a tract of 248,000 acres at its disposal in eligible situations which might be assigned to any object for which the Reserves might have been considered applicable, and the University would be enabled to go much sooner into operation. (Sessional Papers, 1851, Appendix E. E. E.)

In 1827, Lord Bathurst authorized this exchange. (Dr. McCaul's Evidence, Sessional Papers, 1851, Appendix E. E. E.)

On the 16th May, 1827, the Charter of the University of King's College was issued, and on the 29th February, 1828, the endowment was granted to it of 225,944 acres. (Sessional Papers, 1828, p. 78).

Sir John Colborne became Lieutenant-Governor in November, 1828. Trouble immediately arose about the illiberal nature of the Charter, and on 28th December, 1828, it was suspended.

On 19th January, 1829, in reply to an address complaining of the character of the Charter, Sir John Colborne suggested that the first change in the Charter which should be recommended, and which would conduce more than any other to its becoming eminently useful to the Province, was to connect the Royal Grammar School with King's College in such a manner that its exhibitions, scholarships, and chief support might depend on the funds of that endowment. (Sessional Papers, 1829, p. 14).

On the 19th March, 1829, in reply to the Lieutenant-Governor's message of the 19th January, the House replied :—" We are not prepared to express a wish to incorporate the proposed institution with the University, or to confide the former to the care of persons superintending the latter, and we therefore wholly repose in your Excellency to designate, organize, and foster a Royal Grammar School, which we wish to be called "Colborne College," upon the most liberal principles, under the most able masters, and deriving funds from the source already mentioned by your Excellency."

Again (Sessional Papers, 1829, p. 73), the House addressed Sir John Colborne as follows :—" The House trusts that no hoped for modification of the present charter will suspend the exertions of His Excellency to put into operation Colborne College, and by the observance of those liberal principles which His Excellency has already been pleased to patronize and recommend to open with as little delay as possible opportunities of education in no way inferior to those contemplated by the proposed University."

Thus requested by the Legislative Assembly on the 4th January, 1830, instruction in the College was begun.

The House met in the same month, and in reply to an address of the 19th January, asking for information as to what had been done, a message was sent down by Sir John Colborne on the 23rd January, 1830, stating that he had caused a sale of lots in York set apart for endowment of a Grammar School, but that every exertion would be used to induce His Majesty to endow the new College liberally. (Sessional Papers, 1830, pp. 17, 23.)

On the 3rd February, 1830, the House requested further information to which the Lieutenant-Governor replied by a message of the 4th February, 1830, stating that he had no further information to give for the present, and adding:—"Before I leave the Province, I shall endeavour to procure for the institution (Upper Canada College) such protection as may enable it to counteract the influence of local jealousies, or of the ignorance, or vice, to which in a new country it may sometimes be naturally exposed." (Sessional Papers, 1830, p. 80.)

On the 4th March, 1830, the Legislative Council warmly congratulated the Lieutenant-Governor on the foundation of the College.

In January, 1831, the College moved to its own buildings on Russell Square which had been granted to it. The Legislature having again met, and on the 21st January addressed the Lieutenant-Governor for information respecting the survey reservation, sale, or appropriation of certain lands called school townships, on the 2nd February a return was sent down, and on the next day a further return was asked for (Sessional Papers, 1831, pp. 22, 37, and 39.)

On the 7th February, full returns were sent down. These returns are to be found on pages 105 *et seq.* of this volume (Sessional Papers, 1831), and there can be seen the documents above referred to printed in full.

The Legislature again met, in December, 1831, and once more took up the subject of school lands. On the 23rd inst., an address on the subject was presented to His Excellency. On the 26th December, 1831, in reply to that address, the Lieutenant-Governor notified the Legislature of his having set apart 66,000 acres "for the support of Upper Canada College, and for the purpose of raising a fund from which the advances made to establish that Seminary by the University Council and by the Board of Education may be repaid."

The Legislature was not satisfied with this message, and on the 27th December, 1831, requested the Lieutenant-Governor to forward their address of the 23rd December to England. (Sessional Papers, 1831, pp. 57 to 63.)

On the 9th November, 1832, when the Legislature again met, the Lieutenant-Governor communicated a despatch from the Home Government dated 5th July, 1832, in which the decision was communicated, that the sums arising from that portion of the school lands not already alienated should be paid into the hands of the Receiver-General to be applied to the promotion of education the Legislature might direct.

In the same session a Committee on Education instituted a most elaborate inquiry into the origin and then condition of the College, and recommended (pp. 58 and 60) the further endowment of the College and also its incorporation as "filling a link in the great system of education."

This course was adopted in the Act of 1833

Hence we have seen:

1. That the founder of the College was Sir John Colborne, and that the Legislature heartily welcomed his suggestion.

2. That the Legislature of 1829 expressly placed the matter in his hands to "originate, organize, and foster" the Institution, and even requested him to call it after himself. In this year the endowment was set apart for the University.

3. That the Legislature of 1830, when informed that the College had been instituted, congratulated the Lieutenant-Governor on the step taken, as did also the Legislative Council.

4. That the Legislature of 1831 expressed no disapproval of the fact that the College buildings were then in course of erection, although informed of the circumstance.

5. That the Legislature of 1832, although desiring that the unappropriated balance of school lands might be placed under their own management, made no request for the stoppage of work on the College or for its abolition. In this year the endowment was set apart for the College.

6. That the Legislature of 1832, after full investigation, advised further endowment and the incorporation of the College.

7. That the Legislature of 1833 actually incorporated the College, and thus gave legal embodiment to their own creation.

It has been therefore shown that the College was not founded on any act of usurpation, nor was its endowment taken from the University. The latter institution received its full complement of 225,944 acres, or one-half of the whole amount set apart for purposes of education. Nor were the Grammar Schools robbed, as, in 1832, the Crown surrendered to the Province 248,000 acres being the whole unappropriated remainder of the original grant, and being all that could have been claimed on that grant. It will be a matter of gratification to all old College Boys to know that their old school has so plain and honest a record. There has been much misrepresentation, and many unfounded statements have been made in the attempt to show that the College was founded on property taken by usurpation. The evidence collected above is unimpeachable, and speaks for itself. The College was not founded on fraud, but on an endowment granted by lawful authority, animated by a just appreciation of the wants of Upper Canada.*

---

* See Appendix, for list of the lands granted to the College by the Crown.

REGIME OF THE REV. DR. HARRIS, 1830-38.

BY THE EDITORS.

IN A FORMER CHAPTER, we have spoken of the unpropitious character of the era which saw the founding of Upper Canada College. When the enterprise was launched, both man and the elements seemed to conspire, if not to bring it to failure, to detract, at least, from the full measure of its success. Within a year of the opening of the College in its new buildings, the cholera swept over the town, and the boarding-houses were in daily fear of the invading step of the pestilence. Nor was the community free from other alarms. In Canada, as in England, Reform was the watchword of the hour, and the abuses were not few which Reform had then to amend. The issue was the now burning one between popular rights and irresponsible government, an issue which, long and bitterly fought out, was to be decided only after the keenest party strife, ending in rebellion. Already, Wm. Lyon Mackenzie had been repeatedly expelled from the House of Assembly, and the political struggle in the halls of the Legislature extended far outside. The effect of this period of strained political relations and unwholesome excitement can be traced throughout the social life of the time: even Education bore the marks of the upheaval, in the autocratic and non-conciliatory attitude of the ruling Oligarchy. Fortunately there was a firm independent hand at the helm during Sir John Colborne's *régime*, and His Excellency, having shaped his course in his relations to Upper Canada College, and made up his mind as to the sort of institution he designed it to be, did not suffer himself to be turned aside in the pursuance of his object by either executive weakness or popular caprice. We shall somewhat anticipate events if we here make a quotation from a Toronto journal—*The Courier*—written at the close of Sir John Colborne's administration; but the extract so well illustrates His Excellency's interest in the College he was about to found, that we may be pardoned for here embodying it. The reference to the University, still *in posse*, bears out, though with another explanation, what we have previously said about the

Lieutenant-Governor being in no hurry to push forward the more ambitious scheme. The "fling" at the illiteracy of the popular Chamber will be understood by recalling the fact that *The Courier* was a fine old, and well-flavoured, Tory organ. Here is the quotation

> "With indefatigable zeal Sir John Colborne devoted himself personally to the duties of his office. An early riser, and punctual in his habits—he never was without a scheme for the improvement of some part or other of the country. Education, no less than internal improvement and emigration, occupied his early and constant attention. At his bidding, in spite of obstacles innumerable, and of opposition from all quarters, Upper Canada College, with its substantial and appropriate buildings, arose, and a swampy common was converted into a seat of learning. This institution has certainly been his favourite object. He has annually given a prize of the value of ten guineas to the best Latin scholar under a certain age; he has taken a personal and never-failing interest in its minutest details; and encouraged the manly English game of Cricket among the boys. Frequently, when passing the College play-ground on a bright summer's afternoon, he would stop, we are told, and look with satisfaction on the lively and animated scene. And well indeed might he gaze with unalloyed and virtuous pleasure on this, a spectacle of his own creation! A father, and a kind one too, himself, he must have reflected with delight on his having succeeded in bestowing upon the rising generation advantages equal to those which he himself enjoyed at Winchester College; and he must have recalled with mingled emotions those days when 'glowing hot,' he played the very game which was then being contested before him. Had it been in his power, a University would have followed the establishment of a College; but as long as a majority of our Legislators can neither read nor write, nor speak English, we must place the realization of this golden dream among the baseless visions of Utopia."

Let us return, however, to the beginnings of the Institution. In the minutes of the Board for the General Superintendence of Education, under date April 4th, 1829, we find a letter from Sir John Colborne to Dr. Jones, Vice-Chancellor of Oxford University, imposing upon that gentleman the duty of selecting a principal for the new College, also two Classical Masters, and a Mathematical Master—all of whom are to be sent to the scene of their future labours in Upper Canada by November of the same year. With the Vice-Chancellor of Oxford were associated, in this duty of selecting the masters, the Rev. C. Stocker, late Principal of Elizabeth College, Guernsey, and the Rev. Chas. Yonge, of Eton College. The choice these gentlemen made the reader will have learned from the preceding contribution of the Rev. Dr. Scadding. The masters arrived in Toronto late in the Fall of 1829, and at the opening of the new year, as we have already seen, the College began operations, pending the erection of its own buildings, in the Home District Grammar School. The staff consisted of the Principal, the Rev. Dr. Joseph H. Harris; the Vice-Principal (then in the country, and taken over from the headmastership of the District Grammar School,) the Rev. Dr. Phillips; First Classical Master: the Rev. Chas. Mathews; Second Classical Master: the Rev. Wm. Boulton; Mathematical Master: the Rev. Charles Dade; Drawing Master: Mr. Drewry; French

Master: Mr. J. P. de la Haye; Writing Master: Mr. G. A. Barber; Assistant Writing Master and teacher of English: Mr. Padfield; Janitor: S. Alderdice. The staff was immediately afterwards supplemented by the appointment of Mr. John Kent as head of a Preparatory School or elementary form in the College. The boarding school was not organized until some years later, with Mrs. Fenwick as Matron. Lieutenant-Colonel Wells, who was on the Council of King's College, acted for a time as Treasurer of the Board, and Mr. G. A. Barber as Fees Collector. The affairs of the College were administered by King's College Council, the chief members of which were the Hon. John Strachan, D.D., Archdeacon of York, the Hon. Chief Justice Sir J. B. Robinson, the Honourables Wm. Allan, George W. Markland, Duncan Cameron, Peter Robinson, J. H. Dunn, Lieutenant-Colonel Wells, Grant Powell, James Fitzgibbon, C. Widmer, C. C. Small, and Lieutenant-Colonel O'Hara. In the labours of this body, His Excellency the Lieutenant-Governor took a hearty interest.

With the imported and improvised staff we have enumerated, and the organization of a Council of learned and influential gentlemen to watch over its affairs, Upper Canada College set out on its historic educational career, though handicapped by the adverse circumstances of the troubled time, to which we have previously referred. The financial basis of the Institution, as we have already seen, was a land grant of 66,000 acres. This Crown appropriation yielded as yet no income, though presently the Commissioner of Crown Lands was instructed to put the lands on the market, and to pay over the proceeds of sales to the trust fund of King's College, whose Council were to control the affairs of Upper Canada College and advance it money for its immediate maintenance. In addition to the land grant, Government made the College an annual allowance first of £250, which was shortly afterwards increased to £500, and then to a £1000 a year. Its other sources of maintenance were the College fees, from an attendance numbering about a hundred pupils—the fees being two pounds a quarter in the College proper, and one pound five shillings a quarter in the Preparatory School. Five shillings extra, per quarter, were charged both classes of pupils, for quill-pens, ink, fuel and lighting. Though furnished with these various sources of income, the Institution was in no position for a long while to pay its way. New buildings had to be erected for the College; and there was at the outset considerable expense incurred in making the old Grammar School temporarily suitable. Dwelling-houses for the resident masters had also to be built, and these were necessarily of a size to accommodate boarders until a building, specially suited to the purpose, was provided. The staff, moreover, was large and expensive, the salaries ranging from a £100 to £600 a year. The annual cost of maintenance, estimated at the inception of the College, was under £4000. The actual cost, as we learn some nine years afterwards, was between £6000 and £7000 a year. In 1839, on a review of the financial affairs of the College, it seems that the Institution had fallen behind in its accounts over £30,000, most of which was currently met by advances from King's College.

'However disappointing, at a first glance, was this showing of the financial affairs of the new Institution, it did not by any means entail so great a loss to King's College. Nor was the experiment itself fairly chargeable with the discredit of occasioning such a loss. The present-day writer can afford to be frank in dealing with the subject, and the Editors of this volume are not called upon to gloss over any facts. The truth is, the financial management by the University authorities was at first careless and bad. There is nothing to be gained in going now into details, or in exhuming the corpse of a long-buried controversy. But the historian of the period can hardly pass over the fact that, with regard both to the land accounts and to the College dues, there was great administrative laxity, and, in some subordinate quarters, dishonesty. College dues were unpaid and misappropriated, and large arrearages were suffered to accumulate on lands sold belonging to the Institution. In 1839, when its financial affairs were overhauled and put on a more business-like and methodical footing, over £12,000 were due to the College, some considerable portion of which was never recovered.

Where responsibility for this state of things ought definitely to rest, it is difficult, after the long interval, now to say. The country was new, and the management of institutions, either endowed or incorporated, was not then rigidly scientific. The Province, moreover, was in a very anarchic and disturbed condition, and the field for the exercise of good faith and loyalty to public trust was apt to be invaded by the baser virtues. Nor had public opinion, at the period, free scope for the healthy play of censure or of criticism, which the state of affairs demanded, and which would have proved helpful to morality. The country, in truth, was trying a great educational experiment under very exceptional and adverse circumstances. When political institutions are on their trial, and when public life and the reputations of public men become the sport of lawlessness and are enmeshed in the intrigues of faction, we need hardly look for people to be over-scrupulous or honest. The conflict of the period has long since happily died, and it would be poor work for any one now to rake over the dead ashes. Far more profitable will it be to turn to the internal administration of the College. Before doing so, however, let us here take the opportunity of saying, that to make good the advances of King's College, Sir John Colborne caused a deed to be drawn, conveying to King's College Council

18,000 of the 66,000 acres of the land endowment of Upper Canada College, and begged that body to take charge of the remainder of the lands and to direct the Bursar to sell them for the benefit of Upper Canada College. This arrangement, which was made in March, 1833, the minutes of the Council of Education show, was agreed to and duly carried into effect.

There is another matter that here calls for comment, in considering the relations of Upper Canada College with King's College, viz., the fact that while the latter institution was as yet not in existence, Upper Canada College was at the time doing University work in the Province, and that King's College, under the circumstances, need not have been careful to exact the uttermost farthing from the indebted minor Institution. Fortunately it was able, by the arrangement we have just related, to refund to the University the sums advanced it, and, later on, the Legislature gave Upper Canada College an acquittance of the debt. But, had this been otherwise, Upper Canada College might with confidence have claimed a good set-off for the work it was doing for higher education. Its "seventh" form work,—not only in Classics and in the higher Mathematics, but in Philosophy, and in Divinity subjects, such as Hebrew and New Testament Greek, as well as in Surveying and other practical departments,—was the work usually done in a University course. This is a circumstance that was too often lost sight of, in later-day discussions of the early relations of Upper Canada College with the institution afterwards known as Toronto University.

Let us now turn to a more pleasing and less polemical subject—the contemporary record of the educational achievements of the College. A formal report by the Principal, at the expiry of the first year's operations, enables the Editors to show what was accomplished so early in its career. The Report is introduced by a few prefatory remarks of Archdeacon Strachan, commending the founding of the Institution and the year's work. Says the Archdeacon: "What had only been projected a few months before is now happily accomplished, and when the first annual examination took place in December last (1830), the audience and indeed the whole Province might be justly congratulated on the establishment of a seminary equal, if not superior, in its appointments for classical and elementary instruction to any in the Mother Country. The result of the examination was most satisfactory, and when the Board declared, through its President, that the progress of the youth in their various studies had fully answered every reasonable expectation and left a deep impression on the minds of all the members, of the zeal, skill, and ability manifested by the gentlemen to whom their education has been committed, the declaration was fully accorded in by everyone present." From the Report of Principal Harris, we make the following extract, together with a synopsis, in which the old College boy of the period will doubtless be interested, of the work of the year in the respective forms. Says the Principal, writing to the Trustees:—

"The first year of Upper Canada College having arrived at its termination, I beg to lay before you the following statement of our proceedings and progress during that period; and although the average advancement of the scholars is not anything extraordinary, I will yet venture to hope that under all the attendant circumstances the result of our first year's labour has not fallen short of what might have been reasonably anticipated.

"The circumstances to which I allude as tending to retard our progress hitherto, are the difficulties which must necessarily accompany the putting into operation of an extensive seminary in a new country, and in some measure on new principles, with, more especially, the time which is invariably lost in bringing a number of boys who have been hitherto instructed, some on one system, and some on another, to the same uniform plan of discipline and education.

* * * * * * *

"According to the plan on which I proposed to conduct the instruction of the scholars, the College, independently of the preparatory school, is divided into six forms or classes: during the past year the number of forms actually in operation was only five; as it did not appear that there were any scholars who could advantageously be put upon the course designed for the sixth form, though I trust that as we proceed there will be no lack of candidates for the highest degree of instruction which we can impart.

"A detail of the occupation of the several forms will perhaps be the most satisfactory means of conveying a correct idea of the nature and extent of education which a youth may acquire, either in going through the entire course of six forms, or in proceeding only as far as any particular form short of the highest.

First Form.—Rudiments of Latin, embracing some of the leading rules of Syntax; Latin Vocabulary; construing Cordier's "Colloquies" with the aid of a translation. English reading, and on Monday morning memoriter recitation from the New Testament; Writing and Arithmetic. This Form attends the Classical Masters 19 hours; the Writing and English Master 9 hours, each week.

Second Form.—Latin Grammar continued, including the entire Syntax, "Propria quæ maribus," and "As in Præsenti;" construing Corderius and Lectiones Selectæ, without the aid of a translation, and writing Latin exercises from the Eton Exempla Minora. Miscellaneous English reading and Scripture recitation on Monday morning. Elements of French; Writing and Arithmetic. This Form attends the Classical Masters 18½ hours, the French master 2 hours, and the Writing and English Masters 7¼ hours, each week.

Third Form.—Latin Grammar completed, including Prosody; Cornelius Nepos and Phædrus, exercises, etc., Clarke's Latin Elements of Greek; one lesson per week of English History; recitation of Scripture on Monday morning; French, Writing, Arithmetic, and Geography. This Form attends the Classical Masters 16½ hours, the French Master 6 hours, and the Writing Masters 5½ hours, each week.

Fourth Form.—Greek Grammar, to the end of regular verbs; Latin Grammar complete; construing Valpy's Greek Delectus, Cæsar's Commentaries and Ovid's Epistles. Exercises; Valpy's Greek, Ellis's Latin, Latin Verse; English Themes; Roman History, Scripture History, Elements of Mathematics, Writing and Arithmetic, Geography, French. This Form attends the Classical Masters 15 hours, the French Master 4 hours, the Mathematical Master 5½ hours, and the Writing Masters 3 hours, each week.

Fifth Form.—Greek Grammar continued; Latin Grammar entire; construing Greek text, Analecta Græca Minora, Ovid's Metam., Virgil, Cicero. Exercises; Valpy's Greek, Ellis's Latin re-translations of Cicero, Latin Verse. English Themes, Grecian History, Mathematics,

French and Geography. This Form attends the Classical Masters 16½ hours, the Mathematical Master 5 hours, and the French Master 6½ hours, each week.

Sixth Form.—Greek and Latin Grammar entire; construing Greek text, Dalzel's Collectanea Græca Majora; Horace, Cicero, Virgil. Exercises: Valpy's Neilson's Greek, Valpy's Elegantiæ Latinæ, retranslation, and memoriter recitations of Greek and Latin authors, Latin Verse, Latin and English Themes; Mathematics, and French. This Form attends the Classical Masters 17 hours, the Mathematical Master 8 hours, and the French Master 3 hours, each week.

"It is proper to observe," remarks Principal Harris, "that it is not contemplated always to confine the classical reading of the sixth form to those books only which are named in the above detail; but these will be raised from time to time as there may be occasion, and the higher classics introduced whenever there is sufficient advancement to allow of their introduction. Possibly, too, in the course of time, it may become desirable to add other branches which do not at present enter into any course of study. I would also remark of the occasional reading and committing to memory of the Scriptures, that as the scholars consist of the children of parents of every religious denomination, particular care is taken to adhere strictly to the simple text, without any comment or explanation, further than concerns its literal and grammatical sense, and in the Preparatory School, in consequence of a representation made to me, those scholars who are Roman Catholics make use of the Douay Version of the New Testament.

* * * * * * *

"In adverting, in conclusion, to the late examination, I would notice that there were only five forms in operation during the previous year; the extent to which that examination could be carried was necessarily limited to the course prescribed for the fifth form. Future examinations we may expect to be carried to a higher point, as well as to include some subjects, such as History and Geography, which, though not neglected during the past year, were not introduced into the examination, because we were for a great part of that period unprovided with uniform books on those subjects.

"With respect to the proficiency actually exhibited by the scholars at the late examination, I have much satisfaction in stating my opinion, that considering it to have been the first public examination in a new Institution, and also considering that our object has been rather to lay a sound foundation than to make a display of rapid and apparently extensive acquirements, the examination was passed generally in such a manner as to encourage favourable anticipations of the future, both as regards the College and the scholars. And whilst recording this opinion, I beg to be allowed to express my sense of the able and unremitting co-operation of my colleagues and the masters of the establishment in general, by which so satisfactory a result of our first year's labours has been effected.

"To the above report, gentlemen, which I have the honour to submit to you, I have only to add my sincere desire, and I trust not unfounded hope, that the success of so nobly designed an Institution as Upper Canada College may be correspondent to the liberality with which you have provided for its establishment, and that its beneficial effects may equal the wishes of the exalted individual whose enlightened regard for the public good projected and completed it."

      (Signed) JOSEPH H. HARRIS,
             Principal of the College.

We have taken up considerable space with this first Report of Principal Harris, but the reader will doubtless say we have done wisely, as the Report not only attests the great progress already made by the College, but emphasizes the fact that the Institution was in good and able hands, and promises well for the educational training of the future youth of the country. There is a strain of sound common sense throughout the document, par-

THE COUNTESS OF ELGIN AND LADY ALICE LAMBTON RECEIVING BOUQUETS AND THE CREST OF THE COLLEGE, OCTOBER 20TH, 1847, IN THE HALL OF UPPER CANADA COLLEGE.

(Copied from an old lithograph by T. H. Stevenson, dedicated to His Excellency Lord Elgin & Kincardine, Governor-General, &c., &c.)

ticularly in the passages referring to the avoidance of display in the education of the pupils, and in the consideration paid to those of the Roman Catholic communion in the reading of Scripture. Doubtless, Principal Harris's tolerance reflected the spirit prevailing in England, which he had recently quitted, and which had just wisely passed the Catholic Emancipation Bill. The number of pupils admitted to the College in the year which had then closed, was, we learn from the Report, 140. The hours for school work were from 8.45 to 12, and from 2 to 4 o'clock, with a morning session on Saturdays. The general average of attendance at this period was in the neighbourhood of 120. Of this number, it appears, 20 boarded with the resident masters; 84 were College boys residing in the town; and 16 belonged to the Preparatory School. The attendance was at periods affected by the political disturbances of the time; sometimes, also, by the weather and the state of the roads; and, during the Cholera year, when every twentieth inhabitant of York was swept away by the visitation, there was more or less irregularity. Considering the, as yet, primitive condition of the infant metropolis, the school attendance was, however, not to be complained of; and this fact may justly be taken as an indication of how highly the College was prized. In the Harris *régime*, the College had the advantage, as we have seen, of the eager and hearty interest of Sir John Colborne. While he remained administrator of the Province he was able to repress the rising tide of rebellion; and, in no small measure, he succeeded in the endeavour to deal justly with all. "It is less difficult," said he on one occasion, "to discover the traces of political dissensions and local jealousies in the Colony than it is to efface them." To efface them was the work of years and of a happier order of things. Meantime, both the College and the town grew, though it was still a time of trial for both.

With the year 1834, Toronto rose to the dignity of an incorporated city. Rejoicing in its new-found honours, an humble effort was made to improve the King's highway and to extend the planked area of the civic side-walks. The College gallantly responded by bridging, with a culvert, the ditch at its King Street entrance, and guarding its approaches with the defensive dignity of gates. There are not a few old College boys still alive who remember what an undertaking it was in those days to get daily to school. In the present year of grace, less than half-an-hour's drive will bring a pupil from the northern limits of the town: when the city was incorporated it would consume as much time to overcome the obstacles in a short walk along King Street. If the season were Summer, an additional quarter of an hour would have to be allowed for the consumption of an ice at "Rossi's." The Toronto "Belgravia" and "Mayfair" were then just a little way west of the Don. If there was to be a party in that quarter, an evening would often be consumed before the College boarder could get within sight of the dance. The usual conveyance to the scene of the revel was a springless cart, with the swinging pendant of a lanthorn light.

Nor was the environment of the College anything like that seen by the pupil of to-day. The playground was partly a marsh; and to the West of the College was, we believe, a brick-kiln, encompassed by woods. In Winter, the boarding-house was lit by the cheer of a blazing log fire, and without, in Summer, there was the attraction of a cool well and deep oaken bucket. For the pupil boarder, the Easter holidays were occasionally beguiled by a trip to Niagara, in the company of one of the Masters, (it will be found in the bill!)—the world beyond being unlocked to the imagination through the sober medium of "a Father's Letters to his Son." Later on, "Olney," an American text-book, came on the scene, with the useful adjunct of a "Mercator's Chart." But in neither the New World nor the Old was geography, as yet, either the scientific pursuit or the interesting study it is to-day. The story is told of a letter once arriving at the College for one of the Masters, addressed "York, Upper Canada, near Hudson's Bay!"

As the years passed, Time brought its changes within the College as well as without. In 1834, the Rev. William Boulton died, and the Rev. Dr. Phillips retired. The aged widow of the former is still a resident of Toronto, though, we believe, but two of the many pupil-boarders are alive who sat at her table when her husband was a Master at the College. From the lips of one of these the Editors had recently the privilege of listening to a kindly eulogium on Mr. Boulton. In Dr. Scadding's valued contribution, the reader will already have made the acquaintance of Dr. Phillips, the College's first and only Vice-Principal. With the reverend gentleman's retirement, the title was dropped. He accepted a mission at Weston, and up to the time of his death, fifteen years afterwards, he was in receipt of an annuity from the College of a £100. To this, his services entitled him, not only as a Master in the College, but as a faithful labourer in the cause of education in the Home District Grammar School and elsewhere in the Province. The vacant Masterships were filled by the appointment of the Rev. Geo. Maynard, M.A., of Cambridge, and Mr. F. W. Barron, M.A., of Toronto.

There is another event to chronicle in the affairs of the Institution at this period, namely, the departure from Upper Canada of His Excellency Sir John Colborne, the founder and first Governor of the College. This event occurred early in the year 1836, though, having been appointed to a military command, His Excellency did not leave the country until some years afterwards. Fortunately for himself he retired from the administration of the Upper Province before the storm of rebellion burst upon the country. At the period of his leaving Toronto, the sky was comparatively clear, though it clouded over when it became known that the Lieutenant-Governor had yielded so far to his ministerial advisers as to endow the fifty-seven Anglican Rectories. What he had done for education in the founding and endowing of Upper Canada College, was, however, to give him no uneasiness. He left Toronto with many assurances of the debt the City and Province owed him for the interest he had manifested in education In the farewell address of the City Corporation, these words occur: "The benefits bestowed on the Province through the exertions of your Excellency in promoting the education of youth, will ever make your Excellency's name venerated in the Colony. We have no doubt that what your Excellency has so well begun will prove a lasting good to the Province and secure many happy reflections in your Excellency's mind when you are no longer amongst us." Not less interesting, and perhaps more acceptable, to His Excellency, was the "Address of the Former Pupils of Upper Canada College," which we here append, with Sir John Colborne's brief reply.

To His Excellency Major-General Sir John Colborne, Knight Commander of the Most Honourable Military Order of the Bath, &c., and Lieutenant-Governor of the Province of Upper Canada.

MAY IT PLEASE YOUR EXCELLENCY :—

When your Excellency's expected retirement from the Government of this Province is the subject of such deep and general regret, we who have been educated at Upper Canada College, but who are now engaged in preparing for our respective avocations in life, cannot but feel it to be our duty to express the sorrow we experience at your Excellency's departure.

If the generality of the inhabitants of this flourishing Province bear testimony to the numerous advantages which your Excellency's paternal administration has conferred on this Colony, and the uniform energy, diligence, and perseverance so signally displayed in all those matters contributing to the public good, with what feelings of gratitude and esteem should we offer our dutiful and sincere attachment to your Excellency for the foundation of an Institution to which we are indebted for the blessings of an education we now so highly appreciate.

Upon your Excellency assuming the Government of this Province, your attention was happily directed to the then existing state of education, and discovering not only that the growing wealth of commerce but also that the character and genius of its inhabitants demanded acquirements superior to those which had hitherto been attainable, and that unless opportunities were immediately afforded for the instruction of youth in the higher branches of literature and science, they could not be duly qualified for the fulfilment of the various and important duties which society would hereafter require of them, with your characteristic promptitude the foundation of Upper Canada College was determined upon by your Excellency, and in little more than one year this Institution was placed in successful operation.

In giving us the means so eminently calculated to raise the standard of classical literature in this Province, we are happy to observe that the more generally useful though less ornamental branches of education were not sacrificed to those suited to a more polished and refined state of society.

Your Excellency, by presenting an annual prize to the College, for which many of us have contended, has, we are confident, contributed much to the laudable spirit of emulation which generally in its effects is so highly beneficial to the pupils of a public institution.

From the character Upper Canada College has attained under your Excellency's kind and munificent patronage, it must ever remain an imperishable monument of the wisdom of your Excellency's Government.

On this interesting occasion we cannot but again express to your Excellency our unfeigned regret at your approaching departure from this Province, and while you leave in our hearts a grateful recollection of the noble boon you have bestowed upon us in establishing the College at which we have received our education, rest assured that our best wishes for the happiness of yourself and family accompany your Excellency.

> "*Di tibi dent annos, nam de te
> ....Catera munes.*"

G. D. WELLS, *Secretary.*

HIS EXCELLENCY WAS PLEASED TO MAKE THE FOLLOWING REPLY :—

GENTLEMEN :—"An address from those who are now experiencing the blessings of the extensive and liberal education which they have received at Upper Canada College cannot but be received by me with the greatest pleasure and satisfaction. You are among the first who have demonstrated the essential benefits to society which are derived from the establishment of this Royal Institution. May you also ever take the lead in this Province—as Christians, as citizens, as patriots, as members of a community, "*qui consulta patrum, qui leges juraque servant.*" I thank you for the kind expression of your good wishes for myself and family ; and be assured that I shall always watch with great interest the progress and welfare of those who have been students at Upper Canada College."

The following names were appended to the address :—J. Strachan, Jr., A. W. Strachan, S. A. Ridout, R. B. Sullivan, J. O. Heward, W. H. Boulton, G. T. Denison, Robt. Denison, W. W. Fitzgibbon, W. B. Heward, Robert Wells, J. Fitzgibbon, F. Muttlebury, A. Givins, C. Foster, Grant Powell, R. O. Duggan, G. W. Allan, S. B. Smith, L. Ridout, J. H. Cameron, G. Givins, W. Ruttan, G. R. Billings, B. Dixie, R. Cameron, Wm. Bellingham, W. D. Powell, J. Moore, L. Robinson, J. C. Morrison, W. S. Fitzgerald, Thos. Latham, H. Latham, J. Billings, M. Dyett, A. McDonell, W. Dixie, Thomas Moore, G. D. Wells, and John Latham.

The Address, which is both well conceived and well expressed, must have been very gratifying to Sir John Colborne. It is an interesting reminiscence of the early years of the College, of its first founder's connection with it, and of the men who were afterwards to figure, more or less prominently, in Canadian public life. Some of the names appended, it is difficult, after the lapse of time, now to identify ; but it is easy to recognize among the signatories the Hon. George W. Allan, Sir J. Lukin Robinson, Hon. R. B. Sullivan, Mayor Boulton, Col. Wells, Judge Powell, Judge Morrison, J. O. and W. B. Heward, Hon. John Hillyard Cameron, and Colonels G. T. and Robert L. Denison. In the College lists of the period, other well-known names occur of men who afterwards took an active part in the native history, political or social, or were prominent in one or other of the professions. Among these old College boys we find Chief Justice Wallbridge, his brother, W. H. Wallbridge, the Hon. John Beverley

Robinson, Christopher Robinson, Q.C., Larratt W. Smith, D.C.L., the Rev. H. Scadding, D.D., the Rev. Walter Stennett, M.A., the Hon. Adam Crooks, LL.D., Judge Stevenson, the Rev. J. G. D. Mackenzie, M.A., Sheriff Jarvis, Wm. Wedd, M.A., Dr. J. T. Small, Æmilius Irving, Q.C., Dr. W. C. Chewett, Judge W. G. Draper, Judge Kingsmill, Samuel and T. C. Keefer, C.E., Hon. James Patton, LL.D., D. B. Read, Q.C., T. R. and W. Hamilton Merritt, Francis and John O. Heward, Jonas Ap. Jones, James Crowther, Q.C., Henry Hartney, W. H. Weller, W. O. Buchanan, &c., &c.

Not less entitled to honourable place in this Memorial Volume of the College are those who won distinction in the Class Lists of the year and who figure among the Annual Prize winners, during the *régime* of Dr. Harris. Space will not permit us to give any detailed lists of those eager youths, who, judged by their achievements, seem to have been hungry for intellectual food, and were laudably ambitious of showing how well it agreed with them. Their number is a goodly company, and the honours that fell to them make a good showing. Room, however, must be made, for the list of head-boys of the period. It is as follows: 1832, Henry Scadding; 1833, W. J. Fitzgerald; 1834, Wm. Ruttan; 1835, Wm. Fitzgerald; 1836, Thos. Ewart; 1837, Edward Hurd; 1838, John Ewart. Of these, the first seven head-boys, whose names are to be found in the roll of honour in the Prayer Hall of the College, but one or two survive to testify to the able and assiduous labours of the Principal and Masters of the Institution in which they won distinction. Most of them have fallen asleep: not a few of the number, indeed, passed the portals of the other world at an early age. One of these, poor Ruttan, of Cobourg—a youth of great promise and much beloved while at College—returned from his travels in Europe, three years after carrying all before him in the classroom, to fill a consumptive's grave. Great was his love for his *alma mater:* in a letter to a schoolmate, written abroad, he writes "God bless every brick of it!" A most interesting memoir of the youth, prefaced by a funeral sermon preached by the late Bishop Bethune, then Rector of Cobourg, was published at the time, and contains loving tributes by several of his Masters and a few of his cherished schoolmates. One of the bright band—a now venerable and most interesting historical figure—happily yet lives, to treasure the memory of his triumphs, and still loyally to honour the old College in which for nearly a quarter of a century he was himself a Master. The contribution of the first head-boy to these pages, is not by any means the sole service Dr. Scadding has rendered either to the educational literature of his country, or to the historic annals of the institutions of the city which has the honour to own him as a son. His has been a long, honourable and useful life—a life devoted to good works and the service of his fellowmen. In him education, literature, and local antiquities have had a loving, enthusiastic, and life-long friend. If, in a practical way, he may not be called one of the makers of the city, among antiquarian and literary students he is counted, at least, as one of the makers of its fame. Wherever the Capital of Ontario is known, there is, or ought to be, known the author of "Toronto of Old," its learned and loving annalist. In September, 1838, Dr. Scadding was appointed a Classical Master in the College, and in that capacity, for five and twenty years, he laboured well and faithfully in the Institution he so well loved.

Before passing from the early head-boys of the College, it is due to the other head-form prize winners and head-form boys of the period to say, that though others, more fortunate, snatched from them the laurel of the year, they did much by their industry and talent to add to the honours of the Institution. Among the more successful prizemen of the Harris *régime* we find the following: Geo. W. Allan, Larratt W. Smith, Graham Colborne, Christopher Robinson, R. H. Draper, Wm. Powell, J. Lukin Robinson, W. and S. Jarvis, John Breakenridge, John Helliwell, Walter Stennett, D. B. Read, M. C. Cameron, Wm. Vidal, John H. Cameron, H. J. Boulton, James Patton, John Roaf, and Robt. O'Hara. Of these, it is on record that John Breakenridge and Larratt W. Smith won prizes for English verse, the former in 1836, and the latter in 1837. The subject of Mr. Breakenridge's poem is "Canada." It is a warm apostrophe, in rhymed couplets, to his native land, and finds place in a volume of verse issued in Kingston by the author in 1846, under the title of "The Crusades and other Poems." The theme of Mr. (now Dr.) Larratt W. Smith's muse is "The Accession of Queen Victoria," an event which had just taken place, and is commemorated in stirring and loyal lines. The Editors trust to preserve in another portion of this volume some extracts at least from these fine poetical productions, with other prize compositions in English and Classical verse, belonging to a later *régime*. Dr. Larratt W. Smith, throughout his career at College, was also a frequent and diligent prize winner in other subjects than English verse, a proof not only of the versatility of his talents, but of the excellent training afforded at the Institution which has since had the benefit of Dr. Smith's able and unwearied services, through a long series of years, on the Board of Management.

It is interesting here to note the names of two pupils, both of whom in coming years were to be identified with Masterships in the College, and one of whom filled the Principalship from 1856 to 1861. We refer to Walter Stennett and William Wedd, who, though they studied under different headmasters at Upper Canada College, were classmates in the early years of King's College. Later on, both will come before the reader of these pages, one in connection with the history of his *régime*, and the other as the valued contributor of the chapter on the administration of the Rev. Dr. McCaul. An interesting and delightfully reminiscent paper will, in point of time, naturally precede what is written by the one and what is written about the other, in the case of these two gentlemen. We allude to Mr. Wm. Thomson's gossipy " Retrospect" of the College at the era of the Rebellion. In the perusal of this paper by a pupil contemporary with the events which he so charmingly describes, old College boys will have their hearts warmed by the patriotic enthusiasm of the writer, and by his unaffected loyalty to, and long-surviving interest in, the Institution which he proudly owns as a Mother. Appropriate to the subject of Mr. Thomson's paper is the following " memorandum," which we find appended to the official record of the "Distribution of Prizes," for the year 1837. " In consequence," says the minute, "of the public disturbances, which broke out on the 4th of December, the business of the College was necessarily suspended, and the usual examination omitted, which will account for certain prizes, viz., the first and second Latin Grammar, the Greek Grammar, the Scripture, and the College Boarding House, prizes not having been awarded." However jubilant were young Master Thomson, and doubtless many other of his schoolmates, at the prospect of a lively break in the educational routine of the College, the circumstance we have noted could not have been pleasant to the aspirants for prizes and other omitted or withheld honours.

About this period, the College Council was increased by the appointment to seats at the Education Board of the following gentlemen: Attorney-General, the Hon. Christopher A. Hagerman, the Hon. J. H. Dunn, (Receiver-General), the Hon. John Macaulay, (Inspector-General), the Hon. Vice-Chancellor, R. S. Jameson, and John Simcoe Macaulay, Esq. Some additional changes were also made in the College staff, in the Harris *régime*, which should have been earlier noted. One of these was the appointment of Mr. James Duffy as assistant Writing and English Master. A more important change took place, however, in 1833, when Mr. Drewry, the Drawing Master, retired from ill-health, and Mr. J. G. Howard was appointed to "instruct the College forms in Perspective, Planning and Surveying." The College had for nearly twenty-five years the services of this able and experienced Surveyor and Draughtsman, who now for the space of two generations has been well and favourably known as an Architect in Toronto. The venerable gentleman (he is now in his eighty-sixth year), is still a resident of the city, in which he has always taken a loving and public-spirited interest, and to which, some years ago, he munificently donated 165 acres in the Western suburbs, which compose what is known as High Park, including the grounds attached to his private residence, Colborne Lodge.

The year 1838 saw other changes in the College staff. The Rev. Charles Dade, Mathematical Master, resigned, and his post was filled by the transference to it of the Rev. Mr. Maynard. Mr. Dade's retirement was the occasion of regret, for he was a distinguished scholar, a Fellow of his College, and a successful teacher. In the same year, the College was deprived of its first Principal. We need not go over the ground so well covered already by Dr. Scadding, in the sketches he has supplied of these two gentlemen. The retirement of Dr. Harris was a serious loss to the College, more especially as he withdrew from the country, having accepted a living in England. The College Council have given expression, in the minutes of the body, to their keen regret at losing Dr. Harris. We transcribe the minute: *Resolved*, "That the College Council have great satisfaction in declaring that they value most highly the course of arduous service which the Rev. Dr. Harris has sustained during more than eight years in bringing into proper order and discipline the Seminary which he has superintended with so much distinction, and the success by which his exertions have been attended, and in assuring him that he carries to his retirement in England, their best wishes and earnest hope that he will soon be placed in a station where his talents and eminent acquirements may be a source of comfort to himself and of benefit to that country as they have been to this Province. That while they congratulate Dr. Harris on the more immediate cause of his retirement, they cannot but deeply deplore the loss which Upper Canada College sustains in his resignation, and the more especially because they judge it scarcely possible in many respects to supply his place."

This Resolution of "the Chancellor, President, and Council of the University of King's College," in taking leave of the Rev. Dr. Harris, hardly does justice, we incline to think, to the occasion. The retiring Principal manifestly deserved a more flattering testimonial. The College Council, in any case, owed it to themselves to put what little they had to say in better literary form. But these are matters—perhaps trifling matters—of individual taste and judgment. The important thing before us is the loss the College was now to suffer in the withdrawal of its first Principal. Had the College been a proprietary institution, it would be no marvel to find its shares suffer a decline on the retirement of Dr. Harris. As little of a marvel, however, would it be to see them recover their value on Dr. McCaul's succession. It was no light task Dr. Harris had undertaken, in laying the foundations of the Institution over which he had been called to preside. Considering the difficulties of both time and place, the success that waited upon his eight years of arduous labour was most creditable to him. Not only did he bring the College into existence, and leave it a fully-equipped and efficiently working educational institution; but he stamped it with the impress of his own high professional attainments, and set upon it the seal of repute and honour which it was afterwards to bear. "It is not a small thing," writes a proud chronicler of Eton, "to form the characters of men who may one day guide the action of England, or influence the thought of the world." Is not the remark, with some little qualification, in place, in reviewing the work of Upper Canada College under the mastership of Principal Harris?

THE COLLEGE AND THE REBELLION:
A RETROSPECT.

BY W. THOMSON.

Pupil in the Harris Régime.

MY EARLIEST RECOLLECTIONS of Upper Canada College date back to 1830, when I was only six years of age. My father, the late Col. E. W. Thomson, who at that time had a large contract on the Rideau Canal, with the late Hon. George Crawford as partner, had just then removed from Maitland's Rapids to "muddy Little York," and we lived on Yonge Street, about half a mile north of Lot—now Queen—Street. The house we occupied was known as "Elm Cottage," and was quite in the country; a long stretch of open fields lay between us and the town proper. To these fields we were often obliged to betake ourselves, when going to and fro in the land, as Yonge Street was then a mere causeway of clay—and such clay! In the Spring and Fall, and indeed at any time after much rain, it was almost impassable. Scores of times I have seen both horses and ox teams hopelessly mired, even with empty vehicles—but that was not at all a rare sight on King Street itself in those days. Surely a name and place never fitted each other more pefectly than did "muddy Little York," the embryo Toronto. The mud thereof was of a most adhesive and all-embracing nature, and was wont to stick far "closer than a brother,"—indeed it could not by any means be "shaken off." I then little thought that I should live to see a great city, such as the present capital of Ontario, cover the remote places, woods and fields over which the youth of York then disported themselves, or, that in this year of grace 1889, grandson and grand nephews of my own would be attending the Old School. As an illustration of the comparative wildness of the place in those early days I may say, that one day when I was at play in my father's yard, a deer, chased by hounds, nearly ran over me; and the same year I saw a large black bear killed not three hundred yards from our front door!

THE COLLEGE AND THE REBELLION. 67

Upper Canada College was, at this period, located in a large, plain, frame building at the foot of what was then known as March Street, and a most unsavory reputation this street had. Whether it has improved, under its more aristocratic title of Stanley Street, or, as it is now designated, Lombard Street, I do not know. Of course I was at this time too young to attend the College, but my eldest brother did so, and subsequent events, not unmixed with the history of Canada, have fixed upon my memory the names of many of his schoolmates. Among these, if I mistake not, were John and Alexander Strachan, George W. Allan, Percival and Lionel Ridout, Lukin* and J. B. Robinson, F. W. Jarvis, W. H. Boulton, R. L. and G. T. Denison, Edwin Fisher, John Turquand, George D. Wells, Henry Scadding, Ford Jones, T. A. McLean, R. Playter, Edward Scarlett, &c., &c. These were, I presume, the elder sons of their respective families, as the younger sons of the same houses were afterwards my own fellow pupils. As I look back upon this far away time it always seems to me that the students who attended the College during the first five or six years of its existence were much larger and older boys than those who were afterwards enrolled.

Indeed, many of the pupils of 1830-32, appeared to my very juvenile eyes to be almost grown young men; and a most dashing, strapping, vigorous lot of fellows they were. I can well remember with what awe and admiration I used to look upon them as I trudged back and forth to my own school, which was situated on some open ground just west of Yonge Street, and between King Street and the bay. It was conducted by a teacher named Thomas Thompson. Time, however, always brings its compensations, and before many years I, too, was an Upper Canada College boy, and then these hitherto envied mortals did not look half so big and grand to me as in the days when "distance lent enchantment to the view."

In the spring of 1832, my father, who had then sold out his Rideau Canal contract to Mr. Crawford, removed from York to a beautiful four hundred acre farm in the Township of Toronto, sixteen miles from the city. This land was a Crown grant to my father and mother who were both children of U. E. Loyalists, and we had resided upon it before going to the

*On the death of that notable figure in Canadian history, Chief Justice Sir John Beverley Robinson, his son Lukin succeeded to the Baronetcy, while John Beverley, Jr., after an honourable parliamentary career, became one of the best and most popular of Ontario's Lieutenant-Governors. While holding this important office, his popularity, as is indeed the case to-day, was only equalled by that of his excellent and accomplished wife, a daughter of the late Justice Hagerman. In his younger days this gentleman was a great athlete, or rather a great proficient in all exercises requiring agility, in proof of which I may state that I once saw him at the "Olympic Games" in Toronto, stand upright under a bar, and then, with a short run, clear it at a bound!

Rideau Canal. Indeed, your humble contributor was born there, April 27th, 1824, in the first two-storey hewed log house ever erected in that township. From 1832 to 1836, I was "growing up with the country" in the old homestead; and then came the memorable elections of this latter year, when my father defeated the famous William Lyon Mackenzie for the Second Riding of the County of York. Here, I may remark, *en passant*, that out of his twenty contests this was, I believe, the only occasion upon which the sturdy little rebel (or shall we now say Patriot?) was defeated. The result of this election had not only an immediate influence upon Canadian history, but upon my own humble fortunes as well; for at the beginning of the succeeding winter, in order that my father might attend Parliament, we removed to, what had meantime become, the city of Toronto, and my second eldest brother—the late Hugh C. Thomson—and myself were duly entered at Upper Canada College.

I can never forget how nervous I felt when ushered into the presence of Dr. Harris, the then Principal, for preliminary examination. I was a raw country boy only twelve years of age, and although I had been taught the A, B, C, of Latin by a brother-in-law, the late Rev. Andrew Bell, yet I had never seen any of the text-books then in use at the College; and hence was assigned to the Preparatory School. However, I remained there only three weeks, and when I reached the College proper, I was only three months in the "First Form." My brother, being three years older, and further advanced than I, went at once into the "Third Form." I do not know how it is now, but in those days the College was graded from "Preparatory School" to "Seventh Form;" and there was also a Commercial, or as we called it then, a "Partial" Form, for those pupils who did not wish to study Latin or Greek.

Excellent school as it was, Upper Canada College was then literally ruled by the rod. The discipline exceeded justice. It was harsh, and I think cruel. Petty faults, devoid of malice or moral turpitude, such as talking or laughing in class, were punished by from two to six strokes of the barbarous bamboo cane across the bare hand, causing very severe pain and leaving clearly-defined blood blisters wherever it touched. No wonder that high-spirited boys should resent such treatment, or that they should in many cases become so hardened, that, with a fine irony, they would call their blisters "merit marks"! I am now an old man of sixty-five, and have no interest to serve, except that of truth; and yet, with all my love for my *alma mater*, I venture to assert that this system was a mistaken one, —Solomon's proverb to the contrary notwithstanding. On the other hand, had any one of my teachers of those days condescended to speak kindly to me; and for the moment made a boy of himself for my sake; if he had appealed to my generosity and chivalry, and to my better nature, he would have had a loving, obedient and tractable scholar. He would have "spared the rod" and *improved* "the child." Of course, also, what was true of me was true of the generality of pupils. We were all very human boys.

I would not have my readers suppose that corporal punishment was carried to an extreme by the authorities of the College. No; the masters were honourable, upright gentlemen, who performed their several duties conscientiously, according to the best light they had in those days. I remember most of them only with feelings of affection and respect, and could fill a small volume with kindly recollections of them and their ways; but this will doubtless be done by an abler pen than mine. And now to return to my simple narrative. When I first entered the College, being very young, and a stranger in the city, I had no friends or acquaintances among the boys, and for a time I felt quite lost in the crowd. But this soon wore off as I began to know and appreciate my companions. At this distance of time I can recollect only the names of those with whom I came most often in contact, or whom after events caused me to particularly remember. Among them were Stephen Jarvis, James Hagerman, Chris. Robinson, L. W. Smith, D'Arcy Boulton, Wm. Vidal, Waywanosh and Johns —Indian chiefs—R. B. Denison, W. H. and Thomas R. Merritt, Joseph Woodruff, George McMicking, John Kirkpatrick, Frank Dee, Henry Skinner, Richard Dixie, "Charlie" Sadlier, (a wonderful swimmer), two McDonnells, B. Turquand, Fred. and Arthur Wells, Alex. Dunn, R. Dempsey, Will Andrews, Wm. Wedd, Alfred and Walter Stennett, Wm. Dixon, Stephen and "Gus." Heward, John Ewart, Thomas Mewburn, W. R. Harris, George Duggan, Jr., "Sted" Campbell, John, George and Daniel Brooke, George and Harry Draper, John Auldjo, George and "Jack" Munroe, W. H. Weller, Sydney Cousins, two O'Haras, two McLeans, Edward and Jonas Jones, Will Lyons, James Henderson, two Barbers (sons of George A. Barber, one of our teachers and, as well as Mr. Barron, a great cricketer) Hugh C. and A. Thomson, one or two ("Commissariat") Thompsons, M. C. Cameron, James Patton, James Austin, John McKenzie, two Scarletts, two Pagets. J. M. Horne, Walter Boyd. These are all that I can call to mind just now, but among them are the names of many who have since achieved distinction in various walks of life. Upper Canada College boys of that, as well as of a later era, have made their mark in law, politics, and medicine; have adorned the pulpit, the bench, and the bar; and have been gallant soldiers in the armies of their own and foreign countries; have shone as successful explorers, geologists, and engineers; have upheld the honour of their country in civil government, diplomacy, and statecraft; have distinguished themselves in art, literature, and poetry; have become merchant princes and great ship and mill owners; have held high commands in British and Canadian armies; have repelled invasion and subdued foreign and domestic foes; and in numberless ways reflected honour upon the race from which they sprang, and approved themselves good men and true. In the Crimean War were two Upper Canada College boys, Fred. Wells and Alex. Dunn, contemporaries of my own. The latter was among the "Six Hundred" of deathless fame, who charged at Balaclava, and who had the honour to win the Victoria Cross. The name of the former—the gallant son of a gallant sire—reminds me at how early an age a lad may shew an aptitude for military life. After the Canadian Rebellion broke out, in 1837, a number of us young College boys formed ourselves into a company for the purposes of drill. We used to meet on the premises of Mercer Jones, at the foot of York Street, and Fred. Wells was our captain. We were armed with wooden muskets and swords, and worked off our superfluous energies and patriotism at a great rate. But I am getting rather ahead of my story, and must go back to that eventful morning, early in December, 1837, when we boys, ignorant, in common with nearly all the inhabitants of the city, of the events of the preceding night, went as usual to College, only to find the gates closed and the startling news awaiting us that the Rebellion had broken out; that Colonel Moodie had been killed by the rebels, and that there would be no school for six weeks! Of course we were all as sorry as boys could be to hear of the Colonel's death; but all the rest of the news was so entirely delightful, so exhilarating, and altogether so joyous, that with one accord we threw our caps in the air and cheered again and again until the welkin (whatever that may be) rang to the glad acclaim, when we scampered off to our respective homes like a lot of wild young colts suddenly freed from corral. I should say, however, that before we dispersed, and after our janitor—the venerable Alderdice, (what old College boy fails to remember him?) had fully confirmed the good tidings we dashed across to Government House where we were greatly impressed by seeing Mr. Henry Rowsell, of the bookselling firm of Rowsell & Co., walking up and down before the gate, as sentry. He was dressed in his ordinary clothing, but was fully accoutred with buff cross-belts and loaded musket; and although he looked somewhat comical in this unwonted guise, he seemed rather to enjoy the situation. Note here that booksellers of ancient as well as modern Toronto have been prone to fight for their country!

When I reached my own home, which was then just opposite Osgoode Hall, on old "Lot" Street, I burst into the presence of my father, shouting at the top of my voice "hurrah! hurrah! the Rebellion has broken out, and there is no school for six weeks!" My enthusiasm, however, received a severe check when my father, instead of responding with that hilarious alacrity which I thought the occasion demanded, looked exceedingly grave, donned his uniform, and taking down his sword, went at once to Government House, and offered his services to the Lieutenant-Governor, Sir Francis Bond Head. And oh! wasn't Sir Francis a prime favourite with the College boys? They did not trouble themselves about his politics, system of Government, or any such trifling matters. The causes of his popularity were far other than these. In the first place, he was a superb horseman, and scarcely a day passed that he did not ride several times past the College play-ground, mounted on one or other of his fine hunters; then he used frequently to come in to witness our cricket-matches, and once when we had a grand silk flag presented to us (I forget by whom) he "manned the halyards," and hoisted it with his own hands to the top of the lofty staff erected specially for the occasion. Besides, he was the representative of our young Queen, who had then but lately ascended the throne, and who was fairly idolized by the boys—and by their fathers, too, for that matter. But, perhaps, the most potent of all the causes, which led us to look upon Sir Francis as our fast friend and ally, was the fact that when, for some reason or other, weighty in our eyes, we wanted a holiday, he would send a note to the Principal, and obtain it for us. All the survivors of the classes of 1837 will remember the day, shortly after the outbreak of the Rebellion, when a whole crowd of us marched over to the Government House, and gravely offered our services to help to fight the rebels. Sir Francis received us very kindly, and made us a nice little speech, but said—what was certainly true—that adult volunteers were pouring in at such a rate that he felt justified in declining our offer for the present, and that, on the whole, he thought we could best serve our country by remaining at home, and attending to our studies, &c., &c. This Lady Head approved, and, as a solace for our disappointment, invited us into the dining-room, where she regaled us with cake and wine. The prescription answered admirably; and we gracefully retired with three cheers for the Queen, and three times three for Sir Francis and Lady Head; satisfied that if we could not die for country we would at least have all the fun we could while living for it. And fun galore we certainly did have that winter!

As clearly as if the event had occurred only yesterday, I recollect that morning when the two or three thousand loyal, but exceedingly raw, militiamen marched up to Montgomery's Tavern to engage the, supposedly bloodthirsty, rebels, who, however, all dispersed like morning mist before the old-fashioned flint-lock muskets carried by our men could get a chance to work havoc in their ranks. But few of Mackenzie's men were killed: one, I remember, was shot through the head by a stray bullet of the many that were wildly and aimlessly thrown away on that occasion. So very excitable were our militiamen that I remember my father, who was in command of one large detachment, saying on his return that evening that he felt more danger from the reckless firing of his own men than he ever did from the bullets of the enemy in any of the battles of 1812 in which he took part. If I rightly remember, Chief Justice Robinson, Attorney-General Hagerman, Judge McLean, Mr. Draper (afterwards Chief Justice), and all the notabilities of that time took part in this foray; and I think that nearly, or quite, all of the Upper Canada College boys named in the first part of this paper were there too. I know that my own two elder brothers marched in my father's corps, and that I, being then only thirteen years old, fairly cried with vexation because I was not allowed to accompany them. After things began to steady down a little, two regular regiments were formed out of the tens of thousands of volunteers offering. One of these was "The Queen's Rangers," and the other "The Queen's Light Infantry." This last named regiment was stationed in Osgoode Hall, and was commanded by Lieutenant-Colonel Hill (a Waterloo man) and Majors Nash and Thomson (my father). Several old College boys bore commissions in these regiments, but I can recollect with certainty only the name of one, that of George Wells, who was Adjutant in the Queen's Rangers. I do not remember whether John Beverley Robinson, Jr., served in one of those corps or not, (I think, however, he was Lieutenant in the Queen's Light Infantry,) but I know he was about that time appointed an extra *aide-de-camp* to the Lieutenant-Governor, to the huge delight of his old school-fellows. Then, too, was re-organized and rejuvenated Major George Denison's famous troop of Cavalry officered by three ex-College boys, viz., Captain R. L. Denison, Lieutenant George T. Denison, and Cornet Edwin Fisher, while several other old Upper Canada College boys served as troopers. This Cavalry troop, of late years known as "The Governor-General's Body Guard," has now been in existence for, I believe, seventy years, and has, if I mistake not, always been commanded by a Denison, beginning with that stout old 1812 soldier, Major George; then by Colonels R. L., G. T., and R. B. Denison, and later by Colonel G. T. Denison, Jr., Toronto's present efficient Police Magistrate, and author of the well-known work on Cavalry which carried off the Emperor of Russia's prize in face of the world's competition. A signal distinction indeed, and won by an Upper Canada College boy!

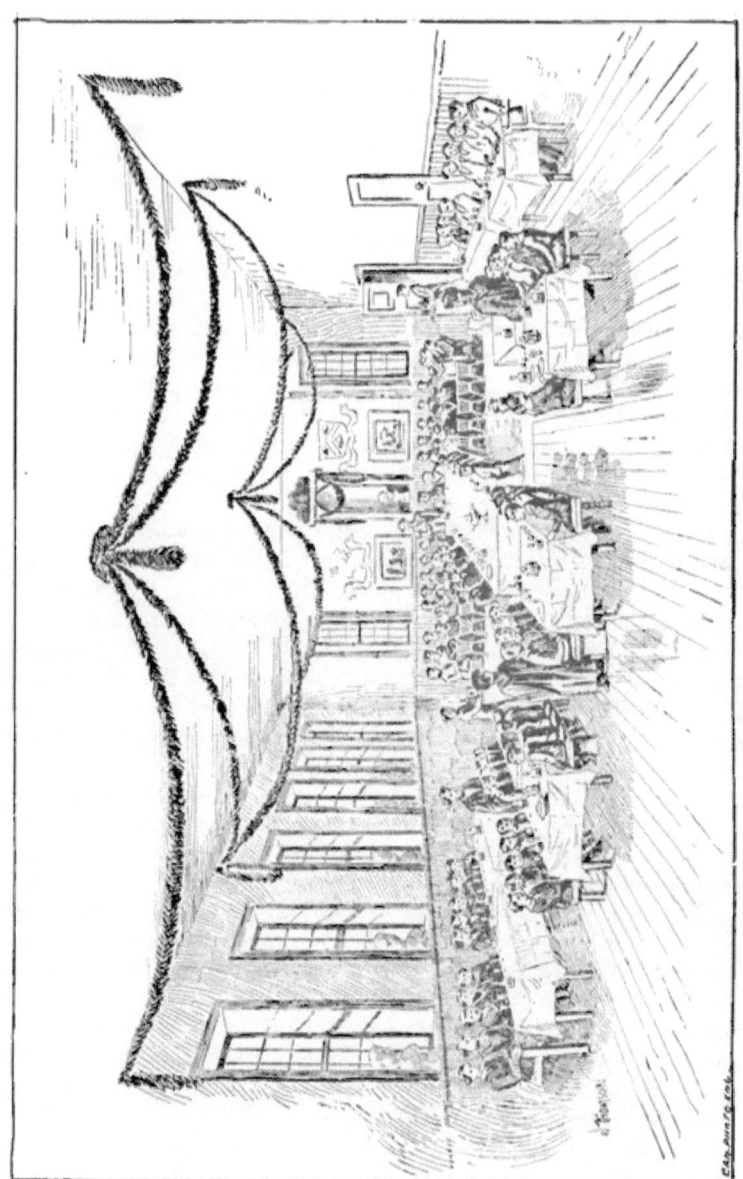

DINNER AT THE COLLEGE ON THE OCCASION OF LAYING THE CORNER STONE OF OLD KING'S COLLEGE, QUEEN'S PARK.

But, a short space back, I referred to the fun we boys used to have in the winter of '37 and '38, and truly the sources of amusement were numberless. Upper Canada College was in a manner a privileged school, and its pupils had the *entrée* to lots of public places and ceremonies not free to the boys of other schools. For instance, at the opening and closing of Parliament a space was always set apart for us in the Legislative Council Chamber where we could at our ease feast our eyes upon the grand display of those state pageants. And to the galleries of the Legislative Assembly we were always welcome—so long as we behaved ourselves—which we generally did. There were numbers of us whose fathers were members of Parliament, and on our Wednesday and Saturday half-holiday we used to go down to "The House" to listen to the debates, and gaze at the "assembled wisdom." Of course, each boy thought his own father was the greatest man of the crowd, and he would wait patiently to see him get up and air his views, and then go home quite satisfied. In connection with the "Assembly" Room there is one little historical fact which I remember very well. It occurred during the first hubbub of the Rebellion, at a time when Parliament was not in session or had temporarily adjourned. The basement of the building, immediately under the Assembly Room was then, for a time, occupied by volunteers. One of these while carelessly handling his musket happened to discharge it, and the bullet passed through the floor overhead, and also through the seat of the chair always occupied by Dr. Rolph when in his place in "The House," This event greatly impressed the boys, but did not hurt the worthy Doctor much, as he was then safe in the domain of Uncle Sam, whither he had betaken himself in consequence of the high value (£500,) placed by the Canadian Government upon his head. Party feeling ran to extremes in those old days, and I am afraid that the few boys among us, whose fathers were "Liberals," (Radicals or Rebels we then called them) had a rather hard time of it. But, once again, time has righted this wrong also. A great many of those same boys lived to see their fathers occupy positions of honour in the councils of their country, and to hear them called by the honourable name of "Reformers." The now free and enlightened people of Canada have long ago ceased to draw invidious distinctions because of party proclivities.

As usually happens in any city where considerable bodies of troops are stationed, Toronto was very gay throughout the winters of '37 and '38, and we youngsters got our full share of the good things going. There were a great many "children's parties" given, particularly by the old Loyalist families; and in going to and from these we used to have lots of fun. At numerous points in the city, especially in front of public buildings and prominent houses, sentries were stationed, who invariably demanded the pass word or countersign from all night pedestrians. It was very often my pleasing duty to escort my young sisters and other little girls to one or other of those parties; and before I left home my father would give me the countersign for the night, with full instructions that when challenged by a sentry with the customary "who goes there?" I was quietly to answer "friends." Then when the sentry should say "advance friends and give the countersign," I was to step forward and whisper the word—Wellington, Waterloo, or whatever it might be. This all looked quite simple, but, for the first dozen or so of our expeditions, the upshot always was that when suddenly challenged, while going round a corner perhaps, the whole crowd would yell out, as with one voice, "*it's me!*"—throwing at once grammar and instructions to the wind. Then, on the order to "advance *me* and give the countersign" we would all shout "Waterloo," or whatever were the words for the night. By and by, however, we got properly trained, as we began to realize that some lurking enemy might possibly avail himself of a pass word so cheerfully published abroad. Then, in addition to our social recreations, and far transcending them in importance, we boys used to have our sham battles, which sometimes bordered very closely upon the real. There was very little snow in 1837, but when an opportune fall did come we would erect great snow forts, and dividing our forces into about equal bodies of loyalists and rebels, determine by lot which party should "hold the fort," and which attack. Some of these battles were contested with great obstinacy on both sides, and many quite painful wounds were given and received; but the result was ever the same. Victory always remained with the legions of the Queen; and for the simple reason that these fought *con amore*, while most of the others were merely acting a part.

And now, as I must have severely taxed the patience of my youthful readers who have followed me thus far, I will close with a humble, but I am sure I shall be pardoned for saying well-deserved, tribute to my native land "fair, free, prosperous Canada." I have been somewhat of a traveller in my time; I have been quite around this globe of ours; have seen many countries and people, and have resided, on and off, for more than a decade in several States of the American Union, and have closely studied their institutions. I freely, and without a spark of envy or jealousy, acknowledge that the Republic of the United States is a great and wonderful country, and that its people are worthy of it and of the grand old stock from which they sprang; and yet I most deliberately say, without prejudice or conceit, that Canada is a still better country, and Canadians, man for man, a better race, and a more free, happy, contented, and law-abiding people; and in sober truth even a more democratic people. And I further say, that

Canadians have sound, solid, and substantial reasons, apart altogether from sentimental ones, for being proud of their heritage. It needs no special gift of prophecy to predict for Canada and her patriotic sons a great and glorious future, which will be enhanced, rather than retarded, by the proximity and generous rivalry of her powerful Southern neighbour. These two great nations, growing up side by side, and always maintaining friendly relations, will, in less perhaps than a half-a-century from to-day, sway the whole civilized world by their combined influence, prestige, and power, while the lustre of their achievements will reflect back upon Old England, the birthplace of freedom and the cradle of liberty!

NOTE:—The Editors desire to express their acknowledgements to the friend of the College who was instrumental in procuring from Mr. Thomson this chatty paper on the Rebellion, with the author's reminiscences of his own College days. From their correspondent the Editors received the following note on Mr. Thomson's prowess as a marksman, which though unconnected either with the College or with education, they append as a biographical epilogue, not without interest, they conceive, to many readers of the present volume:—

"Mr. Wm. Thomson, the author of these Rebellion reminiscences, has been well-known for years as a writer on forest and stream sports, and more particularly as a contributor of many sketches, stories, and verses to the *American Angler*, of New York. Always an expert with rod and fowling piece, he was, as the writer has often heard from the late Col. R. L. Denison, and the late E. C. Fisher, of Etobicoke, a really wonderful performer with the old-fashioned, small bore, short-range rifle. These two gentlemen often testified that they had seen Mr. Thomson, in the year 1849, fire a bullet in a tree at fifty yards distance, and then, at the same range, shoot six bullets upon the first so that the seven were cut out in one lump. On the same day, same witnesses, Mr. Thomson, firing on a challenge to hit ten wild-birds on the head *seriatim*, shot off the heads of nine wild pigeons consecutively, and finished by shooting a blue crane through the head at a measured distance of 135 yards. In 1851, at Dunnville, Mr. Thomson put twelve successive bullets into a four-inch circle at 220 yards distance, and struck a number ten gun-wad sixteen times out of twenty at 75 yards, both of which feats are attested by several living witnesses. In 1863, the present writer saw Mr. Thomson bring down a hovering king-fisher with a single bullet from a Smith and Wesson rifle, calibre twenty-two, and on the same afternoon he saw him kill, with the same weapon, a crow perched on the top of a lofty dead pine situated on the other side of the Chippewa River, from the shooter, a distance of probably not less than 130 yards. In these days, when long-range rifles are the vogue, and accurate shooting at short-ranges little cultivated, one runs some risk of being doubted in recording such feats; but the "old-timers" who remember the practice made with the long, heavy, small-bores of their youth will testify that Mr. Thomson's remarkable shooting was not wholly unexampled. He says himself that his proudest recollection is that he raised a Rifle Company in three days in 1861, at the time of the Trent affair, and drilled it for three months at his own expense."

A. I. KENSHAW.

THE REV. JOHN McCAUL, LL.D., SECOND PRINCIPAL, 1839-1843.

BY WILLIAM WEDD, M.A.

IT HAS BEEN already stated that when the Chancellor, President, and Council of the University of King's College, passed a complimentary resolution in reference to Dr. Harris, on the occasion of his retirement from the Principalship of Upper Canada College, they concluded by remarking that they judged it scarcely possible in many respects to supply his place. And it was evidently owing to the prevalence of this feeling that so many efforts were made, and so much hesitation shown, in the endeavour to fill the vacancy.

On referring to the minutes of the Council, we find that, towards the end of July, 1837, Dr. Harris gave notice of his intention to resign, such resignation to take effect on April 1, 1838. About the middle of March, in this latter year, we see allusions made to unsuccessful efforts, and a statement that no selection had yet been made. At length, under date of May 9, 1838, we have a record of a meeting at which His Excellency the Chancellor (*i.e.*, the Lieutenant-Governor) presided in person—an unusual event, indicating the great importance attached to the object of the meeting. The minutes state that "The Council feeling a strong desire to avoid further loss of time in supplying the vacancy occasioned by the retirement of the Rev. Dr. Harris from his situation of Principal of Upper Canada College, it was proposed and resolved :—

"That Her Majesty's Principal Secretary of State for the Colonies be prayed to procure the necessary appointment to be made by Her Majesty, and it is recommended that His Excellency, the Lieutenant-Governor, in consideration of the great importance of having a suitable person to preside over the College, do suggest to Her Majesty's Secretary of State, that His Grace the Archbishop of Canterbury be requested to afford his assistance and advice in making the selection, in order that the Province may have the advantage of His Grace's intimate acquaintance with the Universities and his perfect knowledge of the qualifications required for the duty."

It was not until January 27, 1839, that the President was enabled to lay before the Council a communication from His Excellency, dated the previous day, and announcing for its information that the Rev. John McCaul, LL.D., who had arrived in the city the preceding evening (January 25), had been appointed Principal of Upper Canada College. It is interesting to observe that Dr. McCaul immediately thereupon signed the prescribed declaration, and took his seat as a member of the Council, thenceforward to attend it with his well-known regularity, until ultimately it ceased to exist, at least under that name.

At a meeting held on February 2, 1839, certificates in recommendation of Dr. McCaul, transmitted by His Excellency, were read, and the following minute in reference to them was directed to be entered :

"The documents referred to gave the Council much satisfaction, as they proved beyond dispute that Dr. McCaul is a gentleman in every respect highly qualified to discharge with distinguished ability and efficiency the duties of the important situation to which he has been appointed."

To this the following addition was made :

"In perusing the Rev. Dr. McCaul's testimonials, the Council are very forcibly struck with the ready condescension and unwearied pains taken by His Grace the Archbishop of Canterbury to secure, at His Excellency's request, for Upper Canada College a gentleman more than usually qualified to become its Principal. So feeling, the Council most respectfully solicit His Excellency, the Lieutenant-Governor, Sir George Arthur, to convey to the Archbishop, in the most acceptable manner, their most grateful acknowledgments for so signal a proof of his paternal affection, and for the deep interest which His Grace has uniformly taken in the spiritual and intellectual welfare of this Colony."

The members present on this occasion were : The Hon. and Ven. the President, the Attorney-General, the Solicitor-General, the Hon. R. B. Sullivan, the Hon. William Allan, and John S. Macaulay, Esquire. Dr. McCaul, in view of the objects of the meeting, was of course absent.

Here would appear to be the proper place to take a slight retrospect, and to state briefly the antecedent training and academic status of the new Principal. Very considerable, it will be seen, are his achievements up to this point. Born, then, at Dublin, on March 7, 1807, he first attended, while very young, a celebrated private establishment in that city, known as "White's School;" subsequently he became a pupil of the "Maravian School," in Antrim, but the year immediately preceding his entrance at the University was spent at the former school. In 1820, when only in his fourteenth year, he matriculated at the University of Trinity College, Dublin. Mathematics particularly engaged his attention for the first three years of his undergraduate course, and it was in that subject that his first college prize was gained, Dr. Sandes, who, in later years was Bishop of Cashel, being his mathematical tutor. Classics claimed his especial devotion during his fourth year, and at this period of his course he obtained several important prizes and a scholarship, tenable for five years, of the annual value of £20. The scholarship also carried with it free rooms and furnished meals in residence. He graduated with the highest honours, having won the gold medal for classics and the Berkeley Greek medal. Among his competitors for these distinctions, it is stated, were the late Dr. Greig, Bishop of Cork, and the late Dr. Hamilton Verschoyles, Bishop of Killaloe, both of whom are mentioned as being then, and afterwards continuing to be, his warm and life-long personal friends. Between the degree of B. A. and that of M. A. (in 1828), he spent a considerable portion of his time in preparing pupils for University examinations, and with such remarkable results, that, when he took the latter degree, he was appointed University Examiner in Classics.

The authority followed in the above statements proceeds as follows:

"Continuing to live in residence, and devoting his whole time to the study of classics and classical literature, Dr. McCaul supplied a long-felt want by writing and publishing a series of works on the metres of Horace, Terence, and the Greek tragedians. These were, for many years, the only text-books on their respective subjects used at Trinity College, Dublin, and are still acknowledged as valuable authorities amongst classical scholars. He subsequently published his editions of Longinus, Thucydides, and the Satires and Epistles of Horace, the edition last named being at once adopted as the standard text-book by the Grammar Schools of Ireland. In 1835, the degrees of LL.B. and LL.D. were conferred upon him by the University, upon his undergoing the prescribed tests, which were, as they should be everywhere, real tests of merit, while the special and very rare compliment was paid him of remitting the fees exacted for those degrees. He had previously been admitted to holy orders—to the Diaconate in 1831, and the Priesthood in 1833, and was frequently called upon to officiate in chapel and elsewhere." (See two exceedingly well written and appreciative articles on Dr. McCaul, by J. King, M.A., in *The 'Varsity*, Oct. 16th and 23rd, 1880.)

In addition to the above works mentioned by Mr. King, I have some recollection as to certain minor writings of Dr. McCaul's during this period: these, unfortunately, were never in my possession, but consisted, if my memory be not at fault, of lectures on Homer, Virgil, and the Dublin University classical course. I mention this from the conviction that even the fugitive products of the learned Doctor's pen should, where possible, be preserved as an appendage to his more prominent volumes; since, whether he was writing an extended and elaborate work, or condensing his genius into some brief inscription, or even merely selecting an appropriate motto, the old saying was still ever true of him—*Nihil quod tetigit non ornavit*. There was, moreover, in everything he either said or wrote that *curiosa felicitas*, that painstaking happiness of expression, which, even when it seems to be entirely spontaneous, is in reality oftener the natural fruit of protracted culture bestowed upon mental qualities in themselves originally refined. For these reasons I would like to see carried out Mr. King's suggestion that Dr. McCaul's literary contributions in the shape of pamphlets, reviews, magazine articles, etc., should be carefully collected and preserved in a more permanent form.

The above condensed retrospect has again brought us down to the time of Dr. McCaul's appointment to the direction and oversight of Upper Canada College. Fresh, then, from the halls of his renowned University, in all the vigour of youth, and with a reputation for brilliant scholarship already well-established, he entered upon the duties of Principal, as it stands recorded in his own handwriting in one of the registers, on Tuesday, January 29, 1839. He found an institution working, as far as possible in a new land, after the great models of the Mother Country, and officered mainly by masters who had been trained in those schools. Being himself of tried learning and a perfect gentleman, he would naturally be led to appreciate, with a delicate sense of honour, all that was scholarly and worthy of commendation in the efforts of the former Principal and his able assistants; and he consequently seems from the first to have been careful to follow, for the most part, the lines already so well laid down by his predecessor, and to have been anxious rather to expand and supplement what had been wisely inaugurated and so far successfully carried forward, than to make changes to gratify personal predilections, or merely for the sake of change. Yet it is admitted on all sides that there was something so marked in the character and bearing of the man—such an indomitable energy and perseverance in all he conceived and did—that he gave a fresh start, as it were, and an abiding impulse to the career of the College.

Dr. McCaul seems at once and permanently to have identified himself with his adopted city and country. This may appear somewhat strange in one of his well-known strong love for his native land—a love so characteristic of all of his nationality. But we must remember that he found the work in which he was engaged a congenial one as far as teaching, at any rate, was concerned. It was, moreover, a fitting introduction to the higher phase of it to which, when we consider how far-sighted he was, it is reasonable for us to imagine he must have looked forward, even if it had not been, as it probably was, held out as an inducement to his coming here.

Again, even supposing it to be true that he may have at times looked back to the old land, and the old associations so dear to one of his temperament, with an intense home-sickness and longing to return, yet we know he made, immediately on his arrival here, very many warm friends. Among these there was one who took a manifest fancy to the young Principal. We refer to the Honourable Mr. Justice Jones, who was a distinguished member of one of Canada's oldest and most influential families, and who then occupied a spacious residence amid beautiful grounds quite close to those of the College. Of course the Doctor was often invited there, as he was to other places; but besides his friendly relations with Judge Jones, there must soon have been an additional attraction calculated most effectually to reconcile the Doctor to his expatriation, for we find that, so early as the October of the very year in the January of which he arrived at Toronto, he married Emily, the second daughter of the learned Judge.

I remember distinctly that, when we boys first inspected our youthful but dignified Principal and his girl-bride (she was then not yet nineteen), we came to the unanimous conclusion that the union was in all respects suitable, satisfactory, and much to be commended. Nor was this conclusion of ours at all influenced by either bribery or corruption; for although it is true that we all were shortly afterwards regaled with a bountiful supply of wedding cake, yet our opinion had been formed antecedently to that occurrence, even, in fact, before we had the remotest idea that such a luxury was in store for us. Now those of us old boys of that period, who still survive and have continued to have opportunities of observing and knowing, are rejoiced to have found that the course of events has fully justified the opinion then formed. Some people may say that the Doctor acted in this matter with his usual wisdom; but then the wisest of men have not always proved wise on these occasions. Others may think that it was in accordance with the Doctor's wonted good fortune; but that surely is a heathenish notion, however classical it may be. No; let us rather look with reverent thankfulness to that Divine Source, whence we are assured by infallible authority that a good wife comes—a true woman, loyal and loving to the end.

The additions and improvements made by Dr. McCaul in regard to Upper Canada College were neither few nor unimportant. Many of them were doubtless but the continuation of what Dr. Harris had pictured to himself in his first report (given in the preceding pages), and had been diligently pursuing all along. This will probably be best understood by a general statement of Dr. McCaul's method, supplemented by some specified particulars.

While Dr. McCaul devoted himself most sedulously to every detail in the whole course throughout all the Forms, the seventh, his peculiar charge, received special attention at his hands. During the abeyance of the University, the idea seems to have largely prevailed that the highest Form of what was then the first educational institution in the Province ought, in a measure, to supply a want which was now becoming more and more felt. It was, therefore, Dr. McCaul's great endeavour to make the instruction imparted in that Form as much as possible of a University character. Thus, in "Subjects of Examination—1841," which I happen to have at hand, we find, in addition to ordinary classical work of institutions of the kind, Sophocles, Œdipus Rex; Horace, Ars Poetica, with other Epistles, etc.; and portions of Plato and Longinus. In Mathematics, besides the usual school work, we see Plane Trigonometry, Logarithms, Elementary Conic Sections, Mechanics, and Natural Philosophy (Astronomy and Optics, Elementary). Also Logic.

Dr. McCaul's mode of teaching, too, was after an advanced style. In the reading of a Greek play, for instance, he paid great attention to making the pupils thoroughly conversant with everything relating to the theatre of the Greeks, even going so far as to instruct them in Aristotle's definitions and critical rules in reference to the drama. Those who bear in mind that Dr. McCaul had before this time given to the world valuable treatises on Horatian and Greek metres, need hardly be told that all questions in regard to prosody and scansion were minutely and exhaustively dwelt upon. Greek, Latin, and English Composition, in prose and verse, and Composition in French prose, also received due attention from him and his staff of masters. Logic was a favourite subject with Dr. McCaul, and was very successfully taught by him. In his capacity of Principal he held fortnightly examinations in the various subjects, for the best annual result of which he instituted and gave the Head Monitor's Prize. In his time, also, Hebrew and German were introduced as optional branches.

Comparing now the prize lists under this administration with those of the former, we find the following changes and additions, some of them gradually, some of them at once, made :—His Excellency the Governor's prize henceforth comes first on the list, the subjects presumably having been changed for which it was given. It was now awarded for proficiency at a special examination in Classics and Mathematics. The next prize was the Classical, similarly decided, the subjects being the same as to Classics as for the Governor's prize, but with other classical subjects added. The next the Mathematical, on a like plan ; then, subsequently, the French, the English, and in 1842 the Hebrew and the German. The Good Conduct and Scripture prizes, the latter for a knowledge of the English and the Greek Text, and for general and critical information thereon, were given a position of greater prominence. In addition to the year prizes for each Form, examination prizes for each were at once added, the intention evidently being to bring out varieties of talent. First and second class Certificates of Honour were also introduced, and of First Places in each subject. Upper Canada College registers were published with prize lists and examination papers appended.

During Dr. McCaul's *régime* sundry improvements were made in the grounds in front of the buildings. These grounds were often much admired. The porch and exterior of the central building were also improved and adorned, and subsequently new gate-posts and gas-lamps erected. The boarding house was improved by building a new porch and by other changes. Dr. McCaul was also mainly instrumental in the foundation by the Council of King's College (in 1841) of twelve exhibitions, open to all Canada, to be competed for by candidates of the final standing of the Fourth Form. These were tenable for three years, the regular number of vacancies in each year being consequently four.

Mention has been made as to the mode in which Dr. McCaul gave instruction in regard to subjects ; let me now say a few words as to the way in which he dealt collectively and individually with the pupils. When it is considered that he had previously had no practical experience in the management of boys, it is wonderful how successfully he ruled those of a large institution like the College. I am indebted to Mrs. McCaul for the substance of the above remark. It is a shrewd and valuable observation— precisely the expression of one of those thoughts, which, when once stated, are so evidently true as to make one surprised that they never occurred to one's self. The circumstance, though wonderful, is strictly in accordance with the extraordinary tact which the Doctor always displayed in everything he undertook. In addition to this, he had such a winning way with him, and his enthusiasm so infused itself into those whom he taught, as to render pleasurable even arduous and intricate studies. He was extremely affable, but withal so dignified that no pupil ever presumed on his good-nature. As to our training in faith and morals, it appears to me now looking calmly back after all these years, that he influenced us not by perpetually harping upon those topics, but rather by an occasional word in season, and by the more forceful, though silent, teaching which his own life and practice invariably afforded. Thus, I think, we were insensibly led on to revere all that is holy, to be obedient to duly constituted authority, to be ourselves actuated by manly and honourable sentiments, and always to show consideration for the feelings of others.

In this connexion I will now narrate a little incident of the class-room which will probably not be without interest to those readers for whom this work is chiefly designed. Characteristic traits pervading Dr. McCaul's whole life were his unvarying kindness of heart and his courtly demeanour towards all—the former constituting a large part of the greatest and the best, the very flower and crown, of the Christian graces; which abides with the good here, goes with them into the hereafter, and "never faileth;" and the latter flowing naturally from the former. Many are able to recount instances, either personally experienced, or as having come to their knowledge, of *great* acts of benevolence performed by him in a quiet and unostentatious manner. Yet it is quite questionable whether the *little* every-day occurrences in a man's life may not be, after all, a truer test of his real self. Old boys who were under Dr. McCaul will readily remember what genuine kindness and encouragement there used to be in his hearty "*Good*, sir," or "*Right*, sir," whenever they gave a particularly happy rendering of some passage, or a correct reply to some difficult question. And, on the other hand, I can tell of a pupil—reading the poet it is true for the first time—who one day, in Horace, and that too in one of the rhythms of most frequent recurrence, said—*At vulgus infidum*—O dreadful atrocity! What must have been the absolute horror of the author of the able treatise on The Metres of Horace!—yet, when he saw that his sudden start, and reproachful look, had moved the wretched delinquent even unto tears of vexation, then his ever-gentle soul at once relented, and he said in soothing terms, "You need not take it so much to heart; you see, ——, you were thinking of *perfidus*." More likely the boy was thinking of the English *infidel*, and the Doctor probably knew that well enough; but the point I want to make is this—how delicate must have been the working of that compassionate CHARITY, which, not content with merely pardoning the offence, could even devise an ingenious excuse for its commission. Oh, when we call to mind the loved ones, who, as he, have "gone before," and when we softly breathe a *Requiescat* for each one, do we not feel our breasts aglow with gratitude while recollecting just such little incidents as these?

It was, however, on the day of the annual distribution of prizes in the old College Hall, that the Doctor, so far as the general public was concerned, appeared to the greatest advantage. Those who never attended Upper Canada College, but in later years were present at University Convocations, will thoroughly understand what is meant to be conveyed. During all the proceedings there was one to whose distinguished and commanding form all eyes were ever and anon turned, as they listened to his still varying but always appropriate eloquence, or were entranced by the occasional outbursts of his now flashing, now glowing, inborn oratorical genius,—whilst he was giving utterance to his friendly remarks, so suitable to each individual case, his witty points, his sound advice, his earnest exhortations, his godly admonitions, his prayerful wishes for future welfare.

One great feature of Prize Day in those times was the accompanying Recitations in all the languages taught. They were either monologues or dialogues, and were taken from standard authors. They were highly instructive, interesting, and some of them mirth-exciting; and for weeks before had given the Principal and Masters no end of trouble in their selection and preparation. But then the way in which they invariably "brought down the house" was compensation ample enough.

At times there were other state occasions, on which the Doctor's perfect familiarity with academic precedent was an additional reason for his having the full arrangement of the whole; for instance, when on April 23rd (St. George's Day), 1842, the corner-stone of the University of King's College was laid by its Chancellor—Governor-General Sir Charles Bagot. The procession was formed in the grounds of Upper Canada College, and, arrayed in full canonical and academic costume, our beloved Principal, as he received the Chancellor, seemed to my boyish mind very nearly, if not quite on a par with His Excellency himself.

It was a grand academic, civil, and military display. The procession, starting from Upper Canada College, proceeded up the Queen Street College Avenue through lines of soldiers of the regular army stationed at equal distances all the way to the site. After the corner-stone was laid, and the procession had returned, there was a sumptuous banquet in the College Hall, the Principal and Masters entertaining His Excellency and suite on the dais, and the boys being at the same time entertained, at the expense of the College Council, in the main portion of the Hall.

A deep impression was made on my mind by the fact, that, at this banquet, we boys had our wants well looked after and were actually waited upon by grown-up ex-pupils of the College. It showed a fine spirit in every way, and, whenever I think of it, much moves me even now. It, however, is only one out of the countless instances, which I have known in the course of a long life, of old and present pupils being ever ready to perform kind offices for members of the same dear old school. Such has been true of the past, and there is every reason to suppose that such will be true of the future.

It was on this occasion, also, that there were addressed to the Chancellor a Greek Ode by Norman Bethune (now the eminent physician) and a Latin Ode by W. G. Draper (the late Judge Draper, of Kingston). His Excellency subsequently sent each of these two Seventh Form boys of the period a suitable acknowledgment in the shape of costly books.

And now there came the day when the sad word Farewell had to be spoken to him who had been so long our example, instructor, and guide. It was on the 20th of March, 1843, that Dr. McCaul, in consequence of his having been appointed Vice-President of the University and Professor therein of Classical Literature, Logic, Rhetoric, and Belles Lettres, retired from the Institution.

The event was marked by the reading in the Public Hall of addresses from the Masters and pupils and ex-pupils—the Masters stating their intention of placing a portrait of the Doctor in the Hall, and the pupils presenting a large, beautiful, and costly solid silver vase, appropriately ornamented and inscribed. On the ample sides of the base there are engraved the names of the pupils. The addresses were in every way worthy of the College and of the occasion, and it need scarcely be said that the Doctor replied to them in fitting, eloquent, and most touching terms. On leaving the centre building the pupils formed a long double line reaching to the Principal's residence. As the Doctor passed through, every head was bared in silent and sorrowful respect—the senior pupils feeling as though they were parting with a kind elder-brother, and the junior with an indulgent father.

A short time afterwards a separate address was presented by the pupils and ex-pupils of the Seventh Form. It was written in Greek, and the Doctor replied in the same language. The reason why this Form, besides taking their part in the former address and presentation, felt it appropriate in them to pay this additional mark of regard would seem to be shadowed forth in the following expression occurring in the Greek document:—'Ἡμῖν γὰρ ἐξῆν τὰ σὰ ἐσωτερικὰ ἀκούειν. This address was accompanied by a massive snuff-box of silver gilt, which they begged the Doctor to accept as a slight token of their respect, gratitude, and affection. It is to be regretted that want of space prevents the insertion here of this and the two other addresses. They all, however, being engrossed on parchment and placed in metallic cases, have been perfectly preserved, and will doubtless be accessible to some future biographer.

Very pleasant would it be to the writer of this article to continue to chronicle Dr. McCaul's course—to describe, however feebly, the energetic and able manner in which he discharged his duties, first as Vice-President, then President, and also as Professor in the University—to tell of the publication of his two great works, so soon and so widely celebrated, especially among archæological and theological scholars; that on Britanno-Roman Inscriptions, and that on Christian Epitaphs of the first six centuries—to bring his academic record even up to the time when failing health at length came upon him, and at the last we, after passing through another double line, of older pupils now, laid his body down with saddened hearts ἐν τῷ Κοιμητηρίῳ, in the Cemetery,—that peaceful Sleeping-place where it awaits the hour, in which the dead shall be raised incorruptible—but my limit is well-nigh reached, and I must forbear.

Let me conclude by stating, that, in going over the records covering this Principal's administration, and comparing them with my own personal knowledge, I became convinced that there were just two born leaders of men, to whom, more than to any others, the distinguished success of the Institution was at this period due. They were persons of widely different type, temperament, training, age; and yet it was remarkable how soon, to employ a word which I have been told was used by the elder of them in this very connexion, they *assimilated*. They continued fast friends, and doubtless a mutual aid and support, as long as the elder lived. They were both preëminently great, but each in his own way; and there are numbers, the writer included, who have particular reasons for reverencing the memory of each in his especial line. Their names are now, and will ever continue to be, historical—the Right Reverend Doctor JOHN STRACHAN, first Lord Bishop of Toronto, and the Reverend Doctor JOHN McCAUL, second Principal of Upper Canada College.

RÉGIME OF PRINCIPAL BARRON, M.A., 1843-56.

BY NATHANIEL O. WALKER, M.A., M.D., PORT DOVER.

MR. F. W. BARRON entered upon the duties appertaining to the Principalship of Upper Canada College in the year 1843, thirteen years after the first opening of its halls under Royal Charter. He directed its internal discipline and teaching, with supervision of the Boarding House, until the year 1856, a period of time equal to that of his two predecessors combined.

The external affairs of the College from its foundation were placed, first, under a Board of Directors and Trustees, until March, 1833, when control was transferred to the Council of King's College. In 1837, by Act of the Parliament of Upper Canada, the College was incorporated with the University of King's College, and became subject to its jurisdiction; and thus it remained until January, 1850, when the University Act came into force. This latter Act, while declaring that the College was still an appendage of the University, transferred the management of its affairs to a Council and Endowment Board of its own. The President of the University retained, however, the power of disallowance of the Statutes and Regulations. The Hon. Francis Hincks was at the same time appointed "Crown member of the Endowment Board of the University of Toronto, and Upper Canada College and Royal Grammar School," as the Governor-General's official appointment reads. This appointment was regarded at the time in the light of "a sop to Cerberus," in order that these institutions might pass safely by the dogs of rapine who sought then, as later on, to mangle the Royal Endowments made for their support.

Again, in 1853, the College, passing through another Parliamentary ordeal, was placed by statutory enactment under the control and management of the Senate of the University of Toronto. This body had power to make Statutes and Regulations for the discipline of "The College and Royal Grammar School;" to exercise supervision over the Principal and Masters; and had charge of the appropriation of the fees and endowment.

This authority was vested by the Senate in a committee of five, constituting "The Board of Management," which, by an Order in Council, was entrusted with the administration of the financial affairs of the College, in regard to the disposition of its income and fees, but subject to the Lieutenant-Governor and Council in regard to its capital and endowment.

These several changes took place chiefly under the *régime* of Mr. Barron, and doubtless were sources of embarrassment and perplexity to both Principal and Masters. The internal management, modelled from the outset after the great Public Schools of England, continued unchanged as regards both the subjects taught and the discipline enforced in the various forms. The changes made after Mr. Barron's time, and the dropping of the Seventh Form which did University work, do not appear to be mentioned in the history of the College under his successors.* The prominence that classics and mathematics had in the curriculum of studies was more marked then than now, for instruction in those subjects was at the time the chief work of the school.

The excited political condition of the Province, incident to the development of self-government, and the hostility of opposing political parties, were doubtless the moving causes of the changes brought about in the external administration of the College. Its internal administration however, moved on quietly, and, despite the turmoil in politics, education made substantial and gratifying progress in the capital and throughout the Province. Much of the credit for this is due to the Rev. Egerton Ryerson, D.D., who in 1850 was appointed Chief Superintendent of Education for Upper Canada. Under his fostering care, and with the aid of Government, the machinery of Common and Grammar Schools was reorganized and largely developed.

The secularization of the Clergy Reserves in Upper Canada and the abolition of Seignorial Tenure in the Lower Province, following the disturbances of 1836-37, had unleashed the dogs of confiscation and plunder, and no endowment was deemed too sacred for the iconoclastic or reforming hand. The preservation of the endowments of King's College and Upper Canada College from perversion and spoliation can now be regarded as almost miraculous. France was hardly yet sober after the intoxicating draughts of "Universal and Individual Liberty," which elevated the Goddess of Wisdom to the throne of the Almighty. The United States after the Revolution were not yet agreed as to "Sovereign State Rights;" a liberty bordering on licence made each individual a

---

* The last appearance of a Seventh Form in the College Register is at the end of the Summer Term, 1860.—THE EDITORS.

UPPER CANADA COLLEGE, 1877-1891.

proselytizing political Agnostic. Tom Paine's writings were, in many quarters, more eagerly read than the Bible, and his political doctrines were freely avowed and quoted by the *hoi polloi*. Each of these sinister forces had emissaries and advocates in the Canadian body politic. Credit is therefore due to those men in whose hands were the destinies of our country and who successfully piloted it through the perilous times.

Upper Canada College emerged from her several ordeals *integra et recta*, and preserved all her proper functions for the education and due correction of the youth entrusted to her care. Among those who stood firm between the fierce opposing factions of the time and the Royal Endowment of the College, the names of our present Premier, Sir John Macdonald, and the Hon'bles. Robert Baldwin and George Brown, must be cited and their memories revered. Many others deserve honourable mention for their unswerving fidelity to this seat of learning. Those mentioned above, however, formed a barrier between their followers and their opponents in our legislative halls, and to their efforts we owe, at a critical juncture, the preservation of the College.

While the angry sea of politics raged without, little was known of it within the College walls. Rarely was political controversy indulged in by the studious inmates, the *esprit* evoked was dominant in influence and led sons of fathers of opposite political camps to fraternize and form but one fold under the *ægis* of *Alma Mater*. The amnesty extended to Mackenzie, his return from banishment, the passage of the Rebellion Losses Bill, the burning of the Parliament buildings at Montreal, the outrage perpetrated on Lord Elgin, the Governor-General and Visitor of the College, and other political events of the period, excited only an ephemeral commotion among the pupils. The only occasion on which the calm, inland waters of education within the College were ruffled was when William Lyon Mackenzie returned to Toronto from his outlawry, and was ejected from the corridors of the Parliament buildings by Sir Allan McNab. This scene and its occasion were hotly discussed for a few days, and some disagreements among the boys were quietly settled in a corner of the playground, according to the Queensbury rules; the gallant knight meanwhile being foremost in the hearts of the boys.

Mr. Barron's personal appearance is easily recalled. He was of medium height, broad-shouldered and full-chested. He had a splendid muscular development, slightly inclined to corpulency, with a fair, round, genial face and bald head. He was upright in carriage and quick in his movements. He wore double glasses on account of nearsightedness. Succeeding to the Principalship just vacated by so popular a man and so efficient a scholar as Dr. McCaul, his *régime* was at first subjected to criticism. Mr. Barron's urbane manner and genial bearing towards both teachers and pupils, the ripeness of his scholarship, and the strictness though thorough impartiality of his discipline, soon however won the hearts and loving confidence of the various forms, and all invidious comparisons made at the outset of his career vanished from the halls of the College. He endeavoured to instil principles of uprightness, truthfulness and self-respect in the minds of all. The higher manly qualities dormant in youth, he sedulously sought to evoke, and, while always preserving and exacting due respect, he yet observed a prudent familiarity, especially with the pupils of his own form. By example, he encouraged all to engage in outdoor sports; cricket, rounders, hockey, running, leaping and jumping were with other sports and games introduced into the playground, there being as yet no gymnasium. Quarrels were frequently settled in the "ring," the monitors and seniors securing fairplay between the contestants. For giving a foul blow or taking a treacherous advantage, boys were incontinently "sent to Coventry" for a week or more. These contests were never too closely inquired into either by Principal or by Masters. Being thoroughly English, Mr. Barron endeavoured to make the boys chivalrous, as well as respectful and considerate, and to sustain the ideal character at all times of an Upper Canada College boy, as being upright, honourable and gentlemanly. The Seventh Form was considered *par excellence* his form; though others, from the First upwards, were occasionally rehearsed by him. The Seventh, however, engaged most of his time, and as its work was mainly University work he took upon himself its chief supervision. The thoroughness of his teaching and superior manner of instruction are borne out by the honours, scholarships and medals which the boys of his *régime* carried off at the matriculation examinations of Toronto, Trinity and other Universities, having earned them in competition with scholars from all parts of the Province and elsewhere.

As Mr. Barron was frequently called to attend meetings of the Board of Management and other councils on educational matters, the Seventh Form was often without supervision. On these occasions advantage was taken to inaugurate a series of so called "tournaments." These consisted of contests in the prayer-hall under the rules and regulations made, as we ambitiously phrased it, at the "Field of the Cloth of Gold." The tournaments, though they lacked the pageantry and splendour of the historic jousts of Henry VIII. and Francis I., at Guisnes, were greatly enjoyed as a spectacle and became the occasions of much fun. They were thus celebrated, and I recall them with still undiminished interest: Janitor Alderdice, junior, with keys of College in hand as sceptre, was installed in the Principal's chair at the head of the room as Master of Ceremonies and "arbiter of the jousts." Challenges were made by a herald, which, when accepted, the gage of battle was thrown down, and when taken up, the herald would then declare "prepare for jousts." The contestants in pairs, two by two, would take their places at opposite ends of the room; a line drawn across the middle of the prayer-hall was the barrier, or division of the lists. The "constable of the lists" (a boy stationed at the bottom of the stairs at the front entrance of the main corridor) would then declare "lists are open" (*i.e.*, the Principal not in sight). Then came the summons "prepare the knight-contestants." The squires would at this call assist one boy on the shoulders of another: head, body, and arms free above, but legs underneath armpits formed part of the horse. Thus prepared at opposite ends of the room, the couples back to back, the herald would shout; "Ready; charge, knights, and let the guerdon be to the most valiant!" At this the pairs would turn and in full career charge upon each other, making as much speed as possible to get beyond the "barrier" with a good momentum. Great was the shock when horse and rider came together, and at times both would "bite the dust." In that case, the rider in whose list the fall occurred was loser. At other times, only one horse and rider would fall and be declared vanquished. Again, it may be, neither would fall at the first encounter, and then would follow a variety of hostile manœuvering, ending with a general scrimmage. The horses would perform a volt or demi-volt, careering backwards and forwards, right or left, as the exigencies of the battle required, taking good care of his own and his rider's legs, and bracing in various ways to sustain the impelling motions of the rider. *Armis naturalibus* the riders would engage each other, pushing by shoulder, pulling by collar, and by every other device seek to unhorse his opponent. Frequently the horses would from sheer exhaustion drop on their knees; but the contest would go on until one or the other engaged in the *mélée* was declared victor.

Puerile as the above may seem in writing, the tournament was a source of great amusement and was entered into with much zest and spirit. The shock in mid-career, when both couples would fall, made the windows of the whole building rattle. The combat on the part of the horse, brought every muscle into play and tested to the full the power of endurance; but on the other hand he was not exposed to so much serious bruisings in the fall. In these contests, I do not remember that any very alarming personal injuries were received: many slight and a few severe bruises and strainings of muscles would sum up the casualties of all placed *hors de combat*. But we made no end of a din. The masters in the other rooms would frequently send to inquire the cause of the concussions heard and felt throughout the building. The answer carried back, "the Seventh Form in the prayer-hall" was deemed an all-sufficient excuse. Nor was there ever a report, so far as I remember, known to have been made to the absent Principal, though on one occasion we were surprised in the height of our revels. The combat, on this occasion, had been so long and stoutly indulged in, that the constable of the lists had abandoned his out-post to witness the fight. Shortly after this desertion of duty, Mr. Barron stood at the open door a spectator of the scene before the joust was concluded. It was some time before he was observed, but when the Master of Ceremonies noticed the well-known figure, he quickly vacated his high seat of honour and command and was Janitor Alderdice once more. Simultaneously, there was a general shuffling back to the seats, and no herald's trumpet was needed to declare the combat off and the jousts suspended.

The sequel may be told in a few words. "Boys! boys! is this *desipere in loco?* Come to my room!" And in obedience to the command, there entered as crestfallen, tired, buffeted and wind-blown a set of boys as ever entered a class-room. The misery on their countenance, and their wearied and bedraggled appearance seemed, however, to touch the good Principal's heart and condone their offence; and the rehearsal of lessons was proceeded with, though with much more effort on Mr. Barron's part to increase the difficulties of the subject examined upon, and to show how little the pupils had studied it.

I can well recall the College staff in my day. Of them all, there remain now alive, I believe, but two—Mr. Wedd and Dr. Scadding. Mr. J. G. Howard has just passed over to the majority at an advanced age. The other masters, with many of their pupils, have also gone hence. If my memory serves me, there were but few changes in the staff during Mr. Barron's term of office. The first that occurred was the installation of Mr. Thompson as writing master, in place of Mr. Gowinlock, who retired. The next was the removal by death of the Rev. Mr. Ripley, second classical master, and the advancement of the Rev. Mr. Stennett to the post. Mr. Wedd at the same time, I think, became third classical master. Although Mr. Ripley was but a short time a master, he was endeared to the pupils by his benignant though firm sway and patient and forbearing manner. Messrs. Stennett and Wedd, being old College boys, their appointment was hailed with delight, each pupil feeling a personal pride in seeing them occupy their several positions. The one was quite a contrast, however, to the other: Mr. Wedd was mild, placable and for those days lenient in the management of his classes; Mr. Stennett was rigorous, exacting, a hard task-master, and mightily in earnest. He was the *bête noire* of all idle and insubordinate boys, for every ill-prepared lesson and every transgression generally entailed a free application of the cane. The use of this instrument was much more common in my day than I believe it is now, and a wholesome corrective I must admit that it was. As a deterrent, at least, we made the most of it in the case of the newcomer. Each new boy, upon his advent (if he belonged to Mr. Stennett's form), would be cheered by his form-mates after the following fashion: "I tell you, if you don't know every letter of your lessons, he will skin you; he will bark you; you won't have a spot of whole skin on you!" With these and such like disconcerting words, the reader may imagine with what sinking-of-heart the new boy would enter upon his first recitation.

For some years, Mr. Stennett's severity in the class was proverbial. There came a time, however—one year, just before the midsummer holidays—when a change appeared to come over him, and he was observed planting flowers in front of his residence and tending them with assiduous care. It was speedily rumoured that he was to be married during vacation, and such turned out to be true, for with a young bride the master returned and took up his old quarters; but where was the anti-holiday Mr. Stennett? In class, suavity, forbearance and even leniency towards the pupils, marked a different man, and great was the praise awarded to the young wife for bringing about the change. But Mr. Stennett's strictness was far more a virtue than a vice, and this was shown in the careful training of the boys under him, and in his rigorously insisting that lessons must be well prepared. In 1856 he was deservedly advanced to the position of Principal of the College.

The cane, though hitherto only casually mentioned, formed no inconsiderable part of the furniture of the College. Each master had a bamboo upon or in his desk; the instrument was generally about three or three and a-half feet long, turned up at one end like a shepherd's crook, and of the thickness of a man's little or ring finger. The usual mode of punishment was by application on the palm of the hand, and nearly all transgressions were atoned for in this way. Flogging was reserved for the Principal, and though the traditions of the College tell of cases having occurred, flogging was but seldom resorted to. Each master had power to administer the cane, and he apportioned the dose to the degree of the offence. From two to a dozen cuts upon the palm were frequent. Some boys were daily punished once or twice, and became adepts in receiving the strokes. The trick of resining the hand well, and of turning the palm from a horizontal to a perpendicular position at the supreme moment, was soon learned, and the trick saved the hand generally at the expense of the cane. In these modern humanitarian days, corporal punishment in our schools is nearly or quite abolished. In Upper Canada College, in those days, the rod was not spared; and the pain of the rattan-cuts on the hand, wiping out as it did the fault and absolving the offender, was preferred by the boys to "a hundred lines of Homer or Virgil," or to the silent record of a black mark held over in menace, to be at some future time enforced when the pupil again lapsed from grace. The cane was an immediate and full expiation, and when administered the culprit was at once shrived and restored to freedom and integrity of spirit.

Monsieur De la Haye, the French Master, was the grim custodian of the stock of canes. Every midsummer, a cart-load was reported to be brought in, to replenish the exhausted arsenal. These were placed in a cupboard in Monsieur's class-room, and thence doled out by him, one or two at a time, to masters, as per requisition when occasion required. At odd times, Monsieur, the custodian, on leaving his room would forget to lock his cupboard or negligently leave the key in the door. Such *lapsus curæ fidelis* always provoked a raid; and it was wonderful how quickly each boy would purloin a bamboo and conceal it on his person. At the end of the division-hour there would carefully file out from the room a curiously straight-backed and stiff-legged set of boys.

Poor Monsieur De la Haye had frequently to bewail his losses, which though recoverable were never recovered. This was a point of honour with the boys. His own cane, I well remember, was the cynosure of canes. It was always the pick of the lot, and when oiled, rubbed, and smoked, as he was reported to prepare it, and duly displayed on the desk, or, as was more commonly the case, held and sometimes flourished in the hand, it challenged the respect and attention of the class.

Monsieur De la Haye was appointed French Master when the College was first opened and continued in that post throughout the whole of Mr. Barron's *régime*. With the exception of English, French was the principal modern language taught in the College. It was commenced in the First Form and carried on to the Seventh. Efficient as a teacher as was M. De la Haye, his usefulness was somewhat qualified by the fact that any industrious lad who diligently applied himself to the study of the master's native tongue would, by his fellow-students, be dubbed "a French fag." The epithet was considered to carry so much opprobrium that the linguistically-inclined pupil was deterred from persevering in the course. Neither Principal nor Masters may have known of this, but it was known to, and especially applied by, the boys themselves.

Monsieur was intensely French, a great lover of Napoleon, and proud of his exploits. Some few forms, perhaps, would have a pupil who could converse easily in French. Happy the form, and more happy the boy ! for the latter was often egged on, in the interest of the class, to start a conversation with the master—and it took little to do this if the theme were Napoleon—and so beguile the hour with an animated recital instead of the lesson. A favourite topic, which then engrossed Monsieur's mind, was the erection of the Parisian tomb for the great Corsican, at the Hotel des Invalides. Sometimes the boys would attempt to play pranks on the Master. One or two of these took the form of gulling a beginner in French, by introducing some words disparaging to the master's nationality in the exercise he would have to hand in, and of which the young "freshman" would be ignorant. Once, I remember, the following was interpolated in this way and handed up to M. De la Haye by the innocent writer of the French exercise: "*La musique des crapeaux et des grenouielles sont aux oreilles des hommes Français très plaisant.*" Another theme was headed, "*Tu as Français grenouille.*" The black thunder cloud that passed over the Master's face when these insulting phrases were observed was disconcerting to the innocent youth who had handed in the *Thème*, though the subsequent "licking" did not elicit the name of the young rogue who had practised the imposition. All that the cane effected was to vary the statement, (in reply to the interrogation of "Who helped you with the exercise?" from "Please, sir, I did it all," to "C—— helped me down along there" [where the interpolation occurred].

Another episode, I recall, which perhaps may be deemed worthy of mention. An old French soldier who had served under Napoleon, was once introduced to Mr. Barron by M. De la Haye, and permission was granted him to instruct any boys who wished to take lessons in "singlestick," "broadsword," or "foils." A few seniors engaged him, and lessons were given in the assembly-room after the regulation hours. A few terms passed and some of the pupils became accustomed to the mien, and the bold "*en garde,*" "*carte,*" "*tiecre,*" "*fond,*" and other professional phrases of *Monsieur, le Soldat.* One day, a senior boy told his comrades that he intended pressing the master with the foils in a bout he was going to have with him. The contest was entered upon, and soon it was seen that the daring youth was pressing hard upon the Frenchman's foil, and made him aware that an earnest contest was intended. Parries, thrusts and returns were quickly made, and the stentorian "*carte,*" etc, of the master ceased, and the youth got in a full, strong "*fond*" on the Frenchman's breast. He fell prostrate, legs in air, mask fallen off, gasping "*Mon Dieu ! Mon Dieu ! Je suis tué !*" The student examined his foil, and, finding the button on, knew that he had not committed a murder. Helping the old soldier on his legs again, he was not long in discovering that he had lost the Frenchman's friendship. No more lessons would he give to this student, and at the end of the term his lessons were discontinued altogether. A complaint was made to the Principal; but a bright, amused smile lit up Mr. Barron's features, indicating thereby that no reprimand or punishment would be given.

These incidents will serve to show how kind and reverent was the feeling, amounting almost to a passion, which bound the students to their Principal. In the class-room, and in exacting strict obedience to Masters in all the Forms, he was rigorous, and applied the "rattan" to transgressors and idle, refractory boys with stern vim, his conduct was at the same time unimpeachable and his administration just. Towards him, the pupils preserve in their minds and hearts a loving regard. Often have we heard old College boys testify to their admiration of Mr. Barron. Communicating lately with an old fellow pupil on the Principal's love of out-door sports and recreations, the following letter was elicited, from which the present writer ventures to make a few extracts. The writer is Mr. A. R. Boswell, ex-mayor of Toronto. "I am not able," says my correspondent, "to say very much of the late Mr. Barron's yachting career, save that he was an enthusiastic yachtsman and until the day of his death he owned a sailboat of some kind. Of late years he lived, as you doubtless know, at Gore's Landing, Rice Bay, one of the loveliest of Canadian lakes, and there he had his little yacht *Donna del Lagos*, and enjoyed sailing her immensely. For many years he was a member of the Royal Canadian Yacht Club. He was an advocate and an enthusiastic lover of all outdoor and athletic sports. Cricke the loved heartily, and he was himself no indifferent cricketer, although short-sighted and compelled to wear glasses. I never heard that he took any interest in horse-racing; but in yachting, rowing, cricket, and skating he indulged in the season for these recreations and was an adept in all of them. In my younger days, I remember being a great admirer of his skating, and he was considered the best and most graceful skater on the Bay of Toronto. There were no rinks in those days. Mr. Barron was also a good fencer. There was no one he was afraid to tackle with the foils. He was also ready to put on the boxing gloves with any one who might care to meet him. The Principal was one of those men who excelled in almost everything in which he took an interest; and though one could not help admiring him for the manly support he gave to all healthful exercise, his greatest charm for me was his cheerful disposition, his interesting conversation, his love of a joke, and his thorough kindness of heart." Mr. Boswell's letter sums up Principal Barron's personal qualities so well, that I am sure he will pardon me for inserting his communication here. The tribute will doubtless be appreciated by all "old boys" of Mr. Barron's *régime*, and especially by those of the manly world with whom he once associated. Peace to his ashes!

THE PUBLIC HALL, 1877-1891.

obtained in European schools. Before entering Upper Canada College he had been a pupil of the district school of the county, under the Rev. Dr. Strachan and the Rev. Dr. Phillips. Leaving Upper Canada College as head-boy, he went to the University of Cambridge, matriculating at St. John's College in 1833, taking his degree in honours in 1837. He proceeded to the degree of M.A. in 1840, and D.D. in 1852. He was early appointed a classical master, and continued as such under Rev. Dr. McCaul, Mr. Barron, the Rev. Mr. Stennett, and Mr. Cockburn.

"It was about the time of Dr. Scadding's first occupying the position of acting Principal that another attack upon Upper Canada College was made. Public notice in the daily papers announced a general meeting of ex-pupils, to take into consideration the affairs of the College; no accusations or open complaints were made, but some slight reflections were cast in the announcement. The writer of this sketch had just returned from England, and, by chance, saw the announcement (it was in February, 1857), and attended the meeting in one of the public halls of the city. There was not a large gathering. The writer challenged the meeting for specific accusations. This challenge was endorsed by M. C. Cameron, a rising barrister, who afterwards became eminent as a jurist and was appointed Chief Justice of one of our Courts. He, in eloquent terms and in fierce invective, demanded to know who were the authors of the public notice, and denounced the unmanly manner in which it was framed as "hitting below the belt," and unworthy of an ex-pupil. Not a single accusation was formulated, nor was there one to stand up to father the notice. The movement collapsed completely. It has always been a mystery whence the inspiration came, but it was shrewdly suspected that some rival educational interests were the "fons et origo" of the attempt.

"Dr. Scadding was beloved by all his forms. He was a conscientious expounder of his own deep classical lore, a lovable man and a sympathetic teacher. The Third, Fourth, Fifth, and Sixth forms were those attendant upon his ministrations. There was but one division in each of his forms, and all were rehearsed in one class, and yet he knew how to address the natural qualities of each. To those at the head of the class the rehearsal was thorough, sharp, and critical; to those midway in the class more leniency and consideration were shown, while to those at the foot he extended careful but long and patient endurance. In teaching the forms, as a whole, at one time and in one division, he was led into dilemmas; while the top were wrestling with his profound, far-reaching and critical questions, the middle boys were little interested and the foot not at all, but occasionally indulged in mischievous tricks.

"On one occasion, while Dr. Scadding was absent from the class in attendance on the Principal, the whole form broke out in one bedlamic saturnalia. The head-boys were piling one another in the wood-box; the middle and foot were buffetting each other with brooms, shovel, tongs (open fire-places and wood were used in those days), and whatever could be got, and in the mêlée one of Dr. Scadding's rubbers was shied, and, missing its mark, went fairly behind the blazing wood and was burnt. This disaster quieted the turmoil, and Alderdice, the janitor, was at once found and despatched in haste to the city for a new pair, taking the remaining one for a pattern and size. These were substituted, and Dr. Scadding was unconscious of the fact that his form had presented him with a new pair of shoes!

"It must be remarked that Dr. Scadding, even in these days, suffered from weak eyes and indistinct vision, and now, in his later years, sad to relate, the malady has so increased that this eminent antiquarian and scholar is obliged to consult his books he loved so well by the light of others' eyes—a sad deprivation to one whose other physical and mental qualities are still intact. Dear master! all your old pupils condole with you in your bereavement and deplore your loss!"

As a supplement to this sketch by Dr. Walker we append the following:—

In 1862 the veteran first classical master resigned his post in the College. The usual trials of a teacher's life had begun to tell seriously on his nervous system, but more especially his eyesight suffered. On his retirement, he was presented by his classes with a claret jug of solid silver on a salver bearing the following inscription: "*Henrico Scadding.... S. T. P. Cantab.....Collegio Canadæ Ulterioris .... Decedenti .... Hoc munusculum....Alumni....Reverentes grate amantes....Dedicaverunt.... a.d. xvi. Kal. Maias....MDCCCLXII.*"

The words, "Reverentes grate amantes," well express the genuine feelings of the donors and former pupils generally towards their old instructor. The wish expressed in the concluding paragraph of the beautifully illuminated address, which accompanied the gift, has been happily fulfilled: "We pray that under the good providence of God your health may soon be reëstablished, that you may long be spared to fill up the measure of your usefulness, and that finally you may be of the number of those who 'crown a youth of labour with an age of ease.'"

Several former pupils of Upper Canada College have been masters in the institution, but the Rev. Walter Stennett, M.A., is the only alumnus who as yet has had the honour of being appointed Principal. He passed through a highly distinguished course at Upper Canada College during the Principalship of Dr. Harris ; and when some years afterwards the University of King's College, Toronto, was incorporated, he matriculated therein, and took part with great success in a competition, in which head-boys of Upper Canada College of several preceding years, and other formidable opponents, were keenly engaged. He graduated B.A. in 1845, being the medallist in metaphysics and ethics, the medallist in Evidences and Biblical literature, and Jameson gold medallist in history and English composition. Besides these high honours he also obtained valuable prizes in metaphysics and ethics, in Evidences and Biblical literature, Latin verse prize four times, English prose prize thrice. In the Faculty of Divinity he won the divinity prize of both years, and a special Bishop Strachan divinity prize offered in the first year. Mr. Stennett proceeded to his M.A. in 1848, but never took his degrees in divinity, although he might either have sought them from the University of Toronto, (since, if we mistake not, the very Act abolishing the Faculty was careful to reserve all existing rights), or have obtained them from Trinity by first taking an *ad eundem statum*.

On referring to the Upper Canada College records we find that Mr. Stennett was appointed third classical master and resident master in the boarding-house in May, 1846, second classical master in 1849, and Principal in April, 1857.

Dr. Walker has already given Mr. Stennett well-deserved commendation as a master. In regard to the Doctor's playful allusions to boys' stories as to severity, etc., we bear well in mind that considerable allowance must be made for the exaggerations which are the result of the force of the imaginative faculty at that early age. Not that we would imply that these are wilful misstatements on the part of youth—indeed we are of opinion that stories of the kind have nearly always some foundation in fact—but we have learnt that such accounts of severity or its reverse must always be received with ample abatement. The desire to augment energy of description by forcing contrasts, a mode of procedure which we occasionally notice even in grave historians of mature growth, does not seem to be altogether absent from the young. Such contrasts we think are sure to be unfair to both parties compared. It appears to us that a juster estimate of Mr. Stennett in this particular can be formed by citing his own words in reference to discipline during his Principalship. He says, "those were days in which discipline was really maintained, with no unkindly but with a firm hand. The cases of corporal punishment during my term of the office of Principal were notoriously few—chiefly, in my opinion, owing to the *certainty* of punishment for proven dereliction of duty. The boys understood the system, and the system worked generally well." Be this as it may, the undoubted fact remains that Mr. Stennett proved himself a most efficient master both in teaching and in discipline, and this probably had a great deal to do with his subsequent appointment as Principal.

Dr. Walker has also alluded to Mr. Stennett's marriage while a master. The lady in question was Veronica Frances, the only surviving daughter of the late venerated Bishop Bethune—an ancient name of high renown which twice graces the Upper Canada College roll of head-boys. The fair and gentle daughter of the good Bishop won for herself, both as a master's wife and as Principal's wife, the esteem and affection of all who were brought in contact with her. She was, indeed, one of those bright and sympathetic natures over which the memory loves to linger, and many an old boy of the time, and such of the then masters and members of their families who yet live, often look back with grateful recollections on those bygone days.

The two head-boys bearing her maiden name are Dr. Norman Bethune, the nephew, and the Rev. Dr. C. J. S. Bethune, the son of the Bishop. This latter head-boy has been for many years Head Master of Trinity College School, Port Hope, a circumstance which suggests to us the thought that Upper Canada College has never been actuated by mean and petty jealousies in regard to kindred institutions. There was a period when the old College undoubtedly took the lead every time, and carried all before it. Since then numerous very excellent schools have arisen, many of them, as the one just specified, under the instruction and rule of her own sons. It is little wonder then, if in the natural course of events she has had to divide the honours, and she feels naught but a generous and friendly rivalry when competing with other schools, either on the literary arena or on the cricket and other kindred fields. She rejoices under all circumstances to see the general cause of mental and physical education prosper.

Mr. Stennett was peculiarly fitted to succeed to the Principalship from the fact that his early training was under the direct superintendence of Dr. Harris, the first Principal; that his University course was under Dr. McCaul, the second Principal; and that he had served as a master under Mr. Barron, the third Principal. We should therefore not be surprised to find in him a combination of the excellencies of them all: and those who are well capable of judging consider such to have been the case.

We have heard the remark made by old pupils that during Mr. Stennett's administration there was no particularly marked feature, but that everything seemed to go on just as usual. Precisely so: that is the very point. What higher commendation could any Principal possibly desire, than that, succeeding such men as Harris, McCaul, and Barron, he should maintain without deterioration the exalted character of the College, and hand it on, in untarnished splendour, to the fostering care of his successor?

But even with all Mr. Stennett's high scholastic and other attainments, this could never have been brought about without infinite pains on his part. It is the universal testimony that he was a most conscientious and persevering Principal—always most anxious to discharge his every duty, always energetic, and ever at his post. He had, however, his reward: for the success of the pupils of his time was most marked, as the various University and other records abundantly demonstrate.

Unfortunately after a few years of faithful discharge of the duties of the office to which he had been promoted, this quiet, unassuming, but thoroughly efficient Principal found his health gradually becoming impaired. This may have been caused, partly at least, not only by the many cares legitimately pertaining to his important position, but also by additional anxieties arising from persistent unfair and unreasoning attacks on the College,—of which, by the way, Dr. Walker has given us a very fair specimen. Mr. Stennett, therefore, came to the conclusion that for the remaining portion of his life the continuous peaceful exercise of his functions as a Christian minister would be in every way more desirable for him. Indeed both Dr. Scadding and Mr. Stennett never forgot their sacred obligations as clergymen. As an instance of this we may mention that the former contracted, while assiduously visiting sick immigrants in pestilential sheds, a fever which nearly cost him the loss of one of his eyes; and that the latter was only constrained to discontinue similar visits by the peremptory command of Bishop Strachan upon the instigation of Principal Barron, who naturally was apprehensive of the danger of contagion among the pupils, although these masters were careful to take all the usual precautions. Here was a clear case of a conflict of duties. The matter had to be arranged somehow, and the good Bishop, if we were correctly informed, would appear to have assumed the responsibility.

Upon retiring from the College Mr. Stennett took country ecclesiastical duty for a time, became examining chaplain to his Bishop, and was finally advanced to a canonry and the important rectory of Cobourg, which preferment he held at the time of his death.

After Mr. Stennett left the College the customary compliment was paid him by Principal Cockburn and the masters of placing his portrait in the College hall. Like that of Principal Barron it is by Berthon, and is an equally life-like and speaking picture. When the secretary, as directed, wrote to Mr. Stennett requesting him to sit for this portrait his reply contained the following words : "Please express to the Principal and Masters my very high sense of the honour they do me, and my cordial acceptance of it. I cannot but accede to a request so flattering to myself and so much in accordance with my own wishes. I feel that it is one which will give me in time to come a visible connexion with that noble Institution in which so many Canadians have received their education, and within whose bounds so many years of my own life were spent."

On the occasion of the death of Canon Stennett, in 1889, Principal Dickson called a special masters' meeting for the purpose of paying due respect to his memory. We extract the following from the minutes :—

"It was proposed by Mr. Wedd, First Classical Master, seconded by Mr. Sparling, First Mathematical Master, and unanimously resolved :

"That the Principal and Masters, having heard with deep regret of the death of the Rev. Canon Stennett, M.A., for many years a classical master and for some years Principal of Upper Canada College, desire to record on their minutes their esteem for the deceased.

"Mr. Stennett was himself an old Upper Canada College boy ; and his distinguished career within these walls was followed by one still more distinguished at the University.

"Both as a master and as Principal Mr. Stennett's regime was characterized by a strict but judicious discipline, combined with kindliness of heart and gentleness of manner ; and old pupils, who were under him, will constantly tell how much they appreciated these high qualities, and the accuracy and elegance of his varied and extensive scholarship.

"Those who knew him best can testify how loyal and how grateful he was to the Institution, which had so well instructed his earlier years. And, indeed, the Rev. Walter Stennett was in himself a proof of the wisdom of the founders of this College in providing, from the first, for a duly porportioned admixture of literary and scientific studies : for while his logical and closely-reasoned arguments showed the mathematical bent of his mind, the melodious flow of his pure and refined English never failed to excite the admiration of all who had the privilege of listening to him as a lecturer.

"But he now rests from his labours: and it only remains for the Principal and Masters to conclude by offering to his widow and family heartfelt condolence under their sad bereavement."

At a subsequent meeting the following letter from Mrs. Stennett was read by the Secretary, who was directed to enter it on the minutes :—

THE RECTORY, COBOURG, APRIL 2ND.

MY DEAR MR. WEDD:

Your kind letter, enclosing "Extract from the minutes of a special meeting of the Principal and Masters of Upper Canada College," reached me yesterday.

The children join with me in thanking you as mover, and Mr. Sparling as seconder of the resolution, and all who were present at the meeting, for their kind appreciation of my dear husband's abilities, and their recognition of his efforts as master and Principal.

We also thank you for your sympathy with us, who mourn. Believe me, your letter and enclosure have done much to comfort, and I pray that the memory of one who loved the old Institution so well may linger yet a while with those he laboured for and with.

Of his personal friendship for you I have often heard him speak; and it is sweet to us all now to hear your gracious and loving words, for you knew and understood him.

I suppose you are aware how great an invalid he had been for some time. We were looking and asking for rest for him: his Heavenly Father has given him "Rest eternal."

  * * *

Again thanking you all for your kindness and sympathy,

   Believe me,

    Yours very sincerely,

     (Signed) JULIA V. STENNETT.

We have ventured to publish Mrs. Stennett's reply for two reasons: First, because it shows, with numerous other instances which might be produced, the spirit in which these kind attentions on the part of Principals and masters have ever been received; and secondly, because her statement that Mr. Stennett loved the institution so well is a proof that his affection for it endured to the end. In order to understand the full force of this testimony, it is necessary to call attention to the fact that this is not the Mrs. Stennett of whom mention has already been made; and, in regard to the Canon himself, that, having been for many years severed from the school, and other ties and other associations, both ecclesiastical and educational, having in the meantime been formed, he might quite reasonably have been supposed to have somewhat weakened in his attachment to it. Most pleasing must it be to all true friends of the College to learn, that such was far from being the case, and to find this succeeding sharer of his heart and home so feelingly alluding to her husband's unabated love for the time-honoured place, and responding, in such beautiful terms, to those its officers who had been anxious to pay him that tribute of their esteem which he had so well deserved, and to offer to herself and family that sympathy which she and they have so fully appreciated.

THE COLLEGE RIFLE COMPANY.

BY THE REV. T. F. FOTHERINGHAM, M.A., ST. JOHN'S, N.B.

AS FAR BACK as 1863, when I entered Upper Canada College, and I do not know how long before, the older boys were assembled weekly for drill under the instruction of Major Goodwin. They were supplied with rifles and bayonets, waist belts and pouches. The room next the lavatory was set apart as an armoury. Out of this drill class the Rifle Company was evolved under the influence of vitality and environment. The presiding genius under whose auspices this took place was the gallant old soldier in command. What boy of that day does not remember him with affection? A strict disciplinarian, yet liking better to silence a frolicsome private with a harmless witticism that held him up to ridicule, than to bid him "fall out." This was the severest penalty he ever inflicted, and it was much more keenly felt as a disgrace than the hundred lines of Virgil which the Principal immediately imposed by way of ratifying the sentence. The kindhearted old Major always seemed sorry the moment after, for in the next breath he would temper his rebuke with a cheery word and good-natured apology for the offender. He was bluff and boyish, although his shoulders stooped and his head was grey. He loved the boys with all his heart, and they fully returned his affection. His quarters in the old Bathurst Street barracks were always free to them, and his happiest moments seemed to be when reciting his favourite "Tam o' Shanter" to an admiring crowd, who never wearied of applauding the really splendid elocution.

The activity of the Fenian brotherhood in 1865 awakened much uneasiness in Canada. Large numbers of volunteers were enrolled, and the Military Schools were crowded with cadets. As in 1837, College boys were not behind in offering their services. Three of us, Fuller, Wilson, and myself, had obtained second-class certificates, and the idea was mooted of transforming our drill association into a company of the "Queen's Own." The consent of the Principal having been obtained, Major Goodwin entered heartily into our plans. The boys met in the Prayer room one afternoon in December, 1865, and amid great enthusiasm elected Frank C.

Draper, an old College boy and ex-officer of the "Queen's Own," as Captain, Valancey E. Fuller, Lieutenant, and M. Wilson, Ensign. William M. Richards, ———— Watson, and myself, were chosen Sergeants. I do not remember the names of the other non-commissioned officers, if there were any. Enrolment went briskly on. The cubits of our stature were measured against the wall of the Principal's room. What heroes we were in the eyes of those whose heads could not touch the ruler held at the standard height! The company was duly gazetted in General Orders of the 12th January, 1866, and attached to the 2nd Battalion, "Queen's Own Rifles."

On March the 8th, some volunteers were called out, and, amongst others, the "Queen's Own." The College Company was not mentioned in the General Order, but the boys would not be suppressed. With the consent of Major (now Lieut.-Col.) Gillmor, then in command, the boys appeared at every parade and march-out,—drilling as faithfully as others, but without any pay. This latter was a consideration to which our knightly souls were utterly oblivious. Class work was sadly interrupted. Every week there were evening drills and a Saturday afternoon march-out. Not one of the company was twenty years old, yet all tramped through the mud with the endurance and light-heartedness of veterans. Woe to the boy who stepped around a puddle instead of marching through it, or grumbled when an unlucky step filled his boot with ice-water. He was the butt of ironical sympathy for days afterwards. Our youthful appearance won us a somewhat patronizing regard from the rest of the battalion, and, in their paternal affection, they nicknamed us "the babies." So far from being offended, the boys shewed the genuine stuff they were made of by accepting the soubriquet, and trying to make the name an honoured one. When, at the close of that period of active service, Major Gillmor complimented the company in his address at the final parade, and three cheers were generously given for "the babies," we felt that the respect of the other corps had been completely won.

At that time many companies had their own marching songs. The College boys, in view of the juvenile position assigned to them, adopted as theirs the nursery hymn "Joyful," fitting to its tune nonsensical words such as—

> "He that hath plenty of spondulics
> And giveth his neighbour none,
> He sha'n't have any of my spondulics
> When his spondulics are done.
>
> *Chorus:* O, that will be joyful,
> Joyful, joyful,
> O that will be joyful, when his
> Spondulics are done."

Other verses followed *ad lib.* "He that hath plenty of sauerkraut, peanuts," &c., &c., until invention was exhausted. The ethics of the song were unimpeachable, and there was not the slightest thought of irreverence towards sacred associations. Anything of that kind would have been treated with scorn as utterly "low." It was simply a boyish response to good-natured chaffing.

Few members of the corps will forget the excitement of St. Patrick's Day, March 17th, 1866. Some days previous a rumour spread to the effect that bodies of men, marching in military order and armed with pikes, had been seen parading the streets after midnight. A guard of citizens was organized and a night patrol instituted. Fears were expressed that the usual St. Patrick's Day procession would be the occasion of an outbreak on one side or the other. In Montreal and Quebec these parades were abandoned, but the Toronto societies determined to display their green banners as usual. Although no one believed that local Fenians would give any trouble, yet there was then, as now, an excitable element of the opposite party who might attack a procession, and those marching in it, fearing such an interruption, might carry concealed weapons. The throwing of a single stone might start a sanguinary conflict. The "Queen's Own" and the "Tenth Royals" were assembled at the drill shed early in the forenoon and kept there until towards evening. The College Company was with the rest of the battalion. Rations were served about noon. Drill and frolic filled up the quickly passing hours, and not a few voted it the jolliest pic-nic they had ever attended. Yet, beneath all the merriment, there were serious thoughts, for we had ball cartridges in our pouches, and many of us remembered the standing order never to fire over the heads of a riotous crowd. It was with feelings of intense relief that the citizens saw the volunteers returning to their homes peacefully that evening.

Although relieved from active service on Good Friday, March 30th, the "Queen's Own" continued battalion drills at least weekly, sometimes oftener. At all of these the College Company was present. There was a lull in the excitement. The O'Mahony wing of the Fenians was making a demonstration at Eastport, Maine, and the Roberts faction was temporarily inactive. The volunteers were recalled from the frontier. A grand concert in the drill shed, which held 10,000 people comfortably, on the evening of the Queen's Birthday, seemed a fitting mode of celebrating the re-establishment of public confidence. Meantime "General" Sweeney had succeeded in effecting a reconciliation of rival factions, and on May 30th was announced as on his way to Canada at the head of the Fenian "army."

Fuller despatches arrived next day, and that night the militia of Canada were again called to arms. In March the Government asked for 10,000 volunteers and were offered 180,000—now the response was no less enthusiastic.

When we assembled in the Prayer room on the morning of Friday, June 1st, Mr. Cockburn announced that the Fenians had crossed the Niagara River and were in possession of Fort Erie, and that the "Queen's Own" had been ordered to meet them. The College Company was also called out, and members would report at once in uniform at the armoury. After a few words regarding the gravity of the occasion, the Principal dismissed the school for the day. The company mustered in full strength within an hour afterwards, only to find to its chagrin that, by special orders of General Napier, it was to remain in garrison and furnish the necessary guards for the armouries and military stores. It was with difficulty that the boys could be restrained from deserting to join the battalion. Many refused to wear their uniform when off duty. The order was an eminently wise and considerate one, but the boys felt that it carried the reproach of "babyhood" a little too far. They resented such an implication of juvenility. One admires their spirit and is not surprised that they failed to appreciate the responsibility resting upon their elders. It was quite true that they were too young for the hardships of service in the field; most of them had been sent to school to study and not to play the amateur soldier, and their parents would have justly blamed the Principal for having permitted the formation of the corps; besides this the duty laid upon them was a necessary and honourable one, and fell most fittingly upon the junior company of the battalion.

For two days the College Rifles were the only troops in the city, and furnished the guard on the Friday and Saturday nights succeeding the departure of the volunteers. I need not describe the excitement of those days. College boys helped to swell the crowds around the bulletin boards and added their voices to the cheers that rang out to the accompaniment of the Cathedral chimes when news of the rout of the invaders arrived. About three o'clock on Sunday morning the volunteers from the country began to arrive. They were marched up from the railway station in companies and dismissed to billets for breakfast. To me, the arrival of these raw troops was a deeply interesting sight. They came evidently from the farm and the workshop. It might be that the first gun of a great war had been fired at Ridgeway,—we did not know. If it was so, every one of these men was ready. There was no noisy frolic or loud laughter among them. Every word of command was heard with painful distinctness in the quiet of that Sabbath morning. When dismissed, one group after another struck up old-fashioned Psalm tunes, and set off singing them to their new quarters. One would have thought that Cromwell's army or a regiment of Covenanters had reappeared among us. With such defenders, we did not fear should Lundy's Lane or Queenston Heights come to be fought over again. Few Churches held service that evening, for nearly every person crowded towards the Yonge Street Wharf to meet the "City of Toronto" with its precious freight of dead and wounded. With another member of the company, like myself just off guard duty, I joined the crowd and was near the wharf when the steamer came in. To my surprise I heard the familiar voice of Lieut. Fuller in command of an escort composed of the College Company. It accompanied the five hearses to their destinations through thronged streets, amid a silence only broken by exclamations of sympathy and sorrow. Every head was uncovered as the dead heroes passed by.

On the Tuesday following a public funeral was held, and the bodies of Ensign McEachern and Privates Defries, Smith, Alderson, and Tempest lay in state in the drill shed. The gallery erected for the concert so recently held afforded a suitable elevation for the caskets. Ranged around these, the boys of our corps stood as a guard of honour, resting on their arms reversed, from eleven a.m. to one p.m. The company took part in all the military funerals of that sad time, and on one occasion, I think the one just referred to, furnished the firing party.

During the fortnight following the raid Toronto swarmed with volunteers, most of whom remained only a few days until formed into provisional battalions. Whilst these were in town, the College Company was released from the duty of furnishing guards. But there was the possibility that a sudden order from Ottawa might remove the guard on duty, and it was accordingly agreed that should the College bell ring at any time out of class hours, the members of the company would understand it as a signal to assemble at the armoury. One night as I was just about to retire I heard the well-known sound. It took very few seconds to resume my uniform, but, before I reached the street, every bell in the city was ringing the "general alarm." The din was enough to warrant the conclusion that the Gael was indeed at our gates. I lived about a mile from the College, and only arrived in time to take my place at the head of the company as coverer and lead the way to the drill shed, then situate between Front and Wellington Streets, at the east end of the Parliament Buildings. A dense crowd was already assembled at the corner of Simcoe and Wellington Streets, and, as we drew near, I heard some one call out:

"It's the College boys, let's give them three cheers!" This they did with a heartiness that made us feel modestly embarrassed. Acknowledging the honour in military fashion, we entered the drill shed, discovering then the cause of the ovation with which we had just been honoured. We were the first company to report itself in obedience to the summons. It was found shortly afterwards that we were not needed. A few companies had been ordered to Prescott, but enough remained for guard duty. In about an hour we were dismissed with not undeserved compliments. On the return of the "Queen's Own" from Stratford, after the engagement at Ridgeway, the College Rifles met the battalion at the railway station and accompanied it in its march through the streets. Although they did not hear bullets whistle, the College boys felt that they had won some slight share in the magnificent welcome the regiment received.

During the summer following the Fenian raid a military camp was formed at Thorold, and the Upper Canada College Rifles united with the University Company to form one corps. The battalion was landed at Port Dalhousie, and marched through St. Catharines to the breezy field on the top of the mountain where the Tenth Royals and the Thirteenth from Hamilton were already pitching their tents. Here the boys again distinguished themselves by their light-hearted endurance of discomforts that would have well-nigh caused a mutiny amongst regulars. The ground was rough and hard—cattle had evidently roamed freely over it when the soil was moist. One had to select carefully for his couch the precise spot whose physical geography was most nearly complementary to the angularities of the human anatomy. The last duty every evening was a field study of the relations between geology and osteology. When it rained, the clay betrayed a most tenacious attachment to boots often ill-suited to such rough usage. The camp arrangements were of the most imperfect character. Plain rations, however, were abundant. One of our number betrayed extraordinary talents in the culinary line, and no "Irish" or "Boston" stew can ever obliterate the memory of his achievements. No coffee and butterless bread ever tasted sweeter than that partaken around our tent pole every morning. The air was pure and bracing, and the drill just enough to make us forget all our discomforts in dreamless sleep. Every one heard with regret the orders to break up camp. To this day pleasant memories linger around the old camp ground. As illustrating the spirit of the boys, I may mention that it leaked out one evening that a general alarm was to be sounded during the night in order to test the promptitude with which the volunteers could respond. We determined that, for the honour of our corps, we should be the first on parade. Not one removed his uniform that night when he lay down. The covering sergeant slept in his boots and cross-belt, with his rifle by his side. To our great astonishment and chagrin the sun was shining brightly when the bugles awoke us at réveillé.

The home march was not uneventful. As we left the camp, and when we marched through the streets of St. Catharines, fair faces smiled from sidewalk and windows, and the battalion sang popular songs, accompanied by the band. We had scarcely left the town behind us when a thunderstorm came on. The "Queen's Own" had proved its ability to "stand fire," but water was another affair and retreat was no cowardice. We quickly found refuge under the grand stand of the race course. On a break occurring in the storm we set out again and arrived betimes at Port Dalhousie, where the "City" awaited us, but alas *quantum mutati ab illis* who one short hour before spread their plumes and tuned their manly throats before the admiring civilians of the "City of the Saints!" Scarcely had we left the friendly shelter of the race course when the storm burst out afresh. The mire of the road was ankle deep and the ditches were brimful of water. Some took to the fields and others picked a careful but tedious path along the fences, while the bolder tramped along as much indifferent to pouring rain and adhesive mud as plucky College boys ought to be. No company in the battalion straggled less than the beardless youths in No. 10. When we arrived at Toronto, our sergeant was the first to spring ashore in response to the bugle call for "coverers," and none marched up Yonge Street with jauntier step than the rain-soaked and mud-bespattered veterans of the rear company.

On the 26th June, 1868, Lieut. George D. Dawson, late of H. M. 47th Regiment, and now Col. Dawson, of the "Grenadiers," was gazetted Captain, *vice* F. C. Draper, who retired with the rank of Brevet Major. The Company re-enlisted under the Militia Act of 1868, but its name does not appear in the General Order of 6th February, 1869, in which the corps who constitute the active militia are named. It seems to have been silently dropped, along with others, which it was not judged advisable to continue in existence. The College Rifles never formed an integral part of the "Queen's Own," but was merely attached to the battalion for administrative purposes. During its brief existence it left a record of which it need not be ashamed, one worthy of an institution which has supplied so many able officers to the various branches of the Imperial service. General Napier did not forget to give us honourable mention in his report.

We old boys cannot contemplate without a feeling of sadness the retreat of our *alma mater* before the resistless tide of commerce. Some ghosts of the olden time will for us ever hover around the spot where we drank the mother's milk of character, and learned to love the noble and the true in ancient song and story. May her new home be consecrated to coming generations with memories as sweet and hallowed as the genius of reverie assembles around the dear old walls. In Reverence, Honour, and Loyalty, may each College boy to the latest generation prove himself a knight *sans peur et sans reproche !*

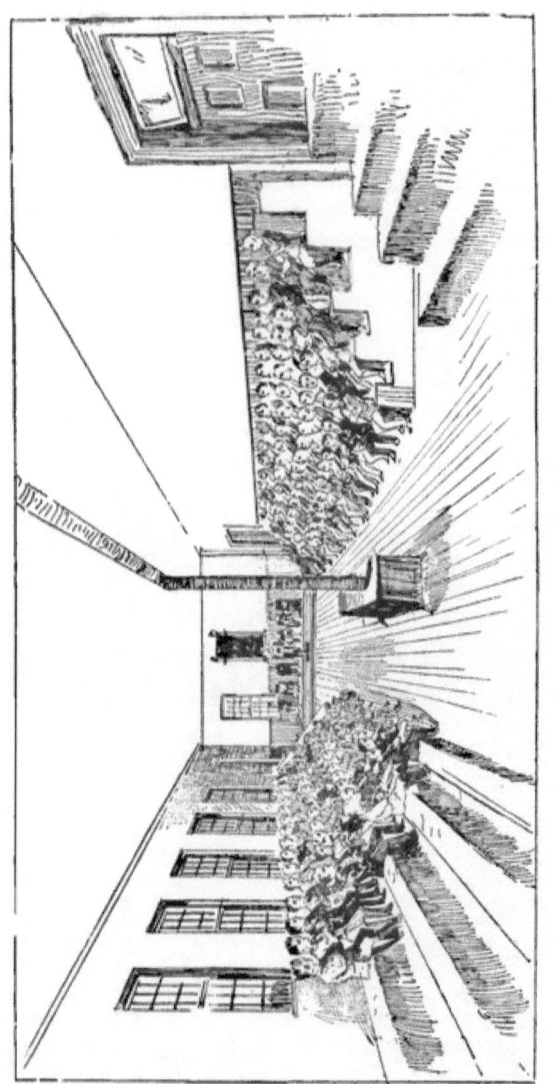

THE OLD PRAYER HALL, 1829-1877.

RÉGIME OF G. R. R. COCKBURN, M.A., FIFTH PRINCIPAL, 1861-1881.

BY D. R. KEYS, M.A.

IN THE YEAR 1861, Upper Canada College was without a supreme head. The duties of this office were for the time being vested in a commission consisting of Messrs. Scadding, Wedd, and Brown—three of the oldest masters of the College. Under such an administration the school had for a year or two been less successful in the race for matriculation scholarships. It had also suffered by the presence of an active rival, the Model Grammar School, which had been established in 1858, by the Rev. Dr. Ryerson, then Chief Superintendent of Education. This school was situated in St. James' Square, but must not be confounded with the present Model School in the same place, nor with the old Toronto Grammar School now presided over by Rector McMurchy. The Department of Education, it will be remembered, had then no control of Upper Canada College, which was under the general supervision of the University Senate, of which the Principal was an *ex-officio* member, but the appointments were made by the Government. That the Minister should consult with the department in reference to the appointment of a principal was not to be wondered at, nor was it altogether surprising that Dr. Ryerson should have recommended the rector of the new Model Grammar School, Mr. George R. R. Cockburn. That gentleman had been selected as head of the new school on account of his high testimonials and his knowledge not only of Scotch, but of German, educational methods. After winning the highest praise from Dr. Leonard Schmitz, rector of the High School of Edinburgh, Mr. Cockburn had distinguished himself at Edinburgh University and had taken a postgraduate course at the University of Berlin, where he entered fully into German student life and gained that familiarity with the spoken language that gave such interest to College "revisals" in German. His success since 1858 in the Grammar School had justified the Doctor's choice, as his subsequent success in Upper Canada College justified that of the Minister.

Yet the experiment was a bold one,—to place at the head of an institution, already a generation old, the head of a rival school that was but a mushroom growth in comparison with Upper Canada College, to advance over masters who had themselves been head-boys in the school and had taught in it for a long period a young man who had been only three years in Canada. To do this was a line of conduct that could only be justified by the very success which it seemed calculated to imperil. But in this case the end justified the means in more ways than one, and it certainly tried the man. Nor were these the only disadvantages the young Principal had to contend against, leaving what might be called personal equation wholly out of account. The condition of the College had been seriously injured by the action of the Legislature in cutting down the staff and reducing the salaries of the masters who were retained and in withdrawing the annual grant of over $4,400. Still further to cripple the finances, the expense of maintaining the Bursar's office, previously assumed by the Government, had been made a charge upon the College revenues, as well as pensions to the amount of $1,900 per annum. To crown all, the College was in debt to the extent of $20,000. Under such financial difficulties Mr. Cockburn assumed the principalship.

As the outlook was most gloomy in the department of ways and means, so the result in that department was most brilliant. There is a saying in Edinburgh that no Scotchman is allowed to enter the service of the Bank of England, even as porter, lest he win his way to the presidency. To this national predisposition to finance Mr. Cockburn added a natural bent of his own. He was aided moreover by the long experience of the bursar, the late Mr. Buchan, no less than by the cordial coöperation of the masters who in this respect, as in all others, shewed their loyalty to their *alma mater* by doing their utmost to assist the new principal. It is neither fitting nor necessary to describe here the means that were adopted to increase the College income; let it suffice to make known the results. The bursar's office was made to pay its own way. The deficiency in the masters' salaries was made up, including the arrears. Not only was the entire debt, due mainly to the building account, paid off, but new buildings were put up and paid for in place of the old ones. In short, an era of business prosperity took the place of the period of depression. Of course, the historical side of all this must not be forgotten: 1857 was the darkest year in the business history of the Province; in 1861 the American civil war began, a war which brought much prosperity to Canada, and affected Mr. Cockburn's private as well as his public life.

Such financial success was obviously dependent also, in part at least, on the success of the school in other ways. Statistics will be found elsewhere, showing the increase in the attendance both of boarders and day boys. The number of masters had also been increased, as well as the accommodation in the boarding-house. The character of the institution had improved, if the standing of the College boys in the University examinations be made the criterion. The most striking evidence of growth in the internal economy of the College was to be seen in the subdivision that took place in the different forms. The form names I. A., I. B. are familiar only to boys who have been at College since 1862. In 1868-9 this division held in the first two forms only. The following year there was a III. B., which afterwards became the Third Commercial, and, later on when the Fourth came to be subdivided, the commercial boys formed the Upper Modern and the third commercial was called the Lower Modern. These divisions were for a time obsolete, under the changed conditions of the College, and the altered requirements for University matriculation.

Indeed the system of education has been almost wholly changed. In the "sixties" and "seventies" specialization had not enslaved the teachers of Canada as it has to-day. Perhaps the most telling way of showing the contrast is to compare the present with the old way of awarding exhibitions. Now they are granted as special scholarships, then they were *all* for general proficiency, the list of subjects in the Fifth form including classics, mathematics, English, French, German, chemistry, and physiology. Not seldom it happened that a boy would gain an exhibition notwithstanding his weakness in one subject, as *e.g.*, mathematics. In one case a boy took only forty marks out of a possible 450 in algebra and very nearly carried off the first exhibition. But in that year Professor Goldwin Smith examined in classics and the late Professor Young in mathematics, and the returns in both subjects were more surprising than the dénouement of one of Gaboriau's romances. So strict indeed was the application of the rule "all subjects must be taken" that a boy who intended going to Germany after leaving College was not allowed to substitute German for Latin verses in the Sixth form. Nor had the era of modern text-books yet dawned. The only Canadian book the writer remembers having studied while at College is "Campbell's Geography," but there may have been others in use in the lower forms. In this respect, therefore, the boys of to-day have an advantage, and it is possible that some of the subjects may be better taught now than then.

Yet as one recalls the days of yore it is hard to single out a master who in his own style could be much improved upon. Each no doubt had his particular faults, but let not "the dram of ill" make "all the noble substance of a doubt." The present writer feels only the great debt he owes to every one of the masters, who, like the Muses, nine in number, had each a special formative influence or inspiration of his own. What wonder if memory brings kindly thoughts of them all? Is not memory the parent of the Muses? But two of the nine remain in the College—Mr. Wedd and Mr. Martland. Of these two gentlemen, who, for at least thirty years, have trained the College youths in the humanities, it would scarcely be fitting to speak at length. Both of them in sympathy with boys, both good classical scholars, and both skilled in imparting knowledge to their pupils, they were at the same time very different in their methods. Mr. Wedd represented the perfervid classical spirit of that fine old Irish scholar, Dr. John McCaul, whose impress upon the learned professions in Canada has been often remarked. Mr. Martland was of the English Public School and Oxford type, accurate to the last degree, and the friend of accuracy above all things, having at the same time an air of the man of the world that the scholar very rarely has and that greatly impressed the youthful mind. His position at the head of the College boarding-house brought him into very intimate relations with the boys, and it would be hard to name anyone in Canada whose influence on the youth of the last generation has been greater or on the whole more beneficial.

The second English master, Mr. C. J. Thompson, was the terror of the First form boys. Perhaps the fact that his room, known also as the writing-room, was the scene of afternoon detention, to which that form was very liable, lent a character of sternness to its principal occupant that he hardly deserved. The impartiality of his severity was admitted by all, and as the boys grew older they found how mistaken was their first estimate of the second English master. After the Fourth form writing was not taught nor was bookkeeping, so that during the last two years we had already graduated from Mr. Thompson's room. Still it was by no means impossible for a Fifth or even a Sixth form boy to be "kept in," and in that case he had a chance to renew his acquaintance with the ink-stained and jack-knife-whittled desks and benches of the old north-west room. The master in charge might happen to be Mr. Thompson himself, when, if it was one of the old boys, he would have a talk about the good old times in I. A. The writing master had a great friend in his opposite neighbour, the late Mr. Schlüter, with whom he used to walk up and down in the hall and around the grounds. Although the head of the commercial department, there was nothing Mr. Thompson detested so much as the rapid off-hand business style of writing. A Belleville boy who came up to Upper Canada College after a term at a business college was sent foot or thereabouts for his "outward flourishes" and only succeeded in getting up near the top by discarding them. Mr. Thompson retired from the College in 1883, and lived several months after, dying in 1884. He had been for fifteen years a master in the old school, and when he left it one of the most characteristic figures had departed.

The position of English classical master was held by the late Charles Connon, LL.D., a gentleman of very striking personality. Already advanced in years when he came to the College, he was perhaps less fitted to make a favourable impression on the youthful minds of his pupils. But the elder ones certainly appreciated his extensive knowledge of our literature and his love of philological research. An annotated edition of the first four books of *Paradise Lost* and an English Grammar, written in the old classical style, were proof of the variety of his reading and the vigour of his pen. Equally vigorous was his use of the cane, for in this respect, too, the doctor was of the old school, and would have scouted the idea of ruling by moral suasion. As an ardent patriot it vexed him continually to have to accept Webster's authority in disputes on spelling. A stripling Yankee roused his ire one day by naming New York as the largest city in the world. "If you put a dozen of your biggest cities together, it wouldn't be equal to London," was the reply with which he silenced the pert youngster. The twenty years that are past since then have seen as great an advance in the subject of English as in the population of the American cities, but with all the new methods no master could be found who would give his pupils a keener relish for the great English writers than Dr. Connon.

Dr. Michael Barrett, M.A., was first English master and lecturer on chemistry. Dr. Barrett had received a part of his own early training in France, and this seemed to be reflected in a certain jauntiness and nattiness that characterized his personal appearance. It also gave a local colour to his treatment of the geography of Quebec and France that might have made a native homesick, had we had any such in the class. Geography was his specialty and was taught with an utter disregard of text-books that made it impossible for the pupil to cram for his lessons. His knowledge of maps was amazing and, after the six years training, which in those days was not thought too much for this important subject, the best pupils still stood a chance of being puzzled by a question on the capital of some Persian province or the position of the rivers in Venetia. With his hands behind his back, and his head bent slightly forward, he used to walk up and down the room with short decisive steps, putting question after question, first on the subject of the lesson, then on all the past lessons, for, with his energetic manner he quickly discovered how much was known or unknown about the lesson for the day. In Dr. Barrett's room, as in Mr. Wedd's, the custom of giving "rounds" prevailed. This curious outgrowth of the marking system deserves a word or two, as it is now, I believe, nearly extinct. The number of questions "passed" from the ignoramuses at the foot of the form to the head-boy gave him more than his due share of work; and, to obviate this, he was allowed on answering a given question to take his place above the boy who had first missed it. To prevent any disputing, a slip of paper with the master's initials upon it was given him and this was the "round." It may give some idea of the doctor's energetic administration of the Socratic method to state that a boy has been known to make a double round of a class of nearly forty, in other words, "to get up" eighty places in half an hour. The doctor's favourite subject has been discarded from the matriculation examination, and will probably be taught in but few of our higher schools, a change, the wisdom of which is questionable, and the making of which he certainly would have vigorously opposed. Geography, however, was but one of the subjects which Dr. Barrett taught with remarkable success. His power as a reader impressed the younger boys, and gave them an excellent model, just such an one as Scott has described in *Guy Mannering*. In his teaching of chemistry, physiology and anatomy, the same mastery of details was apparent as in the geography classes. It was a rare privilege to have a professor in the medical college as our lecturer in anatomy. It is said one must learn anatomy and forget it again seven times before knowing it thoroughly, but the doctor must have been an exception to the rule for his memory could not have failed him so often, and he certainly knew his subject thoroughly. Several of his old pupils are now ornaments to our medical colleges. The skeleton which served for demonstrations in anatomy used to hang in a glass closet, and the doctor sometimes had a little quiet sport by sending the head-boy to fetch this skeleton from its case and hang it up on the gibbet before the class. Apart from the gruesomeness of it, a skeleton is a most awkward thing to handle, and for a tall boy to carry one across a long room in the presence of a score of his classmates, with the skull bobbing up and down, the arms wobbling around his shoulder and the legs getting tangled in his own is a sight to move gods and men to laughter, much more boys. The doctor's humorous smile and rigid justice endeared him to all. He rarely gave, and was never known to take off, a demerit mark. In 1884 Dr. Barrett retired from the College owing to ill-health, but was fortunately restored to vigour and lived to become the founder and first president of the Woman's Medical College, which will be a monument of his energy to future generations. So long as this generation endures his name will call up pleasant memories in the minds of old College boys.

The Rev E. Schlüter, Ph.D., of Halle, was for seventeen years French and German master in the College. Like most foreigners he had certain little peculiarities that afforded constant amusement to the boys. His command of the English language was remarkable in one who had not emigrated until past middle life, and he was never so happy as when displaying his mastery over the various meanings of the words by some far-fetched pun. Should a boy's name afford any chance for such word-play, it was always sure to be taken advantage of. Unfortunately these sallies were invariably greeted by uproarious applause on the part of the class, which would sometimes reach the second classical master's room, like the distant roar of the ocean, reminding Mr. Martland how Homer should be read.

Mr. Schlüter was none the less a good disciplinarian, as well as a thorough teacher. He used to amaze the boys by taking down their rank in the class without calling a roll and in an incredibly short space of time. This faculty, along with his ability to supply off-hand the principal parts of any irregular Greek verb to a "kept-in" Fifth-form boy, made him our favourite among the masters for the position of greatest polymath. A story he used to tell us contributed not a little to this general impression, and as it illustrates human nature as well as the training of bye-gone times, it may be allowable to repeat it here. When undergoing his final examination as a German student one of the exercises was to turn a piece of German into French. As the German was dictated, the quick-witted student wrote it down at once in French, and when the dictation was over handed it all complete to the examiner. But oh, the crabbedness of these examiners! Instead of being pleased at the quickness of Mr. Schlüter's work, his old German professor considered himself insulted by the ease with which his *pons asinorum* had been crossed. At the examiners' meeting he was for giving a second-class to Mr. Schlüter, and succeeded in keeping him down to a first C. instead of a first A. which he deserved. As a moral to his story, Mr. Schlüter warned us never to make light of an examination in the presence of the examiner. The matriculation examinations in French were a perennial source of complaint to the old gentleman, who had his own way of accounting for the fact that an Upper Canada College boy was rarely head at that examination, and as rarely failed to be first at the later ones. But a greater grievance was his being refused a pension when after so many long years of service (during which he had lost but fourteen days by absence), he left the College in 1874. The boys, more grateful than their elders, presented him with a silver service—an act that moved their worthy old master to tears. He lived a long distance from the College on a farm north of Bloor Street, and thither he retired to remain until certain changes in his domestic affairs should permit of his return to the Fatherland. More than one old College boy, in years gone by, has tried to seek out the abode of his former French and German master, but hitherto without success. The other day, however, we chanced to notice the announcement that this faithful old teacher had gone to "that bourne whence no traveller returns." He leaves a kindly memory in the mind of many an old boy.

The first mathematical master during Mr. Cockburn's régime was Mr. James Brown, M.A., who had taken the most brilliant course at the University before the time of Thomas Moss. As a scholar he was all that could be desired, but his subject was one whose unpopularity has become proverbial. The best teaching will not make algebra an interesting subject to the non-mathematical mind and the average mind is of that class. When physics, or, as we called it in those days, natural philosophy, was taught, the lessons became interesting enough and so too with mensuration and surveying. The last mentioned was a Sixth form subject and had the advantage of being studied out of doors and of giving a chance to bring the theodolite to bear on the windows in John Street, whose fair occupants were usually known to the boarders. Although the early mathematical successes of the College boys at the University were not so pronounced as they were in classics, yet, in view of the fact that there were really three classical teachers, for the Principal's specialty was classics, and only one permanent instructor in mathematics, there is no doubt Mr. Brown's boys did even better than could be expected. The aid given him by the second mathematical master was a varying quantity, as that position was the one in which most frequent changes occurred. Thus from 1868-74 it was filled in succession by Mr. John A. Paterson, (now of the law firm of Kerr, Macdonald, Davidson & Paterson); Mr. James MacLellan, (now of the new School of Pedagogy); Rev. Arthur Sweatman, (the present Bishop of Toronto), and Mr. Alfred Baker, who has since become mathematical tutor and professor in the University of Toronto. Only the last mentioned gentleman was known as a teacher by the present writer, for the classical boys remained under the charge of Mr. Brown until they reached the Fifth form. But in that form he met the pupils of the present bishop and was amazed at the celerity produced by Cambridge mathematical methods. Dr. McLellan also made a great reputation both by his originality in the classroom and the strictness of his discipline. But owing to the shortness of their tenure of office none of these gentlemen made a very deep impression on the life of the institution.

In addition to the regular staff the æsthetic arts were represented by Mr. Baigent, the drawing-master, recently deceased, and Mr. Thomas Martin, who has long since relinquished music for painting. In this connection we should mention the gymnastic masters, Colonel Goodwin and his son, and Mr. Andrews. The first named was a survivor of Waterloo, and in his stories to the boys might almost have outshone the famous

Mulvaney of "Soldiers Three." His son was a splendid specimen of manhood, but died of consumption at an early age. Another familiar face was that of the bursar, who seemed nearer to the boys of our form, because two of his nephews, James Buchan and Andrew Freeland were members of it. The latter, now dead, was head-boy of I. A.; the former has gone to the antipodes to spread there the fame of the old school. The bursar was without any sympathy for one class of boys, those who came late with their fees. A laxity had grown up in the matter of paying fees, which it was one of Mr. Cockburn's first tasks to remedy. But boys are naturally forgetful and up to 1869 there were a few who kept forgetting till their names were read out in the prayer-room, a measure that never had to be resorted to more than once for each offence.

In commemorating the officers of the College, we must not forget one who lived as it were in the midst of the boys themselves, the janitor. James Marshall held this position after the Alderdyces, and was succeeded by George Frost at Christmas, 1870. Coming at such a time it would have been extraordinary indeed had he not been rechristened Jack Frost. By that name he still rules the bell rope, and his cheerful face beams a welcome on the old boys who visit the school.

With such a staff, and with his own uncommon administrative ability, it is not surprising that Mr. Cockburn had great success. The financial improvement in the affairs of the College we have already seen; the increase in the number of scholars was due in part to the excellent management of the College boarding-house under Mr. Martland; but the stand taken by the College boys in the University examinations was the result of the combined exertions of all the masters. The various sources of the antagonism excited by this University success are so obvious that we may be spared the disagreeable task of enumerating them; nor is it necessary in such a work as the present to stir up strife by lengthy reference to these "old unhappy far-off things." The controversy was embittered by the introduction of personal animosities, and by its extension to the public press. The whole question as to the management of the College was finally referred to a Parliamentary Commission, which did not materially alter the system. This was in the year 1868. Despite this attack, in 1870 it was found necessary to build a large addition to the boarding-house, and a few years later it became necessary to follow the English plan, and open some of the residences of the College masters, in order to accommodate the increased numbers of boarders.

Nor did the attack affect the success of the College boys at the University. On the contrary, that success increased steadily until, in 1874, the six College boys who matriculated carried off three first scholarships, two second and one fourth, being six in all out of the twelve offered that year. Nor can the decline that seemed to follow this success be justly attributed to any falling off in the quality of the instruction, or in the capacity of the pupils. As a distinguished educator, well acquainted with both sides of the question, has put it, this decline of the College in the competition for scholarships was due to the gradual growth of the high schools. The latter developed wonderfully during the "sixties" and "seventies" under the thorough inspection of such able scholars as the late Professor Young, Dr. MacLellan, Mr. Marling, and Mr. Buchan. The growth of wealth and population aided of course in this development, and under these circumstances it was not to be expected that the College should continue to win half the scholarships at matriculation. Yet at the close of Mr. Cockburn's administration he was able to refer with proper pride to the latest results of College training, as tested by the old University prize lists for 1881, and to point to College boys as winners of four out of the eight medals awarded in the fourth year. "This," he said, "is our latest record, and it is one of which the College may well feel proud."

But the College had fallen upon evil days. The old animosity had by no means died out, nor was there that sympathy with the school in the mind of the then Minister of Education which might have been expected of an old head-boy. Something there may have been of a personal spirit in the opposition that made itself apparent to Mr. Cockburn, as both the Minister and the Principal were men of resolute and uncompromising character. At all events, the old attacks were revived, the papers were again full of letters on the Upper Canada College question, and once again a Parliamentary Committee was charged with an inquiry into the College management. The contrast between the methods of this Committee of 1880-81, and those of the earlier one of 1868, may afford an illustration to the future historian of our constitution, but need not be further alluded to here. The outcome of the inquiry was a decision on the part of the Minister of Education to reduce the salaries of the Principal and masters and to effect a general lowering of expenses.

Such a decision came severely upon the members of the staff. Notice has already been taken of the increase in the number of boarders, necessitating a large addition to the boarding-house. In like manner the increased attendance of day-boys had led to the enlargement of the College Building in 1877. A new hall had been built out in front of the old College, with new classrooms beneath it on the ground floor, allowing the old prayer-room, as it was familiarly called, to be divided up into several additional classrooms.

This old hall or prayer-room filled so important a part in the life of the College that it cannot be dismissed in a sentence. In the old building it occupied nearly all the western side of the upper floor, Mr. Wedd's classroom on the King Street front being excepted. There was an entrance for the boys at the head of the staircases and a master's entrance at the northern end. There were seats for masters along this northern wall and a single seat at the southern end, to which, about the year 1870, seats in the middle of the other two walls were added. The walls were hung with oil paintings of the former principals and emblazoned with the names of successful students, who having done honour to the College were thus honoured in return—a practice much decried by Mr. Cockburn's critics. In this hall it was that morning and evening prayers were said, and here the unsuspecting new boy sitting on a front bench was liable to a sudden shove from the foot of an older boy that would land him on his back on the floor. This was the scene of the weekly "revisals" where two mistakes in Latin grammar meant an hour's detention "to write it out" in Mr. Thompson's room. Here the boys of Mr. Martland's Latin composition class usually did their Latin prose, spread out over the great hall so as to make copying utterly impossible. Here, too, the Fifth and Sixth form boys would get their quota of English poetry to do into Latin verse, a task harder for most of them than for the Hebrews to complete their tale of bricks without straw. One advantage at least was derived from the Latin verse, namely, we usually learned the English piece by heart in the process of turning it into elegiacs or alcaics. Once a week, on Friday afternoon, it was the privilege of the Literary Society to consider the hall their own, and it became the arena of triumph or defeat to the young debaters, who there made their first essays in the art of public speaking. Once a year it was the scene of the distribution of prizes and some distinguished orators were heard within its walls; the stately eloquence of Dr. McCaul gave the boys a foretaste of what they might expect at the University, and the classic English of Professor Goldwin Smith, was heard recalling the memories of his own boyhood at Eton. How it all comes back as we write! The hot close air of the hall, packed far beyond its capacity with the parents and friends of the boys, the brilliant colouring as of some Old World festival lent to the assembly by the resplendent gowns and variegated silken hoods of the masters, more especially that of Dr. Connon; the subdued yet intense excitement of the masters themselves, particularly of Mr. Martland, on whom devolved the duty of marshalling the prize boys, and of Mr. Cockburn, who in the presence of such eloquent speakers as have been mentioned may be pardoned some trepidation; most characteristic of all—the rich heavy odour of the bindings of the prize books, a fragrance that hangs round them still and always brings back the scene of these boyish triumphs.

At rarer intervals the hall was used for more aristocratic functions. When, in 1869, Royalty visited the College in the person of H. R. H. Prince Arthur and, in 1872, eloquence and beauty came in the persons of the then Earl and Countess of Dufferin, it was in the prayer-room that the boys assembled to do honour to these noble guests. The young gentlemen of the Sixth form and the exhibitioners of the Fifth were introduced to their Excellencies, and the whole school was given a holiday to mark the occasion. To the school boys of those days who are old boys now, the College ceased to be the same when the old prayer-room was gone.

To a later generation of boys the new public hall, so soon to be left in its turn, will have its own store of memories. Here it was that Mr. Cockburn took his leave of the College on the 30th of September, 1881,—for the anxieties of the recent controversy had been added to the attacks of a painful constitutional malady and he found it necessary to resign his position in order to seek abroad that relaxation and surgical aid which it was impossible to obtain at home, and by which alone he could hope for a restoration to health. Yet to look at the Principal as he rose before the brilliant assembly to give his farewell address and deliver a last review of his work in the College, the spectator would hardly have suspected the cause of his retirement. His tall figure, well over six feet in height, with massive proportions rendered still more striking by the folds of the academic toga, his head thrown back with the air of a Roman gladiator, the imperious action as of one accustomed to command, made him seem the very ideal type of a man in the prime of life. Nor was this impression lessened when the Principal began to speak. A voice naturally strong and high but not strident, had been cultivated and developed by his years of reading, declaiming, and speaking before his classes, so that it gave an effective expression to the speaker's eloquent defence of his work.

The nature of the occasion assured him of his hearers' sympathy and attention, at the same time that it inspired his own highest efforts, and the result of such reciprocity on the part of speaker and audience was natural. Let us quote the words of an "Upper Canada" boy who was present on that occasion: "Able at all times to give clear and forcible expression to his thoughts and not without a certain eloquence, he on this occasion far surpassed all his former efforts. Smarting under a sense of injustice and injury, and foreseeing, probably, the outcome of the changes which were even then taking place, he reviewed and defended, in sentences that time and again called forth applause from his hearers, the twenty years of his administration of the affairs of the College."

A verbatim report of the address will be found in the Toronto *Mail* of October 1st, 1881. After stating that he assumed the duties of Principal in

June, 1861, Mr. Cockburn proceeded to describe the financial condition of the College at that time and the serious disabilities under which it lay. He went on to sketch the progress which had been made by the institution, in the improvement of its financial condition, the increase of attendance, and the enlargement of its accommodations for boarders and dayboys. Turning then to the question of educational results, the Principal referred to the returns of the last University examinations as a complete vindication of the College from the charge that its pupils were deteriorating in scholarship. A list prepared by Mr. Wedd, who for years has been in charge of the College honour roll, furnished the most indubitable evidence on this question. Of eight medals conferred by the Senate four were carried off by undergraduates owing their previous training to Upper Canada College ; the gold medal in classics, Milner, W. S. ; the silver medal in classics, Armour, D. ; while Gwynne, another old College boy, came next ; the gold medal in metaphysics McAndrew, J. A. ; the Lorne gold medal, Davis, E. P. " None of these medallist at any time lived in Toronto, but they are fair representatives of the provincial youths availing themselves of the training offered by Upper Canada College. In addition to these medals there were carried off by ex-pupils four scholarships, thirty-eight first-class honours, fifty-seven second-class honours, besides ten degrees in arts, three in law, and four in medicine." Such was the latest College record to which the Principal pointed with exultation. After some further general statements in connection with the past history of the College, Mr. Cockburn concluded in the following words : " I have devoted the best twenty years of my life to the old College, which must always be very, very dear to me. My life has been a most happy one, spent as it has been, among the boys, who, I think, have regarded me as their friend, and determined to mete out equal justice to all—though perhaps unknowingly the justice may have occasionally appeared to be tempered with severity. I have enjoyed your respect and affection, and these have been great and sustaining comforts to me in the thousand and one trials incidental to my position. No one can be human and break asunder the ties of two score years' active life without feeling sad at parting. I hope however to return with renewed health to Toronto in a few months, and to renew my acquaintance socially with both my colleagues and yourselves.

" If my bodily health is not what I could desire, it is a pleasure to me to be able to hand over to my successor the College in full and vigorous life, and to assure him that he bears with him in the discharge of his new duties the warmest wishes of both my colleagues and myself." Presentations from the boys and laudatory speeches from several gentlemen followed, the ceremonies concluding with cheers for Mr. and Mrs. Cockburn.

The era of College history thus terminated has certainly been the most important in its annals. The length of his service, nearly a quarter of a century, his strongly marked personality, both as teacher and as administrator, the number of boys that came under his influence, the prosperity arrived at by the College under his rule, lastly, the peculiar character of the institution as compared with the other secondary schools of the Province, all these various causes make Mr. Cockburn's principalship remarkable. Particularly, in the last respect, his resignation terminated an epoch. In its distinctive character as a great public school established on the model of Eton, Rugby, and Harrow, giving a broad, general education of the old-fashioned liberal type, its career was at an end. It must, however be admitted that only by contracting it to the Procrustean standard could the life of the institution have been saved. And we must further admit that the change is after all one of the signs of the times, another of the many proofs that the old ideas are giving place to the new in this part of the American continent, and that the levelling influence of democracy prevails more and more. As we write these lines the local newspapers are calling for tenders for the sale of Russell Square and before this volume leaves the press the old bell to whose pealing we have listened for so many years will be heard on Simcoe Street no more. The old order gives place to the new, and as an old boy of twenty years ago the present writer wishes the College, her Principal, masters, and boys such success in their new home on the hill as shall ensure the continued life and progress of the most notable school that our Province has produced.

THROUGH UPPER CANADA COLLEGE.

CONSULE GEORGIO.

CONTRIBUTED.

"WHY don't you send him to Upper Canada College?" This was the first time I ever heard of the College. We had come from the Southern States, where the war had destroyed whatever educational facilities had previously been found there, to Toronto which even then, over twenty years ago, had a reputation as the city of colleges. So when the above advice was given to my mother by a cousin who had lived all her life in Toronto, we resolved to go down and see Mr. Cockburn.

That visit remains stamped on the memory as one of life's turning-points. The afternoon prayers were just over and the boys were swarming out of the building as we went up the steps of the Principal's dwelling. Shouts of "New boy, new boy!" filled the air, and inspired dismal forebodings in the heart of one who had never before been at a public school of any kind. But the manner and presence of the Principal, though to us awe-inspiring, were at the same time re-assuring. His most striking statement was that the College was the Canadian Eton, and this came with special force to one who had just been reading Disraeli's *Coningsby*. So it was decided that I should be placed in the lowest form, and on the 28th of October, 1868, I was entered as registered number 232, that being the number of boys at the College in the first quarter of 1868-9.

That was a very new and interesting life to registered number 232. There was the morning roll-call in the "prayer-room," at which the head-boy of the College or his substitute—some stentor of the sixth form—called out the 232 names, and each boy answered from his place. Occasionally a boy caused a laugh by entering just as his name was called, and answering it in the doorway. Under this system the boys knew each other better than they did in after years, when each form had roll-call with the form master.

Very awful to the mind of the "new-boy" were the masters seated *en banc* in stalls on each side of the Principal. At the other end of the hall sat one of the junior masters, whose attention was severely taxed to keep order and prevent personation during roll-call. Another master remained in the outer hall to take the names of those who were late, and maintain silence among these unfortunates during prayers. At afternoon prayers the roll-call was a different one, consisting of the names of those boys who had received demerit-marks during the day, and those who were to be detained, or in boys' parlance "kept in."

The small boys of I. A. were never in the "prayer-room" at any other time, except when undergoing the weekly examination or "revisal" by the Principal. This was looked forward to with something of the feeling that high school boys have when anticipating the visit of the Inspector. There being fewer masters in those days, the boys in the lower forms were brought under the senior masters to some extent even in I. A., which gave them a better training in many ways.

During my first year at College, a very striking incident happened at afternoon prayers, which will be remembered by many old College boys. That day it was the turn of the French and German master to occupy the seat at the lower or south end of the hall. Before his entrance one of the Third form boys gave to a I. A. boy, seated in front of him, one of those curiously twisted instruments of torture that schoolboys will probably continue to contrive till the millenium. The pin was put upon the master's chair, but the act was detected and the Principal sent the head-boy to fetch him the suspected article. Every eye was fixed on the lower end of the hall, not a boy dared to remove the biangular dart, and terrible must have been the feelings of that poor little I. A. boy as the proof of his guilt was relentlessly removed and brought to the Principal. But worse torture was in store. " Let the boy who put this pin on that seat stand up ; " came in dread tones from the daïs. For some seconds there was a pause, then with quivering knees the culprit stood up. " Now go into my room and after prayers I'll give you the soundest flogging you ever got in your life ! " The command was obeyed and while the wretched victim waited his prayers were far more fervent than ever they had been in the hall. Nor were they unanswered. For when the awful interview came courage was given him to refuse to disclose the name of his tempter. The first effect on the Principal's mind was very bitter to the young culprit. "Oh! you're more afraid of him than you are of me, are you?" but the answer, "I don't think it would be honourable, sir," was given in a way that bore conviction with it. The inciter very soon gave himself up, whether urged by his own better feelings

UPPER CANADA COLLEGE—VIEW FROM ADELAIDE STREET.

or by that of his classmates I know not. Certain it is that the caning the big boy got was much harder than that received by the little boy. The latter in addition was advised never to be a cat's-paw again, and it is to be hoped he took the counsel for which he had paid so dearly.

In those days the cane was frequently employed, generally by the Principal or by the head master of the boarding-house. With the latter it was a specific for lying, and often in I. A. have I seen boys weep at the invitation "Come to me after three o'clock!"

During the later years of my course the discipline while quite as thorough was less rigorous, the canings becoming, in one sense at least, like angel's visits.

In other respects, too, there was a very marked change in the College spirit. Those were stirring times in the world's history. The great War of Secession had just ended. The two mighty conflicts by which Prussia fought her way to the possession of the European championship took place just before and just after my entering the College. The revival of public interest in pugilism is of much later date, but at Upper Canada College the interest in the prize ring was quite active in those early days. I had not been long at College when I learned that another southern boy had been worsted in the ring. His name, Dan Lick, was against him. This fight I did not see, as we small boys were kept outside the gymnasium, where all the fights came off, while such important contests were taking place. It used to give great amusement to the boys inside to throw sawdust in the eyes of such I. A. boys as tried to peep through at the "mills." However, the I. A. boys had their own innings and had some very creditable "bantam" performances. One in particular comes vividly to my recollection. The two boys were both of Celtic descent, one from Cornwall, the other from the neighbourhood of Dublin. The former had shown me kindness when I was a new boy, the other had charmed me by boyish beauty of face and frankness of manner. It was with mixed feelings therefore that I saw my benefactor knocked out after a quarter of an hour's hard fighting. But the greatest match of this kind that we had in my day was a pitched battle between the champion of I. B. and the two best fighters in I. A. This took place some time in the spring of 1869, and excited great interest. Having been present when the challenge was accepted I can state positively that there were no written articles. There was a verbal agreement between the three contestants that they should fight rough and tumble, but without kicking, for the I. B. hero, a well-grown boy about sixteen or seventeen, wore moccasins and the other boy's boots. On this occasion the I. A. boys were of course admitted to view the fight, which took place after school hours. Goliath stood in the middle of a twenty-foot ring, and David and Jonathan—boys about twelve or thirteen—took up positions one in front of the other, behind Goliath. This added to the novelty and interest of the contest. It showed the grit of these boys that the younger faced his foe, who was nearly a head taller than either of them. I shall only describe the opening of the battle, leaving the rest, after the approved fashion of school chroniclers, to the reader's imagination. When the word was given, big H. wheeled around, struck B. the elder I. A. boy a blow in the forehead that knocked him over and then turned back to get G.'s fist in his eye. By this time B. was on him again from the rear, and it took all the big boy's strength to stay himself up between them, like a Samson tugging at two pillars. It resulted in a drawn fight after all, for the appearance of the boarding-house master put an end to this chancery suit, which after the opening seemed to lag a little. Next morning, however, all the contestants showed signs of the punishment they had received, and it was evident that though H. had managed to get both his opponents heads in chancery he had not been able to keep his own head undamaged.

To these pictures of the bellicose state of the College at the end of "the sixties" the explanation must be added that while there have been as many as three fights in one day, the authorities were strongly opposed to such practices. A rather amusing instance of this occurred when I was in the third form. One of the boys had the misfortune to be hit in the eye with a trapeze and had to remain two days at home, bathing his eye with hot water and milk, returning to the College with an excuse stating as a cause for his absence: "An accident in the gymnasium." The Principal looked severely at the vari-coloured orb, and wrote down (without listening to the explanation) "loses six places," instead of the familiar, "resume place." One of the masters earned that boy's eternal gratitude, by refusing to follow this direction, and restoring the boy to his place.

As time went on this severity proved more effective than in the case of the German duellists, for fighting went out of fashion, and pitched battles were heard of no more. Occasional challenges were given by hot-tempered boys, but so strong was the influence of the Principal that once a sixth form boy refused to fight because he feared the ridicule of which Mr. Cockburn was such a master. At the same time he expressed his willingness to defend himself if attacked, but this was beneath the dignity of his adversary, as prize-fighting in the gymnasium was beneath his own. A curious thing, that dignity! At the present time, I believe, fighting is almost a lost art among the boys and the only regular "mill" that has taken place in the gymnasium of late years was between ex-pupils.

With the decay of fighting there grew up another way of showing enmity which is more characteristic of little girls than of boys—not speaking. There were boys who did not speak to each other from year's end to year's end. There was also a certain lowering of tone among the boys. In those times, twenty years ago, it was an insult to call a boy "a cheat." I remember a fight between two boys on this ground that caused considerable bloodshed. One of them is now a clergyman, and the other a college professor. But as the years passed by greater laxity prevailed until finally the sheep and the goats were about equal in numbers. I have been told that later on the boys who would refuse to be prompted or assisted in their examinations by other boys were the exception rather than the rule.

Those examinations were ordeals that grew more and more trying as the years rolled by. Perhaps the most exciting of all was the earliest—the oral "exam." in I. A. The element of luck was much larger in these than in the later "written exams.," which began in the Second form. At the same time it was much harder to get a high percentage, and when a I. A. boy made forty-seven out of a possible fifty in English grammar, and over ninety per cent. in his Latin grammar oral examination with Mr. Martland, he had a right to be proud of the special prize he obtained.

The inspiration of that examination carried registered number 232 through the next two forms ahead of all his I. A. classmates. But in the Fourth form the "new boy" infusion is usually of a good quality. Many clever boys were in those days sent up from the Grammar Schools to the College, to the great advantage of the latter. Moreover the Fourth form was made a halting-place by boys who had entered the College at an early age, and by their quickness had kept up with their forms so far, but on account of their youth were held back at this stage. Then in this form there was a great advance in the work done. The reading of Greek, Xenophon and Homer, was begun, and the more difficult Latin authors, such as Livy and Horace, taxed the ingenuity of the boys. At the end of this form came the Exhibition examinations; and here again there was a renewed inspiration for registered number seventy, as he had now become. In that year, 1872, the boys who went up for exhibitions had the rare honour of being examined in Classics by Professor Goldwin Smith, and in Mathematics by the late Professor Young. It is not to be wondered at that the Oxford professor, whose Tacitean Latin is at once the pride and despair of his *alma mater*, should have given the head-boy of our form about twenty-five per cent. for his Latin prose. But that two boys who had been fourth and fifth for the year should come out head in classics was an unheard-of thing, and only to be accounted for by the excellence of the

English translation that the boys had learned by heart. It was a matter of no small pride to one of the competitors that he afterwards came out head in Mr. Cockburn's test examination on Livy at sight, and so justified Professor Smith's return. So utterly were the masters' calculations upset by the results, that a re-reading of the papers was suggested. But the idea of an Oxford examiner re-reading his papers!

A noteworthy feature of these examinations was the general character of the work. In this, Upper Canada College presented a contrast to the High Schools. The High School masters at one time made it a charge against the College, that this institution was more intimately connected with the University, and therefore its pupils had a better chance in the University examinations. Whatever may have been the case in earlier days it is certain that during the last six years of Mr. Cockburn's principalship, the tendency, owing to a particular cause, was all the other way. This particular cause was the advance of specialism. That system, which has found such favour with our practical age, owes its origin partly to the influence of political economy, showing the advantage of a division of labour, partly to the example of the German Universities, which in these latter days are supplying teachers to even conservative Oxford; but chiefly to that enormous widening of the bounds of knowledge that has made universal scholarship one of the lost arts. In 1874 there were proficiency scholarships in every year of the University course, and the highest honour a student could win was the Prince of Wales' prize, then given for general proficiency in the fourth year final examination. But already the High Schools were beginning to train up specialists for the different subjects. Not for years later—not indeed until after Mr. Cockburn's resignation—did this system come into vogue at the College. The exhibitions were always granted for general proficiency in classics, mathematics, English, history and geography, chemistry and physiology. To be narrow was impossible. With such a course, coupled with the character of the teachers, was a guarantee against "cram."

Of the masters who taught between 1868 and 1874 but two, Mr. Wedd and Mr. Martland,[*] remain in the school. For more than twenty years these gentlemen have imparted the humanities to generation after generation of College boys. Both of them in hearty sympathy with the boys, both good classical scholars, both skilled in imparting knowledge to their pupils, they were at the same time poles apart in their methods. It was one of the greatest advantages of the school that the teaching was of this varied

---

[*] Both these masters have now (Oct., 1891) been retired.—*Editors*.

character. In Mr. Cockburn the pupils had a teacher whose vigorous, shrewd, and practical mind had enjoyed the combined advantages of Scotch and German training. Mr. Wedd, like the late Chief Justice Moss (one of the staunchest friends the College ever had) and other of Ontario's departed worthies, was a representative pupil of that fine scholar and courteous gentleman, Dr. McCaul, whose far-reaching influence on the mental life of Canada, it would be difficult to over-estimate. Mr. Martland, in turn, was eminently fitted to bring the influence of an English public school and university training to bear upon the College boys, and more especially the boarders. It was customary to read most of the classical authors on the course with each of these masters in turn ; was it any wonder that at the university the classical scholarships and medals were nearly always taken by their pupils?

This breadth was indeed a noticeable quality of the instruction even in the lower forms. Here it was carried into effect by means of the weekly revisals that have been already mentioned. Every old College boy will remember the "vim" which the Principal used to put into these oral examinations on the work done. Entering the prayer-room, with the stride of an Arab sheik, sometimes a little late, owing to the claims of visitors, (once, I remember, just in time to catch a couple of boys in a fight, and send them out to wash their faces) he would take the head-boy's book and then the rush of questions that began to be scattered here, there, and everywhere, till the class was thoroughly sifted and the dregs left at the bottom. Then as the index finger swept more and more swiftly past the foot boys, their names would go down to swell that day's "detention list" and the position of head-boy would grow more and more trying, for he had to act as a net to catch all the hot balls that went through the lower ranks.

Woe to the boy who tried to look in his book or to prompt his neighbour! An incident that took place at one of these revisals is worth commemorating for what it shows of boy nature as the College was then. It was revisal in Ancient History, an old boy was head and the second boy was a new boy who had been working himself up by amazing diligence to the head of the Fourth form. An attachment had sprung up between the two boys who sat together in Mr. Thompson's room. So when the new boy asked the other to tell him a question the head-boy complied. He was caught—it was very rarely that a boy fooled Mr. Cockburn—and told at once to "go foot." He went, and as the hour was nearly over when this happened, he had not risen very far when the end of the recital came. It chanced that the register in which the numbers were kept was not at hand and Mr. Cockburn told the boys to give their numbers to Mr. Martland that afternoon. At dinner time the new boy came to his prompter and after some persuasion induced him to keep his place at the head of the form and let the new boy resume the low place from which he had taken so long to rise. Everybody felt it was a proper thing to do, for he had asked the other boy to tell him. But it caused a wonderful revulsion in the feeling with which the form regarded that new boy. Jealous of the rapidity with which he rose there had been something of "combine" against him. He had been kept down by ways more characteristic of the heathen Chinee than of the Upper Canada College boy. But after that incident there was no bar to his upward progress, and years after, when it became his turn as head-boy of the College to fear the rise of an ambitious new boy, he was often aided by his old chum of the writing-room, who to this day remembers gratefully the magnanimity of W. B. N.

Earlier in the hour during that revisal a question on the Decemvirate had given a rise of twenty places to a boy whose beautiful, classically cut features were in keeping with his knowledge of Roman history. This boy, who had been at Harrow, was the only one that thought N———p's kindness should have been refused. "You should'nt have let him do it," he said. Years after, when the same boy had completed his professional course as a physician, and was still in the first flush of youthful manhood, he was wrecked off the coast of Newfoundland. Swimming up to a boat with another drowning man he learned that they had room for only one more : "Take him, then," he said, and swam away to die the death of a hero!

> "To each his sufferings : all are men
> Condemned alike to groan :
> The tender for another's pain
> Th' unfeeling for his own.
> Yet, ah ! why should they know their fate,
> Since sorrow never comes too late,
> And happinesstoo swiftly flies."

Not the least transient of the joys of College life were the friendships then formed. As the writer recalls the boyish faces of his friends, and remembers how they are scattered : one in St. Louis, another in Winnipeg, a third in the North-West, a fourth, the dearest of all, lost in the Far West and unheard-of for years, he is constrained to cry out against the restless spirit of the times. Many a loyal supporter has it given the old school, whose sons are to be found in every quarter of the globe.

In the upper half of the school the day boys had a better opportunity of knowing each other through the influence of the College Debating Society. It was customary to select a few of the Fourth form boys as members of the society, so as to prepare them for future usefulness, and in one year the wisdom of this plan was shown. The first meeting after we entered the Fifth form was a stormy and eventful one. The lower half of our form was more muscular than literary, and took more pleasure in slamming the benches together than in listening to the debaters. The din had become quite deafening when order was suddenly restored in a very remarkable way. The Sixth form was unusually staid and dignified—more than half of its eleven members afterwards went into theology or law. Their head-boy, President *ex officio*, had in vain called for order ; they had consulted together and now they formally made known the result of their deliberations : they withdrew from the society. This decision having been announced by the President, he left the chair and marched solemnly out of the masters' door, followed by all the Sixth form boys. Thus the great secession was consummated.

This withdrawal of the senior form restored perfect order among the boys who were left. A discussion took place on the course to be pursued, and now the experience of those boys, who were already members in the Fourth form, came into play. Urged on by these and confiding in their judgment it was *resolved* : That the Fifth form keep up the Literary and Debating Society. For that year therefore there were two societies in operation in the College, and the boys of both Fifth and Sixth forms had a doubly good opportunity of becoming debaters. The Sixth form did more, for they published the College *Times*, without any aid from the members of the Literary and Debating Society. Efforts were made to bring about a reunion, but they proved ineffectual and the schism was healed only at the end of the year, when the Sixth form left the College.

JOHN MILNE BUCHAN, M.A., 1881-1885,

BY A. H. YOUNG, B.A.

THOUGH accident of birth would have made him a citizen of the neighbouring republic, John Milne Buchan was through his family, education, tastes and preferences a Canadian and a British subject. Born in Lockport, New York, in 1842, he was brought when yet an infant to Upper Canada. In Hamilton he received his early education, and, after being head-boy of the Grammar School there in Dr. Sangster's time, matriculated thence into the University of Toronto. Here he was contemporary with Hon. J. M. Gibson, Prof. Loudon, Dr. McLellan, Rev. J. Munro Gibson, Rev. Dr. McNish and others who have since made a name for themselves. Never fond of display, and valuing more than prizes and medals that for which they are given, he devoted himself to the pursuit of learning for its own sake, and in due time left the University with a good foundation laid for future culture. The curious may see for themselves in the University class lists how well he stood and what honours and medals he won.

A short time after graduation he returned to Hamilton to become headmaster of the recently reorganized High School. His work in that position was so well done that, in 1873, when a new High School Inspector was to be appointed to represent modern languages, the Chief Superintendent of Education offered him the appointment. For eight years he continued, with Dr. McLellan and the late Mr. Marling, the one an old College boy and the other a former master, to supervise the secondary education of the province, sowing the seed which is now bearing such good fruit. Then, happily he once more returned to teaching when the principalship of Upper Canada College became vacant in 1881, and the Government of the day, desirous of conciliating the High School Masters, offered it to him. That their choice was a good one has never been questioned. Certainly most boys who attended the College in Mr. Buchan's day will appreciate the estimate of him given by one of his Hamilton pupils at the time that death cut him off. "Mr. Buchan was no ordinary tutor or educationist. With a fine education, with the application and enthusiasm in the pursuit of knowledge which makes the cultured man, Mr. Buchan united a humanity which it is given few mortals to experience. Hundreds of young men in Canada have lovingly sat at his feet, and learned from him not merely the knowledge which books impart, but the higher and better instruction of brotherly kindness, of manliness, and of nobleness of character. As a teacher Mr. Buchan had probably no peer in Canada, possessing in a remarkable degree the faculty of imparting the learning he had himself acquired. * * * The personal affection towards him of his pupils was something extraordinary; he won the confidence of his scholars almost at sight, and so heartily, so genuinely did he sympathize with them in all their joys and sorrows, their sports and studies, that almost a brotherly love sprang up between master and pupil."

Great had been the amusement among us boys over the various lists that, from time to time, had been called for by order of the Legislature when the fate of the College was being decided. Had not one lad from a rural district wished to have his father styled agriculturist? And, when asked if that was not the same thing as farmer, had he not scouted the very thought and insisted on agriculturist, when, after all, the man was no farmer but an honest country doctor? And had we not, boy like, got it into our heads that all this row was being raised by the High School masters, and wrongly, as we afterwards found out through Mr. Buchan, concluded that these men were worthy of no consideration at all? Then, we had gone down to the opening of the House and gazed in admiration at our Principal as he stood, a striking figure in his academicals, among the gay throng upon the floor. So, with all our watching and all our listening we were not surprised after the summer holidays of 1881 at the announcement made by the boarders that Mr. Cockburn was going to leave on prize-day; boarders have always been able, for reasons well known to all who have attended the College within the last thirty years, to give early and trustworthy information concerning matters of general interest.

At length prize-day—the day that was to witness the end of a twenty-years' principalship and the coming of a new man—arrived. The last Friday in September was the all-important date. A beautiful autumn day it was, and everything looked its best. The western sun shone brightly in through the great windows of the prayer-hall, one of the monuments of the retiring principal. His predecessors in their frames, and the noble founder of the school, all the better for the recent attentions of the varnisher and gilder, looked down with a frown, a jolly, mirthful smile, or a certain imperious dignity upon the scene about to be enacted. The very curtains, divested for the nonce of their every-day holland dress, did honour to the day in all the glory of their crimson and the gold embroidered crest above them. The uncomfortable, somewhat monk-like, old walnut seats, relics of the older hall, whereon in awful dignity had sat generations of masters, to listen, in appearance at least, to the morning and evening reading of the Scriptures, or to mark out for correction the irreverent and the misbehaving —these seats even, despite their faded damask cushions and valances, looked a trifle brighter while waiting to witness another change in the life of the College, and to receive the throng of distinguished men who had that day come to do honour either to the old, or to the new, Principal.

The gilded honour rolls, not the least beneficial stimuli afforded by the associations of the place, were proxies for those whose names they bore, and in all their pride awaited the coming of the procession from the Principal's room. Soon it came, heralded by cheers for the Governor from prize-boys drawn up at the head of the stairs, and crossed the hall amid the lusty shouts of a couple of hundred boys massed at either end of the room about the places usually sacred to masters. Quickly the ordinary business of the day was done; prize-boys, marshalled from Mr. Brown's classroom by Mr. Martland came in, form after form, in quick succession and then made way for others; exhibitioners rejoicing in their prospective wealth, whether coming from the College treasury or their fathers' pockets, nervously signed the book; the head-boy, now a gay and festive freshman, carried off his load of books and his meed of applause, and the speeches began.

To recount all that was said of the College and the two Principals, in praise of the closing administration or in anticipation of the one just beginning, were here out of place. The interest to-day, of the boys at least, centred not in these, nor wholly in the presentation of an address and memento to Mr. Cockburn. The great pleasure in the latter had been in buying the one and writing the other, connected as they had been with invitations to a farewell dinner party at the Principal's, which had caused not a little trepidation to the boys of the Sixth and the exhibitioners of the Fifth. Never had any of us been at a formal dinner before, so we had to decide in solemn conclave, perched upon the desk in the Principal's classroom, the all-important question of wearing coats or jackets, white ties or black, gloves or no gloves. But to-day the main thing was to see the new man and read his character as far as possible.

Soon, by ways known only to boys, it was found that the tall, thin man, on Principal Cockburn's left, was Mr. Buchan. Dark-eyed and dark-haired he was, rather sombre and mournful-looking, and still only in the thirties, though thought and study gave him the appearance of being older. But he could smile, and what a smile! It made him look many years younger, and at once gave confidence to those looking at him. Evidently a kindly man, yet one not to be imposed upon. Though asked to speak, he preferred to let the old Principal be Principal till the close of the day, and to wait till Monday to introduce himself to his pupils when removed from the embarrassing gaze of curious strangers who had come to criticize.

On Monday morning, contrary to custom, there was not a laggard on the way to the prayer-room. Every boy hurried to prayers as he would have done to play. Already Mr. Buchan was in his place, though the masters still loitered at the head of the stairs exchanging their morning greetings—and their bits of gossip. While they lingered thus, the boys began to applaud. Louder and louder grew the applause, and at last three hearty cheers and a tiger were given for the Principal. At the first "hip" he stood up, uncovered, made a profound bow and, when the noise had ceased, returned a few words of thanks. Then in came the masters, and prayers went on as usual, but well nigh three hundred boys had been captivated by the little act of courtesy done them in the very happy recognition of their reception.

Of course, there came the inevitable putting through to which even principals are subjected; but we soon found that we had in our Principal a friend who respected the rights and feelings of school-boys and was ready to grant us every liberty, as far as the school discipline would permit, and therefore we early gave up the game.

Shortly after Mr. Buchan's coming the Sixth was waiting for him in his classroom just after dinner. To pass the time two of the biggest of them had a scuffle which was interrupted by the opening of the door of the Principal's private room. The two boys were ordered to get up from the floor, which they did, covered with dust and very sheepish withal, slinking off beneath the steady gaze of the Principal. They were quietly told that this time the impropriety of the scuffle would be overlooked, but not the next time. The next time never came.

It was customary in those days for the Sixth form and the Fifth to remain in the building during the noon-hour. Some of the boys, however, wearied of being locked in, had made their way out by one of the windows and back by the same means. This, being found out by Frost, was duly reported. An investigation was held, in which we were all made to feel very foolish, though little was said, and that very quietly. Thenceforward the Fifth, who as generally happened, had been the chief offenders, had to betake themselves to the "Taffy," the "Gym," or the old lunch-room in the basement, instead of enjoying the comfort of a warm classroom at noon.

As St. Andrew's day drew near, the Principal was astonished one day at being asked of what nationality he was, if he was Scotch. He asked "Why?" and was told that it had been customary, as it had been except in the previous year, when the head boy did not think of asking for it, for a half-holiday to be given on the anniversary of the patron saint of the Principal's native country. With an amused smile, one he often wore, he said he was not a Scotchman, but his father was, and he gave the half, without prejudice, however, to future years.

One day in the prayer-hall some announcements were being made, and we were paying no heed to them. All at once the Principal stopped speaking and a hush immediately fell upon us, only to be broken by the ringing of the table-bell which had stood unused for all the weeks of his term of office. We were then given to understand that we were to have no other signal but the Principal's voice to ensure quiet.

At another time there had been a great deal of talking and laughing at prayers, but this was stopped when the Principal very gravely reminded us that at prayer-time we were "in an especial manner in the presence of the Supreme Being, and that it therefore became us to be reverent." To say we never talked or laughed again during prayers would be to say we became goody-goody youngsters, which we were not, but there never again was any necessity to publicly reprove the school for this offence.

But, grave and serious as he was, he was also kindly. A boy never brought a note to school giving illness as an excuse for absence without being asked about his present state of health, or, in the case of family bereavement, without sympathy being expressed by a look, if not by words. A little thing in itself this was, but one often talked about among us.

Among other trying things that happened during Mr. Buchan's first year was the death of one of the boys. The event was all the sadder from the fact that the boy's home was in Jamaica, and that, excepting a brother at school with him, he had neither relatives nor friends in Canada. From the beginning of the illness until the day when the boys followed the body through the rain to the grave, Mr. Buchan was kindness itself.

More joyous memories, though, are connected with both Mr. and Mrs. Buchan. In the Spring when games'-day was drawing near, the Principal took the chairman and secretary of the committee over on Thursday to call on Mrs. Buchan, who, before they took their leave, gave them an invitation for themselves and the other committee-men to afternoon tea on games'-day. Of course not a few of them took advantage of this invitation, and they thoroughly enjoyed themselves. After leaving school it was a pleasure to old boys to call at the Principal's house on games'-day or prize-day and, over a cup of tea, renew their acquaintance with the College and revive old memories.

Just when the school examinations were beginning, and the boys matriculating were about to leave, they were all asked by the Principal to spend a quiet evening with him. Needless to say that every boy put in an appearance and enjoyed to the full the simple entertainment so unaffectedly provided. Except Mrs. Buchan, there were no ladies present, and consequently there was no dancing, but a little music and a great deal of conversation, of which the Principal himself was the life and soul, more than made up for any lack. Delightful and full of interest as this year had been, this little evening filled up the measure of it and made more than one of us feel almost home-sick at the thought of leaving the old College for good, even though we were going to that place of great and varied delights —the 'Varsity.

Going away, we carried with us the knowledge that whatever might happen us we had at Upper Canada College a friend we might be free to consult in any difficulty. We carried with us, too, the deeply impressed fact of the worth of the man who had taught us ;—a man with lofty ideals, who, though he by no means undervalued the little externals that go far to make pleasant the humdrum, work-a-day life, yet had learned not to live for them but to subordinate them to the concerns of his intellectual and moral being, a man who studied in order that he might be worthy, and live a manly, straightforward, kindly and useful life.

II.

It was in the prayer-hall only or in his private room that the majority of the boys saw and knew the Principal as, in his deep musical voice, he read prayers, made announcements, called over the lists at the changing of the seats at the end of the markings, or administered public or private reproof and correction. To the higher forms, particularly the Sixth, he was better known by his teaching them and being consulted by them on various school matters, such as the games, the Literary Society, and the *College Times*.

After the suppression of the journal several years before, on account of its too free criticism and caricatures of the masters, the *College Times* was revived in Mr. Buchan's first year at the school. T. C. Street Macklem (now rector of St. Simon's Church, Toronto) was editor, C. B. Beck (at present a master in the Toronto Church School for Boys) was treasurer, and

Allan Scatcherd, of Strathroy, was secretary. The committee came mainly from the noble or gallant Fifth, it having been stipulated that, for this year at least, no boys who were reading for matriculation in honours at Toronto should have to do with the management. In passing, it may be remarked that the epithets "gallant" and "noble," always applied to the Fifth in those days, were Homeric in their character, and had no specific meaning unless it were a certain tendency on the part of the boys in question to hasten to the John Street fence when a procession of girls from one of the neighbouring ladies' schools passed by, and to most religiously attend evening service at the Church of the Holy Trinity for a somewhat similar reason.

In turning over the dusty pages of the *Times* for that year, one has his memory refreshed concerning little things that had dropped into the background. Now it is little turns of expression peculiar to the masters, but to the Principal in particular; now a chronicle of the games, of prize-day, or the doings of the Literary Society, or some boyish joke at another's expense. A series of sketches of old boys—among them the Hon. Edward Blake, the Hon. Adam Crooks, and Mr. S. Arthur Marling—was one noticeable feature of the paper; while original sketches on a variety of subjects, attempts at poetry and theatrical criticisms were well done—for boys. That almost sounds as though one might be praising himself. If anybody thinks so, he must be content with the excuse which often used to be given by a genial old master who, for some forty years of his pilgrimage through the wilderness of school life, has rejoiced in the name of "Billy" or "Billy Goat." When we nudged each other, with many an accompanying wink, at the announcement that a piece of verse, quoted to illustrate a point in the lesson, was his own, "Billy" would say "Oh well! Boys! That was done so many years ago that I can judge the verse quite dispassionately—almost as though it was the work of another man, you know." Of course we had to know, but there was a chorus of "Oh"!!! The same old master frequently said in an argument with the boys over the marks on a paper, for instance: "Well, boys! I am open to conviction." As surely as he said that, though, we soon learned that no length of argument could bring conviction. It might bring demerits, but they were almost certain to be taken off again if we assumed a properly penitent air, or pointed out to the kind old man the dreadful consequences that would ensue on Saturday afternoon if the demerits were entered, and how grieved our parents would be when the reports went home.

Considering the circumstances that before had led to the suppression of the *Times*, the masters in session in the Principal's room, where they gave counsel on affairs of state and discussed boys' characters and doings, advised

that it be resuscitated only on condition that the Principal should act as
censor. Accordingly, all copy was submitted, but no practical difficulty was
encountered. Little that was objectionable was sent in, for there was no
use in that. It was certain to be thrown out; and woe betide the boy who
put anything in on the sly. The editorial staff would not have stood such
a thing either, for it would have been taking a mean advantage of the Principal. Scarcely any help was given by the masters in editing the paper, the
aim being to make us depend upon ourselves as far as possible. So also
with the Literary Society, and nearly everything else. Advice was given
when asked for, but they were our own affairs and we had to shoulder the
responsibility of failure and were given the credit of success.

After football season ended, something was needed to relieve the monotony of the days before skating had come. A Literary Society was proposed,
consent to establish it was obtained, officers were elected, a constitution was
drawn up, and week by week, or as often as the committee had a programme
ready, a goodly number of boys gathered in the room, then Mr. Martland's
classroom, where now the boys from Mr. Jackson's and Mr. Brock's at least
go through the motions of learning their lessons night after night. The
reading-desk was brought down from the library whither it had been
banished from the prayer-hall. The desk at which "Authority" sat during
the day was taken from the platform and set at the end of the room. The
benches, which, as we had many a time heard in that same room when
lessons had been poorly said, did not communicate learning through the
mere contact of our bodies with them as we sat upon them, were ranged
facing the chair, and proceedings began. Minutes were not always
approved in the formal fashion one generally sees in older assemblies, but
were often discussed and had to be amended. After the reading of minutes
the president vacated the chair to let some other member of committee
sum up the debate and give his decision, while he himself became
a private member for the time being and listened to some, on the principle
of criticism already laid down, not bad speeches on such old-time subjects
as "Is a lie ever justifiable?" "Are early marriages conducive to the welfare
of society?" etc., etc. Early in the society's history, however, that article of its
constitution, which it had copied from that of the society at University College,
prohibiting the discussion of party politics was repealed. Consequently the
meetings became even more lively, all the more so that the elections of 1882
were drawing near. "It is preferable for a college to be located in the
country rather than in the city" drew a large crowd to listen to arguments
founded perhaps, in the speakers' experience, as to the bad effects of
parading King Street, etc. None of us for a moment thought that there

was any serious prospect of our College being located in the country, though even then, one of our number whose father was, and is still, in politics told us as a great secret how the College was to be moved, perhaps, to Scarboro, a new building erected out of the proceeds of the sale of the old site, the residue to be a new endowment, while the old one was to go to swell the revenues of the University. The actual state of things is worthy of comparison with the older scheme.

The most enjoyable of all the meetings of our Literary Society, probably, was the last one. Summer had come, exams. were drawing near, a surplus was in hand (the expenses had not been heavy, so too much credit cannot be given the executive for its thrift), the society might not exist another year, and, if it did, why should our surplus be carried over? The most natural solution of the difficulty, to a boy's mind, was "a feed." From the fact that a sub-committee visited Coleman's (the "Taffy" would not suffice this time), and that the *Times* had the following chronicled in its next issue, all may judge how easily the troublesome surplus was disposed of: "The subject for discussion was: ice cream and cake. Debaters; members (all on the affirmative). After the members had partaken of these refreshments, and after a chorus of spoons vs. plates (borrowed from the boarding-house and due there again at five o'clock) the company showed how they had mastered the Terpsichorean art. The society (led, we suppose, by the singing-class) sang 'God save the Queen.' After three cheers had been given for the president and officers of the society, for Sir John A. Macdonald, Mr. Blake, and Centre Toronto, the society was dissolved, not prorogued." Because of the arduous duties performed by the committee, and because there was not enough ice-cream to give a second helping to every one of the members (forty odd), the committee returned to the prayer-hall to have a second feast free from interruption by the private members, some of whom had, strange to say, joined the society solely to enjoy the privilege of attending this meeting. The treasurer, who has since gone into business, insisted that the membership fee should in every case be paid before the interesting "debate" began.

Though the society was "dissolved," the president had to appear before the Principal on the following morning and explain how his name had been cut on a bench and how the legend "Billy Goat" came to be on another. The meeting had had to be held upstairs, for the piano could not well be brought down from the library, so Mr. Wedd had kindly let us have his classroom, now Mr. Brock's, and, in earlier days, the northern half of the prayer-hall. The return we made him is related above. Of course, boy-like, the president knew nothing about the matter, he having been in the chair.

For once, therefore, Frost was obliged to do the necessary repairing without the levying of fines and without other recompense, for the society's money had all been spent the day before.

It has been already said that the boys came into contact with Mr. Buchan, and learned to know him in consulting him about the games. In this matter, however, it was only in the more general arrangements, such as the day games were to be held on and matches played, that the Principal was spoken to. In the details the master who was always looked to was Mr. Martland, and naturally so : firstly, because he took a real interest in games themselves and in boys, and would walk any distance to see them play a football or a cricket match. Then, he was house master, and, as such, had for years helped the boys to make all their arrangements, and had managed all their affairs in such a way as to make them happy and contented ; and lastly, the games were very largely a boarding-house affair, because the day-boys played on the grounds at recess and noon only, and were expected to take themselves off home as soon as school and detention were over. The boarders, on the contrary, were on the grounds all the time, in early morning, at recess, at noon, and in the afternoon and evening. Such being the case, it was but natural that they should take the lead in sports, and, each year, elect as their president and consult at every turn their old favourite. But it was soon noticed that on practice days, as well as match days, Mr. Buchan turned out to see how the boys were getting on, and stood watching their play by the half-hour. The boys' hearts warmed toward him accordingly.

In making arrangements for the first games after his coming to the College, the writer well remembers in what a difficult position Mr. Buchan was placed. It will be remembered that in the old days there was a graded rate of subscription to the games' fund. The Third paid seventy-five cents a head, but III. A., being made up for the most part of small boys, had no vote and could not be represented on the committee. III. B. was more fortunate, for, being larger boys, they had both these privileges. Here was an injustice, and all wrongs must be righted. So the reformers laid their plans, but, strange to say, the majority of these reformers were candidates who would carry the election if III. A. could get a vote, but would lose it otherwise. The conservatives insisted on adhering to old established custom. The very College would be wrecked if any of these old customs should be changed. Party spirit ran high. Chalk advertisements on fellows' coats and elsewhere solicited the vote and influence of the electorate for one party or the other, and election day was drawing on.

In order to exercise the ancient right of his position, the head-boy had himself excused from Mr. Furrer's German class, and went to afternoon prayers to ask the Principal to summon to the meeting the forms from III.B. up. But a reformer had forestalled him, asking to have III. A. included. Being assured that this was an innovation, the Principal called the meeting in the old way. After prayers III. A. laid their grievance before the Principal, and the head-boy was sent for from the meeting which had already begun in Mr. Martland's classroom. Once more the question was decided against III. A., but the reform leaders still persisted, and came with the Principal to the meeting, where nominations were already being received. A consultation was held with the whole Sixth form, and, they agreeing with the head-boy, the Principal finally withdrew, saying he could not interfere. Thus he was always careful to change as little as possible the old usages of the College.

Needless to say the meeting was none the quieter for the dispute, and the reformers were beaten. By way of retaliation the III. A. vowed they would not pay their subscriptions, but a threat to exclude them from competition in the games and to give them no invitation cards broke down their opposition. The games went on, and had the success that usually attends them.

To Mr. Buchan's first year belongs one innovation which deserves mention. For years the boarders had had their minstrel show at Christmas, but no day-boy had ever been present at it—unless he had stolen in. This year, however, an invitation to the supper and show was given by the committee to all the exhibitioners and, if the writer is not mistaken, to all the boys of the Sixth who were day-boys. Early, for promptness has always been a virtue of the house, the day-boys presented themselves and were received by the head-boy of the boarding-house in Mr. Martland's drawing-room. Thence, after a short delay, they were marshalled in state to the dining-room. (There was only one in those days, though now the seniors have betaken themselves to what was the senior study to eat.) Here memory fails to recall the enormous quantity of oysters said by the boarders to have been bought for the feast. All sorts of Christmas good-things were heaped on a dinner plate at each boy's place, beside which also was a box of candies. On the box, in many a case kept to recall the jolly night, was

UPPER CANADA COLLEGE BOARDING-HOUSE.

A MERRY CHRISTMAS AND A HAPPY NEW YEAR.

SAFE HOME AND SAFE BACK AGAIN!

Supper over, the dining-room was cleared, and we all went upstairs. There we ate our good things, scattering nutshells from one end of the house to the other, regardless of the housemaids' extra flourishes of the broom, and equally heedless of the feelings of our schoolmates when they should get into bed.

As we were going up-stairs several fellows whipped out pillow-cases and made it known that they were ready to receive contributions of cake, apples—anything eatable. One lad who was particularly fond of eating, received in his slip a glass of lemonade to wash down the more solid provisions. He did not appear, however, to approve of that way of taking lemonade.

On going back to the dining-room at the ringing of the bell, we found it had become a theatre, with stage, curtains and scenery. Mr. Martland's piano, with tambourines, banjos, guitars and mouth organs, made up an orchestra to accompany the chorus. The interlocutor's questions, the endmen's jokes, the speech, the witticisms at the expense of principal, masters, steward and servants have nearly all faded from our memory, but, in thinking it over, the same feelings of delight are almost felt again ; with them comes regret that there was another side which finally led to the suppression of this entertainment. It always did not a little to make a Christmas feeling in the house, and was one of those pleasant things which used to make boys glad to have been at Upper Canada College.

III.

Genial as the glimpses we obtained showed him to be in private life, kindly and judicious as he was in all his dealings with us, it was in his teaching that Mr. Buchan shone most of all. To give an adequate idea of it were impossible, and yet, on the other hand, one's appreciation of it might lead to exaggeration. For the first week or so the old time-table was in force ; following it, the Principal took Horace. Though he appreciated the beauties of that author, his sympathies did not go out to classical studies as they did to certain others; hence the teaching was not at all inspiring. But what a change when the new time-table came into force and he took his favourite subjects—History and English ! He no longer seemed the same man ; he was enthusiastic. The afternoon hours, often the dullest and most uninteresting since they came just after dinner, were now looked forward to more than any other. Not lecturing but simply talking, asking a question here and there to make us think, to have us give him ground to work upon, and to find out whether we had read the lesson or not, he in a certain measure made us realize that the Greeks and Romans and the men they fought with, their writers and their statesmen were men of the same flesh and blood, and of like passions with ourselves ; that the social and political problems presented to them were, after all, much the same as those we have to solve in our day ; and that History, the unfolding to us of cause and effect, was not merely a collecting and memorizing of certain facts, but a most instructive study to warn us from the rocks on which so many men and so many nations had struck and sunk in days of old ; a beacon to guide us as citizens in doing our duty to our country.

In the art of questioning he was a master, and many a time did the simple word "why" disclose to us the fact that, underneath many a point we thought quite clear, there were depths still to be explored and explained. When our embarrassment at not being able to suggest a reason, or at suggesting a wrong one, showed itself in our faces, the amused smile, so often noticeable, came into his eyes and he would proceed to tell us all about it till no obscurity remained.

But delightful as these lessons in History were, those in English were still more so. Why they should have been will be best understood from what he himself said at various times and in various places. "The study of English Literature is better calculated to cultivate the intellect and the heart than that of any other subject." Again, "He who acquires such a taste (that of the study of literature) not only places within himself a fountain of perennial pleasure, but ennobles his nature, and makes himself capable of rising at will above the trivialities of everyday life to contemplate themes worthy of the intellectual being." And once more, "The savage, as he faces the mystery of life, finds no footprint on the sands of time to guide him ; the civilized man, on the contrary, sees before him the traces of the great and the good of preceding generations who, though dead, yet speak to him in melodious verse or eloquent prose."

From his introductory lecture, in 1876, to the Ladies' Educational Society, formed under the presidency of Mrs. Ewart, the widow of an old head-boy, when as yet women had not been admitted to University lectures, from his introductory lecture in literature to this society, which had his fullest sympathy as well as that of the late Prof. Young and of others equally prominent, we may gather something of what were his views of teaching English. Nor, from what has been already quoted, shall we be surprised. "I do not regard myself as a pump and each one of you as a bucket into which, through my agency, are to be conducted so many gallons from the Pierian Spring. No, my conception of the duty I owe to you is far different. I do, it is true, intend to pump a certain quantity of facts into the reservoirs of your memories, but I intend to do more. I shall attempt to show that these facts have a meaning fraught with interest for ourselves if we can only get at it."

In another place, when dealing with methods of teaching English, which until recent years was, by reason of the methods pursued in most schools, made as wearisome and uninteresting a subject as any on the programme of studies, he writes " Parsing, the analysis of sentences, the derivation of words, the explanation of allusions, scansion in the case of verse, the pointing out of figures of speech, and the hundred and one minor matters on which the teacher may easily dissipate the attention of his pupils should be strictly subordinated to this great aim. The masterpieces of our literature were written not to serve as texts whereon exercises of various kinds might be based, but to convey to others in the most attractive form the thoughts and feelings which pervaded the minds of their authors, and the chief benefit which any reader can obtain from them is to imbibe those thoughts and feelings and to inhale for a time the atmosphere by which they are surrounded. The essential thing is, that the mind of the reader should be *en rapport* with the mind of the writer. There is something in the influence of a great soul upon another soul which defies analysis. No analysis of a poem, however subtle, can produce the same effect on the mind and heart as to read the poem itself."

These were his views when, about 1876, he and his fellow inspectors were able through their representations to have an English text put on for the Junior Matriculation into the University of Toronto ; when, later on, he became an examiner in the University ; and lastly when by virtue of his being Principal of the College he took his seat in the University Senate. But, best of all, they were the views he put into daily practice in his classroom, where, with benches drawn up close to his desk, we listened to him as he talked of the glorious Elizabethan age and showed us how Shakespeare fitted into it, or of the artificial Frenchy age of Dryden and Pope, and of the revolution brought about by Cowper and Goldsmith. Richard II.'s woes were more pitiful, the public and the private character of the man were made clear to us ; the " Deserted Village," always beautiful, grew upon us ; and even " The Garden " with its cucumbers, sewers and stercoraceous heaps seemed fit subjects for poetic composition. Day by day we gave him our understanding of passages or he gave his to us, or, listening to his reading of the poems in his deep, rich voice, we were thrilled through and through, and day by day imbibed more of his spirit and had our tastes formed by his. Whatever love and appreciation of the beauties of English literature any of us has to-day is due mainly to those pleasant after-dinner hours spent in the large classroom adjoining the Principal's private room.

Mr. Buchan's main object in life, as we have seen, was to study "that he might be worthy," and, after that, to make others love what he had found to be worth loving. He, therefore, did not confine himself to History and Literature alone, though these were the only subjects he taught in the College. Early in life he took up the study of Botany; his reasons for so doing may fairly be drawn from an essay on "Our April Flowers," read before the Hamilton Association. "It is for their influence in the formation of character that the pursuit of the physical sciences is especially valuable. The love of truth, patience in investigation, fertility of resource and habits of accurate observation required for the successful study of any of the physical sciences are qualities which cannot easily be over-estimated." Again, "an occasional ramble is very pleasant, but a regular morning or afternoon tramp becomes monotonous as the treadmill. Under these circumstances the study of some physical science furnishes the needed incentive to exertion, and while it exercises the body, refreshes the mind by turning thought from its ordinary channels. The ideas gained enlarge the mental horizon, life becomes easier because mind and body are healthier, and more enjoyable by the addition of one more mode of pleasant exertion. The ardent entomologist or botanist will have thews and sinews worth speaking of, and a plentiful lack of indigestion, nor will mental thews and sinews be wanting, and he will have a heart full of the love of all pure and beautiful things—the best safeguard against the entrance of impure thoughts."

Anthropology with its kindred subjects was another study to which, with its many problems, he turned in even his busiest days with unchanging delight to keep his mind from deteriorating by contact with immature minds. Freshened by contact with master minds, he was always ready for his work, and always had an elevating influence upon his pupils, while his attainments in science and literature were rewarded by his election and re-election to the presidency of the Canadian Institute.

IV.

Despite his connection with the Canadian Institute and the University Senate, not to speak of other public duties, Mr. Buchan never allowed his work as Principal to be neglected. Throughout his régime the school prospered, so far, at any rate, as can be judged from increase of numbers and from the standing of pupils in the matriculation lists—neither of which, however, is in itself ever a sufficient standard by which to judge a school.

As to the former, the causes of increase are quite evident. The first undoubtedly was the quiet his appointment had brought to the school; no school, especially a boarding-school, could do its best work amid such turmoil and uncertainty as his predecessor had had to contend with during the latter part of his principalship. Full allowance being made for the effects of this quiet, as well as those that a change of itself brings, everyone will agree that the manly, straightforward character of the new principal did not a little to influence parents in the choice of Upper Canada College as the place to send their boys. His answer to a lady who asked him to take a special interest in her boy was characteristic, " Madam," said he, " I cannot take more interest in your boy than in any of the others, and I shall try to take as great an interest in each of the other boys as in yours." It certainly was not the answer of a worldly-minded man or of a time-server. Another cause of the increase was the obligation the new head of the College felt resting upon him, merely by virtue of his receiving a boy into the school, to get rid at once of any boy who clearly showed by his conduct that his further presence would be hurtful to the institution and to the other boys. This disagreeable but necessary duty was performed with his usual consideration, the boy generally being informed at the end of the term that it was not desirable that he should return after the holidays. After all, the pursuance of this policy was the chief reason for the masters' houses being filled with boys, one after the other, as they fell vacant.

As for matriculation scholarships and the like, whoever wishes to know the College's standing from 1881 to 1885 must consult the honour rolls given in the present volume. To dwell upon them would be an insult to Mr. Buchan's memory, for he never dwelt upon them himself, in anything of that spirit, at least, in which a jockey might with some propriety be allowed to speak of a horse he had trained and ridden to the winning-post. Apart from other considerations, he knew too well that one cannot always count on having clever boys to win the scholarships. Indeed his definition of a clever boy was " one who had a capacity for work." Though they may be naturally clever, boys vary in this capacity for work, while there may happen in one or two years to be really dull boys. Therefore, as a mere matter of policy, one can see the wisdom of his not setting much store by scholarships and honours as such, and certainly one would not expect him to advertise his school as an honour-getting establishment. Another quotation from the " April Flowers " will emphasize this idea. " We are all continually tempted to forget that there is something more valuable to a nation than wealth and power, that is the character which makes it possible to acquire wealth and obtain power." Accordingly, he strove to build up a good character for the school and allowed its reputation to take care of itself.

Under ordinary circumstances, it would have been an especially difficult task to come to the school as Mr. Buchan did, and yet to achieve success.

It was the difficulty that might naturally be expected by a comparatively young man coming to be principal over men older than himself in years as well as in experience, one of whom at least would have been offered the position, had it not been for the peculiar circumstances in which the College was at that time placed. Happily the staff received Mr. Buchan with the greatest cordiality, and everything ran smoothly.

Again, he came as the representative of a policy of retrenchment. But on this point he himself soon saw the difficulty of living, even quietly, in Toronto on salaries which appeared large when compared with those paid in High Schools. To manage to live and work comfortably year in and year out with men whose pockets had been affected, if not by his coming, at least contemporaneously with it, would have been no easy task if there had not been on both sides a determination to do their duty fairly the one toward the other.

No easy task either was it for a man who had had but little experience of boarding-schools to take the headship of one whose superintendent had been managing the house for nearly twenty years, and had done his work well in spite of many difficulties and drawbacks. Yet he himself, as a study-master in the College early in Mr. Cockburn's and in Dr. Barrett's time, and afterwards in his own home in Hamilton, had learned to know that the best interests of the school required him to be Principal only and to take cognizance of those house matters alone which were referred to him. Thus he followed the good example set him by his predecessor.

Not only a policy of retrenchment, but one of change was his to be, as any one who wishes may see in the report on the College prepared by the late Minister of Education. Formerly all boys intending to matriculate had been obliged to pass through the Sixth Form whether intending to write for honours or for pass only. Of recent years the opinion had become common that this extra year was a waste of time, and it was, therefore deemed advisable to establish a matriculation class for pass boys separate, from that for honour candidates. Thus the College was brought into line with the practice that prevailed in the larger High Schools. Since that time, inasmuch as the University is now crowded with boys instead of men, the question has presented itself as to whether the extra year is really, or in appearance only, wasted time.

Another change contemplated by the Government when it placed Mr. Buchan over the College was the re-establishment of the Modern Forms which had been abolished some years before. It had been necessary for every boy in the school to take Latin, while an option was allowed in the case of the other languages. Now, however, it was regarded as useless to make boys grind away at Latin and Greek if they were going into business, while certain other branches would be of more practical benefit to them. Accordingly, in 1882, the old order was restored, and boys intended for business were enabled to take advantage of the finishing given in the boarding-house, and at the same time pursue a course in Modern Languages, mathematics, chemistry and bookkeeping, and were thus in some measure fitted for their work after leaving school.

Besides these changes in the classes, there was one which was not popular with the boys—there are no conservatives like boys. It tended also, perhaps, to divert their attention to specialties rather than to the general all-round learning for which Upper Canada College had justly been celebrated. Such diversion, it is hardly necessary to say, was not the reason for the boys' disapproval of the rearrangement of the exhibitions, but the fact that the money was less in amount than it had been. Prior to the session of 1882-83 there had been four exhibitions for general proficiency tenable in the Fifth and in the Sixth, the first two in each form being worth respectively eighty and forty dollars, with tuition; the other two entitled the holders to tuition only. Now, there was to be but one for general proficiency in each form, while the other three were to be given for modern languages, classics, and mathematics, thus following the lead of the University of Toronto toward early specialization. As has been said already, the unpopular part of the new scheme was the manner of dividing the money. Hereafter no boy could win eighty, or even forty dollars, since no more than thirty dollars (with free tuition) was attached to each exhibition. Moreover, no matter how many he might win, a boy could hold but one exhibition.

In text-books and methods little change was made, since there was a strong feeling that it was not well to have too much uniformity in educational matters, and that Upper Canada College had a good field in which to work out its problems in education after its own fashion.

Other changes, but of minor importance, also took place. Now disappeared the row of frames that used to hang on the wall of the downstairs hall. In these, written in old Mr. Thompson's neat, round hand, had been displayed the honour rolls of the Forms at the end of every marking— a source of gratification to fond parents when they visited the school, and of course to the boys themselves. But the pupil whose ambition was to be foot did not mourn their disappearance.

The "revisal," or examination of the forms that had been wont to be held periodically by the Principal in their various subjects of study found no place in Mr. Buchan's time-tables. Many a hapless youth who had heard with much quaking the familiar formula, "Three to four, and write it out," was devoutly thankful that revisals were no more. With them also vanished the time-honoured general detention presided over by all but the house masters in turn down in Mr. Thompson's, or, as it was often called, the writing-room. Sundry carvings, drawings, and etchings on the forms and long old desks showed how the boys had *not* learned their lessons, while a goodly collection of College paper to be found in their rooms afterwards gave evidence of their forethought and thrift.

Of all the customs of the College the ancient system of going up and down in class, and marking accordingly, was the most sacred; it was therefore suffered to remain with but slight modification. The Sixth, all reformers this time, not long after Mr. Buchan's entrance upon his new duties, made a most respectful request that the old system might be changed —so far as they were concerned at least. The inevitable "why" made it necessary for them to call into play all their logic and powers of persuasion to shew what a premium the system placed upon cheating, etc. With the usual promise for consideration we had to be content for a day or two; but that was easy, for we already knew that once a matter was taken into consideration it would not be forgotten. At length we were told that the markings would hereafter be on the results of examinations held when we had finished a subject, or a part of it. Rejoicing in our triumph, we did not know until years afterwards when turning over the leaves of the minute-book for the masters' meeting that there had been a formal discussion of the question. We had won our point; that was the main thing.

There may have been other changes, but they were not of importance enough to impress themselves upon the memory. Whether brought about at the suggestion of the Government or otherwise, those that were made were followed by no calamity, as some had seemed to fear. On the contrary, the College was even stronger than before, while opposition almost entirely disappeared. Whatever may have been the expectations of those who suggested Mr. Buchan's appointment to the principalship, and they were doubtless high, they cannot have been disappointed. The same manliness, uprightness, and simplicity of character, the same devotion to learning, diligence in business, and conscientiousness in the discharge of his many duties, and the same gentleness and kindness which had won and kept the love and respect of many in his student days, in his earlier manhood as a schoolmaster, and, in the succeeding years, in the exceedingly difficult position of Inspector of High Schools, caused him to be loved, respected, and after his death sincerely mourned, by those College boys who were fortunate enough to know him. No mere matter of form was it, no mere consideration of the proprieties, that prompted them to go on the funeral day to show their sympathy with the mourning family, in the short autumn days when more of them were in town to send a boyish address of condolence to Mrs. Buchan, and later on to erect in Mount Pleasant a simple stone recording the dates of his birth, principalship, and death. To them generally it was clear that, in becoming Principal, it was not so much he who was honoured, but rather he who had done honour to the College. In them, though dead, he lives again, an inspiration to the doing of noble deeds.

A TRANSITION PERIOD.

BY G. MERCER ADAM.

THE old order giveth place to the new. After sixty years, institutions, like men, are apt to suffer change. In the case of the College, it is, however, not easy to see why change should come to it, save that in these democratic times little is venerated, and the socialistic leveller is permitted a fatal facility in tampering with old-time State endowments. Insidious, from the first, has been the cry against Upper Canada College. The voice of envy loved to taunt it with being a privileged institution. The charge was that it was designed only for a class. Even from those who might be expected to be its friends sympathy was withheld from it, because it was unshackled by the Departmental Machine and had immunity from Government Inspection. The same critics objected to it because its staff was paid too highly; forgetting, seemingly, that to cheapen salaries at the College was to lower the rewards of the educational profession generally. Contemporary with these cries, came one from a still more interested source, which was plied through a long series of years with artful, and finally, with fatal persistence. This was the charge that Upper Canada College had, in its early years, been a heavy burden on Toronto University and owed it a large amount for overdrafts on maintenance account. Whatever truth was in the charge, and we shall deal with that presently, there were set-offs which should have squared the account, to say nothing of injustice to the College arising out of a scandalously loose system, in the early years of both institutions, of financial administration. Still further did self-interest seek to prejudice the public mind against the College, by re-enforcing the last charge with one which investigation subsequently proved to be utterly without warrant. This new device of the enemy called in question the legality of the College endowments, a charge which, as we shall see, was as unfounded as that which aspersed the College for preying upon the funds of the Provincial University. These and other sinister objections were from time to time made the subject of parliamentary inquiry; but unhappily they were not always fairly dealt with, even when strenuously rebutted, and where statements founded on them were emphatically disproved. As years passed, hostility to the institution increased, and the "College Question," as it was called, came annually into the evil arena of politics. The result, despite the heartiness with which its friends rallied to its defence, could not be doubtful. The legislature was not always wisely informed as to facts, and Committees dealing with the subject had perhaps an unconscious bias, imparted, if not by active opponents outside the College, by a spirit within the assembly apparently inimical to the higher culture. Before investigation had proceeded very far, and before the College's defence had been heard, public opinion was influenced adversely by the cries to which we have referred, cries which in a popular assembly not over-scrupulous in its regard for public faith or even careful not to traverse the will of former legislatures, were sure to prevail. It is possible also that the House was not altogether free from a certain prejudice against the provision for the maintenance of the College made at a time when the provincial administration was in ultra-Tory and autocratic hands. Present-day Radicalism might be excused for resenting, for instance, the tone of Sir John Colborne's message to Parliament, in which he advised it of his intention to provide for the College in such a manner as to place it above risk either of failure or overthrow. "Before I leave the province," said the far-seeing though, perhaps, not politic founder, "I shall endeavour to procure for the institution (Upper Canada College) such protection as may enable it to counteract the influence of local jealousies, or of the ignorance or vice to which in a new country it may be sometimes naturally exposed." Unhappily, Sir John Colborne's safeguards were not proof against spoliation, still less were they proof against the spirit and temper which is apt to breed vandalism.

Vandalism in the provincial legislature we do not say there was, though more than once debates on the College question betokened designs not quite guiltless of that taint. In the heat of discussion much, of course, has to be excused to a speaker who has taken a pronounced side on a public question; but the spirit was not acrimonious merely that demanded the abolition of an institution which for over half a century had been a bulwark against ignorance and, educationally, was a sound and strong pillar of the State. Nor was the clamour for the diversion of its endowment creditable to legislators who might claim to be above the arts of the demagogue and in sympathy with higher aims and aspirations. If vested interests, hallowed by many and tender associations, were not sacred in the hands of representatives of the people in parliament assembled, to whom should we look for the permanance of our institutions, and even for the integrity of the State?

Not only insidious but prolonged was the agitation against the College. For fully twenty years its enemies kept up a current fire of detraction and flung at the hapless institution almost every missile which envy or selfishness could invent. Even denominationalism was dragged in as an ally of the enemy in the fray. This was done in concert with the movement to bring about college federation, and to augment the resources of Toronto University, with which the denominations were seeking affiliation. To bear the expense of the enlarged teaching staff and a more thorough equipment of the University, when the federation scheme was projected, more funds were needed. For supplying these, the ill-favoured design was then formulated, to lay hands upon the endowment of Upper Canada College, which for a number of years had been a trust of the University; and later came the outrage of expropriating even the College's old historic site. How the provincial legislature came to sanction these ruthless misappropriations, and subsequently to ratify what was a gross violation of a sacred trust, we shall with amazement presently see. Only an obtuse or a commonplace mind could have been misled by the perversion of facts by which the iniquity was justified in parliament and before the country, and only a conscience unresponsive to the promptings of honourable dealing would have given effect to the wanton spoliation. We write, as we feel, strongly on this matter, for, in respect of the whole question, we hold that there was nothing in the circumstances of the case to justify so sacrilegious an act as the government and parliament of the province ere long committed. Nor can we see any reasonable consideration of public policy to warrant the despoiling the College of its endowment, and, at the instance of selfish rivalry, tearing it up by the roots.

Looking back now upon the whole controversy, when a forced acquiescence in the results of recent legislation has stilled the agitation and cooled the blood of the most ardent defender of the rights of the College, one is abjured to write dispassionately. In briefly reviewing the history of this crisis in the affairs of the institution—which we have termed " A Period of Transition "—we shall endeavour to write dispassionately. We have stated that the agitation against the College lasted for fully twenty years. In its more virulent form, the clamour may be said to have broken out in the year 1868, when the provincial high school masters made common cause against the institution, as a privileged rival, burdened the press with interested outcries, and brought their grievances to the bar of parliament. Some ten years later, the College bore the brunt of a still more bitter onslaught, from pretty much the same partisan sources. A general indictment appeared, in the form of a pamphlet, issued under the auspices of the Grammar School Teachers' Association, which became the arsenal of the Philistine weapons used in the fray. The grounds of attack at both periods were in the main alike, though at the second outbreak, fuel was added to the flame of enmity by the proposed expenditure of $30,000 for additions to the buildings used as the College residence. The College was spoken of as a pampered institution, designed for the sons of Toronto plutocrats, inefficiently conducted, and wasteful in its management—charges which were far from the truth. Nor were the tactics of its assailants merely Philistine : they sought not to reform, but to abolish, the institution. With this iconoclastic aim, they accused it of enjoying its endowment illegally, and averred that it subsisted only by the grace of the other secondary schools of the Province, which were starved to maintain the institution. This calumnious statement the now well-known history of the College endowment conclusively refutes. The statement was at the time met by Mr. G. R. R. Cockburn, then Principal, who also replied to the other items of indictment contained in the pamphlet issued under the sanction of the Grammar School Masters. Mr. Cockburn's rejoinder was addressed to a Committee of the Provincial Legislature on Education, in 1869, and is an able and exhaustive refutation of the charges made by the enemies of Upper Canada College.

In the years 1880 and 1881, the attacks on the College were renewed. To meet them, the Hon. Mr. Crooks, then Minister of Education, prepared a special report on the history, working, and condition of the institution, which was submitted to the Legislature. In this report the origin of the College endowment is traced historically to its source, in the Crown appropriation of public lands for the general purposes of education made when the Province was founded. This appropriation consisted in a land grant of 500,000 acres, set aside to endow a University and four Royal Grammar Schools, one in each of the four districts into which the Province was at first divided. The Royal Grammar Schools were intended as feeders to the projected University, after the model of the great public schools of the motherland. Of the 500,000 acres, one half was set apart for the University, and one-fourth of the other half (66,000 acres) was devoted to establishing " Upper Canada College and Royal Grammar School," its long-time official designation. Public documents are extant to prove the validity both of the original provision for the general purposes of education, covered by the specific grant of Crown lands, in 1798, and of the later appropriation, in 1831, of the 66,000 acres for the endowment of Upper Canada College. These conclusively attest what we are more immediately concerned with— the legality of the College's endowment, a legality which has since repeatedly been confirmed by Acts of the Provincial Legislature.* In defiance of

---

* In Mr. R. E. Kingsford's paper, in the present volume, this has already been pointed out. The reader is further referred, in confirmation of the matter, as well as to the general history of the College endowment, to page 27 of Principal Cockburn's "Statement," prepared for the Legislature (Toronto, 1869), and to the "Memorandum" of the Hon. Mr. Crooks, submitted to the Legislature in 1881.

the facts, once more here set forth, it was contended during the College controversy (the financial connection of the two institutions, and for a time their common administration lending colour to the charge) that the College had been endowed from lands specially devoted to the erection and support of the provincial university. Another assertion of its enemies was to the effect that the College drew its maintenance from lands styled "Grammar School Reserves," which it was claimed had passed under the control of the Provincial Board of Education, established in 1821. Both statements, it need hardly be said, are untrue. Despite proof to the contrary, however, much wrong was done to the College by the dissemination of the misstatement while the agitation was in progress. There were other charges brought forward at the period, but of a minor though equally unscrupulous nature; and these we should weary the reader by retailing here. Unfortunately, with the sum of the other and more weighty charges, they adversely influenced public opinion and insidiously prepared the Legislature for the perpetration of a great wrong.

We may be suffered a word here of what may frankly be admitted as the only vulnerable point in the armour of the College, if even this concession is due to its assailants. We refer to the administration of the institution, which its enemies deemed wasteful and inefficient. During its long existence, Upper Canada College fell at various times under a more or less indifferent management, both of men and of systems. At first it had a council of its own, under which, the provincial university not being in existence, or rather not having been launched on its academic career, it practically did University work. When King's College went into operation, the institution fell under the control of the long-projected University. But King's College did not, in name at least, attain to the dignity of a University until 1850, and when it did Upper Canada College was given back its own council. Three years later, another change came to it. It was then placed under the management of the Senate of the University, which appointed a standing committee of five members, who were entrusted by order in council with the "administration of its financial affairs, so far as regards the disposition of its income, and subject to the Lieutenant-Governor in Council as to its capital and endowment." Under this Board of Management its affairs have since been administered, though at Confederation the Education Department of the Province, through the Minister of Education, has had the practical disposal of its affairs, subject to the approval of the Legislature. Under the early years of this diverse management the College had a somewhat chequered career. We have already seen that for a time there was indulgence in collecting and laxity in accounting for the College fees. The general methods of finance were, in like manner, at first easy-going

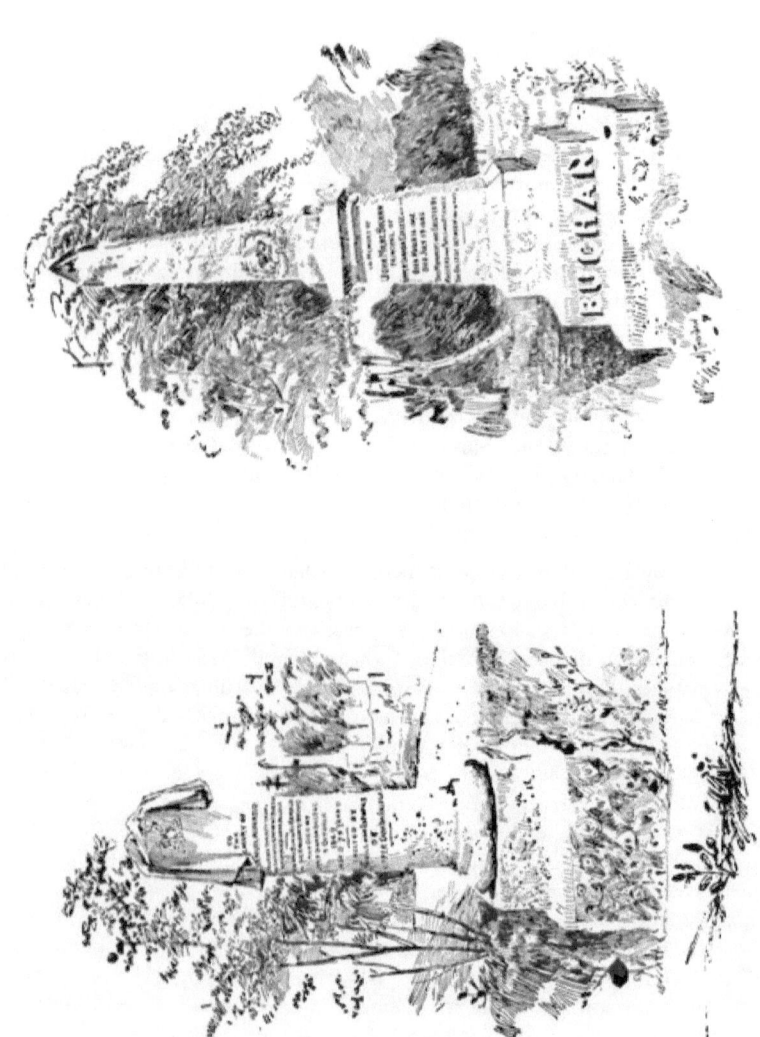

A TRANSITION PERIOD.

and, in relation to the University, somewhat complex. But each institution had its own endowment, and the common Bursar, writing in 1868, when the affairs of the College were being closely looked into, is authority for saying that "neither from the University Permanent Fund nor from its Income Fund has any grant been made to Upper Canada College since I took charge of the endowment."* While the College has had its financial difficulties, and while the administration at periods might have been more wise as well as thrifty, it is gratifying to know that the institution has been no pecuniary burden to the Provincial University, and that for its maintenance it has drawn on its own resources. It has been difficult to eradicate popular belief in the reverse of this statement, but the evidence is too overwhelming to admit of it now, or at any future day, being questioned. Justice, though tardy in its coming, should at last be done to the College in this matter. We submit also, that the College has never had full credit given it for the work it accomplished in its early years, when as yet the University had no existence, and when the College, for ten years at least, not only did its own work, but that of the University.

Equally satisfactory is the College's claim to the possession of its own lands. Where there was a doubt as to the legality of some portion, at one time claimed by the Toronto Grammar School, doubt was set at rest by the Executive Council of the old Province of Upper Canada, in a report of a committee of the body. Candour requires it to be said, however, that financially speaking, it was not always smooth-sailing with the College. Doing the work it did, and that at a time when it was most important to the country that its work should be done, and well done, it was necessarily at heavy expense to maintain itself. Nor, as a distinctive and invaluable provincial institution, was it always fairly treated by Parliament. In 1860, in a fit of economy, Parliament withdrew its annual money grant to the College of over a thousand pounds currency. This occurred at a most inopportune time, when the institution had to honour drafts on its income for pensions or gratuities to retired or retiring masters. This drain, some $2,000 per annum, continued for over seven years, and to meet it entailed a *pro rata* reduction of the salaries of all the staff. Despite this and other drawbacks, the College, during "the sixties," set forth on a highly prosperous as well as most notable career. The credit of this is largely due to Principal Cockburn, whose régime, as we have seen, covered the period from 1861 to 1881. These twenty years were perhaps the most critical in the history of the College. They are those that saw the institution rise to the full stature of its lusty manhood, under one of its most vigorous

---

* Letter of Bursar David Buchan to Principal Cockburn, appended to the latter's "Statement to the Committee of the Legislature on Education," Toronto, 1869 (page 31).

and efficient heads. Never before did the College shine as it shone during these couple of decades. Only that fact could have triumphantly carried it through the long series of assaults to which it was then exposed. But manly, as well as aggressive, was the defence made for it; and Principal Cockburn's "Statement," to which we have referred, testifies to the effectiveness of the rally to its aid, no less than to the unscrupulousness and bitter character of the attack.

The Government's course at this time respecting the institution added in no little measure to the perplexities of the position. The affairs of the College, though nominally controlled, as we have seen, by a Committee of the University Senate, were really controlled by the Minister of Education, acting for the Provincial Government. The institution was thus brought within the untoward influence of politics. When its affairs came to be discussed in the legislature, the government, properly enough, had to give ear to the will of the House. There, the government, in its relation to the College, was however under two fires—the fire alike of its supporters and its opponents—for on the College question there were foes on either side, and opinion in the House traversed party lines. Nor was there a common ground of hostility to the College: one section of the enemy sought its abolition to augment the revenues of the University, the other, to supplement the government grant to the Grammar Schools. Why the College endowment, anciently set apart for a sacred, and surely commendable, purpose, should thus be gambled for, and its confiscation bruited, was intelligible to no honest mind. The act that would legislate Upper Canada College out of existence might be made to legislate out of existence all the secondary schools in the province, and, with them, the University itself. Ply the axe at the root of one institution, was the current reflection, and what other was safe? Nor, as we have already said, was there anything in the circumstances of the case to warrant the threats of the despoiler. The institution had fallen upon evil days; it had not fallen, however, into decadence. Never had it been doing better or more useful work. To alienate its funds, was, at any time, to do a great wrong; to raise the clamour against it at the period was utterly and wantonly unjust. To speak of it as a local institution, maintained for a class in the capital of the province, and doing work equally well done by the High Schools, was quite misleading, if not wholly untrue. The College had been, and still was, distinctively national; it was, moreover, a residential school; and in this respect it filled a place filled by no other institution of its scope and character in the Province. It is true, it educated the sons of well-to-do Toronto residents, but it would be strange if the wants of this class were not entitled to consideration, even if it did not seem reasonable that they should take advantage of the facilities supplied by a local institution. Besides, were not the parents of these pupils the main supporters of the College, and that despite the fact that they were taxed to maintain the Public Schools of their localities which they did not use? The city pupils, it is calculated, averaged less than half the number attending the College, while they contributed fully half the revenue. If a parallel is to be drawn between the circumstances of the College and those of the High Schools of the province, the advantage, in one notable respect, will not be with the latter. In the matter of fees the contrast between them is a sharp one; for while the College contributes from this source some forty-five per cent. of its total receipts, the High School contributes only five per cent. Happily there is to-day little need to repeat these contrasts or to take up afresh the old brands of warfare in defence of the College. In the history of the period with which we are dealing, it is however necessary that the case should, as far as possible, be fully presented, especially in a volume such as this, where essential facts may be looked for that throw light on the controversies of the time, with some record of the vicissitudes through which the institution has passed. Nor must it be forgotten that though the College had its enemies, it had also its friends; and it is due to such to indicate at least the lines on which the battle was fought for the preservation of the institution.

Nor need the charge that the College was an aristocratic institution be seriously confuted: the character and career of its long roll of distinguished sons absolve the writer from undertaking so trivial a defence. What the College had to impart in the way of tone and manners was a desirable, certainly not an undesirable, element in the education of democratic youth. Nor as an educational agent, looking to the character of its work, is it difficult to repel the charge that the College was inefficiently conducted. In now meeting this point, there is no need to underrate the achievements of the Provincial High Schools; but, as was aptly remarked at the period, "their unquestioned usefulness is no argument against the existence of an institution which has served to most of them as a conspicuous model." The contention often heard at the time, was, that the High Schools were doing work almost equal to that done by the College, while some of the Collegiate Institutes were abreast of it in special work. It would be ungracious to make invidious comparisons; but the writer is happily relieved from this in being able to quote from the Minister of Education conclusive evidence of the status of the College and unimpeachable testimony as to the character of the attacks then made upon it. "In getting up a cry against the College," said the Honourable Mr. Crooks in a debate in the House in 1881, "the selfish instincts of certain interests had been appealed to, and the petitions resulting therefrom were no indication of public opinion."

"From 1867 to 1879," the Minister went on to say, "about four thousand pupils received their training at Upper Canada College,—an average of three hundred yearly—so that the usefulness of the institution had not ceased. The reason of the endowment was that an institution of a provincial character, such as Upper Canada College, should be supplied to give secondary education. During the ten years forty University scholarships had been taken by the College against sixty-six by all the High Schools. * * In three years from 1877, the College had obtained twenty-three scholarships in arts, while in four years from that date all the High Schools (over a hundred in number) had taken only thirty-six. * * It was not true, moreover, that Toronto as a municipality got any special advantage from the institution, since the parents of the pupils contributed about $12,000 a year towards its maintenance. * * To abolish an institution which had confessedly been of great use for fifty years was a singular proposition, unless it could be proved that the College had failed in the object for which it was founded. The same proposition could be made in regard to the University endowment, on the ground that the local colleges were doing good work." Not less conclusive, and we hope we may say not less impartial, was Principal Cockburn's reference to the record of the College, in a speech made at the annual distribution of prizes in the previous year. "At the examinations of the Toronto University alone, for 1880," said the Principal, "the students of the College had carried off one gold medal, three silver medals, six scholarships, sixty-five first-class honours, twenty-eight second-class honours, three degrees in medicine, eight degrees in arts, and one in law." The College record, again, from 1867, when the institution was transferred to the care of the Provincial Government, to the present time, showed that the following students had matriculated at Toronto University alone during that period: 175 with first-class honours, 204 with second-class honours, and fifty-two scholarships—making a total of 431 honours or distinctions, apart from special prizes, or 30.79 honours for each matriculant, and four scholarships. This was apart from honours obtained at the Universities of Oxford, Cambridge, Trinity (Dublin), Edinburgh, London, McGill (Montreal), and at the examinations of the Law Society, Military College, and similar institutions." Better testimony than this to the efficiency of the College, and to the high standard of work it was doing, could hardly be furnished: it is its own and a sufficient answer to the attacks made upon it. While we say this, we are not unmindful of the truth that the efficiency of a school is not to be measured merely by the number of university honours its pupils may obtain. That the College is, or was at any time, a class institution, is belied by the statement made at the period by one of its many loyal sons. "During my three years' course," writes an 'old College boy' from Belleville, "I sat beside and competed with the son of a shoemaker, the son of a journalist, the son of a mechanic, three sons of merchants, two sons of lawyers, two sons of clergymen, and two sons of farmers." Only Philistinism or a petulant prejudice could remain hostile to testimony such as this. More reason, perhaps, had the High Schools to complain of the College, in attracting their pupils to it by its offer of annual exhibitions, and in appropriating credit for the honours won by them at the University, after perhaps only a year's coaching at the College. While the exhibitions were maintained, there was no doubt a grievance here; but it was a grievance which did not call for more than a protest from the High School Masters, certainly not for the obliteration or the dispoiling of the College.

The College happily withstood the onslaught in the Assembly of 1881. The local and municipal spirit, which, abetted by the jealousy of the High Schools, had laid covetous eyes on its endowment, was not then gratified. Mr. Crooks, who, as an old College head-boy, had been loyal in the defence, had, however, not wholly triumphed. He and the government had saved the institution from wreckage, but Cerberus had for the time being his sops. These and the general results of the agitation were briefly as follows: authority for the expenditure on the residence was, from politic motives not pressed in the legislature; the College's affairs were to be more closely looked into; economy was to be rigidly enforced; and the institution was to be made to come more effectually under the Provincial Educational system. Some of the masters, moreover, were to have their salaries reduced while others, long in service, were to be retired. The instituting of these changes, and doubtless the application of the pruning knife, had an untoward and, at the time, unlooked-for sequel. It brought about the resignation of Mr. Cockburn, as Principal. This occurred on the reopening of the College after the midsummer holidays in 1881; when, as we know, Mr. J. M. Buchan, then Inspector of High Schools, was installed in the Principalship. Regret, as well as surprise, was of course manifested at Mr. Cockburn's resignation. The friends of the College naturally looked upon it as ominous of further change. In this respect, the enemies of the institution had won a point; and policy appeared to have dictated that the new Principal should be an old High School master. The appointment of a successor brought about the no doubt intended result; it allayed, for some years at least, the storm of agitation, and the College once more set forth on its now reposeful and beneficent career.

Principal Buchan's régime was uneventful, since unhappily it was brief. His death, which was greatly regretted, occurred in 1885, after four years of able and careful administration. Under him, the College was permitted to pursue the even tenor of its way and continued to do excellent work. It was said that the controversy over its affairs had done good, since it put the staff anew on its mettle and had an inspiring influence on the management. Possibly this may have been the case, though there is no reason specially to credit the agitation with giving the institution a spur beyond that which it had always had from the zeal and high sense of duty exhibited by its governing heads. One mercy, during Mr. Buchan's period of office, the College was manifestly thankful for ; it was let alone. This, as we have hinted, was in part due to the politic appointment of Mr. Buchan, who was greatly esteemed by the High School masters, and was himself, for many years, one of their number. It was doubtless, in part also, due to the concessions made by the Government in the new administration of the College, which for the time being disarmed, but did not uproot, opposition. All too brief, as we shall presently see, was the respite from attack. Mr. Buchan's lamented death once more brought the College and its affairs into the arena of discussion. The vacant Principalship was worthily filled by the present incumbent of the office, who, like his predecessor, stood in the forefront of the teaching profession in the province, and had long been known as one of the most able and successful of headmasters. Principal Dickson's régime dates from 1885. With his installation, the College made a further leap in a career of progress, as well as of efficiency and usefulness, hitherto hardly paralleled in the history of the institution. Largely animated by the modern spirit, Principal Dickson brought to the headship of the College just those requisites which the institution found most valuable in the new dispensation which had been forced upon it. In his new sphere, as has been truly said of him, Principal Dickson's power of organization, good discipline, and thorough business-like administration, combined with his all-round scholarship, fine teaching ability and faculty of imbuing students with love of their work, soon manifested themselves, and gave a new impetus to the old historic school of the Province. On his appointment to the Principalship, there were signs of a renewal of the old agitation against the College, and the new incumbent in office could scarcely fail to perceive that, if doom was not actually impending, a period of transition, at least, would have to be faced. Faced it was, and loyally faced, for the new Principal from the outset determined that whatever crisis might ensue, the College, so far as he was concerned, should suffer no eclipse of its fame. Under his administration, it continued to flourish, and that not merely by the grace of sentiment or from consideration of its traditions and old associations. Whatever might befall, it was said, its future, under its new and capable head, need cause no uneasiness to any friend or " old College boy." This has since been abundantly demonstrated, not only by the satisfactory routine work done within the College, but by the high standing of its pupils at the annual examinations of the national and other Universities, pitted, as they were, against all comers, and in competion with the best educational training the country could supply. Whatever designs were still harboured against the institution, the excellence of the work it continued to do could not be mistaken by any unprejudiced observer, or its substantial results for a moment doubted. That what we have said is not mere rhetoric or partisan comment, the statistics of the College are in evidence. These were presented by the Principal on Prize Day, 1888, three years after he succeeded to the headship of the institution. "There were enrolled," said the Principal, "during the year ending June 30th last (1888), 415 boys, of whom 180 were resident pupils, the percentage of average attendance to the annual enrolment being eighty-three. In 1883, the annual enrolment was 243; in 1884, 255; in 1885, 296; in 1886, 346; in 1887, 369; and in 1888, 415! Now that we cannot increase our classrooms, we have reached the possible limit of attendance in our present site. Last session two new class-rooms were opened, and two additional masters employed to meet the demands then made upon us. This year we could have increased our attendance far beyond that of last year if there had been room for all applicants eligible for admission. Our pupils come from the Maritime Provinces, from British Columbia and the North-West Territories, from Central America, Bermuda, and from the Hudson Bay Country. Of the forty-one counties of Ontario no fewer than thirty-one are represented on our enrolment; about ninety per cent. of our pupils come from our own province. The boarding-houses, which form an integral part of the College, have always been filled; and at the present time we have a long list of applicants waiting for admission." As shewing the success of the pupils for the year on entering the Universities or engaging in the practical avocations of life, Principal Dickson proceeded to say, "that of the boys who left the College eleven entered the various faculties of Toronto University, two entered Trinity University, two Queen's University, three McGill College, two Osgoode Hall, one the Royal Military College; while twenty-three entered mercantile or manufacturing life, four entered banks, and five took to farming." The matriculation class of the year won at Toronto University, he added, "eleven first-class honours, five second-class honours, and no fewer than five of the seven scholarships annually offered for competition among the High Schools and Collegiate Institutes of the Province; namely, the first mathematical scholarship, the first modern languages, the first and second general proficiency, and the Prince of Wales' prize. The last named scholarship has been awarded seven times by the University; it has been won no less than five times by College boys!" Of the comparative standing of the College pupils in the University class lists, the Principal observed, that "the College ranked in a matriculation class of upwards of 250 candidates, drawn from the best schools in the Province, as follows:—first and tenth in mathematics, first, fifth, and sixth in French, first in English language and literature, first in history and geography, fourth in classics, and fourth, fifth and eighth in German."

Comment on results so excellent as these statistics indicate, is superfluous; yet in presence of these figures, and the good work and high standing of the College which they imply, envy looked coldly upon the institution, or churlishly averted its face. Well for the College had this been the extent of the disaster! Worse, on the contrary, was in store for it. The old cries once more broke out, and unhappily gathered strength, from the fact that something at previous agitations had been yielded to the enemy. Concession had already brought the institution into line with the Collegiate Institutes and High Schools of the province, and an advance, it was thought, could easily be made on what was then gained by the adversary. Importunity well knew, also, how to gain its ends: while security slept selfishness made haste to get in its work. Nor was the situation improved when a land boom broke over Toronto, and, at an inopportune hour, placed a fictitious value on the old College site. The school, it was true, had outgrown its home; but there was no reason why that home should not be enlarged. The enemy saw the chance; either lever could be worked; the College wanted increased accommodation; to rebuild where it was would require the sanction of the Legislature; this it should not have, for the site was too valuable. Such was the first reasoning of the adversary: the second was like unto it: if the College could not do where it was, it might accept a new site; agreeing to this it would surrender the old one. The next step was an easy one; surrender of site might, under agitation, be made to include surrender of endowment: obtaining the latter then would come partition of the spoils, afterwards—happy thought!—possibly abolition!

What the friends and "old boys" of the College thought of all this, may be seen from the public press of the city towards the end of March, 1887. In the "Old Boys' Rally" for the preservation of the College, the gravity of the situation, as well as the truth of the above presentation of the enemy's argument, may in part be realized. Should the "Rally" fail to make its due impression, the curious inquirer into Parliamentary dealings with the College is directed to the journals of the Legislature in the session of 1887, when the College question was once more under debate.

The meeting of the old pupils took place in the public hall of the College on the evening of the 22nd March, 1887, and was of a character, with respect both to numbers and influence, such as to carry weight with the Government. The late Senator John Macdonald was in the chair, supported by many prominent citizens of Toronto, either "old boys" or friends of the College, who had rallied to its defence when menaced by the hand of the spoiler. Among these were Chief Justice M. C. Cameron, Hon. J. B. Robinson, Senator Geo. W. Allan, Principal Dickson, ex-Principal G. R. R. Cockburn, Judge Macdougall, Dr. Larratt W. Smith, Rev. Dr. Scadding, Colonels R. B., G. T., and Fred. Denison, Col. Jarvis, J. O. Heward, S. M. Jarvis, D. B. Read, Dr. J. A. McLellan, A. R. Marling, Rector MacMurchy, Rev. D. J. Macdonell, Rev. G. M. Milligan, R. E. Kingsford, G. M. Evans, A. R. Boswell, W. H. Beatty, J. T. Small, F. Arnoldi, G. G. S. Lindsey, Z. Lash, W. H. VanderSmissen, F. Cayley, G. W. Badgerow, E. Langtry, John A. Barron, M.P., Allan Cassels, E. H. Duggan, G. T. Blackstock, James Morris, Q.C., G. H. Robinson, William Houston, C. E. Romaine, G. Mercer Adam, and others. The motive and designs of the "Rally" will be gathered from the following resolution, which was moved by ex-Principal Cockburn and supported in a convincing speech :—

"Whereas, Upper Canada College was established over half a century ago as an institution for the promotion of the liberal education of the youth of this Province, and was granted an endowment of certain lands for that purpose, and

"Whereas, this institution has fulfilled and is fulfilling efficiently the aim of its foundation, in furnishing an education in a way that is not provided for by any other institution of the Province, and of the need of which there is no reasonable question ; and

"Whereas, if the endowment of this institution be applied to other purposes than those set forth in the charter, or than those for which it was granted, a dangerous precedent will be thereby created, perilous to all state endowments, and thus subversive of the highest interests of the Province, and a precedent will be established which the Government in the future will find it hard to resist ; therefore be it

"Resolved, That this meeting regards with alarm the proposal to deprive the College of its rightful endowment, or to interfere with its present usefulness in any way whatever, and that it further expresses the earnest hope that no argument of mere expediency will prevail with the Government to adopt a course of action that cannot fail to cause distrust of our system of self-government, to place our established institutions for secondary and higher education in peril, and to extinguish one of the forces that gives rise to and fosters amongst the youth of this Province a true national spirit."

In his remarks, Mr. Cockburn dealt at some length with the College endowment, insisting upon the fact that it had a sure historical foundation, that nothing had been done to impair its stability, that the College had in no way trenched on the funds of Toronto University, that it was "fulfilling efficiently the aim of its foundation," and that therefore its friends "should combine in resisting spoliation, and insist upon its opponents keeping their hands off." Other speakers followed in much the same vein, expressing at the same time loyal adherence to the interests of their historic *alma mater*. Chief Justice Cameron, amidst loud applause, strenuously resisted interference with the vested interests of the College and expressed surprise at those who were moving in the Legislature to despoil the institution of its own. Such, he said, had not really considered the enormity of the act they wished to perpetrate. He insisted that the endowment granted to the College should be held as sacred as any land deeded by the Crown to a private individual. "No one," he continued, "should attempt to lay hands on it. Had not this institution rendered that service to the country which was contemplated at its foundation? He felt proud as a Canadian of its record and of its antiquity, and affirmed that it would be ruinous to the best interests of the University to owe success to the spoliation of Upper Canada College. The University, he believed, might in its turn be injured in a similar manner by the denominational colleges."

The meeting was further and eloquently addressed by the Rev. D. J. Macdonell, by Mr. John A. Barron, M.P., son of a former Principal of the College, by Dr. Larratt W. Smith, and Mr. R. E. Kingsford, ex-pupils, and members of the Senate of Toronto University, by Senators G. W. Allan and John Macdonald, and by Lieut.-Col. G. T. Denison, Judge Macdougall, Mr. A. R. Boswell, and Dr. J. A. McLellan. The latter gentleman's rally to the aid of the College, in its hour of trial, was not only a courteous but a generous act, since he might have been expected, as one long connected with the Provincial educational system and for many years Inspector of High Schools, to be in sympathy with those who sought to abolish the College and to make partition of its endowment for the benefit of the High Schools. Such, however, was not the case, and Dr. McLellan's presence on the occasion was, therefore, the more gratifying. His experience, moreover, of the secondary schools, which claimed rivalry with the College, gave increased value to his testimony as to the unique work done by the old historic institution. "No system of national education," remarked Dr. McLellan, "could be sufficient that did not provide amply for higher education. Those who opposed higher education were mostly demagogues. In such a national system an institution such as Upper Canada College was a necessary link. The historic schools of England had made that nation great. They were necessary for the complete development of the national life. There was not a school in Canada," he added, "that could give the education that was received in Upper Canada College. Nor were there any boarding schools in connection with the High Schools." Dr. McLellan concluded by offering the following resolution:—"That this meeting, while protesting against any interference with Upper Canada College, would rather be prepared to support the original intention of its founder, and suggest the establishment of similar additional residential schools in other sections of the Province, so that the benefits now conferred by the present institution may be even more largely distributed throughout the country." With the passing of another resolution, proposed by ex-Mayor Boswell, deputing a delegation " to wait upon the Legislative Assembly to request to be heard at the bar of the House in support of the College, and lay the views of the meeting before the Government," the " Old Boy's Rally " of 1887 came to a close.

What was done in the Legislature, and what the Government, under pressure even of its own supporters, seems to have been forced to do, are now familiar matters of history. The agitation against the College, when it introduced itself on the floor of the House, cut across the lines of political party. This we have already shewn, as we have also shewn the vicious grounds on which the Legislature demanded the abolition of the College or its serious impairment, by laying hands on its endowment for the benefit either of Toronto University or of the provincial Collegiate Institutes and High Schools. Circumstanced as the Government was between two fires, it was, as we have seen, indisposed to steer a course characterized by inflexible loyalty to the College. The case, in every respect, demanded such a line being taken. A Government morally as well as numerically strong would have hazarded everything to achieve this. That line at the outset, however, was not taken, and each passing year saw the agitation spread until it was too late to maintain inviolate the rights of the College and respect the sanctity of the Crown's appropriation on its behalf. What followed was a compromise. The College was not abolished, though its valuable and historic site was confiscated, and its endowment made over to Toronto University. In lieu of the expropriated King Street site it was given a new home, built for it in the northern suburbs of the city, with thirty acres of land for ornamental lawns and playgrounds. Both the site and the new buildings, which have been especially designed for the enlarged modern uses of the institution, are happily such as to atone, in some measure, for the ruthless act of confiscation. We say this frankly, with the intent of being fair to the Government, by whose grace so much of a restitution was made from the diversion of the endowment to the University and the expropriation of the College site for the behoof of the Province. But nothing, in our judgment, can justify the confiscation or palliate the wrong committed. Well will it be for public morals, and well also for the Province, if no further outrage or excess of Parliamentary license is made easy by pointing to this indefensible College precedent. The Government's position, we repeat, was a difficult one. Had it been firm, however, from the first and refused to give ear to local jealousy and Philistinism, as well as abstained from sanctioning an act fraught with the gravest evil in itself, the difficulty, we apprehend, would not have been created. What it finally had to do, we must in justice say, it did creditably; and, in the person of the Hon. Mr. Ross, Minister of Education, the path of transition was made smooth, and the College moved to its new home with as little wrench as was possible under the circumstances.

The summer months of 1891 witnessed the desertion of the familiar old quarters on King Street, replete with memories dear to thousands of the flower of Canadian youth, and hallowed by the tender associations of sixty long years. There was a pathos in the act of removal which smote not a few hearts among those who from boyhood's days had known the College and been loyal to it. Chiefly, we can well imagine, however, must the disruption have affected those old masters who were now not only parting with the College haunts, but were severing the ties that had long bound them to the institution itself. Keen as their regret must have been, theirs was the solace of duty well done, and the consciousness of meriting approval where, faithful service claims, even though it may not always receive, its reward. Nor without satisfaction must the thought have been, that the College, while betaking itself to a new home, had passed the dangers which had long beset it, and been set free, finally it is hoped, from the perilous fortunes of political vicissitude. In entering on a new phase of existence it did so with the honours which it had so well won, added to the advantages of historic reputation and traditional interest. These should count for much in the new home it now occupies, and have their influence on the hearts and minds of the coming generations to be nurtured under its spacious roof. Nor can the new and enlarged College buildings, with their improved modern equipment, and the ample academic groves which will in time encompass them, fail to have their æsthetic influence and become a potent instrument in refining the taste as well as in cultivating the imagination of the trooping Canadian youth who are to throng its beautiful halls. In the annals of the institution, as elsewhere, history significantly repeats itself. The College had its beginnings, surrounded by nature's wildness, when Toronto was but partially hewn out of the forest fastness; to-day, like fabled Antæus, "it renews its life by falling back on the bosom of its mother."

Not only the situation, but the vast area and architectural design, of the new buildings at North Toronto are handsome and attractive. The spacious grounds lie back of the ridge that bounds Toronto on the northward, and the fine tower and ample front of the new building are striking objects of interest as the visitor approaches the College by way of Queen's Park and Avenue Road. In many respects, we frankly admit, the College has gained by removal from its old-time site. Not only has it freer and more ample surroundings; it has a palatial home and more extended and improved equipments. The edifice in which it is housed is in appearance distinctively academic, and as a residential school it has now the advantage of having the dormitories and refectories, as well as the public hall and class-rooms, under one roof. The value of this, socially and morally, was aptly pointed out by the Principal, when speaking, on the first prize-day in the new building, of the formative influences of a little commonwealth like that of Upper Canada College. Nor in the new quarters of the College has provision been stinted for physical culture and recreation. In all the appurtenances of the modern home of the College—in the playground, the gymnasium, music hall, library, and laboratory—the demands of the time have been fully met. With such facilities and an enlarged and reorganized staff the old institution once more takes a new departure, the sun of its meridian life gilding alike the future and the past. The reorganization of the staff was in part necessitated by the retirement of two of the oldest and most valued of the masters. Mr. Wedd, first classical master, and Mr. Martland, second classical master and superintendent of the boarding-houses, retired from the College on its removal. In Mr. Wedd's case there had been over forty years, and, in Mr. Martland's case, over thirty years' faithful service. The memory of these services may well be treasured in the annals of an institution which has so long borne the impress of their work.

The retirement of the two long-time masters, endeared as they are to all old boys of the College, would, under ordinary circumstances, have made it difficult to fill their places. But happily the College, in its six decades spent in the training of youth, is not left dependent on outside aid to carry on its work. It can now, as it could from the first, call on its *alumni* to assume the mantle of its retiring preceptors and hand on the torch of learning to succeeding generations of scholars. Pleasant is it to see the "head-boys" elevated to the position of masters in the institution, and with the best results to the *esprit* and *morale* of the school. Successful and time-tried masters are properly also given preferment, where, as in the case of Mr. Jackson's installation as Dean of Residence, the interests of the College are subserved by the appointment. It is thus that an institution like Upper Canada College maintains its time-honoured traditions and hands them on with added zest to relays of "new boys" who enter the venerable and venerated institution.

An incident connected with the last day's work in the College before the final break up, in July, 1891, well deserves to find record in these pages. On the morning of the closing day, when the College bell had for the last time summoned the pupils together in the King Street building, there entered the Prayer Hall with the Principal and the Masters Mr. John Ross Robertson, a well-known ex-pupil and the generous donor of the annual Ross Robertson prizes. Mr. Robertson had been repeatedly invited by the Principal, and at the solicitation of many of the boys, to be present on some prize-day or other public occasion, in order that the school might honour a munificent benefactor and one of the most warm-hearted and loyal of its sons. Circumstances, added to Mr. Robertson's own modesty, had prevented his earlier complying with the request. The spirit of the hour, when the College was about to close its career on the old site, now however overcame Mr. Robertson's reluctance, and on the morning referred to he honoured the school with a visit and gratified the pupils by a brief talk to them. We need hardly say that this generous patron of the school was received with the most hearty acclaim and with an applause almost boisterous in its fervour and intensity. Principal Dickson, in appropriate and felicitous terms, introduced the visitor and acknowledged the almost princely character of the gifts Mr. Robertson had showered upon the College.

Mr. Robertson, when he rose to speak, was greeted with a storm of cheers, and it was with difficulty that silence could be obtained to permit the audible delivery of his remarks. Substantially, Mr. Robertson spoke as follows :—

"Mr. Principal and boys. The last time that I had the pleasure and privilege of standing in the public hall of the old school was some forty years ago in response to an inquiry of an animated character from my old teacher, Mr. Barron, who was anxious to have an explanation as to how a small portion of cayenne pepper mysteriously managed to find a resting-place on the top of the long box stove, which then stood in the centre of the old public hall. My memory does not serve me as to the exact result of the explanation. Sometimes I think it was satisfactory, but at times I have vivid recollections of being directed to write out a thousand times, in legible hand, the familiar heading to be found in your copy-books which reads : 'Evil communications corrupt good manners.' As I stood at the door of the *Evening Telegram* office yesterday and heard the old bell calling the boys of the College for the last time in this building to their afternoon's work, the days of long ago came rushing back to me, and the promise made to Mr. Dickson, some day or other to say a word or two to the boys, came freshly to my mind. As I stand here to-day memory fills this room with the forms and faces of those who were as you are, and in this sad and sacred hour my mind goes back to the old days when as a boy of ten years I struggled through the old preparatory form, then to the second, third, and fourth, winding up my career in the sixth form after seven years of College life.

"If I am not known personally to the majority of the boys, I am at least known to many of you by name, and nothing gives me greater pleasure than to feel that I have been enabled, in the sphere in which Providence has placed me, to do what I can to encourage the boys and keep up the interest in the work of this old school, and no delight is so great to me as when some of my old friends come with joyful faces and tell me in pleased tones that their boys have taken the 'Robertson Prize.' It is indeed an incentive to me to stand by the old boys, and to-day, with even all the cares of business and family, there is no spot on earth which has a warmer corner in my heart than this old building, bright with so many memories—a building, which has sent forth from its walls some of the brightest and best minds of Canada. This school is greater than the building or the grounds which have so long been its home, and in another pile, surrounded by more spacious grounds, the standard which has so long waved over this roof will again be set up. Upper Canada College is, my boys, but in the morning of its glory. These old walls, the dear old sward, are all joined to the infancy, not only of the school, but of the country. The place where I stand to-day, is a relic of the old colonial days, the days of the pioneers, and if some of those who were connected with the earlier work of the Old Blue School and the infant days of Upper Canada College, could stand in this room and look on these boards and see the names of those who have carried away honours, they would indeed be proud of the institution which they founded, and feel that when Upper Canada College was established, it was on a permanent basis, reflecting credit not only on this section of the country but on the whole Dominion of Canada. I do not believe that the old days were the best days. Year after year the work of this College has gone on with increased prosperity, and although in my opinion and that of a great many others, the institution has not received the fair play to which it was entitled, and through the selfishness of a larger institution and the eccentricities and ignorance of legislators, has been robbed of a large portion of its patrimony, still, withal, it is climbing the ladder of success, and notwithstanding all the difficulties and obstacles which have been thrown in its way, the prejudices which the rival educators, biassed by sectarian influences, have endeavoured to create against the College and its work, lustre will yet be added to its name, and the great work which has been accomplished in the past will be but a shadow of what will be done in the future, when in another place, with renewed life and vitality, Upper Canada College will hold front rank among the educational institutions of this Continent.

"While it is gratifying to me to stand here and see your pleasant faces and listen to your kindly applause, I know that to-day is an important one to you, boys, for it not only is a closing up of the examination work, but it is the day when the trunks and bundles which I see in front of the different boarding-houses, will go with you to your homes. I had it in my mind to come up yesterday afternoon, but I knew that you boys would feel that to take ten or fifteen minutes from your play hour would hardly be the proper thing, even if it were to listen to a talk from an old boy, and therefore I am here this morning to speak to you, without encroaching upon your play hour, but rather taking the minutes from those which are allotted to work. I can only tell you that this morning, this very hour, will always be to me one of pleasure, a red-letter morning in my life, and, believe me, that so long as I live I shall always have pleasant memories of the visit.

"I am glad to know from my friend the Principal that the prizes which I have given year after year, are competed for with eagerness, and it is a satisfaction for me to know that in the College course no prizes are more anxiously sought after than those which I give to you. Satisfactory as they have been, not only in selection, but in number, in the past, I hope they will be even more so in the future ; and so deeply do I feel the honour of being an ex-pupil of this dear old school that I shall so arrange it that certainly during my life-time, and after I have passed away, the boys of the College may always have the Robertson prizes to try for. I have occasion many times to speak to large audiences, but, believe me, boys, were it the applause of an audience of ten thousand of my fellow-citizens it would not touch my heart as the generous cheers and hurrahs which you have bestowed upon me on this last visit to the old school. May you all go home and enjoy, whether in city or country, your lengthened vacation. May those of you who will return to your studies come back reinvigorated for your work, and you who have finished with

College and are entering the busy paths of life prosper and succeed. Remember in your journey through life that you were pupils of Upper Canada College, and wherever you are, and whatever you do, forget not that you carry with you the honour of this old school, that its escutcheon, like your own, must never be sullied, and may you look back upon your College days with pleasure and profit, and be able, perhaps, to tell your children's children of the old school where you learned the rudiments of education, and where were formed your habits which have made you good, moral, truth-telling, and loyal citizens of the Empire, whose drum-beat is heard in every corner of the globe."

The proceedings closed with cheers for the speaker, which made the old public hall fairly shake to its foundations.

We may fitly close this chapter by chronicling two additional events which marked, by the display of a loyal and touching enthusiasm on the part of its sons, the transference of the College from its old to a new site. On the 29th of August, 1891, there was played on the old grounds a farewell cricket match between former pupils of the College, which brought happily together a number of the old athletes of the institution, who having had their sport on the field retired to the familiar dining-hall to season the "loving cup" with stories of by-gone "matches" and other genial College reminiscence. The day was joyously closed by another rally round the banqueting board, at a well-known city restaurant, where *alma mater* was again loyally pledged, and all, for the time being, came under "the spell of other days." The other incident which signalized the removal of the College was the reorganization of the Old Boys' Association, founded with the object of "promoting the interests of Upper Canada College, the renewal and perpetuation of the associations and traditions of the school, and the preservation of its records." An enthusiastic meeting of ex-pupils was held on the first prize-day (October 14th, 1891), in the new building, under the presidency of Mr. W. T. Boyd, and the honorary presidency of the Principal and the venerable first head-boy of the school, the Rev. Henry Scadding, D.D. The Association, on this occasion, adopted a constitution and elected officers. It took at the same time for its motto the legend, *solum non animum mutant*, with the idea of marking the fact "that the change to its present new position from the old-time hallowed premises in which the College was commenced, and where it has been so successfully carried on, has not changed or diminished the affection of its old boys." The motto in this respect is appropriate, and it may be taken as an earnest of the good-will and kind feeling which actuates every "old boy" of the College towards the institution which prepared him for the duties of life. Very beautiful is fellowship such as this, mind kindling mind in the common desire to honour an ancient and honoured seat of learning. In the fresh start taken by the College towards still nobler things in the domain of education, hardly anything could be more encouraging than the sympathy and loyalty of her sons.

THE OLD BLUE SCHOOL.

THE COLLEGE CLOCK.
(The time-keeper for over sixty years).

THE OLD BLUE SCHOOL.

THE SCHOOLS OF EARLY YORK—THE HOME DISTRICT SCHOOL OF DR. STUART, AND THE DISTRICT SCHOOL AND THE OLD BLUE SCHOOL OF DR. STRACHAN.

BY J. ROSS ROBERTSON.

THE first Legislature of the old Province of Upper Canada debated with interest the means and methods by which the rising youth— the sons and daughters of the pioneers who had cast their lot on British soil—should have the advantages of education in all its branches. Indeed, one of the first acts of those who sat at the council board at Navy Hall, in the old town of Newark, now Niagara, was for organization with this object in view, and Governor Simcoe, who, from his advent, had recognized the necessity for a public school system, gave diligent thought to the subject.

The result was the founding of District Grammar Schools, and, at a later period, of colleges for higher education. This was accomplished in 1797 by a memorial to the Imperial Government. The plans for the establishment of these schools did not materialize until 1807, when the sum of £800 currency was apportioned for the payment of the yearly stipend of the masters of eight grammar schools, one school being maintained in each of the eight districts into which the old province of Upper Canada was then divided.

These headmasters were selected by the trustees, appointed by the governor, and the selection was confirmed or sanctioned by the governor-in-council. Governor Simcoe had been transferred to another colony, and, consequently, did not share in the anticipated pleasure of seeing a system of popular education inaugurated in the province. It is not pertinent to this chapter that further reference should be made to any of the schools other than those in the town of York. The procedure had been laid down, and on the 16th of April, 1807, the Rev. George O'Kill Stuart, D.D., was appointed by Governor Gore as the first headmaster of the Home District Grammar School, at York.

Of the many preceptories for the enlightenment of youth in the ancient town of York, none occupied the exceptional position of the far-famed Home District School, better known as "The Old Blue School," and its near neighbour, the Central School, a rival institution which, under royal patronage, also has a claim to primitive eminence as an educational crucible in which youthful brain-power was tested and refined.

The centre of trade and commerce in the eastern section of the modern capital was in the vicinity of George, New (Nelson) (Jarvis), Church, King, and Palace (Front) Streets. Indeed, every foot of the locality from Yonge Street east was more or less not only the business but the residential part of the town. The inhabitants who could afford it sought homes and habitations in the west between Yonge Street and the Garrison, in open fields and pastures new that to-day are studded with mansions and palatial residences of enriched descendants of the pioneers of York.

In the summer of 1803 the residents of York first saw the benevolent-looking face and stately figure of the Rev. Dr. George O'Kill Stuart, the first rector of the Anglican congregation, which worshipped in the cathedral of St. James, and who, at the same time, was the founder of the first public school in York, so well known to succeeding generations as the Home District School. The plot of ground on the south-east corner of King and George Streets the rector held in fee simple, and, with the purpose of living near his charge, erected a substantial frame house, with bow windows looking out on King Street, the entrance being on George Street. The external part of this structure was painted a light brown colour, with green Venetian blinds as a protection to the smaller windows. This was the home of the rector. At the eastern side or gable of his house, and attached to it, he erected a small one-storey stone building that might be rendered serviceable for any purpose, either as the habitation of man or beast. When this structure was erected the stone was rough as when first extracted from its native quarry. In order, however, that the contrast between the home structure and the stone house might not be unfavourably noticed by passers-by, a sheathing of half-inch boards covered the quarried boulders which composed the walls.

In this primitive school-house the first public school of York was established, and on the roll of pupils one may read the names of boys who became rich and prominent men, and of girls who blossomed into belles of the growing capital. The school-room was about fifty feet in length and fully twenty-five feet in width. The classes opened on the 1st of June, 1807. Here we find that the townspeople of York sent their children; indeed a reading of the names gives us almost a directory of the inhabitants of the first settlement. A score or two of those entered on the first rolls should be mentioned: William Pilkington, Thomas Playter, James Givins, Benjamin Anderson, Robert Anderson, Harvey Woodruff, William Smith, William Cawthra, Robert Gray, John Gray, Henry Ernest, Gilbert Hamilton, William Robinson, Charles Reade, Daniel Brooke, Richard Brooke, Marshall and Henry Glennon, Bernard Glennon, James McIntosh, Philemon Squires, Peter McDonell, William Bowkett, George and William Jarvis, John Hayes, Charles Small, James Edward Small, Donald McDonnell, Alexander Chewett, Charles Boulton, Edward Hartney, Charles Ruggles, John Moore, Allan McNab, Robert Ross, Wilson Hamilton, Alexander Hamilton, Angus McDonell, William Stanton, Robert Stanton, George S. Boulton, George H. Detlor, Thomas G. Hamilton, William A. Hamilton, John Ridout.

This old corner was the business centre of York, even as late as 1832, for we find an advertisement in the *Upper Canada Gazette*, of that year, offering for sale a lot directly east of the old school as "one of the most eligible lots in the town of York, and situated on King Street, in the centre of the town." The labours of Dr. Stuart were continued with great success for six years. In 1813, he resigned his charge, sold his property to Colonel Duggan, and accepted a call as the rector of St. George's, Kingston, and archdeacon of the diocese. He was succeeded by Dr. Strachan, who, having presided with energy over the Cornwall Grammar School, gave renewed life to educational matters in York, by a reorganization, on a broader basis, of the system of training which had been so happily introduced by the Rev. Dr. Stuart.

The District School, which at a later period was more particularly identified with the interests of Upper Canada College, was a structure of primitive architecture, without an attractive feature, the aim of the architect being to rear a pile that, framed in heavy timber covered with clapboard and plastered inside, would give the active youths of York room for lung exercise guided by the eagle-eyed instructors, who surveyed their juvenile audiences from a pedestal-mounted desk, which ornamented the east end of the main or ground floor of this academic institute, from which graduated, in later years, many of the brightest lights of our University.

Let us, however, wander back to the second decade of the century. We stand at the south-east corner of King and Yonge Streets, and observe on the north-east corner a neatly built, two storey, white painted frame building, with a neat porch half hidden with vines and faced with a sharp pointed picket-fence that ran around the structure, shaded as it was by huge willow trees which shielded the inmates from the sun-rays of summer and the snow-whirls of winter. This was the house of Mr. Joseph Dennis, whose sons were the first lads on the roll of the District School, which, at its foundation, was temporarily accommodated in a very ordinary frame building that stood about a hundred feet east of the Dennis House, in later days the Ridout corner. The building had been a barn, and was readily improved by Dr. Strachan, when he bid farewell to his Cornwall pupils, and favoured York with his energetic presence in the early days of 1813.

In an old plan of York, dated 1797, the six acres directly north of the square occupied by St. James' cathedral, is marked "School." The plan is official, and its correctness is certified to by "D. W. Smith, D.S.G., 10th June, 1797," with the countersign of "In Council at York, June 10, 1797, Peter Russell." At a later date, in 1819, another plan was issued by "T. Ridout, Surveyor General," on which this plot of ground is marked "College Square." The authorities had evidently made the selection with the intention, that within the limits of this stretch of green, buildings for the purposes of education would be erected, from which would radiate the knowledge that might illume the understandings of the striplings of York. The King Street building had served its purpose from about 1815. Under Strachan apt pupils of the early days had gathered a mental strength that was a credit to the master. Parents recognized the vigorous efficiency of the founder of the school, and felt that they could entrust the intellectual development of their sons to the guidance of a man whose heart was in the work, and who strove to impart knowledge that would be bearing fruit when their children had climbed into manhood.

The progress of the King Street school was phenomenal. Success had crowned the early designs of the master, and the limited accommodation soon compelled a flight to more commodious quarters. The six acre field, originally laid out by Mr. President Russell, was selected as the site of the improved building, and the summer of 1816 saw the timbers felled from the forest, north of Lot Street, now Queen Street, for a more stately erection than the rude structure which for years had served the purpose of a school near King and Yonge Streets.

The "School" or "College Square," north of the "Church Square," had no particular claims to beauty. The tall pines, the drooping willows and the forest oaks which adorned it when the town was originally laid out, had become martyrs to the axe of the pioneer woodman. The field was nothing more than a green sward, dotted with stumps of the monarchs of the forest and divided by a half sluggish rivulet, that finally assumed the proportions of a pond, which, in winter, was haunted by boys. These urchins smoothed the soles of their Wellington boots on the half acre of ice, which formed at the bidding of the thermometer, and thus afforded untold enjoyment to specimens of future manhood who were fond of sport. In summer the field was the arena for games of hockey, and the lads tumbled over the stumps, and, perhaps, landed in the shallow pools of water which formed in the field, to return to the parental roof with torn attire and mud-bedrabbled boots. A sight of their children no doubt made mothers feel, as mothers from the beginning of time have always felt, that such rude experiences were a part and parcel of the life of the genuine, practical, every-day boy.

An old pioneer, whose face the writer welcomes, even as the century folds its arms before sinking into the calendar of time, recounts the raising of the frame of the Home District School in 1816; the timbers, dovetailed into each other, stood waiting for the shingled roof and the half-inch clap-board sides. The structure occupied a site near the south-west corner of the square, a hundred odd feet north of Newgate, or Adelaide, Street, and the same distance from Church Street, directly east and north of the line of the present Public Library. The school building was nearly seventy feet deep, with a frontage of forty feet. The structure was two storeys high, its gables faced the east and west, and light streamed into the structure through ten windows on the north and south sides—five above and five below; while the east end was pierced by four windows—two above and two below; and the west end was honoured by the entrance door, with three windows above and two to the south of the doorway, the tread of which was scraped hourly by the juvenile horde that made the welkin ring as, at the close of the school day, they eagerly sought the unconstrained atmosphere of the six-acre play ground. The boards which covered the stout frame-timbers had been smoothed by a vigorous jack-plane, and thus yielded more gracefully than when in the rough to the arm of the painter, who, brush in hand, at a low price per yard, covered the entire outside with a dull slate-blue that defied not only the scorching sun of summer but the Arctic frost of the old-time Canadian winter. To vary the monotony of colour the door and window frames were painted white; a not uncommon mode of treatment in early buildings by the deft artists of York. Surely it has been by right inscribed in print as "The Old Blue School." The designer had not much difficulty in apportioning the space at his disposal. Once inside the door the pupils found themselves in a long lobby that extended from the north to the south along the west gable of the building, the only decoration of which was a long row of iron pegs and brackets for the hats, caps and coats of the pupils. At the east side of the lobby a stairway ran up to the second storey which was not used for school purposes, but served occasionally as a public hall for concerts and lectures. A door opened from the centre of the lobby into the lower school-room, of sixty by forty. It was a roomy apartment, with the conventional plastering of the period. The angles made by the walls and ceiling were not ornamented with the moulded projections or curved lines of cornice work; indeed, the severity of treatment was doubtless intended to prevent dust and cobwebs accumulating in the corners that are special targets for the activity of the broom. The stringers, which grasped the frame of the building, and which in turn strengthened the roof, had additional support in four square upright pillars of pine which rested on a stone foundation, and within a few feet of the angles of the room, helped to support not only the main roof but the ceilings of the upper and lower school-room. The guiding mind in the school-room occupied an elevated position behind a long pine desk that stood on a platform and commanded a full view of the pupils whose minds and characters were being formed to suit the requirements of life. The furniture of the room was in harmony with the woodwork. Friendly as had been the painter's brush with the exterior of the structure, it was a perfect stranger—indeed, had not ever had a bowing acquaintance—with the interior. The woodwork bore evidence that the active and regular movements of the carpenter's elbow had made rough places smooth and rendered the pine presentable, and it was not many months ere both the woodwork of the building and the furniture caught that dark, sienna look which is the sombre result of smoke, dirt and age. The benches and desks were ranged on the north and south sides of the room. Every boy owned an ink-cup of glass, which dropped into an auger hole the size of a half-penny, and was replenished as regularly as the supply was exhausted, out of earthen bottles that were labelled "London Writing Fluid." The faces of the boys at these side desks were turned towards the wall, while on each side of the centre of the room was a set of double-sloped desks. In the centre stood a long box-stove of government pattern, that consumed the beech and maple without the aid of the traditional bucksaw. The school was as all primitive schools are. The boys were as varied in character as those of to-day. Studious lads were commended by the master; those who struggled and persevered were encouraged by a kindly word; while the perverse youth, who could but would not digest the mental diet, was invigorated and quickened into activity by the aid of rods, cut from the McGill and Jarvis property, which lay north of Lot Street, and at a later day by the assistance of a strap, fashioned by an artizan who in these days would be called a shoemaker, but whose appellation in olden times was that of "cordwainer." We have no desire to perpetuate, even in the memories of the descendants of the boys of the Old Blue School, the physical treatment administered for any infringement of regulations.

Yet the dignity of standing up alongside of one of the ceiling supports, with jacket or coat turned inside out made the victim prominent for the rest of the lesson. The mishap of allowing a pocket-full of marbles to roll over the floor meant an extra half-hour after the other boys had retired for the day, and the sly bite of an apple during school hours, on one occasion, resulted in an inventory being taken of every earthly article in the youngster's pocket. An old scholar whose pocket pence had been invested in a jew's-harp, inadvertently tested its notes in school hours and had, as a punishment, to favour his much amused mates by rendering, on the top of a desk, an air that had more life and vivacity in its chords than musical rhythm. The old pioneer who relates to the writer so many of the incidents of early York, smiles as he recounts his efforts to cut, carve, and engrave, with the aid of a jackknife, his name in the slant of one of the pine desks, and he declares that a photographic view of any of the desks in the school would pass for the hieroglyphics on some Egyptian monolith. Other volumes have told the story of the loved old schoolmaster, whose familiar face and careful step are bright in the memory of hundreds to-day. There are still among us those who remember Dr. Strachan, not only in the sere and yellow of old age, but in active and lithe youth either presiding over the primal school, in Cornwall, or as director and central figure of the District School of York. Dr. Strachan was born in the north of Scotland, in 1778. He was the teacher of the parish school at Kettle, although some years prior, he, at the age of sixteen, had charge of a smaller school, where the sons of small farmers of the surrounding gentry and clergy imbibed knowledge from their youthful instructor, who possessed an executive ability in his vocation that would have been creditable to one of older years. His store of knowledge was replenished by keeping the terms and lectures held during the winter months, at King's College, Aberdeen. Before seeking a home in the new land over the sea, Dr. Strachan had a position in the school, at Denino, where two years "as happy as any in my life" were spent. Here, under the guidance of Dr. Brown, the parish minister, and the Rev. Thomas Duncan, the doctor states that they "corrected many of my false notions. I learned to discriminate between hypothesis and fact, and to separate the ebullitions of fancy from the deductions of reason." At Kettle there were nearly a hundred pupils, and, amongst them, the renowned David Wilkie, whose work as an artist in "The Village Politician" first found fame in the Royal Academy of 1806, just as he stepped from the confines of youth into the arena and welcome of manhood. Captain Barclay, who fought so well at Put-in-Bay, Lake Erie, in 1813, against Commodore Perry, was also a pupil, and the poet Campbell, whose "Hohenlinden" and "Exile of Erin" are familiar to the boys of all schools on recitation day, was likewise a scholar.

The school at Cornwall had an excellent reputation. At its desks sat the scions of all the leading and prominent families of the old Midland District, while from the Home District many were sent to obtain the advantages which York from 1800 until 1815 did not possess. The names of the scholars enrolled are familiar on the pages of Canadian history, and their gratitude was marked as late as 1833, when forty-two of the old pupils testified their love for their old master by presenting him with an engrossed address, accompanied by a substantial piece of silver plate. The address was a pleasant exposition of the views of the old pupils, in that it admitted that : " Our young minds received there an impression which has scarcely become fainter from the time of the deep and sincere interest which you took, not only in our advancement in learning and science, but in all that concerned our happiness, or could affect our future prospects in life." This generous tribute to the teacher's skill touched the heart of the reverend doctor, and in his reply, pregnant with many truths, he said : " It has ever been my conviction that our scholars should be considered for the time our children ; and that, as parents, we should study their peculiar dispositions if we really wish to improve them, for, if we feel not something of the tender relation of parents towards them, we cannot expect to be successful in their education. It was on this principle I attempted to proceed ; strict justice, tempered with parental kindness; and the present joyful meeting evinces its triumph ; it treats the sentiments and feelings of scholars with proper consideration ; and while it gives the heart and affections full freedom to show themselves in filial gratitude on the one side and fatherly affection on the other, it proves that unsparing labour, accompanied with continual anxiety for the learner's progress never fails to ensure success and to produce a friendship between master and scholar which time can never dissolve."

We have the printed order of exercises at the examination of the District School on the 7th August, 1816, and the " recital " of the prologue was given to John Claus, of Oxford, whose father, in 1804, was one of the lieutenants of counties in Upper Canada. This office, a counterpart of which may be found in England, was not perpetuated in Canada. Among the names of the pupils we have John Skeldon, and George Skeldon, Henry Mosley, John Doyle, Charles Heward, James Myers, John Ridout, Charles Ridout, John Boulton, William Allan, Allen McDonell, Henry Heward, James Sheehan, Saltern Givins, John Mosley, John Fitzgerald, William Myers, Daniel Murray, David Shaw, Warren Claus, Henry Nelles, Robert Baldwin, John Harraway, David McNab, James Strachan, William Lancaster, Horace Ridout, James Givins, John Knot, K. de Koven, George Baldwin, William Baldwin, James Bigelow.

At this period His Excellency, Francis Gore, was Lieutenant-Governor of Upper Canada, previously Governor of Bermuda, and frequently visited the school, and on examination day paid a special visit. The prologue of the head pupil was of course the *piece de resistance*, not only as an original composition but as a bit of rhetoric, which probably had been carefully examined by the master prior to its delivery. Indeed we have many examples of the poetic gift in the work of Dr. Strachan at his Cornwall school. This prologue, in the concluding lines, asks that His Majesty's representatives pay some little attention to the educational interests of the country. The last two lines were of a topical character, and must have amused the Governor, as he sat in a high chair which, with others, had been borrowed from the cathedral church for the occasion. The youth thus spake:

> "O, think what honour pure shall bless thy name
> Beyond the fleeting voice of vulgar fame,
> When kings and haughty victors cease to raise
> The secret murmur and the venal praise;
> Perhaps that name, when Europe's glories fade,
> Shall often charm this Academic shade,
> And bards exclaim on rough Ontario's shore,
> ' We found a Wellesley and Jones in Gore.'"

The system pursued by Dr. Strachan in the school at York, and previously at Cornwall, was in harmony with the sound methods adopted in the parish schools of Scotland, followed out in early days at the schools of Kettle and Denino. In the advanced classes the pupils prepared for one another a series of questions on topics selected, this interlocutory exercise being carried on in the presence of the master, whose word was useful in the correction of any errors that might occur. Another favourite method of inspiring emulation was for pupils who were versed in rhetoric or elocution, to challenge one another in a reading or recitation, after which, in the presence of the class or entire school, the contest took place, the voice of the school awarding the palm of victory, subject to review by the teacher— and a possible reversal of the award.

Dr. Strachan realized that in a new country the difficulties in the way of imparting information were many and serious. Men who had to earn the bread and butter of life had but limited time to give to an intelligent study of the arts and sciences, and the hours snatched from that enlivening time which begins in the pinafore season, and ends when long boots and trousers are assumed, was a limit within which information had to be instilled prior to entrance upon the toils and cares of business life. So many of the Cornwall pupils achieved honour in the highest positions—mercantile and judicial—and stand prominent in public work in the annals of Canadian history, that one must feel that Dr. Strachan's methods were the results of careful thought. He himself saw the situation. He admitted the peculiarities of the position, and said to his pupils at Cornwall, in 1807: "The time allowed in a new country like this is scarcely sufficient to sow the most necessary seed; very great progress is not, therefore, to be expected; if the principles are properly engrafted, we have done well. In conducting your education, one of my principal objects has always been to fit you for discharging with credit the duties of any office to which you may hereafter be called. To accomplish this, it was necessary for you to be accustomed frequently to depend upon and think for yourselves; accordingly I have always encouraged this disposition, which, when preserved within due bounds, is one of the greatest benefits that can be acquired. To enable you to think with advantage, I not only regulated your tasks in such a manner as to exercise your judgment, but extended your views beyond the meagre routine of study usually adopted in schools, for, in my opinion, several branches of science may be taught with advantage at a much earlier age than is generally supposed. We made a mystery of nothing; on the contrary, we entered minutely into every particular, and patiently explained by what progressive steps certain results were obtained. It has ever been my custom, before sending a class to their seats, to ask myself whether they had learned anything, and I was always exceedingly mortified if I had not the agreeable conviction that they had made some improvement. Let none of you, however, suppose that what you have learned here is sufficient; on the contrary, you are to remember that we have laid only the foundation. The superstructure must be raised by yourselves."

Again, in 1809, in a small publication, issued by himself, he refers to his method of teaching arithmetic. He writes: "I divide my pupils into separate classes, according to their progress. Each class has one or more sums to produce every day, neatly wrought upon their own slates; the work is carefully examined, after which I command every figure to be blotted out and the sums to be wrought under my eye. The one whom I happen to pitch upon first, gives, with an audible voice, the rules and reasons for every step, and, as he proceeds, the rest silently work along with him, figure for figure, but ready to correct him if he blunder, that they may get his place. As soon as this one is finished the work is again blotted out, and another called upon to work the question aloud as before, while the rest again proceed along with him in silence, and so on round the whole class. By this method the principles are fixed in the mind, and he must be a very dull boy indeed who does not understand every question thoroughly before he leaves it. This method of teaching arithmetic possesses this important advantage, that it may be pursued without interrupting the pupil's progress in any other useful study. The same method of teaching algebra has been used with equal success. Such a plan is certainly very laborious, but it will be found successful, and he that is anxious to spare labour ought not to be a public teacher. When boys remain long enough, it has been my custom to teach them the theory and give them a number of curious questions in geography, natural philosophy and astronomy, a specimen of which may be seen in the questions placed before the appendix."

The venerable preceptor fully realized the incongruities of disposition, character and mind, to be found in the primary schools of a young country, and, in another part of the same address, he writes in jubilant strain, and justifies his methods of inculcating instruction. He states :—

"One of the greatest advantages you have derived from your education here arises from the strictness of our discipline. Those of you who have not already perceived how much tranquillity depends on the proper regulation of the temper will soon be made sensible of it as you advance in years. You will find people who have never known what it is to be in habitual subjection to precept and just authority breaking out into violence and outrage on the most frivolous occasions. The passions of such persons when once roused, soon become ungovernable, and that impatience of restraint which they have been allowed to indulge embitters the greatest portion of their lives. Accustomed to despise the barriers erected by reason, they rush forward to indulgence without regarding the consequences. Hence arises much of that wretchedness and disorder to be met with in society. Now the discipline necessary to correct the impetuosity of the passions is often found nowhere but in well-regulated schools; for, though it should be the first care of parents they are too apt to be blinded by affection, and grant liberties to their children which reason disapproves. * * * That discipline, therefore, which you have sometimes thought irksome, will henceforth present itself in a very different light. It will appear to the teacher a habit of the greatest consequence in the regulation of your future conduct; and you will value it as the promoter of that decent and steady command of temper so very essential to happiness and so useful in our intercourse with mankind."

The writer of this has in his possession a copy of the programme of the school at York for 1819. The list of names recalls to mind many familiar faces, all of whom, except old Mr. John Ridout, have gone into that higher country—beyond the lowlands of life. The examination days were so regulated that the classes, when not engaged in exercises and lessons, exhibited their power in retaining knowledge and ability as memorizers, in recitations and debates.

"Order of the examination of the Home District Grammar School at York, Wednesday, 11th August, 1819. First Day. The Latin and Greek Classes. Euclid and Trigonometry. Thursday, 12th August. Second Day. To commence at 10 o'clock. Prologue, by Robert Baldwin. Reading Class.—George Strachan, The Excellence of the Bible; Thomas Ridout, the Man of Ross; James McDonell, Liberty and Slavery; St. George Baldwin, The Sword; William Murray, Soliloquy on Sleep. Arithmetic Class.—James Smith, The Sporting Clergyman; William Boulton, Jun., The Poet's New Year's Gift; Richard Oates, Ode to Apollo; Orville Cassell, The Rose. Bookkeeping.—William Myers, My Mother; Francis Heward, My Father; George Dawson, Lapland. First Grammar Class. Second Grammar Class. Debate on the Slave Trade.—For the Abolition: Francis Ridout, John Fitzgerald, William Allan, George Boulton, Henry Heward, William Baldwin, John Ridout, John Doyle, James Doyle. Against the Abolition: Abraham Neils, James Baby, James Doyle, Charles Heward, Allan McDonell, James Myers, Charles Ridout, William Boulton, Walker Smith. First Geography Class. Second Geography Class. James Dawson, The Boy that Told Lies; James Bigelow, The Vagrant; Thomas Glassco, The Parish Workhouse; Edward Glennon, The Apothecary. Natural History.—Debate by the Young boys: Sir William Strickland, Charles Heward; Lord Morpeth, John Owens; Lord Hervey, John Ridout; Mr. Plomer, Raymond Baby; Sir William Young, John Fitzgerald; Sir William Windham, John Boulton; Mr. Henry Pelham, Henry Heward; Mr. Bernard, George Strachan; Mr. Noel, William Baldwin; Mr. Shippen, James Baby; Sir Robert Walpole, S. Givins and J. Doyle; Mr. Horace Walpole, James Myers; Mr. Putteney, Charles Baby. Civil History.—William Boulton, The Patriot; Francis Ridout, The Grave of Sir John Moore; Saltern Givins, Great Britain; John Boulton, Eulogy on Mr. Pitt; Warren Claus, The Indian Warrior; Charles Heward, The Soldier's Dream; William Boulton, The Heroes of Waterloo. Catechism.—Debate on the College at Calcutta.—Speakers: Mr. Canning, Robert Baldwin; Sir Francis Baring, John Doyle; Mr. Wainwright, Mark Burnham; Mr. Thornton, John Knott; Sir D. Scott, William Boulton; Lord Eldon, Warren Claus; Sir Samuel Lawrence, Allan Macaulay; Lord Hawkesbury, Abraham Nelles; Lord Bathurst, James McGill Strachan; Sir Thomas Metcalf, Walker Smith; Lord Teignmouth, Horace Ridout. Religious Questions and Lectures.—James McGill Strachan. Anniversary of the York and Montreal Colleges anticipated for 1st January, 1822. Epilogue, by Horace Ridout."

These public examinations were red-letter days with the parents of York, and the paternal and maternal relatives of the house were always there in full force. Fond friends and the usual retinue of sisters and cousins and aunts, donned their best gowns to witness the results of the year's study. Sir Peregrine Maitland and his staff, seated on a slightly raised daïs, covered with cloth of crimson hue, were usually interested spectators in the proceedings. To make the occasion more joyous than the ordinary dismissal at Christmas, the midsummer vacation day was celebrated by a lunch or *dejeuner*, at which contributions of jellies, preserves and pastries from the pantries of the best people in York combined to make the pupils, who had been "cribbed, cabined and confined" for six months, feel that there was one day in the year on which life was worth living.

The central figure at the opening was young Robert Baldwin, whose name and memory to-day are green in the hearts of all Canadians. His verse travelled over the whole range of European history. It lauded the work of Warren Hastings in India, the "Asiatic Researches" of Sir William Jones, the English Orientalist, the founding of Calcutta College by the Duke of Wellington, and the advantage of a similar institution in Canada was suggested by the lines:—

> "Yet much remains for some aspiring son,
> Whose liberal soul from that desires renown,
> Which gains for Wellesley a lasting crown;
> Some general structure in these wilds to rear,
> Where every art and science may appear."

Perhaps the day dream in Baldwin's fertile brain was the erection of Upper Canada College and King's College in the early future, and then with a few lines which must have warmed the heart of the distinguished visitor, he adds:—

> "O, Maitland blest! this proud distinction woos
> Thy quick acceptance, backed by every muse;
> Those feelings, too, which joyful fancy knew
> When learning's gems first opened to thy view,
> Bid you to thousands smooth the thorny road,
> Which leads to glorious Science's bright abode."

The Epilogue was pronounced by Horace Ridout. An extract from this, which was a mixture of machine poetry and doggerel, will suffice. The reciter is supposed to be a pupil, who complains of the conduct of the master.

> "Between ourselves, and just to speak my mind,
> In English Grammar, Master's much behind;
> I speak the honest truth—I hate to dash—
> He bounds our task by Murray, Lowth and Ashe.
> I told him once that Abercrombie, moved
> By genius deep, had Murray's plan improved.
> He frowned upon me, turning up his nose,

> And said the man had ta'en a maddening dose.
> Once in my theme I put the word progress—
> He sentenced twenty lines, without redress ;
> Again for 'measure' I transcribed 'endeavour,'
> And all the live-long day I lost his favour."

There are many reminiscences which might be written concerning the District School. The venerable Dr. Scadding, the chronicler, in "Toronto of Old," has given us the story of the old school-house and its founder. The Rev. Dr. Bethune, the successor of "The First Bishop of Toronto," and who, by the way, assisted as teacher in the early days of the school, has also epitomized his recollections in the cheerfully told story of the life of his mentor and patron. He thus alludes to the first visit he made to York, in 1819, when guided by the principal he for the first time saw the inside of the school-house. His story runs :—

"On entering it for the first time, with the reverend principal, on a bright September morning, fresh schoolboy feelings were wakened up at the sight of forty or fifty happy young faces, from seventeen down to five years of age. There was a class of only two in Greek, who took up Horace and Livy in Latin; and there were three Latin forms below them—the most numerous and most sprightly reading Cornelius Nepos. None were much advanced in mathematics, and, with the exception of the senior two, had not passed the fourth book of Euclid. Everything was taught on the same plan as at Cornwall, but at York the pupils' were much less advanced, and the headmaster rarely took any share in the actual work of instruction. I had had the opportunity of seeing both schools, and, though the glory of the former was never approached by the latter, still there are reminiscences connected with the school at York more fresh and lively than could be awakened by the more celebrated one at Cornwall. With the schoolboys of the former—now in the sere of life, and owning children and grandchildren, I can exchange daily greetings ; but few are left who were my associates in the latter ; one by one they are dropping fast away."

After 1820 Dr. Strachan's public duties prevented his active participation in the work of the school, and he resigned his connection with it in July of 1823, for on the 26th of May of that year he had been appointed General Superintendent of Education for Upper Canada. His position for many years had been more that of a director to those who assisted in the conduct of the classes than of a master. Mr. Rosington Elms, a tall, well-formed, well-educated Englishman, was one of the principal assistants, and some years later the entire charge of the school fell to the lot of the Rev. Samuel Armour, M. A., whose home on James Street will yet be remembered by old boys. Mr. Armour was a graduate of Glasgow university, a scholarly man, who had taken high honours in the Scotch commercial metropolis, and who, at the same time, had a mind of sporting turn, which enabled him with unerring aim to bring down a percentage of the flocks of wild pigeons, which occasionally passed over the town. Dr. Scadding gives an incident in the career of this master, illustrating two views of his character. The doctor says :—

"In those days there was not a plentiful supply in the town of every book wanted in the school. The only copy that could be procured of a Eutropius, which we ourselves on a particular occasion required, was one with an English translation at the end. The book was bought, Mr. Armour stipulating that the English portion of the volume should be sewn up ; in fact, he himself stitched the leaves together. In Mr. Armour's time there was, for some reason now forgotten, a barring-out. A pile of heavy wood (sticks of cordwood whole, used to be thrust into the great school-room stove) was built against the door within, and the master had to effect, and did effect, an entrance to his school through a window on the north side."

Mr. Armour having taken orders in the Church of England, resigned his post, and officiated for years in the Anglican church in the township of Cavan. His successor was the Rev. Dr. Thomas Phillips, of Queen's College, Cambridge, a master of a school at Whitchurch, in Herefordshire, who arrived from England to take charge of the District School. With the advent of Dr. Phillips the curriculum of the District School was changed. The doctor, who had taken his B.A. in 1805 was one who inspired respect and regard. He was the ideal country clergyman of English parish life. His hat was typical of clerical style, and his closely buttoned frock coat, with the prescribed leggings, added to the benevolent features of the old gentleman's appearance. When he migrated from British soil, he brought with him many traditions of his educational life. He ranked in England as a teacher of note and introduced the Eton Latin grammar and Eton Greek grammar, thus displacing some of the text books, which had endeared themselves to the classical teachers of Little York. The new principal was an extremely affable man, with kindly voice for all who sought his friendship, an educationist of tried experience, one who possessed the faculty of planting seeds of scholastic knowledge in the brain of every boy who showed the slightest aptitude for the acquirement of mental food, which would be useful in fighting battles in the business fields of after-life. To know him was to love him, and his personal contact with the boys, who valued his friendship and training, left an impression that was productive of the best results.

Dr. Phillips assumed charge of the old school in the autumn of 1825, just five years before its removal to the location at the east end of the "College Square." The old building was much the same as in its pristine days, although, at his coming, the western end was improved by a shed-like erection, which was a protection to the pupils during the summer showers. The structure was fitted up with a few bars and poles, that earned for it the name of "Gymnasium," the first title of the kind that was attached to any of the early schools. The ground surrounding the school which, in primitive times, was slightly undulating, had been cleared of the stumps, and a space of a few hundred feet square, was selected for the good old English sport of cricket, which was cultivated from 1825, under the enthusiastic direction of Mr. George Antony Barber, who accompanied Dr. Phillips to York, as his principal assistant in the school, and who was well known as the father of cricket in old Upper Canada.

The District School continued to exist in the square north of Newgate (Adelaide) Street, and its prosperity was attested to by no other feature than that the tuition was perfect, and the school popular.

In 1828 the reins of government in Upper Canada passed into the hands of Sir John Colborne, a gentleman whose interest in educational matters in Guernsey, where, as governor, he had revived the "School of Queen Elizabeth," founded by the maiden Queen in 1563, was an augury of good for education in Upper Canada. He had obtained a royal charter for the founding of a university in his new charge and laid his plans for a better class of school than the old District, the result being the establishment of the school, known in its early years, as "The College of Upper Canada," or the "Minor College," afterwards "Upper Canada College."

The first record we have of the intention of Sir John Colborne to found a school, as the successor of the old Blue or District School, is in the minutes of the Board of Education of Upper Canada, dated 4th April, 1829. At this meeting Dr. Strachan, the Ven. Archdeacon of York, presided, and submitted to the Board, composed of Hon. Joseph Wells, Hon. Geo. H. Markland, and John B. Robinson, Esq., a letter from Sir John Colborne to Dr. Jones, Vice-Chancellor of Oxford, giving the plan of organization. As the correspondence, indeed, the minutes of this Board, have never seen the light of day since 1831, and, as portions are so closely linked with the founding of Upper Canada College, the writer ventures to include in this chapter excerpts from the original and official documents, which will, it is to be hoped, be read with interest by all who take pride in being pupils of the old school.

THE NEW PUBLIC HALL, TAKEN MAY, 1891.

The enthusiastic Governor was heart and soul in his work. He desired a preparatory school for the proposed university, and wanted the masters "forwarded" with as little delay as possible. His closing lines are unique. If he had been writing of "a cargo" of school-boys, one could appreciate the situation; but when he wrote of "a cargo of masters" the enthusiastic Governor evidently thought that those learned in classics, science, or art, were kept duly parcelled and labelled, on shelves, ready for shipment by the first sailing vessel.

The President read the following despatch : "The Lieutenant-Governor has requested His Majesty's Government to grant £1,000 per annum from the Territorial Revenue, for the support of this school. If these arrangements should be carried into effect the revenue of the college will be £3,050 per annum. It is recommended that the buildings for the school and masters may be erected on the part of the military reserve, adjoining Peter Street, and parallel with it. The houses may be completed for £5,000.

"It is intended also to attach several exhibitions to the college. With proper encouragement, the Lieutenant-Governor is persuaded it will flourish and prove in every respect advantageous to Upper Canada."

The following resolution was proposed and adopted unanimously : "Resolved, That the treasurer be authorized to place in the hands of Messrs. Thomas Wilson & Co., Warnford Court, Throgmorten street, London, agent for the Bank of Upper Canada, at the credit of Dr. Jones, Vice-Chancellor of Oxford, the sum of £1,500 stg., for the purpose of enabling him to advance an outfit of £100 stg. to the principal and to each of the masters, in consequence of the letter of His Excellency Sir John Colborne, dated the 31st March, 1829, and also such further sum out of the remainder as they may require on account of their future salaries.

"Resolved, That the treasurer be authorized to make such arrangements with the Bank of Upper Canada as will enable him to carry the above resolution into effect."

The letter to Dr. Jones was then submitted. It read :—

York, 31st March, 1829.

My Dear Sir,—I am about to impose on you, I am afraid, an unreasonable task, but, as I know you will agree with me in thinking that there is no place in which education is required more to be encouraged than in Upper Canada, I trust that I may calculate on your assistance in establishing a seminary, which is destined to supply the intended university with students.

I therefore will proceed in communicating my plan of obtaining, through your good offices, three classical masters and a mathematical master. We wish the gentlemen, that you may be able to enlist, forwarded to Upper Canada College before October next, if possible.

We shall call our college the Upper Canada College. The head master shall be styled the Principal. The second master is now at York, and will not object to take the situation I have offered him.

The Principal will have a fixed salary at £600 sterling per annum. He will be provided with a home, allowed to take boarders, and will regulate the studies of the whole school, which will consist of four classical masters, a mathematical master, two French masters, two writing masters, and a drawing master. On the reputation of the Principal the College will chiefly depend. Therefore much care will be required in selecting one whose name will give support to the institution. He must have taken a first-class degree in classics and mathematics. As a generation may pass away in corresponding across the Atlantic, I and the trustees of the College give you full power to select our Principal, and the two classical masters, and the mathematical master. But if you should not wish to be charged with the responsibility entirely, I beg you to have the goodness to consult Mr. Stocker, of the Guernsey College, who has had, during three years, much experience in the selection of masters, and Mr. Charles Young, of Eton College.

Thus, probably, these gentlemen may have no objection to decide among the candidates that may offer. The two junior classical masters will receive £300 per annum for their fixed salaries, and will also have a house provided, and will be allowed to take boarders. The mathematical master will have the same advantages.

I must trouble you to have the following notice inserted in the Oxford and Cambridge newspapers:

"The headship of Upper Canada College being vacant, a Principal is required to carry into effect the system of education to be adopted at that institution. He must be a graduated member of one of the Universities, and possessed of high classical and mathematical knowledge. He will receive a fixed salary of £600 sterling per annum, and will be allowed to take boarders, and will be provided with a house for that purpose. Candidates for the appointment may make application to the Vice-Chancellor of the University of Oxford for further particulars.

"A mathematical master is required for the same College, and two classical masters. They will each receive a fixed salary of £300, and will be provided with a house, and permitted to take boarders."

I am in great haste to save the post. I am persuaded of your zeal in the cause, and reckon upon it to overcome all the difficulties that you may encounter in completing the cargo of masters for Upper Canada before next winter.

(Signed),   J. COLBORNE.

In this letter, and in the accompanying memoranda, we have the gist of the deliberations, which led to the founding of Upper Canada College.

In the original suggestion for the selection of a site, the location was on a plot west of John Street and east of Peter Street, what was afterwards the site of the General Hospital, now occupied by private residences, and the property of the Hospital Trust. Some discussion prevailed among the members of the Board of Education as to the proposed site, for we find that at a meeting of the Board on 30th April, 1829: "The President reported that he had made known the opinion of the Board, respecting the intended site of the College of Upper Canada, and that it seemed most expedient to him to place it at the west end of King street, that His Excellency, however, still continued to prefer that part of the military reserve he had before fixed on, as it would create an additional demand on the funds to procure the other, and might cause delay."

At this meeting the plans were submitted, and it was resolved, "That the plan of a school-house, exhibited by Mr. Ewart, be adopted, with this difference, than the third storey of the wings be taken away, and a balustrade substituted.

Resolved, "That the outline of the house be adopted, removing the third storeys, and reducing them to a scale of forty feet clear.

Resolved, "That two of the houses be so built so as to accommodate two families each.

Resolved, "That an advertisement be immediately inserted in the newspapers, and distributed by handbills, that proposals for building a school-house, and four dwelling-houses, will be received on the 1st June next, the plans and specifications to be seen at the College Council office after the 12th May next."

At the meeting of the Board on the 13th May, 1829, it was resolved, "That an extra allowance of £50 be allowed to Mr. McFarlane on account of the loss stated to have been sustained in printing Mayor's spelling books on cards."

And it was also resolved, "That Lieut.-Col. O'Hara, and Grant Powell, Esq., and James Fitzgibbon, Esq., be constituted a committee to superintend the buildings, about to be erected, during their progress."

It was also resolved, "That the contracts be received for each building, and that persons making tenders be told that expedition in the completion of the work will be considered a ground for preference," and "That a sum, equal to half the amount of the security given, be advanced for the contractor, in order to facilitate the work, and on producing, afterwards, a certificate from the Clerk of the Works, that further work has been performed, eighty per cent. of its value be advanced."

At the meeting of the Board, on the 27th May, 1829, the question of the site again came up.

In consequence of a notification from Mr. Markland, that His Excellency, Sir John Colborne, was pleased to submit for the decision of the Board, "whether the site of the College of Upper Canada shall be upon Russell Square, or on part of the military reserve, near the woodyard, it was unanimously resolved that, in consideration of the increased convenience which will be afforded to the youth of the town, it is expedient to place the buildings for the College on some part of Russell Square, to be hereafter determined upon."

It was also directed to postpone the opening of tenders, until the 8th of June, and that Mr. Rogers, an architect of Kingston, be allowed three per cent. for superintending the work, in conjunction with that of the Parliament Buildings, which were then being erected on Front street.

The advertisements for tenders which appeared in *The Loyalist*, read :

> Minor College—Sealed tenders for erecting a school-house and four dwelling-houses, will be received on the first Monday of June next. Plans, elevations and specifications may be seen after the 12th instant, on application to the Hon. Geo. Markland, from whom further information will be received. Editors throughout the province are requested to insert the notice until the first Monday in June, and forward their accounts for the same to the office of *The Loyalist*, York.
>
> York, 1st May, 1829.

The first tenders that were opened for the college buildings and the residences of the masters amounted to £5,626, and this, being the excess of the intended expenditure a further extension, until the 1st August, 1829, for the receipt of tenders, was ordered. The speedy execution of the work had, it was thought, contributed to produce these high figures. The delay resulted in a tender, by a contractor, for £5,268, and the selection of Mr. John Ewart to superintend the work for two and a-half per cent.

On the 27th June, 1830, the Board met and decided to offer for sale the ground known as the college or school square, in the centre of which stood the old Blue School. The ground was laid out in lots 26 x 90 feet, and on the 10th July was sold to the highest bidders. The extreme east end of the old square was reserved for the Central School, which was a preparatory school for children, prior to entering the College. The building stood on the north-west corner of Newgate (Adelaide) street and New (Nelson) street. North of it was a vacant space, all of which had been reserved for the Central School; but, it having been found that there was quite sufficient room on the reservation to place the District School-house, it was resolved to move the old building from the western centre of the square and place it at the south-west corner of March (Lombard) and New streets. This was resolved upon in August, 1829, and the contract was awarded to Mr. John Cuthbert, for the sum of £64. The work was superintended by Mr. Wilcox, a builder, an American, who was working for Messrs. Thomas Helliwell & Brothers, and who undertook the task of removing the school building to the north-east corner of the square, at the junction of March, or Lombard, and New streets. The contract was not a light one, and Mr. Thomas Helliwell, now of Highland Creek, tells the writer with gusto how well he remembers driving up with Wilcox every morning from the Don, while the contract was in progress. Finally the work was accomplished. The position of the building was retained, the east and north sides being brought within a few feet of the corner, with space enough to permit the erection of a six foot close-board fence, which protected the lower windows from the mob of urchins that have, even to this day, retained a preceptive right over that particular locality.

Prior to this move the Board had considered the question of laying out Russell Square. It was resolved that the College and buildings should be placed on a line with King Street, one hundred and thirty-two feet from the street, and with this idea the foundations were laid, the period for the completion of the College being considered the 1st January, 1830, and for the dwelling-houses 1st September, 1830.

In the meantime, the work of selecting masters had progressed. Mr. J. P. de la Haye, who had been appointed French master, was the first to arrive, and was duly introduced to the Board by the Governor, who presided at a meeting held in September, 1829.

Sir John Colborne also handed in a memorandum, with regard to the action of the authorities at Oxford, to this effect :—

"The Vice-Chancellor of Oxford, the Rev. C. Stocker, late Principal of Elizabeth College ; the Rev. C. Young, one of the masters at Eton College, met in July last at Oxford for the purpose of examining the testimonials of candidates for the headship of Upper Canada College and other appointments at that seminary, and elected the Rev. Dr. Harris, of Clare Hall (5th Wrangler); the Rev. Mr. Dade, of St. John's College, Cambridge (12th Wrangler); Mr. Matthews, of Cambridge (2nd Wrangler); the Rev. Mr. Boulton, of Queen's College, Oxford (2nd class). Mr. de la Haye, for some time employed at the College of Louis le Grand, at Paris and at Vincennes, a native of France and an experienced instructor, is appointed French master, and Mr. Drury, an eminent artist, drawing-master.

"As the whole of the masters may be expected at York early in November, it is very desirable, in preparing for their reception, that every exertion should be made to enable them to open the school as soon as possible after their arrival. With this view, the present school-room should be repaired and fitted up immediately, in such a manner as will afford a class-room for each department.

"Much advantage would arise from all the masters connected with the institution being accommodated in the new buildings, and from their being encouraged to take boarders at a low rate."

It was also decided "to prepare for publication a scheme of the College of Upper Canada, fixing the commencement for January, 1830."

The District School-house had, in the meantime, been moved, repainted and improved, and fitted up for the accommodation of the new college, pending the completion of the new edifice. The third week in December saw the furniture in position in the old District School-house, and on the 17th December, 1829, the *Upper Canada Gazette* contained the following announcement:—"Upper Canada College established at York. Visitor, the Lieutenant-Governor for the time being. This college will open after the approaching Christmas vacation, on Monday, the 8th January, 1830, under the conduct of the masters appointed at Oxford by the Vice-Chancellor and other electors in July last. Principal, the Rev. J. H. Harris, D. D., late Fellow of Clare Hall, Cambridge. Classical Department.—Vice-Principal, the Rev. T. Phillips, D.D., of Queen's College, Cambridge; First Classical Master, the Rev. Charles Matthews, M.A., of Pembroke Hall, Cambridge; Second Classical Master, the Rev. W. Boulton, B.A., of Queen's College, Oxford. Mathematical Department. The Rev. Charles Dade, M.A., Fellow of Caius College, Cambridge, and late Mathematical Master of Elizabeth College. French.—Mr. J. P. de la Haye. English, Writing and Arithmetic.—Mr. G. A. Barber and Mr. J. Padfield. Drawing Master.—Mr. Drury. (Then follow terms, etc.) Signed: G. H. Markland, Secretary of the Board of Education. York, Upper Canada, December 2, 1829."

The contractor for the new College had, however, undertaken a work that he could not accomplish, and, accordingly, the work was taken out of his hands and finished under the superintendence of officials appointed by the Governor.

The College classes were, at this period, in the meantime carried on in the old District School until 1831, when the entire staff was removed, with the pupils, to the time-honoured pile on King street west. The Grammar School was then closed, and although on the 2nd May, 1831, it was ordered by the Board that "the District Grammar School should be put in a fit state of repair for the accommodation of the Central School," it does not appear to have been done. We find that in July, 1832, the Roman Catholic Bishop requested "the use of the old school-house for Catholic children, until one, which is being built, can be finished," but the request was not complied with, as it had been represented by Mr. Spragge to be absolutely necessary for the children of the Central School. Whatever may have been the requirements, the school was not used for some years. The Central, which had been built about 1826-27, had its location in the southern part of the lot, the north-east corner of Adelaide and Nelson streets, and the removal of the District Grammar School, its staff, pupils, and even its janitor, made Upper Canada College the direct and only successor, the heir to all the glory and prestige of the noted Home District School of George O'Kill Stuart, the District School of the Rev. Dr. Strachan, so well known, even to the men of to-day, as the Old Blue School.

Some years afterwards, in 1836, after an agitation on the part of the inhabitants, who desired a school in the eastern part of the city, the building known as the Home District School, was again occupied for school purposes, under Mr. Charles Cozens, who was appointed headmaster. In 1838 Mr. Cozens received an appointment as resident master of Upper Canada College boarding-house, and Mr. M. C. Crombie succeeded to the vacant position.

The following notice in the *British Colonist* of 1st November, 1838, reads :

HOME DISTRICT SCHOOL.

In consequence of the appointment to a situation in Upper Canada College of Mr. Cozens, the late master of this school, applications will be received from candidates for the mastership thus made vacant, till Saturday, 1st December next.

Testimonials are to be addressed to the Honourable and Venerable Archdeacon Strachan, Toronto.

A salary of £100, Halifax currency, per annum, is attached to the situation.

And at a later date, on the 10th January, 1839, we find a paragraph to the effect that "the Home District Grammar School was reopened on Thursday, 10th January, 1839, at the District School-house, under the superintendence of M. C. Crombie, Principal."

This is the story of the Old Blue School.

THE JANITORS OF THE COLLEGE.

THE ALDERDICES, FATHER AND SON — OLD SAM, OF '32 TO '49, AND
YOUNG DAVY OF '49 TO '67 — THE JANITORS OF THE
OLD BLUE SCHOOL AND MODERN COLLEGE.

BY J. ROSS ROBERTSON.

BEADLES in the universities of the Old and New Worlds, and janitors in the great schools of England and America are generally well-known characters to the students. To the boys of Upper Canada College none could be better known than the two Alderdices—father and son —who for nigh half-a-century, with broom and duster, kept the floors, benches and the chipped and carved desks free from the dust that, as a consequence, gathered when the young colts of the modern city kicked what they could of the early York mud from their shoes and carried the remainder into the dozen class-rooms of Upper Canada College. Indeed, the janitor of to-day would be dumb with horror if his life ran on the lines of the servitor of sixty years ago. Whatever may be said of the modern causeway, whether of wood, stone, or asphalt, the pavements of the young metropolis were laid with a scrupulous desire to economize material. Possibly, too, the boys were somewhat indifferent. Between short cuts from home, in the eagerness to be on hand for the roll-call, and trampling on the ungravelled soil, which bounded the grounds of the College, they managed to bring into the class-room more of that real estate which is now so valuable in Toronto than was, at that period, yearned for by him whose face and form were familiar both within and without the College fence.

How pleasant it was for the writer, a lad of the days of 1849, '50, to commune with the grey-haired sire of 1829, '30, and to chat with one of the old boys, whose eyes sparkle as he is reminded of school days and the familiar name of the old caretaker. Old Samuel Alderdice! What a host of half-forgotten memories of the College spring into life again with his well-remembered name! Before the mind's eye rises a two-storeyed, red brick building, of many windows, with spacious, sanded porch, a miniature belfry peeping over to the roof, right and left, detached houses of reddish brick, fronted with little gardens, fenced, redolent with roses and honey-suckle, and an occasional sunflower, interspersed with shrubs and trees, the background to the two velvet lawns which, divided by a great gravel walk, led from the main building to the principal street in early York. This was Upper Canada College. This was the fountain of learning, at which some of the bright boys and most distinguished of Canada's sons first drank in the inspiration which has since guided them to high places in the history of their country.

Old Father Alderdice! With rounded shoulders, and stooped form, bent down with age, clad in a faded but well-brushed brown coat, his long gray locks escaping below his high hat, his quick but infirm step, his bunch of keys in hand, he remains as distinct a picture to the boy-student of that time as the venerable College itself. Was it not his hand that rung the "accursed bell" which summoned trembling souls, conscious of unprepared lessons, to the presence of the masters? And was it not he who pealed forth the joyous sounds that freed the lads from bondage and sent them home to play and liberty? Can we ever forget him—that warm-hearted old man, who looked upon all boys as under his special care?

Old Samuel Alderdice was, in truth, a celebrity. The masters respected the old man and the boys revered him. Indeed, Sam had a kind heart for all lads who were, as he would say, "not downright bad." He knew that boys would be boys, and made due allowance even if legitimate pastimes occasionally exceeded the bounds of decorum. Then he had grown up with the school from its foundation in the Old Blue School and before removal to the King street structure. He felt therefore as if he held not only the building but the boys in perpetuity until at last the youths bowed a final farewell to the four walls of that historic piece of ancient architecture.

Samuel was an Irishman by birth. His character was strong, and he deemed his duty, as the guardian of the College, as essential to a happy existence as was his daily bread. He first saw the sunlight in the town of Armagh, Ireland, just when the war cloud darkened the empire in the gloomy days of 1774. In youth he had a short probation at a local school, where knowledge was engrafted on the youthful mind by a brusque old pedagogue, who swore that he had "fought with the army in Flanders," and who, in lieu of mask and foil, for he was an expert fencer, displayed his athletic skill by handling his ruler as a drum major would his baton, bringing it down with a touch on a boy's knuckles that made even the hard-fisted son of an Irishman groan. Sam never forgot the merciless manner in which he was pounded, and, as hourly and daily he met the boys, he tried to be the antithesis of his old master in the marble-paved town of the Green Isle.

The senior Alderdice, the father of Samuel, was a joiner by trade, and Sam, of whom we write, graduated from school and as time progressed developed into a full-fledged mechanic, who could push a plane and use the tools with a deftness that was creditable to his parent's teaching.

The field for employment in the old land was then, as now, limited, and the son yearned for a sight of the new world. With enough saved from his earnings to pay a passage to America, a few sovereigns and a godspeed to cheer him, he said good-bye to the old folks at home. He and his family journeyed to Belfast and after being buffeted on the Atlantic for nearly six weeks he saw the flag flying from the citadel of Quebec late in the summer of 1822. With a light heart Samuel Alderdice stepped ashore cheerfully, into the dawn of a strange life, with bright hopes of happiness in the new and promised land. His wife, a thrifty and tidy matron, of Irish Presbyterian stock, was with him, and four children, Robert, Samuel, William, and a young daughter named Sarah, or as the boys used to call her, "Sallie." The oldest boy was about twenty, while the others ranged between ten and fifteen. Davy, the fifth child, of whom more hereafter, the only Canadian of the lot, had not appeared upon the scene. The family lived for about three years in Montreal before they sought their home in the west.

Samuel, the janitor, in whom we are more particularly interested, was a central figure in College life, as well-known and as well-liked by the boys, better, perhaps, than some who were high in authority in the building. He began life in Upper Canada as the janitor of the Old Blue School. Other pages of this volume tell of the organization of the College classes in the Old Blue or Home District School, on the corner of Nelson (Jarvis) and March, afterwards Lombard, streets. Alderdice was well up in years when he first arrived in Toronto, and here it is that we have the first full view of the good old fellow whose portrait, taken, of course, when he had almost filled the allotted span, graces this volume. To the boys who saw the closing days of the old District Grammar School and the first decade of College life, Samuel seemed a fairly active man. He was the janitor who, from about 1831, had charge of the Old Blue School, a structure erected to encourage mental activity in the youth of early York, and who, with some of the masters, migrated to the King street edifice when it was finished in 1831. The portrait given is the veritable visage of the old guardian. It is an excellent likeness, and scarce needs the aid of pen to tell his story. Alderdice's face was that of the typical Irishman of northern birth, a man of medium frame—not large, but broad-shouldered, long-armed, and one who, in early years, must have been active and powerful. His head drooped as would a full stalk of grain, and, in the days of 1830-40, was covered with greyish hair, mingled with black, kept neatly brushed, even if it did lie loosely on the collar of his Sunday coat, a garment of bluish cloth which, with its velvet collar, was the product of an Armagh tailor anxious to have his old friend carry old-world fashions across the sea.

The janitor's face was emblematic of good nature, and his nose, sharp and yet prominent, was, so to speak, guarded by two thin lines of whiskers, which in colour matched his hair, and seemed to strengthen those two little bright grey orbs of his which beamed with kindness, and yet were so keen that wayward boys would oft declare that Sam could "see around the corner, or through a college door." His voice was one to be remembered— not harsh, but sharp, and yet guttural, a marked dialect, not of uncertain sound, but sometimes of a high treble, vigorous and decided, with variations of tone suited to the particular occasion that called his lung power into exercise. If a boy shied chestnuts from the head of the stair-landing at some victim at the foot of the staircase, Sam's wrathful bass voice, in vigorous, sharp and decided North of Ireland accents, pursued him at express train speed. If, on the contrary, "a young man conduct himself as a young gentleman should," Sam was sympathetic and kindly. At noon orders were always given that the class-rooms should be locked, but boys who lived at a distance and who wanted to enjoy their lunch in comfort, either waited in the rooms until the masters had gone, stuck a piece of wood under the door latch, so that it would not fall when the door was closed, or, as a last resort, would vault into an empty wood-box and watch the master close the door. Sam sometimes was suspicious, and on more than one occasion was up to the trick, and in his sharp Celtic tones insisted that "Yez must open the dure," or there would be trouble. He looked about the same all the year round, never older nor younger, methodical in his habits, quick and pleasant in his actions. His style of dress did not change with the fashions. A long, brown frock coat, a vest to match, a pair of grey trousers, and a high silk hat of antique vintage, composed the principal items in his attire, as he marched along the street, swinging his arm, either on an errand for the Principal, or, perhaps, to bring from Rowsell's book-store a bunch of canes made of wicked bamboo, and designed by Providence for the hands of cross-grained boys.

The old janitor, when in the building, ever had his hands in his pockets, a habit acquired perhaps from carrying a bunch of keys, which were always on his person, and which he oftentimes jingled, as he ambled from hall to room, or stopped to answer the query of some youth who bothered him with useless questions. He said that he always went on the principle of "Speak when you are spoken to; go when you are called," and while unobtrusive and obliging, never was very chatty with the boys. His day, from sunrise to sunset, was an ever-moving panorama of work, and not a moment was wasted. His thumb touched the College latch at half-past six in the summer and seven in the winter, and in about an hour he had the rooms aired, the fires lighted, the class-rooms dusted, after which he yielded twenty minutes to breakfast, and returning opened a box which ran half-way up to the ceiling in the north end of the main hall of the College, in which was kept the bell rope from the prying hands of playful boys, and at fifteen minutes past eight the air echoed with an invitation to College to half-sleepy youths, who groaned as angered fathers or doting mothers called them to the matutinal meal, with its proverbial *menu* of porridge and milk. The sound of the second bell, at twenty minutes to nine, which seemed to be heard in every house, had scarce died away when the door of the Principal's room would open and Dr. Harris and, at a later date, Dr. McCaul or Mr. Barron, would march across the end of the hall through the north door of the prayer room or public hall, followed by the masters who, bowing to the Principal as they took their seats, faced the boys seated on the east and west of the hall, waiting for the monitors to call the roll. Sam generally stood with hands folded, as if at ease, within the shadow of the doorway, undisturbed by the "tramp, tramp" of the boys, as they crowded around the doors of the class-rooms, waiting for the masters to emerge from the public hall. Then he followed the Principal—who, by the way, always called the janitor "Allerdice"—into his inner room, and behind that red baize door, noted in his mind the orders and messages for the day, and then with a respectful "Good morning, sir," retired.

Old Sam did not remove his household goods when the College first opened on Russell Square. The main buildings were the first erected, along with four large, double houses for the masters, while the little cottage at the west end of the ground was not framed until about 1832, a year or so after the classes had left the Nelson street building, where the old man lived. Robert, his son, had struck out for himself, but William, Sam, and Sarah were under the parental roof, with a baby boy named Davy, who, born in 1832, in the old rooms at the east end, was tenderly and carefully wrapped in a heavy blanket, and carried by the old man to his new home in the College grounds. Sam and Sally were old enough to help their father, and, years afterwards, when Davy became big enough to assist, his elder brother learned his trade as an engineer, and turned the water of Toronto off and on at the old Furniss Works at the foot of Peter street. The janitor always basked in the smiles of the masters. He was so obliging and attentive that none could find fault. In winter his work was heavy. In those days the stoves were all made for wood burning, and the task of bringing in the wood, building the fires in the open fireplaces of the classrooms and in the big box stoves of the upper and lower halls, kept all his muscles in motion. As coal was not used, Sam, when he had to light a new fire, brought live coals in a covered sheet iron pan or shovel, which he carried about as carefully as if it were a child. "De yez mind, now?" and "Whisht, now whisht" were favourite expressions of his. His gait was as uniform as his temper. He never moved faster than a walk, except, perhaps, when the boys in winter would catch him at a disadvantage as he walked between the College and his cottage, and was good-naturedly snowballed into his own door by urchins daring enough to serve a bishop as they would the old janitor. His wife enjoyed the fun herself, as she met her better-half at the door and knocked the snow off his coat. The life-partner of the veteran caretaker was a woman small in stature, with a very pleasant face, showing that old Sam's taste, when he selected her for a helpmeet, had not been far astray. She was, as the old boys say, "very jolly," with enough knowledge of the economies of household life to make her husband comfortable. An excellent mother, she trained her family in the path of right and duty, and in her daily life realized that where her home was there she was happy. The old dame had a noted recipe for making potato cake, and it is said that some boys—one of whom is now an ex-Governor—who were her special favourites, were occasionally feasted at the porter's lodge. Mrs. Alderdice could cook fish to perfection, and at frying frogs' legs the old lady excelled. Some of the boys in residence were her particular friends, and the catch of all fishing excursions was invariably cooked at the little cottage. Her youthful friends always remembered her at Christmas, as they did her husband.

A warning, or "first" bell, rang at a quarter-past eight, and then followed the regular twenty minutes to nine peal. When not at this work, or when cleaning and messages were not on the daily programme, Sam carried about the absentee book, which recorded the names of missing boys, and for which duty he cared as little as did his son who succeeded him in after years. However, it was duty first with the old man, and while the masters were inditing the names of those who had not seized the opportunity for knowledge on that particular day, Sam would make up the fire in the room, sweep up the ashes, and then carry away the absentee book in one hand, and in the other a shovel full of coals to replenish some distant fire that was languishing in another class-room. Through some unaccountable means, on one occasion, the woodwork in Mr. J. G. Howard's room, in the front of the College, became ignited, and considerable damage was done. How the room caught fire was always the mystery of the janitor's life. Our old friend "Nobody" was there, as he always is in every house in the land where mischievous boys, in vacation hours, keep the family circle in a constant state of terror.

The College bell did not grace its belfry until some months after the opening, and perhaps the first to hear its notes was a boy who is as loyal as ever to the old school, no less a person than the Hon. John Beverley Robinson, who, with boyish curiosity, climbed up the slim ladder, and, crawling along the rafters, saw the men at work placing "the big bell," as the boys used to call it, in position in its picturesque turret. He gave it the first swing, and it has been swinging and ringing for sixty years. Every boy had not a tug at it, for Sam regarded it as a peculiar honour, and those who had the privilege, if they jerked the rope or varied the regular monotony of the peal, would soon bring the old man in haste to the rope, with "Whisht, now, whisht, now! Stop, didn't I tell yez?"

The old man would stand not a little torment, but to quicken the tones of the bell was an offence that roused him. He good-naturedly avenged himself with the aid of a cane, which he kept in the box that enclosed the bell rope, and made a raid upon the offending boy, who, perhaps, had jumped the bannister and disappeared down the stair-case while the janitor was getting the surroundings in his mind. But his good-nature was not always proof against ingratitude, and the base betrayal of his confidence. A great delight was to have a pull at the bell, and to obtain the coveted permission, any amount of youthful eloquence, worthy of a better cause, was put forth. Then the old man, with many cautions, would place the bell rope in the boy's hands. This was eagerly seized, and was generally pulled with due moderation and discretion. But there were evil-disposed boys, whose hearts, as the Indians say, were "bad." They would give a few rings as all properly constituted College bells should be rung, and then would come a pull that turned the old bell completely over, and so complicated the internal anatomy of the belfry that no after-persuasion could elicit any sound from it but a kind of grunt. This indeed angered the old janitor and shadowed, for a time, his otherwise cheerful existence.

The most vigorous peal the old bell ever rang out was when John Powell, afterwards Mayor of Toronto, an hour or two after midnight, on 4th December, 1837, roused old Sam to alarm the town, in the fear that

Mackenzie and his men would, before dawn, have the city in their grasp. The old man made the wheel whirl round, and, in half-an-hour, had every inhabitant in the neighbourhood, masters included, up and buckling on their armour.

Once the old janitor did come in for a shake-up by a pupil. For two or three years after the opening of the College, there was only one ringing of the morning bell, and that at twenty minutes to nine. One day, however, without notifying the boys, Principal Harris, who occupied the eastern resident master's building, and kept half-a-dozen boarders, gave orders to Alderdice to ring a preparatory or warning bell, at a quarter before eight. This roused everyone within its sound. The boarders, with fleet foot, rushed to the main building, and one William McNider, a pupil from Montreal, and the oldest and tallest boy in the College, who had been having a before-breakfast struggle with an intricate Latin exercise, was particularly wrathy. He bounded up the well-worn stairway in his shirt sleeves, and as he landed at the top he threw one eye on the big clock in the upper hall, and another at Alderdice, and taking the old man by the collar of his brown coat, shook the tall hat off his head exclaiming, "You old rascal! Only half-past seven and you frighten us in this way, half-an-hour before the time—breakfast all spoilt—I'll pay you for this." "Whisht now, whisht now," said the old man, "the Principal tould me to do it, and yez ought to know it yoursel, living as ye do, at the same place, so yez ought." McNider was furious, and was about to grapple with him again when the old man's Irish blood commenced to boil, and in his sharp-keyed voice he faced the youth, and declared: "If yez don't make off, or dar to touch me again I'll bet ye feel the weight of these keys, me bye," brandishing as he spoke the large bunch, with its iron ring, in McNider's face. The angry youth seeing trouble ahead dashed down the stairway to master his lesson and finish his breakfast.

The Hon. John Beverley Robinson, who relates with relish this story, was a College boy at the time, and came on the scene just as McNider was pouring his wrath upon the old janitor. The old fellow often told the tale himself, and enjoyed a good laugh over it, twinkling his small bright eyes as he described how he whipped out his keys and "saw me young gintlemen skip down the stair."

Undisturbed by the hopes and disappointments of a larger ambition, Alderdice day by day faithfully discharged the simple duties of his office, and lived a contented and even life. His character was not chequered by the lights and shades of eccentricity. The boys all loved and respected the kind-hearted old janitor, and recall the early days with pleasure, when the snows of many winters are falling heavily upon the brows of the lads who saw the dawning days of College life.

Let us look at the old soul as in the years of long ago. It is four o'clock. The bell has toned the closing hour. From the class-room doors a host of joyous boys rush to the large prayer room to take their seats. The roll is called, the clear and melodious voice of Dr. Scadding has offered up prayer, and the fiat of dismissal has gone forth. Down the stair-case troop the pupils with shouts that make the long halls echo and re-echo. The happy youngsters speed for home or playground. The old janitor plies his broom till nigh sundown. The day is closing. The black-gowned masters have disappeared. The front of the building is quite deserted, save for one bent figure, outlined against the porch. The right foot is on the highest step, the left on the next below, one hand holds the latch, the other is turning the key. It is old Samuel Alderdice, performing the last office of the day, locking the doors of the College, preparatory to his return to his little home by the piney woods. The janitor was not only popular with the boys but with the public in general. He was well-known all over Toronto. On one occasion when the Hon. John Cameron was appointed Solicitor-General of the Province, a banquet was tendered him at Government House, which was unoccupied during the summer; a large number of the old boys were among the guests, and old Samuel making his appearance was given a place in the room at a small table, where he not only enjoyed his dinner, but the feast of eloquence which accompanied it.

After 1845, Alderdice began to feel the effects of long service. His rounded shoulders and enfeebled frame—for he then had passed threescore and ten—indicated that his health was failing. Sam, his son, had left the parental roof, and David, his youngest boy, helped him to carry wood and ply the broom. Three years rolled on. The heavy work was done by Davy, who had learned his trade as a carpenter in McBean & Withrow's shop on Adelaide street, near Yonge, but who gave up his trade when he became his father's helper. When the leaves in the College ground began to turn in the autumn of 1849, the faithful father and keeper saw that the shadows were deepening around him. He had seen the sunshine of summers and the snows of winters for nigh fourscore years, and firm in a belief in the Promise, surrounded by his wife and children, as the old bell chimed the close of the College day, as if at evening, the old man passed away, and, followed by the boys he loved so well, and who truly mourned his loss, he was gathered to the last rest of all. His grave is marked by an obelisk of stone, surmounted by gown and keys, within sight of the little

church in the Cemetery of St. James, telling the visitor that it is a testimonial :—

TO THE MEMORY OF SAMUEL ALDERDICE,
DURING TWENTY YEARS THE PATIENT AND FAITHFUL PORTER OF
UPPER CANADA COLLEGE.
HE WAS BORN AT ARMAGH, IN THE KINGDOM OF IRELAND,
AND DIED AT UPPER CANADA COLLEGE
9TH OCTOBER, 1849, AGED SEVENTY-FIVE YEARS.
ERECTED BY THE PUPILS AND EX-PUPILS OF UPPER CANADA COLLEGE.

But who does not remember "Davy" Alderdice, the janitor of the fifties and sixties of College life, "the son of his father," the youngest hopeful of the stooped old man, whose memorial in that hallowed acre of the dead—the Cemetery of St. James—was the tribute of boys and youths, who, from the opening of the College, had deep regard for the old janitor? No, it was not the venerable porter, whose story has been told, but the youngster of twenty, who, when an infant in 1831, had been carried by his father, rolled up in a blanket, to the College residence, and who, when his father had gone to the "narrow house and the long sleep," stepped into the old man's shoes and donned the toga that graced the shoulders of him who made music in the air with the old bell that at twenty minutes to nine ushered in the College day and called many a willing and unwilling pupil to Russell Square to enjoy or endure the daily task of wresting knowledge from the bagful of books which fond parents had provided.

Davy was a quaint piece of human mechanism. His life was not to him a burden; indeed, many thought it lay in pleasant lines. His cosy cottage stood, as in the picture, close by the boarding-house gate, a neat and tidy example of pioneer architecture, clap-boarded and primitive enough in its style, and yet, by the aid of nature, made pleasant to the sight of all boys whose ideas of architecture had not sought higher flights under the skilful guidance of J. G. Howard. The gravel roadway and narrow wooden pathway that led to the boarding-house ran past Davy's habitation, and when the long, black hands of the family clock, which, twenty years before, was a Christmas gift to Alderdice, senior, touched the hour of seven, Davy, with his well-blacked "T. D."—his solace after the evening meal—would leisurely saunter out, and, bringing the big gates together with a satisfied air, as if he were the warder of a castle, drop the bar into its iron sockets, shoot the bolt that held the smaller side gate, turn the key in the heavy padlock, and return to his cottage, as one who had done his whole duty. In summer time, the little cottage just nestled in roses, and the wreaths of vines, which gracefully folded their tendrils around the front door, made the drab-painted home of the porter slightly picturesque.

Davy's personal popularity was exceptional. His character was an admixture of good nature, tempered with a show of humour, a tolerable amount of practical, every-day common sense, such as the descendant of a North of Ireland "mon" might justly claim. His whole mental system was tinged with a general desire to be friendly with all, save those "imps of Satan," who either "turned the bell, and threw the rope off the wheel," or "knocked down the piles of cordwood" that flanked the Adelaide street entrance to the school, or, what was in his eyes the unpardonable sin, of "stealing the absentee book," which, on one occasion, was mysteriously transferred to his own home, and placed under his own pillow, by one who now works in Christian fields, and sermonizes with eloquence in "Talks to Young Men on the Follies of Youth." This last-named crime—for, with Davy, it was the crime of crimes—led to his being the principal figure in a walking match, for he searched every room, and even climbed the long, steep ladder that led to the belfry. On a previous occasion the book had taken wings and flown to a refuge alongside the old bell. An old schoolmate—the rival journalist of the writer's College days—E. H. Tiffany, reminds the writer that on one occasion while passing through the avenue on the west side of the plot in front of the College buildings, he saw a man a short distance from him striking the air and jumping about in a most extraordinary manner. On coming up to him he found it was Davy, who had been attacked by a swarm of bees. They had settled on him, and stung him on the face, head, neck and arms. He was taken to his home and was laid up several days as the result of his encounter.

Alderdice, when he assumed the reins of power—and he was a power, too—was in his eighteenth year, and an active and persistent worker, whose broom, as it sped over the floor after school hours, made the dust fly. He was an artist in sweeping. He could cover more square feet in a minute than any janitor of modern times in an hour. Before the boys had swarmed out of the prayer room Davy had at least two of the class-rooms in half decent condition, and his temper was never known to fill the void of the apartment save on one occasion, when a lad whom Davy had reported for appropriating the key of the old clock in the upper hall and setting the hands forward ten minutes, revenged himself by colouring the contents of the water can with dregs of ink from the glass bottles which graced the pine desks in the room of Mr. Thompson, the writing-master.

Then Davy fairly foamed, not viciously, but with a deep-hearted wish that he could get his massive hand anywhere within reach of the youth who had sought this method of revenge. The janitor's wrath, however, was not long cherished. His evening meal and the enjoyment of his pipe were harbingers of peace, and when he sought his pillow his anger lapsed into a feeling of forgiveness, with a mental reservation that possibly indisputable evidence as to the guilty one might provoke a gentle reminder of the game that had been played upon him.

The absentee book was the bane of the boys. It held the names of absentees, and every hour Davy sauntered around and as regularly did the names of the absent boys go down. In the morning round Davy would walk up to the desk of the master, in the afternoon he would stand within the doorway and call out "all present," wait for a reply and retire. This was the only duty for which Davy did not thirst. It was dull, monotonous and objectionable—it seemed like giving his boy-friends away. It was the black book which told fond mothers and indulgent fathers that their progeny had not filled the allotted hours in the class-room, and it led, on one occasion, to a misdemeanour that, somehow or other, got Davy into trouble, and the boys also. It has been said that sometimes Davy's favourites were not marked down, that apparent forgetfulness to click the latch of the class-room, and walk to the master's desk with the book, was more design than accident, and one of the liveliest scenes ever enacted in the building was when it was found that in one of the upper forms, the rounds of the porter had been honoured in the breach rather than in the observance. The paternal sovereign of a household had occasion to visit the College on a matter of business, and, after satisfactorily transacting it, asked the kind-hearted Barron to show him the class-rooms of three youthful scions of his house, and guided by the College "board," which hung in the hall, indicating the subjects and time of study, the classes were visited. A twelve-year-old colt, in the Preparatory was found in the writing room, caught red handed, just as he had finished carving his name in the long pine desk, with one of his fingers blackened with ink, endeavouring to cover up traces of his work in the art of carving, and for which he paid the penalty by writing out that favourite headline, "Evil Communications Corrupt Good Manners," one hundred times. The other rooms were visited, but the familiar faces of the two remaining striplings did not greet the father's eye. How could they? Enquiry proved that, instead of "pushing pencils" in Mr. Howard's room the youths were down at Mrs. Masterson's, at the foot of Bay street, busily engaged in painting a skiff, that had been bought in a trade, or rather exchanged for half-a-hundred pigeons, that the bargainer was anxious to get rid of. This brought Davy into the throes of dispute, but he cleverly extricated himself, by reminding the Principal that he had been three times that week on messages to the University, and that, as a natural consequence, he could not be "here and there at the same time." This saved the porter, but the boys suffered.

Impositions, in those days, were varied in character. Some masters, especially Dr. Barrett, favoured the Scriptures. Others thought that the second book of the Æneid was more appropriate for purposes of punishment, so that many a lad passed weary hours in covering foolscap with "The Book of Proverbs," or "The Song of Solomon," "so many timely texts for boys," as Dr. Barrett would say, or the second book of Anthon's Virgil, as another master would direct. These impositions were dreaded with a horror that pen cannot express. The writer recalls penning twenty pages of Lucian for the simple offence of being one of five who, quite accidentally, dropped the contents of a cayenne pepper bottle on the long box stove which ornamented the centre of the prayer room.

This, however, is a departure from the story. No one sympathized with the boys in their troubles more than Davy, and he has been known to help many a poor unfortunate by getting others to aid in inditing the manifesto of misery. A thoughtful boy once suggested that, when a chapter had to be written out twenty times, the first and last sheets would look well in the handwriting of the delinquent, while the intervening pages might be the work of sympathizers, who could make a fair imitation of the caligraphy of the martyr to College law. A victim, who was reminded that copying out the Book of Genesis would add to his store of knowledge called for volunteers, of which the writer was one, and, with their help, completed his task in an amazingly quick time. An obdurate master was, struck with the pleasing variety in the handwriting and observed:

"Your hand varies a good deal."

"Does it, sir?" replied the unabashed boy, "it must be a difference in the pens."

"Well," his heartless oppressor retorted, "you had better write this out again with one pen." Davy often regretted that he was not gifted in the writing art, for, said he, "Boys, you know, I could earn many a dollar."

The red-letter days in Davy's life were two in each year. To a certain extent he recognized the fact that pleasure is the confectionery of life, and that Christmas Day was one that made his pockets jingle with coin. His good nature was refreshing in December, and of the two hundred—yes, three hundred—pupils who surged out of the hall and class-room few indeed forgot "a quarter for Davy." It was the balm of Gilead for Alderdice. When December was welcomed, whether in snow or rain, Davy wore one continuous smile. The boys might have torn down the building, taken the tongue out of the quick, clappered bell, strewn the floor with haws and chestnuts from the grove, and Davy would never have murmured, for the fifty or sixty dollars, added to the not extravagant wage from the bursar, bought many a luxury, and enabled Davy to enjoy his mug of ale and whiff the air with a brand of tobacco that would be the envy of a veteran of the pipe.

Another day dear to Davy was the "Twelfth of July." While not bigoted Davy felt that when William landed on English soil at Torbay, he was guided by the hand of a special Providence. As for the victory at Drogheda on the Boyne, in Davy's opinion no struggle of ancient or modern times should be classed in the same chapter, and when the boys, knowing his predilections, would refer to Marathon, Thermopylæ, or even Waterloo, Davy would shake his head, and venture the remark that if he had the selection of the subjects in history he would make the boys learn the story of the fight on the Boyne by heart, and thus try to instil it into the minds of youths, who enjoyed the day more for the music and the procession, than for the memories it served to brighten in those from the Emerald Isle, who, like Davy, enjoyed the parade. Fortunately for him, his favourite pleasure day hit the calendar in the summer holidays, and thus he had full and free scope for his enjoyment. The Toronto boys, as they watched the procession, were not long in singling out the old porter, as, with his black silk hat, that had seen many a Twelfth, his breast ornamented with a broad band of orange and blue ribbon, he kept step to the tune of "Rise, Sons of William, Rise," or "The Protestant Boys," with his brethren of No. 301.

Alderdice retained his post for nearly twenty years, and then his health began to fail. The seeds of consumption, whether by heredity or neglect, were visible early in the sixties. His health had so far given out that an assistant, who did the heavy work, had to be called in. Years before, the little cottage by the grove had been dismantled, and in 1861 the brick lodge by the north gate was built. Davy, in November, 1852, had married a comely, frugal wife, one Mary Ann Anderson, had a family grown up, and the new home was commodious and more comfortable than the nest where he with his father had lived so long. It was here that he died. It was in midwinter. The boarding-house was closed, and many of the masters and day scholars were in the country for vacation. Few knew of Davy's death till the sods had covered his grave. The masters, with Principal Cockburn, followed the remains, and, with the writer, made up the procession that, on a bright winter afternoon, which followed the New Year's Day of 1867, wended its way from the porter's lodge to the Cemetery of St. James, where, within the shadow of the shaft of granite erected to the memory of his father and predecessor, another grave was opened to receive the remains of a faithful fellow, whose memory will be for ever green in the hearts of the boys, who thought kindly of him who, for nigh an ordinary lifetime, had called them from the belfry to the lessons of the day.

From 1867 until 1870 one James Marshall and others handled the broom along the corridors of the College. While, however, they did their work efficiently and to the satisfaction of the authorities, none of them could see as deep down into the hearts, or, for that matter, into the pockets of the boys as the janitors of the bygone days, who had endeared themselves to the youthful collegians by many acts of kindness that were well remembered at Christmas time, when the traditional quarter-dollar, the shilling of our ancestors, made peace for past offences. Of all those who followed the Alderdices, while they could use the broom, somehow none seemed to grasp the idea that boys were human, that if they did turn the bell, water the ink, or hide the broom, such acts were part and parcel of the *menu* of boy-life, dishes not exactly ready but "extra, if not on the bill of fare," and without the "fifteen minutes to wait for cooking." No, fifteen seconds were sufficient in some cases to half craze a janitor, who would walk into a master's room, and, as he swept the watering-pot around his manly form, find that, instead of the floor being covered by *aqua* Ontario, it was *aqua collegio*, a pigment that was scarcely up to the standard of a civic health officer.

There are janitors and janitors, and while the actual duties pertaining to the office were few, yet tradition supported the belief in the minds of the boys who had just entered College that if there was a gold medal for a janitor, to secure it the examination paper would be so stiff that unless the candidate possessed exceptional abilities, he might pass as a good all-round, go-as-you-please janitor, but it would require a high standard of excellence to come up to the mark of the Alderdices, whose names were endeared to thousands of the old pupils.

The dawn of 1870, however, brought with it one who is now well-known to College fame, one who had not only a civil but a military history, a brave fellow who, in an old town in England, in 1860, was so charmed with the gay colours of the enlisting sergeant that, with Her Majesty's shilling in hand, he inscribed his name on the muster roll of the Fourth Brigade of the Royal Artillery, and for ten years at garrison towns, such as Aldershot and Woolwich in England, Kilkenny in Ireland, and Quebec in Canada, spent the noonday of his life in soldierly activity.

My friend, Mr. Leacock, an old boy, and now a popular master, remembering the advent of this favourite janitor, writes :—

"Those of us who are old College boys of the last two decades remember well the mental shock that we received long ago when we first scanned the list of dignitaries in the College circular, and found, under the heading 'Janitor and Messenger,' the ambiguous word 'Frost.' The bitter disappointment at finding our half-hatched witticism ruined by the Christian name of George, probably remains in our minds. Nor less so our delight, on the other hand, when we entered these classic precincts and found the individual in question actually living, breathing and moving, not as we had feared as George, but as 'Jack Frost.' Boys generally entered College at the age when Santa Claus and Jack Frost have hardly faded from real beings into abstract personifications. The anthropotomical tendency of the child's mind asserts itself, and 'George,' the real and baptismal, gives place to 'Jack,' the imaginative. Thus has Providence seen fit to thwart the wishes of George Frost's godfathers and godmothers when they 'stood' for him, and the sobriquet of 'Jack' has clung and will cling to him for life."

If, in the army life of George Frost, he did not have the opportunity of seeing service in the field, he merited the good-will and esteem of superiors, and when his term of service expired in 1870, he was mustered out with not only an unblemished character, but a strong letter of recommendation from his commanding officer, Colonel Williams; for as body servant to the Colonel, Frost had by faithful service made himself indispensable to the comfort of the gentlemen in command of Her Majesty's Fourth Brigade.

If Frost made his mark in military life, as he rode with folded arms and soldierly visage on the box of an artillery waggon, certainly he eclipsed himself from the day he donned the clothing of a civilian and found himself installed in the routine of work, which made him for ever part and parcel of College life. He was without doubt not only "Jack of all trades" but master of many, a genius in a mechanical way, one who accomplished everything that he undertook, and when expert mechanics were baffled, Frost, in his unostentatious and quiet way, rose to the occasion and succeeded where others failed. He was a plumber, carpenter or blacksmith, just as required. He could give a pair of skates just the right edge, adjust a mouth organ out of gear, clean a watch or insert a mainspring, flood a skating rink, or stick type, build a tobogganing slide or tune a piano, clean a rifle or make a mattress, splice a cricket bat, erect a flag pole, in fact, repair anything from the lip steel of a jewsharp to a breakage in the internal economy of a steam engine. Truly he was a wonder in mechanical skill—an obliging fellow, who left no stone unturned in his effort to serve all, from the headmaster down to the small boy in knickerbockers—for in the eyes of the latter Frost was something more than a marvel. If a machine went out of order in the physical department, he was summoned from the humbler pastime of shovelling snow or flooding the rink to adjust it; in the working of electrical apparatus, it was his delight to lay aside the broom, and, with the air of a scientist, give the nerves of the inquisitive youngsters a reminder that, if not a pupil of Edison, he had at least some notion of how that gentleman carried on business. When wind from the west interfered with the ventilating and heating of one of the master's rooms in cold weather, Frost inserted a wooden flue or chamber, which carried the air in and sent the thermometer up many degrees. When the blackboards faded and the colour material was not to be had in the city, Frost compounded a mixture that put all others out of the market. When a small steam engine gave out, and was pronounced by an expert city mechanic, after a day's labour, too far gone to be repaired, Frost's keen eye discovered that the cause of the trouble was the expansion of a pin in the cylinder, which stopped the piston, and when he sheeted the gymnasium, laid a new floor and straightened all the apparatus, a small boy's comment was, "Well, he beats the world." He is as faithful as the needle to the pole. He has no hours and will work eighteen a day if necessary, and loyal as he was and is to the old flag, under which he served, his fidelity to the College is so sincere that, if he had his own way, he would remove every stick and stone—yes, the very sod of the lawn—to Deer Park.

And yet, while Frost is the happy possessor of so many useful faculties, he has a bit of temper which occasionally asserts itself. It is rarely tried, but when the stock of patience which a janitor should possess is exhausted, and the youthful scions step beyond the regulation line, and the tranquillity of janitorial routine is interfered with, the broom of office is thrown aside and the absence of the offender lends enchantment to the view. His conversational powers are excellent, and if the offender has not glided out of sight, he may have a lesson from the book of College Etiquette, edited by Frost, who alone holds "the author's copy."

An old boy once remarked, as he was leaving the Sixth, " What would we do without Frost?" Well might he say so, for to the boys the janitor is like the two-faced god of Rome—an omen at once of joy and sorrow. His duties are too numerous to mention. He smiles, as he brings around the announcement of a special holiday, while his countenance is darkened by sorrow as he leaves in allotted places the bundle of bamboos. He takes pleasure in distributing letters from the post, and the very routine of his functions is so allied to his inner thoughts and life, that he justly regards himself as a human annex of the old school, with which he has been so long identified.

LIFE AT THE BOARDING HOUSE.

EARLY DAYS AT THE RESIDENCE—LEAVES FROM THE MEMORIES OF
OLD BOYS—THE FROLICS AND FANCIES OF THE LADS WHO
SAW THE BEGINNINGS OF COLLEGE LIFE.

BY J. ROSS ROBERTSON.

LET us take a walk through the old boarding-house—not the pile we see to-day, but the wings which ran east and west, the original structure that about 1840 was amplified by a southern extension. Let us, arm-in-arm with one of the boys of 1830-1840, see life as it was in those early days, and, as we chat, recall the scenes of boyhood, the "scraps" in the study when John Kent's eyes were away for an odd quarter of an hour, the memories of tough beefsteaks, and the battles with the city boys, whose domain was strictly defined to be without the old gate that creaked on its hinges at seven p.m. and shut the young saplings of the land of the maple leaf within four walls until another sunrise. Our friend, who refreshes his mind as we sit in one of the old rooms, was one of the lads of 1834-1844—a youth whose good father shipped him from a distant part of Upper Canada, so that he might possibly shine at the bar, on the bench, or in the halls of Parliament—and I wot he has excelled in all three departments of usefulness, and has not yet seen the sere and yellow of old age. He was not a good boy—that is, not a very good boy. Nor was he a bad boy—not real bad—a sort of a cross between Tom Brown and Tom Sawyer, with just enough of Huckleberry Finn thrown in to weary the life of fond parents, who gloried in the thought that the scion of their house would wheel away in a handcart the gilt-edged prizes, or open his pocket-book to receive the twenty odd pounds of Halifax currency for which brainy boys of the fourth form struggled. Would it be fair to deny that there were not within the College walls exemplars in the fine arts of study and deportment? And yet, it goes against an old boy's grain to admit that a youth of the wild stripe could be found in the loved old spot. Our friend was a sort of medium boy, an average all-round youth, such as you could pick up within or without the boarding-house, one who could knock off Latin verses with one eye open, translate at sight the satirical lines of Lucian into decent English, render the stanzas of Horace in every-day speech (and, perhaps, use Anglo-Saxon too freely in so doing), see clear through a mathematical problem, and, after thus performing his duties to himself and parents, swing a cricket bat, run a foot race, jump a hurdle, swim across the bay, enjoy a pillow fight, and then declare that if he were a member of parliament he would pass an Act to hang old Morgan, who provisioned the boarding-house with steak that was an infringement upon an india-rubber patent, and selected sour bread, that he might have something that would harmonize with a not very delightful temper.

The bricks worked into the structure of the College and adjacent houses were made in the clay grounds on Adelaide street, between Peter and Bathurst. Directly west of the College, on Russell Square, was the large, squarish building of the General Hospital, a structure that, by the way, was built due east and west, which accounted for its slanting front— for King street, my reader must know, does not run in a straight line from east to west. Back of the Hospital proper was a long row of wooden buildings, known as the cholera sheds, and these were the dread of the boys, especially the resident pupils. The first cholera epidemic came in 1832, and then every boy in the College had his tiny bag of camphor hung around his neck, an amulet, so the youngsters claimed, that was proof against that dreamless sleep into which so many sank to rest in that dread year.

The sorrows of life thickened in 1832 about the Irish immigrant, and his welcome to the new land was sad indeed. As the little long box waggons, their only ornamentation four smallish wooden plumes, were drawn to God's Acre in the Potter's Field, one's heart went out for bright-faced Irish boys and girls, strangers in a strange land, who with fathers and mothers had been cut off in life's prime, their only mourners being the light-hearted driver and the soft-hearted old sexton, who with his mattock and spade made room in the sandy soil for another whose soul had gone beyond the Dawn. The dread messenger was in other lands in 1833, but revisited Toronto in 1834, the year that the boys were housed in the new boarding-house. Some still remained at the masters' houses, but the majority, with a score of new recruits, moved to the College residence. The second attack of cholera was worse than the first. The emigration from the Emerald Isle was very great, and, as the boys could see the hospital grounds from the windows in the rear, they gazed with sympathetic eyes on the covered waggons that hourly gathered up the dead for burial and brought the sick to the meagre comforts of the hospital sheds. Fortunately the boys escaped infection; indeed a bag of gold could not have tempted them to go near the dismal sheds, where the sick and the dying held grim communion, while the dead lay on their "lone couch of everlasting rest." Thus the boys for years remembered the sad scenes, to be recalled in 1849, when, once more, homes were desolated, and the Irish immigrant again tenanted the Field of the Strangers.

The boarding-house was not built until a few years after the erection of the College pile. The plans were drawn, but the work on the main buildings was more important; and, to meet the temporary difficulty of providing for the comfort of boys from a distance, the masters, whose residences were east and west of the College building proper, were permitted to take pupils. Dr. Harris, the Principal, lived, with a houseful of boarders, at the east end of the grounds. Mr. De La Haye had several boys from out of town. Dr. Phillips the Vice-Principal, who lived in the extreme western building, had two or three, while the Rev. Mr. Boulton found room for eight over whom he had special purview. At last, about 1833, when the boarding-house was opened, there were quite a number of applications. Some boys left the masters' houses and sought quarters in the boarding-house, while new faces, from different and distant parts of Canada, made up a houseful of good-natured, noisy lads, many of whom have made a mark in life's calendar and reflect credit on College training. A Mr. Morgan had charge, but his reign was unsatisfactory and therefore brief. His ideas of catering were very limited. He thought that "growing boys should not have too much meat," that "oatmeal with good milk" was an excellent groundwork for a day's schooling, that "fish strengthened the brain," so that the boys "need not grumble, for the fare was better than what you got at home." Had they known anything of the immortal Squeers of Nicholas Nickleby, the boarding-house keeper would certainly have been put down as a relative of Dickens' character. In theory Mr. Morgan might have been right, but his theory and practice did not travel on the same line, for the meal was ill-cooked, the milk ofttimes sour, and the visits of the finny tribe so rare that the boys had no physical acquaintance with the anatomy of the inhabitants of the blue lake, the waters of which sparkled in sight of the College grounds. Morgan's reign was a short and unhappy one, and, when he stepped aside to make way for Mrs. Fenwick, of Niagara, the boys sang pæans of joy, and wished him a journey to the setting sun or some locality quite as remote.

LIFE AT THE BOARDING HOUSE.

Mrs. Fenwick was a kindly woman, one whose early life was not strewn with roses, eking out a modest livelihood at Niagara as the presiding genius of a young ladies' seminary, or, as the boys irreverently called it, "an angel factory." But Mrs. Fenwick's experience with the gentler sex served her well when she came across the lake to take charge. The boarding-house proper was under the ken of a resident master, a Mr. Kent, up to 1838, when Mr. and Mrs. Cozens assumed control, and continued until 1845-46, when Dr. Barrett took charge, with Mr. Thompson and Mr. Dodd as assistants. But in the early days, of course, the pupils were few and their cares were light, and Mrs. Fenwick was an excellent manager. She was very popular, and the change was welcomed as a revolution in domestic cookery. The boys were delighted, and a modern Delmonico could not have tickled their palates with more tempting dishes than those Mrs. Fenwick provided, and one boy declared, after the first meal, that an extra line of thanks might be annexed to the College prayers as a recognition of the welcome act of Providence for sending Mrs. Fenwick on earth. The lady in charge did not, however, come alone. She brought with her a niece, or granddaughter, a Miss Rutherford, an educated and refined woman, not particularly good-looking, but so full of common sense and good judgment, that she captured the heart of a Canadian missionary, who desired a comforter in the wilds of Africa. Miss Rutherford seemed to have a roving commission, and looked after Mrs. Fenwick's interests when that lady was absent. The fare at the boarding-house was plain but substantial. The delicacies supplied were not "the best that the market afforded," and even the enjoyment of these after sundown was due to the good graces of three or four smart Irish girls, who waited at table and between times did general housework. Every morning fifty spoons touched fifty plates of oatmeal porridge, and the milk supplied would make the owners of cows of the present day blush to the eyes. Pumps were not as common as in these degenerate modern days, and consequently the milk had a richness and a colour that was a certificate of good character. Treacle, which to-day is dignified in the shop windows as "golden syrup," was a sort of *entrée* twice a week, and when Mr. Kent did order extra fare it had the same effect on the boys that a fat refresher would have on a special pleader. The pantries and the lockups were looked after by an expert housekeeper, a Miss Arnold, who, it was to be regretted, was subject to fits, which on one occasion created a panic amid a band of boys who were at their lessons in the upstairs study. Mrs. Fenwick's life was saddened by the death of two young men, her nephews, brothers of Miss Rutherford, who were subject to epileptic fits. Both lads had been out on the bay in a skiff. One fell overboard in a fit and his poor brother, anxious to save him, jumped in, and both were drowned.

Mr. Kent lived at the east end of the boarding-house. He ruled that the boys should view the golden sunrise at six o'clock on summer mornings, and at seven in winter; indeed, he had a general supervision of the boy boarders and was not a hard taskmaster. He read prayers in the evening, and stood well with his charge. He was English, young, bright, and courteous. A man of remarkably good literary taste, of good family, his father having been a rich merchant in England. He was, in the opinion of many, one of the foremost men of his day in point of literary taste and acquirements; a perfect master of his own tongue, he was equally familiar with Latin and Greek, and could read and write in either language in prose or verse fluently. After leaving the College he educated and was travelling companion to the late Earl of Carnarvon, and was held in such esteem by that noble family that he was regarded at the family mansion as one of themselves. There he was always welcome, and for years lived with and acted as private secretary to the late Earl. Although his life-long friend and patron has gone over to the majority, Mr. Kent still survives, and at the patriarchal age of eighty years and upwards, is residing at Funchal, Madeira. He is one of the very few still living of those with whom he was so closely associated in those early days. In the fast thinning ranks of the old guard are still standing Chief Justice Hagarty, Sir Thomas Galt, and the Rev. Dr. Scadding, while scores of others of equal celebrity have long since passed away.

Mr. Kent after he left the College edited *The Church* newspaper for several years. Before Dr. Boys became Bursar of King's College, he was offered and refused that position, preferring to return to the old country where work of a literary character more congenial to his taste awaited him. He was peculiar in temperament, quick in thought, sharp in manner and prompt in punishment. His linen was immaculate, and his white tie and clean-shaven face reminded one of the man who always looks as if just out of a bandbox. He urged the boys to be neat in their attire, and certainly by example encouraged them to practise what he preached. He was fond of music, and, as in thought he went back to his College days in the motherland across the sea, he made it a point that the boys in residence should practise for a few days before each summer vacation, and assemble in the study to sing in Latin, "*Domum, Domum, Dulce, Domum*," a song that touched their hearts, and has kept John Kent's clean-cut form and kindly face warm in the memory of the young choristers, who looked upon him as a friend, rather than a teacher. The monotony of boarding-house life was varied with happenings common to all resident schools.

During the earlier years of boarding-house life there was no such thing as fagging, but in later years the writer remembers well that the old world practice of the big boys having "a fag" was considered quite in order. The tenderling of twelve or fourteen was therefore in demand, and if he did not use his pins and fly on messages for his tyrant, he had to stand the kicks and cuffs that make juvenile life uneasy—not to say unhappy. Some fellows fagged their little vassals with a vengeance, and the writer remembers one colt who in desperation, filled the air in the neighbourhood of his liege and master with a half-filled inkpot, a ruler, and if he could have managed it, would have sent a "Liddell and Scott" to improve the aerial march of the other incidentals of school equipment.

The raw country lad whom fate had selected for a term at the boarding-house had to stand the gentle hazings that accompanied residence in the town. To bantams of eight or nine years this was not entertaining, and yet the infliction was a mild one, that, however, gently lowered the miniature bank account of the new-comer. Ginger beer and bulls' eyes are the concomitants of a boy's life, and the pence and halfpence speedily disappeared from view in the tiny cash drawer of the taffy shop on Simcoe street, that received material support from its patrons, the many pupils of the College. One youngster, with whose advent came a royal feast, was overtaken by dire disaster when three of a-half dozen corks flew from under arms laden with ginger beer bottles, in full sight of the boarding-house and the boys, who from the windows watched the unfortunate in his manly struggle to reach home.

The rules about going down town were not as strict in the first twenty years of College life as from 1850 to 1860, and the penalty for infringing the rule against wandering into the embryo metropolis was an imposition that would keep a boy with pen in hand for many an hour. Indeed this class of punishment was always a convenient one for the masters who did not believe in physical warfare with the boys. A youth at the boarding-house, who has since become a master, one loved by all, for merely remarking to the resident master that he thought the fine weather would soon be gone, as dark clouds were advancing in shape of a crowd of coloured men going down Adelaide street, was quickly ordered to "memorize 'Gray's Elegy' and perhaps you'll change your mind about the weather." In those times the boys all slept in large dormitories, seven or eight in one apartment. There were four rooms, and a pillow fight was an occasional feature before retiring. The pranks of the youths as they pranced up and down the halls, in long nightgowns of different colours, made an innovation on the ordinary quiet of the sleeping quarters, and led to unpleasant consequences, especially if the linen suffered. An old game of the boys was to have without leave an evening outing, particularly if a theatrical company—one of the early barn-storming, one-night stand combinations—came to town. One of the primitive theatres was in the rear of the Shakespeare hotel, now the Metropole, at the corner of York and King streets. It was a rickety old structure, a barn in every sense of the word. It was dubbed "the Theatre Royal," and on one occasion four boarders feasted their minds for two hours on "The Taming of the Shrew," and although the curtain fell at the close of the play, there was another act not down in the "Bill of the Play." A resident master spied the boys in the gallery and sauntered home in their wake. He witnessed the sight of the youths mounting the playground fence, jumping the boarding-house gate, and nimbly climbing up a ladder that led to the roof and within hail of a second-storey window, where a friend was on watch, dexterously letting themselves in. After breakfast, the guardian of College morals, calling the lads up, said that as they had seen the players give the Taming of a Shrew, he would entertain them with a new play called the "Taming of a Boy," and that they could individually star in the title-role by each writing one of the four Gospels, giving them the privilege of drawing lots for choice.

The writer jots these reminiscences down as he talks to an old boy who saw the sunrise of boarding-house life and the pranks and frolics of boyhood in the old school. "Yes," my old friend of 1834 says, "I think it was in 1834, or perhaps 1832, that I first stepped into the arena of College life and with thirty or forty boys found a residence at the boarding-house. Pocket-money was not over plentiful, and when some special pleasure was in view a common fund was formed by all concerned. Amongst the boys were some who followed old Isaak Walton with hook and line, and the Easter holidays saw a score of the boarders make up a fishing party to the Humber. Mr. Kent gave us permission, and fully equipped with tent, bag, and pole, we started for our camping ground. One acted as commissary and expended our slender resources with care. In order that our advance might be duly heralded as we were *en route* the Vice-Principal's brother loaned us a splendid huntsman's horn. We had in the party, I think, the Wallbridges from Belleville; the Meyers boys from Trenton, cousins of the Wallbridges, and the four FitzGibbon boys, sons of the brave fellow who fought so well at Beaver Dams, and who later on risked his life to labour night and day during the cholera seasons of 1832, 1834 in aid of the suffering and dying immigrants; the Givens boys, who lived up in the woods at Pinehurst on Dundas street; the Wilmots, of Newcastle, Sam and his brother John, the former well known as the director of the fish-hatcheries of the Dominion; the Robinsons, sons of the Chief Justice; the Wells boys, from the hill back of the old town; the Smiths of Port Hope, and the Hewards, of Toronto.

In this connection it may be said that the first white settler in Belleville was, in 1797, a fur dealer named Wallbridge. Belleville was called at one time Meyers' Creek, after an Albany Dutch family. The father of the Meyers' boys who were at College, was a Hanoverian and their mother a Wallbridge. It was a procession that had in it not only resident pupils but many from the town. A leading spirit led the way with the huntsman's horn and made it lively for all concerned. The other boys carried the kettles, pans, and supplies. As we marched along we kept step to the notes of a College song. An hour's walk brought us to the Grenadier Pond, at the present High Park, and within sight of a fish trap, in which had been caught sunfish, perch, and bass. To our shame be it said—unheeding the voice of an energetic and petticoated Milesian—we appropriated the fish and made off up the river. A few miles further we found a camping ground, close to piles of cordwood cut ready for the wood scows from the city. We fashioned our tents out of boughs of trees, lit our fires and cooked our fish and turned in at midnight, to turn out long before daylight, as the piles of cordwood, a mass of fire, caught from our camp, lit up the surrounding country and hastened our exit. The boys were up quickly. Half awake and half-dressed we attempted to extinguish the flames but without success. To add to our terror the cry came that canoes were coming down the river with men bearing lighted torches. The men, whose faces were blackened, threatened to seize our belongings, but recognizing the fact that we were strong in numbers gave us time to stampede while they claimed to be waiting for reinforcements. We parleyed, palavered, struck camp and much to the surprise of Mr. Kent, landed, bag and baggage, the day after our outing. We loafed about school for holidays, fearing an investigation might take place, and were terror-stricken when one of the older boys declared that a letter had been received; that the town police were on the search for the " fire bugs "—and our surprise was great and our relief still greater when we found that our tormentors were none other than senior boys of the school. The Rapeljes from Simcoe, who, with Askin and Fisher, had been spending their holidays with relatives on the Humber, and knew of our camp, had come down in canoes to give us a scare, and extinguished the fire after we left."

During winter, College life was sometimes irksome. Opportunities for sport were not as in summer, and with short days and long lessons the outlook was barren. All kinds of schemes were devised for vacation hour. By special permission boys might skate upon the bay; but the privilege was on one occasion revoked, when it was found that a half-dozen boarders and day-boys on a Saturday afternoon fired the marsh, at the east end of the bay, calling out the fire brigade and raising quite an excitement. Of course nobody did it. Nobody ever does. The boys hankered after theatricals, and "Lucinda; or, the Mysteries of a College Pudding," an unheard-of production in one act—the literary invention of a couple of the boarders—was placed upon the stage. A short farce was to follow. Lucinda was the presiding genius of the College cooking stove. The good priest had, at her father's bidding, called her Bridget, but when she touched Canadian soil the old name was dropped, and without the intervention of an Act of Parliament the new one was adopted. Lucinda was sensitive, and when she heard that her merits were to be discussed by "yez players," she declared that the supply of bread and butter, which had heretofore been surreptitiously conveyed out of the kitchen window to her favourites would, without further notice, be stopped. The upper loft in Dr. Phillips' carriage-house was selected as the place for the performance. It was cleaned and made presentable. The boarding-house supplied benches and chairs and the residences of the masters were levied on for curtains and decorations. The boys were well up in their parts. A large audience assembled. Some of the folks from Government House were on hand. The late Chief Justice Robinson and his family were spectators, and Dr. Phillips and the masters and other local dignitaries were patrons. On another occasion, when the boys of the boarding-house had amateur theatricals, an interesting incident occurred. The trunk-room of the boarding-house had been adapted for the purpose. The play, or rather the farce, was "Like Master Like Man." The stage was small and the scenery rather crowded. Wilmot and Ingalls dressed as women were to be discovered. The audience, amongst whom was Mr. Matthews, the first classical master, were all anxiety for the rise of the curtain. The bell rang, but the boy whose particular duty it was to manipulate the curtain was not on hand, and a youth seized the rope, but had hauled only a few seconds when he heard roars of laughter, screams from the ladies and shouts from the small boys in the background, as the wooden roller caught in the skirts of one of the female players, now a venerable and prominent government official, and gave the audience a scene not on the bill. Need it be said that he quickly slacked the rope, achieving better results on his second attempt.

Across the street from the boarding-house were the fine garden and orchard of the Hon. Alexander Macdonell. At the corner of the street and back from the front, stood the mansion of the affable old gentleman, whose face, up to 1842, was familiar to many of the boys. The orchard ran east along Adelaide street, about 500 feet, and north about 200 feet to Richmond, occupying fully one-third of the entire square. There was no orchard in Toronto like it. Apples, pears, berries and currants were as plentiful behind that high board fence as if the region were a fruit market. The windows of the boarding-house overlooked the tempting landscape, which was occasionally enlivened by the guardianship of a couple of ferocious looking bulldogs, whose sole duty was to test the quality of cloth in the attire of uninvited guests. Apples have charms for boys, and pears possess a relish which always makes the owners of keen and youthful appetites brave danger. The day-boys were no better than the boarders. Their desires were mutual. To climb the fence in daylight meant certain capture. Darkness, therefore, as the friend of evil-doers, was accepted as an ally. The boarding-house gates were locked at seven; evening prayer at nine saw the household between blankets. The small boy then as now was an aggressive agent of mischief, and after the clock had struck ten, sheets and towels were fastened into ropes, and youths of ten and twelve were let down, with pillow-slips in hand, and orders to load up with all the varieties of fruit that could be obtained. As the rascal who supervised the pillage said to the intending pilferer on one occasion, "gentle youth, you take all the apples you can get and you need not stop to count them." A boy who now stands prominent in one of the principal departments at Ottawa, declares he has a vivid recollection of being lowered out of that second storey window and seizing his quota of apples. Another, in ermine who now dispenses justice to evil-doers, being detailed on a great occasion to secure fruit, was caught in the clutches of the gardener just as he was preparing to vanish. The angry old gardener told the boy he would have to bring him before Mr. Macdonell, but the little fellow pleaded for liberty as effectively as in later years he pleaded for freedom for men who stood in the dock. And he returned in triumph to the boarding-house, not only free but with a pillow-slip full of apples, which had been carried away by another boy, while the principal sinner was pleading for liberty.

While school training was carefully looked after, the religious side of life was not neglected, and the prayers of the morning and afternoon of the weekday, were strengthened by a discourse at the Cathedral of St. James, where the boys repaired every Sunday morning. Some rather kicked over the traces and objected to this march. The Episcopalians really envied the Presbyterians, for the latter were looked on as nomads, who could go to church or not, just as they willed. At any rate the followers of Knox had not to take part in the Sunday procession; so many of the young Tartars sacrificed Church, State and Creed, and entered the Presbyterian fold to secure the privilege of avoiding a morning tramp through town.

Then the College bell sounded out at seven in the morning to awaken the College residents; but on one notable occasion it rang much earlier. It was truly before cock-crowing. The incident is briefly referred to in the chapter on the College Janitors, but it will here bear repeating. The boarders were sound asleep, and had been for hours in bed. The masters, even those who burned the midnight oil, were deep in slumber. Old Samuel Alderdice, who had been hard at work all day, was in the land of dreams. About two in the morning, Mr. John Powell, who had been out Yonge street, rode hurriedly back to warn the Governor that Mackenzie was on the march to the city. The messenger almost banged the door of the janitor's cottage to pieces, as he called him out to ring the bell, and sound the alarm to the inhabitants. The old man was up like a flash. If he had one virtue, it was loyalty, for he was an Orangeman and a Tory and oft declared that Mackenzie would get his due some day for declaring that Upper Canada College was but "a Preparatory School for young Tories." The bell rang—that part of the town was aroused. The church bells took up the alarm. The boys in the boarding-house were startled. Some arose thinking it first bell, others thought that some one was playing tricks with the bell. Mr. Wedd, who, a boy at the time, was asleep in one of the rooms, arose to dress and wondered that it did not get lighter. Sleep, however, being more important to boys than study, the lads went to bed again, to awaken, however, in the morning and see Mr. Lewis, brother-in-law of Mr. Rowsell, the College bookseller, on guard at the Government House, and the Rev. George Maynard, the mathematical master, dressed as a private, ready to do his duty in defending the city. All was excitement at the boarding-house. The College classes were broken up; a piece of paper pinned on the front door, and another on the Adelaide street gate, notified the day pupils that an unlooked-for vacation prevailed. The boarders who could get home were hurriedly packed off, and those who could not were looked after by the masters. At the boarding-house provisions were served on a war basis, so an old master informs me, and on the morning after the excitement broke out, about the 7th of December, four loaves of bread were all of that valuable commodity that could be put upon the table. The town bakers had to supply the militia and citizen soldiers, and for a day or two matters looked bad enough. There were no troops in the Province when the rebellion broke out. Sir Francis Bond Head had allowed them to go to Lower Canada, making it his boast that they were not needed in Toronto. My friend, Dr. Larratt W. Smith, one of the old boys, ever loyal to his *Alma Mater*, relates to me an interesting reminiscence. He says: "I saw the 24th Regiment, the last to leave, defile up King street and down Simcoe street, as they marched to the boat, and when William Lyon Mackenzie, who sat in his buggy at the corner of King and Simcoe streets, saw the last of them pass he remarked in a loud tone of voice, 'I'll make it hot for you before you return.' I, with the other College boys looking on, threw stones at him." Another old boy tells me that Samuel Alderdice, the janitor of the College, was standing within earshot of Mackenzie at the time and when he heard the disloyal remark he used rather emphatic language.

After the troubles of 1837 were over, the College itself seemed to advance in popularity throughout the Province. The boarding-house was over-crowded, and more accommodation had to be provided. The brain of J. G. Howard was, like Adoniram of old, utilized and drew plans on the trestle board and fashioned a wing, which extended from the south side of the original boarding-house. In those days tenders were advertised for by handbills, posted about the streets, copies being sent to leading contractors. In the *British Colonist* of September 20th, 1838, we find the following announcement :—

UPPER CANADA COLLEGE.

The College will re-open after the summer vacation on Thursday, the 27th of September. The College boarding-house has been considerably enlarged, and affords ample accommodation for at least seventy boarders.

CHAS. MATTHEWS, A.M.,
Acting Principal.

And we also find in glancing at an old file of the *British Colonist* of April 5, 1838, a notice of the sale of the furniture of the late Dr. Harris, which reads that the furniture was sold by J. M. Strange by auction, on the 9th of April, 1838, with a "quantity of particularly fine Madeira port, sherry in bottle, eighteen years old, also two pews in St. James' Church, Nos. 76 and 112." From 1838, on the appointment of Mr. Cozens as resident master, the boarding-house took a new lease and was much improved.

In December of 1842, we find a notice in the *British Colonist* of the 7th to this effect :

UPPER CANADA COLLEGE.

In consequence of the prevalence of scarlatina the pupils of this institution have been dismissed for the vacation at an earlier period than usual.

The recess will extend from this date to Wednesday, January 4th, 1843.

The annual public examinations will commence on Monday, January 16th, and the regular business will be resumed on Friday, January 27th.

JOHN McCAUL, LL.D.,
Principal, U.C.C.

U. C. College, December 3rd, 1842.

This sent the boarders as well as the day-pupils home two weeks earlier than usual.

Dr. Barrett afterwards became resident master, assisted by Mr. Christopher Thompson, writing master, and Mr. John Dodd, master of the "partial form" or commercial form, the class of the latter in the College being dubbed "the refuge for the destitute" by the boys who studied classics, as opposed to those who could not or would not delve into the intricacies of Latin prose and verse. The additional space gave much more sleeping accommodation, and the large rooms of the early days were divided into dormitories, framed of lattice work, about seven feet by eight in extent, each dormitory being provided with a single bed, a washstand, and a few pegs for clothing, and a door, which was so hung that when closed it could not be opened without jingling a bell in the main hall that would wake the Seven Sleepers. This bell business was a disagreeable innovation. At ten o'clock the boys were supposed to have retired, with each door closed, the bell set, and usually quiet prevailed, but not always. One of the boys, a genius in his way, secured a piece of wire and dexterously twisted it so that he could slip the snap without disturbing the bell. Once out, of course, he could emancipate the entire army. Occasionally, on Friday nights, the boys held high carnival, parading the halls on tiptoe, and then winding up with an old-fashioned pillow fight, that brought Mr. Thompson and Mr. Dodd on the scene. The urchin on watch, hearing the masters approach, gave the warning, and the boys, recognizing the truism that silence is golden, were in a few seconds safely in their beds, apparently very sound asleep, but possibly with their ears still open, listening to the footfalls of the half-dressed masters, who were astonished at the transformation from chaos to order. But all was taken in good part. The boys must have their fun; and on another occasion, when carnival reigned, a night or two before the summer holidays, Dr. Barrett held an inquest upon the remains of some pillow-slips, the verdict being that every lad whose pillow was torn was kept within the College grounds until able to memorize perfectly a few verses of Scripture selected with great care by Mr. Dodd, a master presiding in the evening preparation of lessons. These memory-tests plagued the pupils. They could grind out an imposition, with the aid, perhaps, of friends, but there was no device that could be combined to get over the memory-tests. As a Brockville boy remarked, it was "the extracted essence of refined cruelty" to exchange the time-honoured punishment of the imposition for this new method of imparting information. And yet, as the masters would often admit, the boys averaged well in deportment. True, the masters' gardens—a row of seven on the east side of the hill that sloped into the playground—were sometimes despoiled of favourite plants; a riot might occur at the tea-table, if the fare of the steward was not up to the standard; a fight might take place in the grove, between boarders who thought best to settle their disputes that way—but all these things are the natural methods that boys have of finding vent for their surcharged feelings. On one occasion, a luckless lad from Eastern Ontario, was careless enough to let lighted matches fall between the wainscotting in the long study, and then there was a clatter. Water was plentiful and the fire was soon out, but the penalty paid was one that makes the writer shudder as he still thinks of it. For four weeks the boy viewed the scenery of the outside world from the top of the College fence—he was within the law if he did not cross—and, as a further punishment, three hundred verses of the Good Book, extracted at the rate of five per day, were not only to be memorized, but also presented in College ink, on College foolscap, with instructions to dot the i's, cross the t's, and give the commas, semicolons, and full points the positions they were entitled to in Holy Writ. The boys sympathized and poured forth their condolences, but the edict had gone forth and there was no help for it.

The reader has in this chapter a fair picture of life at the boarding-house. In the days of Dr. Barrett the *régime* improved, and since that time, with the knowledge of modern experience, the boarding-house is a model for all schools—and the boys of to-day, as their fathers tell them of the happy days of early life, may well feel proud that they with their fathers can call the Old College their *Alma Mater*.

COLLEGE JOURNALISM.

BY AN OLD COLLEGE BOY.

To GO back to the days of nearly forty years ago, and pick up pebbles from the shores of a memory closely identified with the youthful typesetters of old Upper Canada College is a somewhat difficult though not unpleasant task. Interesting are the experiences of the boys, who, as they climbed into manhood, thought more perhaps of the art preservative than they did of their daily toil in the school room. We all know that it is an effort, not unattended with difficulty, to train a boy's mental faculties just in the way they should go, especially when the trend of his inclinations is in another direction, and he fancies, as many boys do, that the master at the desk is a modern Legree, sent on earth to "belt and welt" the life out of every one whose thoughts run counter to what the boy would term the mind of the literary slave driver.

With feelings not very remote from these the early printers at the College had to contend. Obstacles were varied in character, and one has to smile as he thinks of the divers devices which afforded relief from educational toil. The time thus gained was used in order to have the paper out on time, with the latest cricket news and College gossip. These items were jotted down by some, who, in later life, availed themselves of this early practice in order to earn the conventional bread and butter of life, and who by their pencillings have made for themselves name, fame, and reputation, either as the ubiquitous reporters of the daily press, or in the forum of debate at Toronto or Ottawa.

The College of the fifties was a different institution from that of to-day, and these words glide from the pen with a great deal of real love for the old masters—some yet to the fore, others gone into dreamland—as well as for the old pile of brick and mortar smoothed with winds, which swept the face and curled around the corners of the weather-beaten building, now by the march of modern improvement hidden from view in an elevation that certainly has more charm, as a thing of beauty, than the severe, four-cornered, low, slant roof designed by Mr. Ewart in 1829.

We may be pardoned for taking a preliminary canter ere writing the history of the College press. One cannot pass down the old halls, and peep into some of the old rooms, without a thought of the happy days of long ago, when the precious five minutes at the end of every hour was not only made available to change the classes, but also to do a little business in the way of orders for work, for it was " Your name and address, on good paper, in the highest style of art for seven cents," or " *The College Times*, with the best news for the boys, only fifty cents a year." It was remarkable the volume of business transacted in those precious five minutes. Orders were taken, accounts collected, and work delivered, with a cheapness, a neatness, and despatch, that would do credit to a metropolitan Caxton.

There were half-a-dozen boys who dabbled in printer's ink. With some the fad was only for " a quarter," as the session or term of those days was called. Others clung to it for a longer period—but only one made it a stepping stone in the realms of active business life.

The College of the fifties and sixties was divided into seven " forms " or classes, with a preparatory division for the " twelve year colts," who struggled with Latin grammar, as the only method by which they could attain a knowledge of English grammar, for, in the halcyon days of the College, English grammar was an unknown book—the grounding therefore had to be through Latin, and to be of as substantial a character as the foundation of the city of the Cæsars. Even if a surgical operation were necessary to get " Hic, hæc, hoc " into the youthful skull it was performed with the skill of a veteran Esculapius. The year 1860, by the way, saw the last of the seventh form.

Some of the juvenile striplings were enthusiastic patrons of the first College press, for to have one's name immortalized in cold type at seven cents a dozen, even if it did take a week's pocket money, was a sacrifice that was made without a grumble. While the toddlers of the College were content with an investment in a dozen labels—or even half-a-dozen, at four cents—the boys of the first, second, third—the commercial—a form that has just been revived—and the fourth, preferred larger quantities on special paper, for which they willingly gave the printer a special price. The label had all the advantage of typographical ornament, and with the name surrounded by a fancy border, of unique style, it made an attractive inside to the cover of the well-thumbed school-books, that did duty, in turn, for a whole family of boys.

Let us picture, in *fac simile*, one of the early productions of the College Caxton. The type was bold and readable. The boys cared little whether it was a Clarendon, an Antique, or an Ionic letter, so long as it described the invincible right of property in the book into which it was pasted.

It was somewhere after the Christmas holidays of 1856-57, that the monotony of College life was disturbed by the competition of the rival boys who engineered diminutive printing presses in the homes of fond parents, who, no doubt, thought that the time given to the types could be more profitably employed in filling the respective brains of their progeny with knowledge that would be more serviceable in after life. The writer recalls the names of a few of the juvenile typos, all of whom, save one, have written their names on the title page of time in fields of labour not akin to typography: J. Ross Robertson, eldest son of the late Mr John Robertson, the well-known Toronto dry-goods merchant; Edward H. Tiffany, son of Mr. George S. Tiffany—a descendant, by the way, of the Tiffany Brothers, who printed the *Upper Canada Gazette and American Oracle*, at Newark or Niagara, in 1798; King Arnoldi, son of an eminent physician, the late Dr. Arnoldi, and Henry Prettie, son of a prominent Toronto builder of the early days.

Mr. Robertson was a partner in the youthful enterprise, successively with Mr. Arnoldi and Mr. Prettie, and is to-day the proprietor of *The Toronto Evening Telegram*, which was founded in 1876. Mr. Arnoldi followed architecture as a profession, and his designs as an architect at Ottawa are a credit to himself and his country. Mr. Prettie has achieved fame as a merchant, and occupies a seat in a western legislature. Mr. Tiffany delved into the mysteries of Blackstone, and measures out law, as one profound and skilled, in the village of Alexandria, Ontario.

The printing of labels for books received such encouragement that higher flights in art were attempted, and the publication of a journal that would be the voice of College opinion was discussed. Robertson and Tiffany were rivals in this field. The father of the former had gladdened the heart of his son with a fifty dollar bill, an offering which sprang out of a feeling of thankfulness to a merciful Providence for sparing the life of the youngster who, playing truant for an hour, in the midsummer of 1857, was not a disinterested spectator in the Brown-Cameron election riot at the corner of Queen and Simcoe streets, on the last day of that famous contest. Let me give the incident as it occurred:—

The election was a hot one, and the boys, after the fashion of boys, had their likes and dislikes in matters political as well as in school quarrels. The pet of the College in this contest was John Hillyard Cameron, for he was "an old boy." The lads were anxious to see the fun, and a few of the "big uns" thought that instead of spending an entertaining hour with our old friend Lucian, under the watchful care of the now venerable Dr. Scadding, or struggling with the second book of the Æneid with Mr. Wedd, an hour in the practical field of everyday life would be more profitable. Accordingly, half-a-dozen names were marked down in the absentee book that afternoon. The polls closed at five o'clock, and the school at four, and an hour before David Alderdice rang the closing hour of the College day, the boys who proposed seeing the fun, were over on Queen street, between St. Patrick's market and the corner of Simcoe and Queen. It was open voting in those days, and the Cameron men had possession of St. Patrick's market poll. In full force they were assembled on Queen street, armed with newly broken macadam, which lay in piles along the roadway that bounded the property of Sir John Beverley Robinson, on the south side of Queen street. The Brown men made their stand at the corner of Simcoe, William and Queen. In those days Simcoe only ran north to Queen; the street was continued north of Queen under the name of William, as far as the present Anderson street. Robert Moodie, a local politician, popularly known as "Bob Moodie," was at that time a Reformer, and was as vigilant on his political side as the partizans of Cameron were on the Conservative. About half-past four the respective crowds had mustered perhaps 500 each. Word had been sent up " the ward," as St. John's was familiarly called, that there was to be trouble at St. Patrick's market, and the reply came in a score of cab and waggon loads of men, headed by Moodie, arriving on the scene of action. Mr. Clinkenbroomer, the watchmaker, was building a new house on the north-west corner of Queen and William. A pile of brick about twenty feet in length by twelve feet in breadth and as high as an ordinary man, stood in the roadway ready for both trowel and mortar, but fate had ordered otherwise. The crowd gathered in the situation and the bricks at the same time, for in ten minutes the height of the pile was well lowered. The men from the market came slowly down the street, driving all before them. The windows on both sides were, unless where protected with shutters, riddled with stones.

The cover of Dr. Hodder's buggy, driven by the old gentleman himself down Dummer (William) street, was riddled with a shower of stones as it turned into Queen, and when the opposing crowds met opposite Sheppard's marble works, located fifty feet west from the south-west corner of Queen and Simcoe streets, just by the old stone which marked the first mile from the City Hall, the fight became fast and furious, and the shattered windows and roadway literally alive with brickbats, loose macadam, and formidable paving stones, revealed a state of affairs that happily came to an end by pure exhaustion, rather than from the waning energy of the score of policemen who watched the city of thirty years ago. Young Robertson and his friends were surveying the situation from the front of Sheppard's works, when an ill-natured, many-pointed piece of macadam, pitched from the western side of the battle landed through the strap and peak of Robertson's cap and laid him on his bed for a few weeks. Convalescence was a day of joy in the family, and the fifty dollar bill was invested with William Halley, manager for D. K. Feehan, the agent of the Montreal Type Foundry, in a font of long primer, with display type, which fitted up the first printing office of the College, from which was issued *The College Times.*

The other College mind of typographic turn was also seeking an outlet for his opinions, and Tiffany, too, had equipped an office that would meet the requirements of College trade and from which was issued *The Boys' Own Paper.* The connection of Robertson with boating, debating societies and cricket circles of the College, gave him an advantage with the boys, and, as an active participant in sports, the boys showed their fealty by rallying around him in his enterprise. They did so, not only in financial support, but assisted as contributors and made the columns readable and entertaining. So many years have passed that only a few names can be recalled. The work of typesetting was performed by Robertson, and editorial matter frequently flowed into type without even a line of the usual MS., while play hours were occupied with the business of collecting subscribers and subscriptions. Other boys joined in— James T. Morgan, a noble specimen of boyhood, a generous, pleasant fellow with a face that beamed with brightness, contributed to the poetical column. A few stanzas are remembered by the writer. "Jim," by which Morgan was better known, was a son of Mr. Peter Morgan, an old resident of William street. His brother Charles, also an old College boy, is now manager of the Merchants' Bank at Perth. "Jim" ground out poetry to order—sometimes when sitting with the writer, having a quiet smoke, in the top of the tall pines which long ago stood on the east side of the College gymnasium, but usually at the writing hour when, in a back seat in Thompson's room, Jim and his old friend would coin verse with an assurance of excellence that caused a general laugh when, at lunch time, it was read over to connoisseurs in the verse-making art, who were adepts at versification, and who had carried off honours in that line.

Thomas S. Reid, brother-in-law of the late William Hay, the Toronto architect, and now a resident of Bermuda, was a prose contributor. Reid was a brother of Dr. Thomas Reid, the eminent psychologist. His efforts were of the sober and reflective kind, and yet with enough mischief in them to form the subject of a miniature libel suit, which interested the boys for the greater part of one term. Reid, in 1862-75, was actively engaged in commercial pursuits in Halifax, Nova Scotia.

The College Times first saw light in September, 1857. It was a sheet 7 x 12, or about the size of ordinary letter paper. It was a four-page production. The matter was set two columns wide, in long primer type, and was issued monthly. The type was set up in a small room in the house of the Robertson family. Stout oak chases, instead of iron, were used, and the type, as set, was read over carefully, and proved and corrected in the "stick" and then emptied into the primitive chases and carried down to the old *Globe* office, where the edition of five hundred was worked off by Upton, the pressman, on a Washington hand-press, the most rapid piece of printing machinery that the leading job office of those days possessed.

For the first issue the paper was known as *The College Times*, but this title led to trouble before the sheet was well off the press. The College authorities—those who sat in council as a committee of the senate and looked after the welfare of the boys—had determined that the south hundred feet of the playground should be sacrificed for building lots, for in 1857 the real estate boom had struck Toronto with a force proportionate to that of 1887-90. The boys were up in arms and determined to assert their rights, by all possible means to preserve their much valued playground from spoliation. Robertson, Reid and Tyner, with a score of others, organized a meeting in the prayer-room after College hours, which was largely attended. A resolution was enthusiastically carried to appeal to His Excellency the Governor-General of Canada as *ex officio* Visitor of the College, Sir Edmund Walker Head, Bart., who then resided in the old Government House, opposite the College, in the welfare of which he took considerable interest, his son having for some time been a pupil. The appeal to the "fountain Head" resulted most favourably, the distinguished scholar and educationist supporting the contention of the College boys in every particular by vetoing all the proceedings of the Senate in the matter, which produced among the boys a revolutionary action to save every inch of soil which they deemed sacred ground. The Rev. Walter Stennett was then principal of the institution and his views did not coincide with those of the agitators. The chief preceptor did not take a lively interest in sports, as did the honoured Barron—whose memory will forever be green in the minds of boys, who have dismal recollections of lengthy impositions and birchings with the typical bamboo by the old principal—and the young publisher was not disappointed when he heard that his enterprise was frowned upon by the head master. *The College Times* made its debut. Its advent was the talk of the halls. The boys were more eager for it than for their lessons. It came at last. The proprietor added to his duties those of editor, type-setter, publisher, and distributor. Four hundred subscribers had been secured among the boys and among the friends outside, many of them in the offices of the old government of Canada, for in those days the seat of government alternated between Toronto and Quebec. Sir Edmund Walker Head, the Governor-General, was appealed to as the official Visitor of the College. A copy of *The College Times* had been sent to him by the publisher. The Governor was impressed and the College block was kept intact, all due to the juvenile spirit of patriotic duty which inspired the movement.

The leading editorial was a powerful and explicit demand that the boys should not be robbed of their play ground. It must be admitted that the language was energetic, but respectful ; indeed the late Chief Justice Moss, one of the bright boys of the College, said it was quite justified by the facts. Principal Stennett objected, not only to the paper but to its tone, and stated that unless the name, at least, was changed, and revolutionary articles refused insertion, the paper should not be distributed in the College building or grounds. This edict was an augury of future success. Indeed he informed the rival Caxtons that they might choose between the desire to continue as publishers and expulsion from the College. This threat, which was, of course, beyond the power of the principal, was never carried out. The boys were up in arms. Every friend became a canvasser, and subscriptions from outside poured in with a bountiful hand. The name of the paper was changed to *The Monthly Times* and, headed by the proprietor, a couple of active agents distributed the sheet at the King street and Adelaide street gates, to the delight of the boys, and amid the kindly smiles of some of the masters, who rather relished the little cloud of rebellion, which enlivened the even tenor of College ways. The College boarding-house was to be specially guarded, and David Alderdice was warned that, if he saw the emissaries of the printing shop pass his cottage, which stood east of the old gateway that led to the boarding-house, his vocation would either be gone, or some unheard-of penalty would be inflicted. But Davy was a good soul, and, like his father, had a heart for boys who, unasked, never let Christmas pass, as we have already seen, without some token, however small, of the esteem they had for the plodding messenger. The paper found its way into every class-room. Every boy had a copy in his pocket. The dormitories at the boarding-house were well supplied, and the satisfaction of all concerned, both publishers and subscribers, was unqualified. The agitation against the real estate deal had, however, its effect. The notices of " For Sale " were taken down, and the surveyors' stakes pulled up out of ground, in which they had been buried deep by the indignant three hundred.

The November issue of the paper found the title changed to that of *The Monthly Times*, and in May, 1858, to the *The Boys' Times*, as being more appropriate to the constituency which it proposed to represent. It was also made a semi-monthly publication. Its success was phenomenal, and its circulation generally averaged about five hundred. It was an outspoken organ of juvenile opinion, and if its editorial range did not extend to the higher flights of literary writing, it was good enough for the boys, and its day of issue was looked forward to with as much eagerness as is the five o'clock edition of *The Evening Telegram* of to-day by the people of Toronto.

A glance through a file of the paper shows that it improved as the months progressed. A continued story, "The Haunted Hall," was a feature. The cricket column records a meeting of the "Wellington Cricket Club," with W. B. Nicol, president, G. B. Nicol, vice-president, and A. Brunel, secretary. The Nicols were sons of Dr. Nicol, and Brunel was the son of Mr. Brunel, the City Engineer. The Wellington Club met in the Brunel grounds, on the corner of Front and Brock streets, the old family home of Mrs. Jameson, wife of Chancellor Jameson. George B. Nicol is now the popular Clerk of Assize at Toronto, and W. B. Nicol is a barrister. The same issue gave the officers of the U. C. College Cricket Club, with G. P. Gildersleeve, now of Kingston, as president ; D. F. Bogert, now Rev. D. F., of Belleville, vice-president ; and F. A. Read, formerly of Cayuga, secretary. The issue of June 1st recalls to the mind of subscribers the fact that "as printers cannot altogether live on atmospheric suction, something must be provided for their sustenance * * we hope then that our friends will save us the trouble by remitting the needful." This was headed "An Admonition to pay up."

On June 15th the proprietor of the paper offered prizes for proficiency in gymnastics to all boys above ten years and to all boys below that age, but made the condition that competitors "must be subscribers to this paper for six months." In the issue of 1st July, 1858, we have a report of a libel suit tried by a jury of College boys, and brought by Robertson against K. M. Arnoldi. It was a business dispute in connection with an interest in the paper. The court was a self-constituted one. It met in Dr. Barrett's room. A. C. Tyner, the Tyner of the College and University, presided. Charles Crawford, son of the Hon. Geo. Crawford, of Brockville, T. S. Reid, now of Bermuda, and D. F. Bogert, were for the plaintiff— a great array of counsel. Fred. A. Read was for the defendant. The verdict was rendered in a peculiar manner. The paper states— " The presiding officer, Mr. Tyner, then charged the jury. The jury retired, and after a short deliberation brought in a verdict for the plaintiffs and $4 damages. A member of the jury expressing his dissent from the verdict delivered by the foreman, the jury again retired and brought in a verdict for the defendant." After this jump from plaintiff to defendant, the former thought it would be well to have a new trial. The points were argued, but "Mr. Tyner stated that he had no power to grant a new trial. The case had been tried by consent of both parties, and as this was not a legally constituted court, the matter would remain as it had been before the trial." Thus ended the great suit. The audience at each sitting varied from seventy-five to one hundred, and the efforts of the counsel were watched with great eagerness. Happily at this writing and for the past thirty years the parties to the suit are good friends and enjoy with gusto a talk about the great trial.

In the issue of July 21st, 1858, we have the opening chapters of "The Sea Lion, or the Privateer of the Penobscot," by Sylvanus Cobb, jr. It is worthy of remark that when the American paper in which the story originally appeared did not arrive in time for *The Boys' Times*, the proprietor ventured to fill the necessary gaps and trust to luck to make the connection in the next number fit into the genuine production of Cobb. This July number was called "the Holiday number" and it was made attractive by engravings of Toronto Public Buildings borrowed from a city printing office. It also contained a woodcut of the old Royal Lyceum, which thirty years later proved very valuable in making engravings of the old playhouse.

The issue of the 15th September, 1858, had the announcement that " Mr. E. Tiffany, having discontinued the publication of his paper, is handing over to us his subscription list." A letter also appeared from Mr. Tiffany, as proprietor of *The Boys' Own Paper*, confirming this notice, thanking the boys for support, and stating that owing " to serious losses," he had been "obliged to discontinue" and hoping that *The Boys' Times* would meet with support as "a highly useful and instructive paper." The issue of the 15th September, 1858, had an editorial on a new division or "scheme" of studies made by the authorities. The editorial said:—

UPPER CANADA COLLEGE.

"The College reassembled after the midsummer vacation on Thursday the 10th September.

"A new scheme has been devised by which we observe that German and English classics have become part of the College course.

"Another important change is the sub-dividing the commercial form (now called the English department) into five parts, The epithet, 'Refuge for the Destitute,' which with proprietory applied to it, will no longer be

UPPER HALL-WAY

THE LONG STUDY

applicable. Those students whose nostrils cannot appreciate the odour of the Latin and Greek classics, will not find a refuge now in the English department. They will be taught to know that there are such things as English Classics. Avoiding Scylla they will fall into Charybdis."

The issue also contained the welcome intelligence that the College playground was to be levelled and sodded. The issue of October 1st, 1858, contained an editorial which reflected on the University authorities for their treatment of the boys at the laying of the cope stone of the new structure. It appears that the boys were invited to the ceremony, which took place on the last week of September, 1858. They were to fall in, on the laying of the stone, and after the ceremony apples and cakes were to be provided. The boys were dismissed from their classes at 10 a.m., and were ordered to assemble at the Park at noon. The *elite* of the city were there—the Governor-General and party, and Lieut. Goodwin had command of a detachment of artillery. After the ceremony the graduates and guests lunched in the library, and then the editor goes on to state:—

"The College boys were directed to enter at the Medical department, where it was understood the above-mentioned refreshments would be served. To the astonishment of all, however, one of the masters, assisted by some other officials, kept pitching apples and cakes among the boys outside. Some obtained with difficulty one apple, others half a one, while others, still disgusted with the proceedings, went home.

"A more luke-warm reception, we believe, was never before given to the College boys. Invited, as they were, to take part in the ceremony, they ought to have at least received some little attention. Had even, we say, the few apples and cakes been distributed in a civilized manner, the boys would have been satisfied. Instead of that, however, they distributed the fodder in a manner that they would not have done to any other species in the animal creation.

"College boys have always held a high reputation, and have been respected wherever they went. At every demonstration they have been heartily received. It is rather strange that they should have met with such a reception from the University."

The boys, were of course, indignant and even Dr. McCaul declared that it was a shame that those who in time would fill the lecture rooms of the University, should be "treated like a lot of hungry paupers."

The *Grumbler*, a weekly satirical paper, published by Erastus Wiman, had half-a-dozen anonymous verses on the subject. The verses are worthy of reproduction.

THE COLLEGE BOYS' LAMENT.

'T was on a windy afternoon,
   Just at October's birth,
When the maple and the chestnut
   Dropped their tribute to the earth,
They went to lay the coping stone
   Of a pile now reared to knowledge,
And thither in high feather marched
   The boys of U. C. College.

The graduates and students passed
   In togas to the hall,
From the greenest of the freshmen,
   Up to Dr. John McCaul,
The band blew out a merry blast,
   The students took their dinners,
But no turkey's leg, or chicken's wing,
   Was pitched to us poor sinners.

We heard the noisy gownsmen then
   Hurrah with might and main,
And fifteen score or more of corks,
   Pop from the brisk champagne,
A little beef would have sufficed,
   Our teeth were getting all edge,
But nor beef, nor veal, nor bread was there
   For the boys of U. C. College.

At length an unshorn porter came,
   Through the place meant for a door,
And, as to pigs, some apples green,
   Poured forth upon the floor.
And this, while they were swigging
   Their champagne, hock and claret ;
We gathered up the beggar's fare
   And pelted Dr. Barrett.

But what more galled us than it all
   Was the speech of Mr. Stennett,
And the *Globe's* absurdly flattering puff
   Of the hospitable Senate.
The " sumptuous repast " he gave,
   Did our Principal acknowledge,
But what it was and where it went,
   Beats the boys of U. C. College.

Such was the entertainment rare,
   Which in the autumn's prime,
When the north wind whistled through the trees,
   At half-past eating time,
When they went to lay the coping stone
   Of that pile new-reared to knowledge,
They gave the poor, unhappy wights,
   The boys of U. C. College.

In the December issue we have a few stanzas from Morgan, the poctaster of the paper. If the facts are not lost in a tangled maze of memories these verses were written in Dr. Barrett's room the day before the winter holidays, when the good old doctor had been called away to a meeting in the Principal's room to decide the fate of some boys in the boarding-house, who the night before had raised pandemonium in the dormitories with a first-class pillow fight, in which the linen of the College had suffered to an extent that demanded complete renovation. A few of the verses read:

A CHRISTMAS PEAL.

What joy is depicted on every chap's face,
Each quietly sitting with delight in his place ;
That joy, in truth, which in youth knows no care,
All troubles have fled, but we cannot tell where.

"Christmas holidays," Mr. S. n w declares
Will commence (by jove ! boys,) just after prayers,
From prep. to the seventh what buzzing goes round,
Each trying to speak, themselves do confound.

The Boys' Times is published and out for this month,
And so would another be, if it were not defunct,
A Christmas number full of mirth and of fun,
Says the agent, "subscribe, a new volume's begun."

The editor also returns thanks for past favours, stating that :—

"The publishers beg to return thanks for the support and encouragement tendered them during the present year ; and to say that they have made arrangements for publishing the paper weekly. The publishers in taking this step are perfectly aware of the expenses attending it, but hope that they will receive such additional support in their hazardous enterprise as will amply repay their efforts.

"They have engaged a new staff of writers, who will sustain the well-earned reputation of this Journal. Our columns will always be filled with an interesting story, and a plentiful supply of original matter, written on subjects of the greatest interest to boys, and odds and ends calculated to excite and amuse.

"The publishers wish it to be distinctly understood that this is strictly a boy's paper; being written for, and conducted by boys. Many little inaccuracies have occurred in many of our numbers, but we are assured that few will be found in the coming volume."

The issue of 5th January, 1859, opened with a few verses by J. T. M. (J. T. Morgan). The maker of the rhyme had just left College, although he still contributed to the paper. His lines had particular reference to Mr. John Dodd, the excellent teacher of the commercial form.

Morgan also gave in this issue the opening chapters of a thrilling tale entitled "Hessian Bedrearn, or Ottoman Tyranny," which opened with the lines :

"'Allah is great! he must die,' were the concise words uttered by Pasha Del Keder, to a youth of about twenty summers. His crime! what was it?"

The development of the plot was, perhaps, of the dime novel order, for the hero was carried in successive chapters through a series of adventures that could only exist in the mind of an author that had a lively imagination, fed by perusal of the Arabian Nights or the annals of Don Quixote.

The issue of January 12th, noticed the advancement of an old boy. Ensign R. G. Newbigging, of the 89th Regiment promoted to a lieutenancy. The regiment was stationed at Neemuch, in India.

The next issue has a meeting of the College Debating Society, of which A. C. Tyner was President, S. F. Lafferty, Vice-President, and J. Ross Robertson, Secretary and Treasurer. Mr. A. C. Tyner was the son of Mr, John Tyner and brother of Mr. Christopher Tyner. A. C. was an exhibitioner and one of the brightest pupils that ever studied at the College. He carried off high honours at the University and engaged in the newspaper business, editing with the late W. A. Foster the *Daily Telegraph*, a paper published in Toronto from 1866 to 1872. Christopher Tyner was the well-known editor of the Hamilton *Times*, and subsequently on the *Daily Telegraph*. He was an ex-pupil and attained high honours at the University. S. F. Lafferty was a pupil who, in his College days, distinguished himself particularly in mathematics. He is now a Barrister in Chatham, Ontario.

In the issue of February 9th, we find the debating society discussed

" Has the freedom of the press been productive of good results? "

Affirmative—Messrs. E. H. Tiffany, McCaul and Rossin.

Negative—Messrs. Tyner, Crawford and J. Ross Robertson.

Vice-President Lafferty will take the chair at 4 p.m. precisely, when a full attendance is respectfully requested.

E. H. Tiffany was the publisher of the *Boys' Own Paper*. McCaul, or "Doctor," as he was familiarly called, was the son of the Rev. Dr. McCaul, and Rossin was Julius Rossin, son of the owner of the Rossin House, now a wealthy merchant, a resident of Hamburg, who recently endowed the University with a scholarship valued at a thousand dollars. The others have been referred to before.

In connection with this debating society, a humorous handbill was circulated, giving the proposed programme of a drama and a comedy which never materialized. The playbill read:

V.  R.

TIMBUCTOO DEBATING SOCIETY.
KING STREET WEST, TORONTO.

POSITIVELY LAST PERFORMANCE,
Prior to the appearance of a new company.

☞ BENEFIT OF MR. JOHN ROSS ROBERTSON,
PRINTER TO THE "COLLEGE."
Rossin's Splendid QUADRILLE BAND will be in attendance, and Perform during the Evening.

THIS FRIDAY EVENING, MARCH 25TH, 1859.
Will be performed the Celebrated Drama, in Three Acts, adapted for Representation in the British Provinces for Mr. T. S. Reid, entitled

COLLEGE AS IT WAS;
OR,
THE DAYS OF OLD.

Dan O'Trot	J. R. Robertson.
Ragged Pat	Topney Crawford.
Neil O'Carolan	Mr. Thompson.
Conor O'Flaherty	" Montizambert.
Mons. Voyage	" Tyner.
Slang (a Cockney)	" Reid.
Gossoon	" Harris.
Magistrate	" Rossin.
Flunker	" Lafferty.
Doctor	" McCaul.
Judy O'Trot	Miss Julia Bogert.
Honor	" K. Jones.
Florence	" Julia Read.

The Evening Entertainment to conclude with the Sterling Old
English Comedy of

RESPONSIBLE GOVERNMENT.

Sloucher	Mr. A. C. Tyner.
Charles II	" Manson.
Rochester	" Read.
Edward	" Bogert.
Caucus	Miss Kate Jones.
Lady Clara	" Julia Bogert.

Boxes 50 cents; Pit 25 cents; Family Circle 25 cents.

Doors open at Half-past Seven. Commence at 8 o'clock.

GOD SAVE THE QUEEN.

"Topney Crawford" was a son of the Hon. George Crawford, of Brockville.

Thompson was the son of Mr. Thomas Thompson, Sr., the King street merchant, and is now an expert shorthander on the Grand Trunk. Montizambert is now the well known Medical Officer of the Dominion, at Grosse Isle. A. C. Tyner was the second son of the late Mr. John Tyner, of Yonge street. T. S. Reid was a brother-in-law of the late Mr. William Hay, the architect. Joseph Harris the son of the late Mr. Harris, of Buchanan, Harris & Co., of Hamilton. He now resides in Marton, New Zealand. S. F. Lafferty was the son of a Yonge street storekeeper, and is one of the brightest mathematicians in Canada. D. F. Bogert is an Anglican clergyman, resident at Belleville; and Read for some years practised law at Cayuga.

This month noted the formation of the College Boarding-house Debating Society, of which Messrs. Foley, son of Hon. M. H. Foley, Dewar, Benjamin, son of Hon. L. H. Benjamin, Radenhurst, Ranney, and Turquand, son of Dr. Turquand, of Woodstock, McKee Rankin, afterwards the actor, Bell, of Belleville, Jessup, of Brockville, now of the Dominion Land Office, Winnipeg, Austin, the Rev. Henry, of Gananoque, Hoyles, of Newfoundland, and others were leading lights.

In the issue of April 20th, 1859, we find verses written by an ex-pupil of the College in the *Grumbler* entitled " The College Boys' Complaint." The state of the College playground was so bad that an appeal had to be made to the Senate of the University and the lines were eagerly read by the boys, many of whom will recognize the poetical effort.

THE COLLEGE BOYS' COMPLAINT.

Respectfully dedicated to the Senate of the University of Toronto by the Boys of Upper Canada College.

Cheerily ring the voices of Spring,
   O'er the shrill cool April blast;
The birds twitter forth their opening hymn,
   And the leaflets are opening fast,
Through the dusky pine, in a dying whine,
   Old Winter his death dirge sings,
But no merry shout of boyish glee
   From the walls of the College rings.

The beavers peep from their wintry sleep,
   The beetle drones out its mirth,
And the trees shuffle on their garb of green
   To gladden the wakening earth.
Joyous and free in its fresh spring glee,
   Chirps even the meek little cricket;
But an acre of mud is all we can get
   For the bat, the ball and the wicket.

We'd a verdant lawn in the times agone,
   Where we gambolled and played at our ease,
Till our playground was ruthlessly spoiled
   By that odious Senate's decrees.
The dear old spot must in silence rot,
   Or in building lots be sold,
Oh, it galls our hearts as we sigh and think,
   On the good lost times of old.

E'en the squirrel now, from bough to bough,
   In its joyous gymnastics may spring,
But never a swing, a bar, or a pole,
   From the Senate can College boys wring,
The time has been in summer's sheen,
   Many hours we sported away,
But an old flag-staff in a desert of mud,
   Is all that is left us to-day.

"All work and no play" is as bad, sirs, to-day.
   As when you, old griffins, were boys;
Our playground give back, with its coating of grass,
   And hurrah! for our old College boys.
And this we can tell, we shall travel as well
   On the hawthorny pathway of knowledge,
If you give a free rein to the play-hour sport
   Of the pupils of old U. C. College.

Cheerily ring the voices of Spring
   O'er the shrill cool April blast;
The birds twitter forth their opening hymn,
   And the sternness of Winter is past,
In the old playground, let our voices resound,
   At old British cricket once more,
And with bats, as with books, we'll beat all the world
   As we did in the good days of yore.

In April of 1859 the boys determined to make an appeal to the Senate so that the playground should be placed in proper condition. They did so in the following petition, which was shaped first into existence on a slate in Mr. Dodds' room, and was then written in a good fair hand by Smallwood, the only coloured boy in the College, a clever fellow, who wrote a fine, large round hand, that could be read as easily as printed matter. The petition read :

"The petition of the pupils of Upper Canada College humbly sheweth, That—

"Whereas the playground appropriated for the use of the pupils of this institution was levelled during the month of September last, and left unsown and unsodded, it is at present in a state totally unfit for use, and that as the season for cricket playing is rapidly approaching, unless steps are immediately taken to render the said ground fit for the purposes to which it has been hitherto applied, there will be no possibility of the pupils enjoying it during the approaching summer.

"Your petitioners, therefore, humbly call the attention of your honourable body to the state of their playground, and earnestly impress upon you the necessity of taking immediately such measures as will render it suitable for use, and enure to your petitioners the advantages which they so eagerly desire. And they, as in duty bound, will ever pray."

In the issue of May 5th, 1859, J. T. M. gave his views on "The College Bell." He opened with the stanza :

> How many tales of cares and woe,
> Could that old bell unfold ;
> Back in my memory doth it grow,
> So, come, it must be told.
> *   *   *   *

And closed—

> But for me 'tis past that good old time,
> Would that 't were back again ;
> Yet the College bell still rings in rhyme
> To the air of the "Crack o' the Cane."

We also find that at a meeting of the debating society, "Is pestilence more to be dreaded than war?" was discussed by Messrs. Rossin, Tyner, Vandersmissen, Crawford, Jones and Foley. Mr. Vandersmissen is the University German Professor of to-day.

The exhibition competition at the College was in the early days the cause of great rivalry and excitement, and the results were always looked for with anxiety. Young Snider, of Eglinton, was a competitor in 1859, and his efforts were immortalized in a few stanzas by J. T. Morgan.

A rapid run through a portion of an old file of *The Times* gives an idea of the style of the paper. Not that it was up to a high literary standard, but as a paper turned out by boys in every department it was popular and entertaining to the youthful mind it catered for.

In the fall of 1860 Robertson left the College, and migrated to the Model Grammar School under Mr. G. R. R. Cockburn, where his spare hours were devoted to the publication of *The Young Canada*. It was a larger, better printed and edited sheet than the old *College* or *Boys' Times*. The experience gained in the old paper was a great advantage, and it was made attractive by outside contributions, and its circulation was more general. In the Upper Canada College about three hundred were sold, while in the Model Grammar and Model schools, about a hundred and fifty copies were subscribed for. In the year 1861 the name of the paper was changed to *The Young Canada Sporting Life*, a large portion of the space being devoted to sports and pastimes.

Robertson had from 1859 till 1862 devoted all his odd hours to learning the trade of printer in the old *Globe* office, in Alexander Jacques' office and in the *Guardian* office, so that in a very few years he became an adept with the composing stick and was in a position to manage a moderately sized office. Some of the first type he ever handled was some that was given him by the late Wm. Lyon Mackenzie. Wm. Mackenzie, the son of the Reformer, was a pupil at the College, and a strong friendship sprung up between him and the youthful type setter. The noted Reformer owned a printing office, from which he issued his celebrated "Message," and it was from that place that part of the type came. Robertson had a long chat one day with the veteran journalist, and gave that gentleman his views as to how a daily paper should be conducted, little dreaming that he would one day have to profit personally by the advice he was tendering.

The title *Young Canada* was dropped in 1860, and that of *The Sporting Life* adhered to. It was printed and published in a job office, which was formed out of the *Boys' Times* and *Young Canada* offices on King street, over what was then Brown's exchange office, one door east of the Rice Lewis building on King street, east of Toronto street. It was the first sporting paper in Canada.

To return to the rival paper, to *The Boys' Times*, we find that March of 1858 saw the issue of *The Boys' Own Paper* at Upper Canada College. It was typographically a handsomer sheet than the *The Boys' Times*. Tiffany had more resources at his command than his opponent, and consequently was enabled to turn out a larger and more entertaining paper. It was three columns wide and the type was set up by Tiffany, who was then an amateur printer, an adept at the art. The paper was excellent, both in its editorials and selections, and the printing was as good as could be produced. The investment was not, however, a satisfactory one, and it ended in the merging of the paper into *The Monthly Times*.

In 1862, Robertson visited Europe, and, on his return, was assured of a permanent situation, as either a junior in the old Commercial Bank, at $200 a year, an ensigncy in the army, through influential friends and relatives at the War Office, or a situation in the dry-goods establishment of his father on Yonge street. Of the three evils, the least was chosen, and copying letters, marking bales and cases for customers, whose families had ample chance to grow while their notes were in process of payment, was the apparent fate of one whose appetite had been sweetened by the magnetism of the composing stick, and whose muscle had been developed by a frequent pull at the arm of a Washington press. Three weeks at the work was about all that was necessary, and, with a "good-bye" to dry-goods and all its departments, save and except as regards personal attire, Robertson took hold of *The Grumbler*, the weekly comic paper which was edited by Erastus Wiman, W. J. Rattray, W. A. Foster, James Wright and Edgar Judge, and in 1862 continued the publication, with W. J. Rattray, W. A. Foster, James Wright, now of *Grip*, and James McCarroll, the author of the Terry Finegan letters, as contributors. *The Grumbler* flourished until 1864, when its proprietor went on the staff of the *Globe*, as city editor. In 1866 Robertson and J. B. Cook, of the *Leader*, started the *Daily Telegraph*, which ran for five years. Walter Barrett, son of Dr. Barrett, wrote his first paragraph on *The Telegraph*, and has since then successfully improved his opportunities and shown marked ability as financial editor of the New York *Times*, one of the leading dailies of the metropolis of the American continent.

On the 30th of January, 1871, the publication of a journal at the College was resumed. It was styled *The College Times*, which, it will be remembered, was the name of the first paper issued at the College in September of 1857. This new venture, had a continuous publication from 1871 until the 27th June, 1873, when its editors, in a farewell article, thanked the "outside contributors for their assistance, the advertisers for their patronage, and the public for their appreciation of our humble efforts." From the 30th January, 1871, until the 26th June of that year, the paper was issued bi-monthly, with Messrs. F. W. Kerr and Len Harstone as editors, with a committee of management consisting of Messrs. J. A. M. Aikins, R. Atkinson, W. A. Biggar, J. H. Cameron and W. A. Langton. The proceedings of the College Literary Society, the Cricket and Base Ball

Clubs, were duly chronicled, while the paragrapher and those skilled in making poetry had ample space at their disposal. In the issue of 13th February, Mr. W. A. Langton was the joint editor, Mr. Kerr exchanging positions with him on the committee of management. The issue of 26th June concluded the closing number of the series, and in a piquant article of a column the announcement was made " This issue is our last. The allotted ten numbers have now been issued and here is the last of the series number one of *The College Times*, undoubtedly and without question the greatest newspaper the world has ever seen."

As a literary production this revival of the College paper was popular with the boys. The pabulum supplied pleased its patrons, who, by the way, were not confined to the youthful constituency. City merchants were glad to secure space at ten cents a line, and when one King street mercantile light, whose bills for clothing against College paters would reach from the Atlantic to the Pacific, hesitated about signing an order for space, a youthful member of the committee, whose father was a journalist, suggested that " a drop of ink makes millions think," which so tickled the tailor that, without a word, he sent the boys away happy.

As we turn over the old files we find many lively and interesting sketches—an account of the Convocation at the University of Toronto, which appeared in *The College Times* of 26th June, 1871, from which we extract the following:

" At three o'clock the beautiful Convocation Hall was crowded with youth, beauty and intelligence, as the procession of dignitaries filed in. First came the Undergraduates—the throng of lesser stars ; then the Graduates—after them the Senate and Professors; the whole tapering to a very fine point in the person of the Chancellor, escorted by the Esquire Bedels of the graduating year—Messrs. Fletcher and Dale, the successful candidates for the Prince's Prize and the gold medal in classics, both of them U. C. boys. We ourselves now looked around us and prominent among the distinguished guests, we noticed the Church School, the Medical Board, the Rev. Mr. Punshon, the Lunatic Commission and our own reporter. In scarlet majestic, terrific in pink sleeves, arose Dr. McCaul to present the medals in classics. ' He had examined many men in classics (cheers) but he had never examined men who had answered his very trying questions and those of his colleague, Mr. Bell, and passed (cheers and laughter) such an eminently successful examination (cheers) as the men who now stand upon the platform (cheers).' Here follows, fully, one of the Doctor's ablest addresses. ' Mr. Loudon had the pleasure of presenting Mr. Ballard, who was born in 1847, in England, and was christened in the following year.

He had early displayed great mathematical talents, and at the Whitby Grammar School had become a prodigy and was sent up to take the gold medal, which he had done. Mr. Teefy, on the contrary, was born in 1849, and his baptism, he believed, was also registered; at the age of ten years he went to Richmond Hill Grammar School, and after remaining there $x+5$ years he came down to the University, and now stands before you in his $x+9$ year. And both of them live in the ardent hope of following up their mathematical successes and of figuring for $y+m$ years in the larger arena of the world."

"The Chancellor then presented Mr. Fletcher with the Prince's Prize, a beautiful ink bottle, neatly engraved, with his name on one side, and on the other, Blue black writing fluid." So sportively and naively runs the whole account, ending with what must be as great a source of pride to U. C. C. boys now as it was then—" We cannot help adding that four gold medals, one silver medal, and the Prince's Prize in Arts, the two scholarships in law, one in medicine and eight in arts, had been taken by U. C. C. boys."

On the 19th February, 1872, after a lapse of seven months, under an article headed "Not Dead Yet," *The College Times*, phœnix-like, revived again to the great delight of the boys. Mr. W. A. Langton was now the managing editor, the editing and executive committee being composed of Messrs. W. A. Langton, Chairman ; J. G. McKeown, Secretary ; R. D Richardson, Treasurer; W. H. Biggar, H. E. Hodgins, R. Atkinson, H. E. Morphy, J. A. Paterson, W. N. Ponton and E. B. Brown. The leading editorial reviewed the most important events in the history of the College during the year. The College Debating Society had passed away, and its place was acceptably occupied by the formation of the Upper Canada College Literary Society. The progress of cricket and other games and pastimes was duly noted in the article, the paragrapher closing up the last column of the first page by a reference to a boy correspondent, who wrote : "We used to hear long ago that the curse of Cain was upon us all. We do not think the curse of cane exists in Upper Canada College." "This," writes the paragrapher, "was sent in by a marvellously intelligent boy in the Third Form, who had probably narrowly escaped a licking." In another paragraph, under the head of "Vaccination" a boy reporter writes : "Ritualistic practices are on the increase in the boarding-house. On Ash Wednesday the boarders mortified the flesh by undergoing the operation of vaccination."

Every issue down to 29th June, 1872, was bright and readable, and at that date the issue ceased. The plan of publication was to print ten numbers in the year, the last being issued prior to the summer holidays. The work of revival was apparently left to new editing committees, and one of these, with the determination and pluck which are the distinguishing characteristics of College boys, marked the 24th of January, of 1873, with " Vol. III. No. 1, whole No. 21" of another series of *The College Times*. This year Mr. E. B. Brown, the son of J. Gordon Brown, was " Editor-in-Chief," the editing and executive committee consisting of Messrs. E. B. Brown, Chairman ; W. N. Ponton, Secretary; J. C. Harstone, Treasurer ; E. A. Bowes, T. A. Ridout, A. W. Sprague and R. Kennedy. This series continued from January to July. On February 25th, 1873, Mr. W. N. Ponton became Editor-in-Chief, while Mr. Brown assumed the duties of Chairman of the Editing Committee, and Mr. H. W. Aikins succeeded Mr. R. Kennedy, who had left the College. It is no reflection upon past issues of the new series to state that Mr. Ponton made a capital editor, and that the committee turned out a very lively and interesting sheet. The issue of 25th February contained a clever and laughable sketch of " An Afternoon with the Masters," being the report of an alleged meeting, or rather " A Stormy Debate " held by the Masters. The article was continued in the succeeding issue, but the opening chapter is worthy of reproduction :

"STORMY DEBATE."

" On Friday afternoon, the 15th February the Masters met in the Council-room.

" All felt that a crisis was impending, and that a storm was about to break forth which would astonish the world around, have no little effect on the stock market and might even cause a change in the administration of the country. Grave were the countenances of the Masters as they sat around the board in the Council-room. Graver was the countenance of the presiding officer himself, the great Principal of Upper Canada College, who knew right well that the proposition would that day be brought forward —but we anticipate.

" After routine, the first Mathematical Master rose to his feet. He had a duty to perform, a duty from which he would not shrink ; no one regretted more than he that anyone present would be personally objectionable to any other person present, but he would show both by reason and example before he had finished that he had good grounds for what he was about to say. He had for many years, in common with the rest of the Masters, placed the fullest confidence—despite the hypercritical hallucinations which would sometimes equivocally influence the most just and impartial minds—in the character of the Principal, for it was about that gentleman, his friend (if he would allow him to call him so), that he had to speak. He was grieved, chagrined, to have to change his mind. On a former occasion, his honourable friend, the First Classical, had occasion to make some remarks upon an unconstitutional phrase, which he, the Principal, had adopted. Would that it had stopped there! But no, the inexorable fates, which wield the destiny of men, declared that the Principal should once more err and violate the fundamental principles of the constitution, which ought to be the proudest boast of every man present. (Loud and prolonged cheering. A voice from the reporters' gallery: 'Hold on, old boy, till we take down the exact words.') He alluded to the constitution of the College governed by the Masters in Council. Many new innovations had the Principal introduced during his term of office. Not the least noticeable among them was the improvement and refinement, which he had introduced with regard to the Marking System—the proudest boast of the College, the Magna Charta of the Constitution, the great stronghold of the Masters! (Repeated cheers). It had been lately stated in a journal, to which he need not allude by name, that the Marking System had been introduced for the purpose of keeping the Masters up in their arithmetic. It did not so act with *him*. *He* worked the results by a very simple formula, a judicious mixture of algebra and trigonometry, which he had been in vain endeavouring to teach to the Sixth Form for the last six years. But he digressed. (Hear, hear). What he had to say simply was that the Principal had made a dangerous violation of the constitution in actually (mark his works) *giving a form seven markings with a view of changing their places upon one examination paper.* He (Mr. B.) was now prepared to cry hold! 'The subject who is truly loyal,' etc. What Mr. C. had done was an arbitrary measure, and this Mr. B. would never advise nor submit to. Was not this running the Marking System to its death? Seven markings! Surely three were enough; but seven! Why not eight, ten, or twenty? (Huge applause.) His disagreeable duty was now at an end; he had remonstrated in a few feeble words with the Principal for the course he had taken. He would now take his seat. His honourable friend, the First Classical (if he was not mistaken), had a motion to make, which his honourable friends would hear immediately. (Loud cheering.)

"The First Classical Master moved: 'That in consequence of the manifest ill-conduct of the Chairman of this august Council (the Principal), the First Mathematical Master be elevated to that post.'

"'This motion will come up for discussion next Friday,' quoth the Principal, and the Masters adjourned. The odds being freely taken, two to one against B———n by the betting men."

The "Answers to Correspondents" in the issue of 11th March, 1873, are full of humour. We select three by way of sample.

"Willie—Our space will only permit us to give the public the substance of your long letter, viz.: The architectural design of the 'four walls with a roof on,' and appliances for comfort therein are sadly in need of reform. Suggestions to the Government to 'fork over' some of the surplus for this purpose, instead of establishing lunatic and inebriate asylums, etc., etc. Sentiment good and concurred in. Composition bad."

"Charley—Canada has a good many authors, but the Shorter Catechism was not, we believe, written by a Canadian."

"G. Nuptus—We would have been most happy to have published your piece gratis, had you given us the first refusal of it. As we make it a rule never to print anything which comes 'second hand' should you wish to obtain *cinclyta fama gloria*, please favour us with your pieces *before* the editors of *London Fun*. Many thanks, however."

The weather paragrapher on the 7th April, 1873, was evidently in ecstasies of delight at the approach of spring when he wrote as follows :

"As we go to press a fine, drizzling rain is falling, permeating and perforating the remaining snow, and acting as the harbinger of the ethereal and long delayed spring."

Some claim that *The College Times* was the foster mother of *The 'Varsity*, the ablest of all College papers on the Continent. Indeed, in the days of the first issue of *The College Times*, in 1857, many of the old pupils, who had passed through the College and University, contemplated a publication in the interests of the students of the latter institution, but the idea was not at that time carried into effect.

The College Times, of 7th of April, in this year, had an announcement of the coming University journal, in the following paragraph :

"University College.—We may mention that the students at University College are taking measures for the starting of a journal. Supported as it will be by all the talent and ability for which that Institution is so celebrated, and also by experienced journalists (many having been on the staff of *The College Times* for the last two years), it will, no doubt, prove completely successful, should the enterprise be found to be practicable."

The issue of 27th June, 1873, wound up the series. The leading article was on "A Sixth Form," by Mr. Goldwin Smith. As it is most interesting we extract the following :

"It has been suggested to me that I should contribute something to *The College Times*, on the subject of the functions, which may be usefully discharged by the Sixth Form in a Canadian School. I would gladly do anything in my power to throw light on the subject, as well as to assist the editors of *The College Times ;* but I fear I can do but little. The moral authority of a Sixth Form, and the possible scope of its duties, must depend in great measure on social sentiment, which always pervades schools and colleges, as well as society at large ; and as to the social sentiment of Canada in general, or of Canadian schools in particular, I, a recent immigrant, am not very well qualified to judge.

"Nobody would recommend the mechanical reproduction of the English system in Canada. We should miscarry as ludicrously, and, with more serious consequences, than the Chinese, who produced an exact imitation of a steam vessel, only omitting the steam, and putting a quantity of lighted straw to make the smoke.

"However, the fact is, that there is no uniform system in England. I was myself at Eton, which I suppose I may call the most typical as well as the largest of English public schools. I have little doubt that the system of Sixth Form authority, and the cognate system of fagging, had there descended from the middle ages. In the middle ages strict subordination was the rule of every household, and the noblest youths waited as pages on their elders at table ; such service was, in fact, regarded as a regular part of the education of the young nobility. These traditions had remained unbroken in the old scholastic household founded by the good and pious, though unhappy, King Henry VI. The example of monastic life, to which that of places of education in the middle ages, always under the rule of the clergy, had some affinity, tended in the same direction. When I was at Eton, there were twenty Sixth Form boys out of a school numbering seven hundred, and which now, I believe, numbers a thousand. These boys had certain privileges, and enjoyed a certain personal inviolability, if the word is not too grand. In return, they were expected to put down, or in extreme cases, to report to the masters everything very disgraceful, especially bullying, fighting and blackguardism of any kind. No power of inflicting personal chastisement was ever formally delegated to them, though they sometimes exercised their authority in rough and ready ways ; nor were they ever treated as regular parts of the machinery of government and subordinate colleagues of the masters. Equals, or nearly so, in practical importance to the Sixth Form, were the 'captains,' or senior boys of the boarding-houses, among which the 'Oppidans,' or boys not on the Foundation, were distributed. The boarding-houses were some twenty in number, and of course, in many of them there was no Sixth Form ; but the senior boy, whatever his standing might be, was invested with the authority and responsibility of a Sixth Form boy so far as the house was concerned. The privilege of fagging belonged not only to the Sixth but to the upper part of the Fifth. Whatever it may have been in more primitive

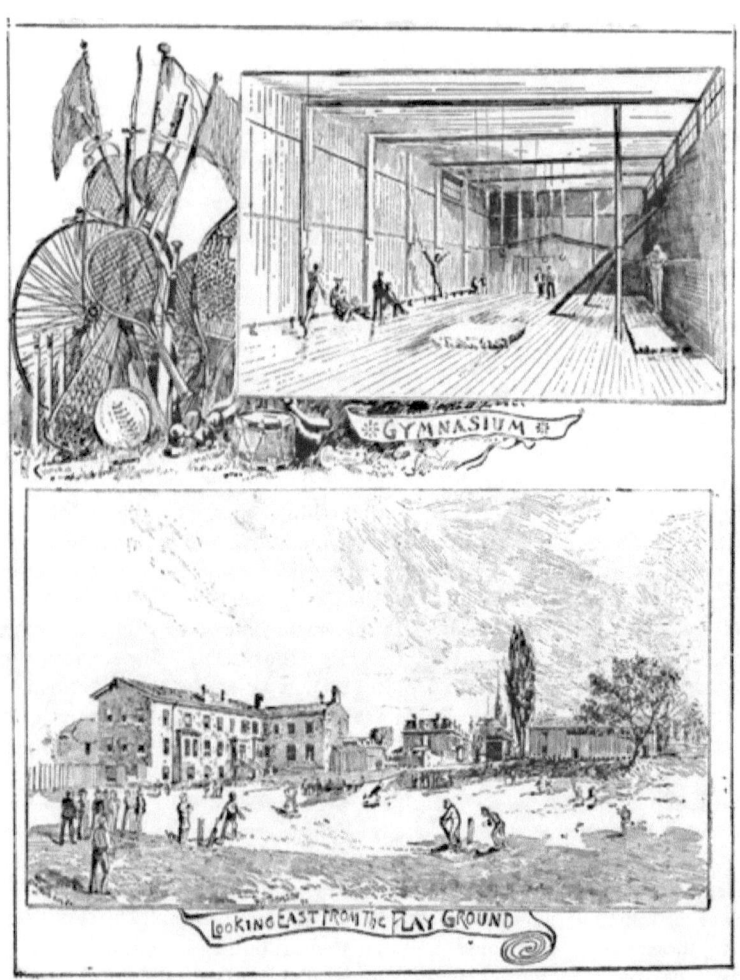

times, I can truly say that in my time, and as I experienced it, it involved neither cruelty nor degradation. The principal part of the fag's duty was to lay the things for the upper boy's breakfast and tea. These meals we took in our rooms. Dinner we took in the hall of the boarding-house, and the attendance at table, as well as the domestic service generally, was abundant. Indeed, we lived, I suspect, in too great luxury. The upper boy, while he received from his fag these slight services, owed him in return advice and protection, which to a new boy were invaluable. The result, I should say, on the whole was good. Eton, in my time, was not distinguished by industry ; I am afraid that I must say that for the mass of boys it was a very idle place, though the clever and ambitious were encouraged and stimulated by a great amount of personal attention and an almost lavish system of prizes. But it was a happy place, and it was comparatively free from ruffianism and blackguardism, if not from all kinds of vice. I can attest that a weak and sickly boy might enjoy there a remarkable immunity, not only from bullying and cruelty, but from molestation of any kind, till he grew stronger and was able to do as other boys did. I shall say, too, that foul language and filthiness of all kinds were considerably kept in check. I do not say, nor do I believe, that the moral standard was high, but the point of honour was ; and to lie to a master, which is too often deemed venial, was certainly deemed dishonourable at Eton. This, however, was probably due rather to social traditions brought from home than to anything in the system of the school. However, I speak of Eton as it was in my own time. Schools are continually changing in tone as well as in other respects ; and thirty years have now passed since I stood in the great quadrangle crowded with boys, by King Henry's statue waiting for the school hour, played on those broad lawns stretching along the Thames, from which the pile of ancient buildings rises ; or took my evening meal with my chosen friend in the snug little room, the separate possession of which, I have no doubt, was the important element in our civilization. Even in those days, everything, including Sixth Form rule and fagging, was much rougher among the Foundationers than among the Oppidans ; but the Foundation has since been greatly improved. Fagging, no doubt, even in its mitigated form, is too repugnant to the sentiment of the present day to last much longer, if it has not already been abolished."

On the 14th of March, 1882, Vol. IV. of *The College Times* once more became a living factor in College life. It was issued every third Thursday in the College year and was a vigorous publication, with plenty of dash and enthusiasm, filled with readable verse and entertaining prose, keeping up a general interest in current news, with kindly references to young ladies' seminaries, which were situated within sight of the College. It may not have been as great a pecuniary success as former efforts in College journalism, but it was perhaps the best edited of all its predecessors.

The name of the editor is not given. All literary contributions were "to be addressed to the editor." Mr. W. N. Ponton was one of the principal contributors. The "make-up" of this sheet differed from that of its predecessors. The type was larger and there were two columns to the page instead of three. This series which composed Vols. IV. and V., closed on 6th July, 1883.

The new publication made its bow to a College public by announcing that :

"After an interval of nearly nine years *The College Times* again makes its appearance—excellence cannot be hid for ever. The literary spirit of the College lay smouldering for a time beneath the smoking ruins of the paper that has to-day revived with more than a flickering flame; but smoke though it may often assume shapes both pretty and amusing, was felt to be of too dull and glowing nature to suit the brighter intellects it was overshadowing, and the love of literature has at length dispelled the cloud, and resolved itself into a tangible form—*The College Times*. The pupils of the College take a lively interest in their new venture, and will spare no trouble to bring about the success they so heartily desire. It is not, however, among the present pupils only that the resuscitation of the old paper meets with approval, but also among those of many years back, who still feel a warm interest in anything connected with the 'old College' at which their younger days were spent so happily and with such advantage to themselves. *The College Times* of the former regime, we are told, was eagerly read by the boys at the earliest opportunity and freely discussed and criticised—of course, in the ablest manner. We hope that its present namesake may enjoy like popularity, and suffer as little from adverse criticism, and we, for our part, will endeavour to make it deserving of such indulgent treatment."

Then, in a jocular vein, it noted the exodus to the Island of citizens, who fly to a cooler clime when the thermometer jumps into the nineties. The editor writes:

"Already people are beginning to think of forsaking the noisy city and luxurious home for the Island, to revel in a few months of comfort in half-furnished houses, where the plain (but not planed) pine floors will persist in running splinters into one's foot; where the wet sand gets into the island sojourner's hair and clothes, and above all into his boots; where on every rainy night the water leaks in through the roof right on to the top of his nose, until, after enjoying this kind of nightmare for half-an-hour, he awakens with the exclamation: 'Confound it; do you think my nose is a cistern?'—where in fact everything that is charming and heavenly can be enjoyed to its full extent; and yet in spite of all these 'comforts,' who can help feeling just a little envious, when looking at a happy, jolly party, lazily grouped around a blazing camp-fire, singing and talking, and forming a perfect picnic of lazy, careless, quiet enjoyment?"

Then some inquisitive boy reporter found out that at an aristocratic seminary on Peter street, where co-education of the sexes was not advertised in the curriculum, a colt of ten years—a relative of the lady director, studied in the class with the fair ones, who two by two took their afternoon constitutional past the College, guarded by a keen-eyed governess. This discovery was food for a paragraph in the following terms:

"The attention of our Argus-eyed janitor is called to the fact that certain young ladies from an adjoining seminary of learning, in which the co-education of the sexes is practised, have made certain breaches, both of the College fence and discipline, by perforating the former at the N.-W. and S.-W. corners of the playground, in order to spy out the gallant boarders in their moments of relaxation."

Another extract commends itself as being an alleged copy of a set of notes by a boy, who in the double role of contestant at the College games and competitor at an examination in the second book of the Æneid, went off into dreamland the night before the physical and mental fray, and between the two got sadly mixed. The notes were evidently more useful for athletics than classics.

"*Notes in Virgil.*—'Jamque dies exoptata aderat,' quoth many a boarder as he closed his eyes on Thursday night to dream of the coming games.

"'Conticuere omnes, intentique ora tenebant,' as the wheel-barrows come hustling along, each dragging a small boy behind it.

"'Et quorum pars magna fui,' said each youthful magnate, as he described the athletic sports to his wondering sisters.

"'Fidens animi, atque in utrumque paratus,' might have been said with truth of each of the contestants in the steeple chase.

"'Omnis opes puerorum, et coepti fiducia belli "ancoræ" auxiliis semper stetit,' as the Sixth formed in line for the tug-of-war; but the boys at the other end of the rope smiled half pityingly and thus remonstrated: 'O Miseri, quæ tanta insania, pueri?' Creditis that you can pull us over? "go way.'"

For years after this the boys did not dabble in printers' ink. The projectors of the last revival did not care to invest in what might be an unprofitable speculation, and although editorial talent was always available and ready paragraphers were willing to sacrifice the midnight oil in order to provide "copy," no juvenile capitalists presented themselves with the financial sinews, without which enterprises cannot succeed.

At intervals between 1884 and 1886 some of the senior boys ventured to trifle with the pen, and at irregular periods produced the " Scholasterion," a publication in manuscript, brightened with pen-and-ink sketches of persons and passing events. This paper, however, had not the local name and fame which immortalized other juvenile productions, and yet it was a model of excellence, written by those who penned paragraphs with a freedom, which inspired respect from even those who sat in high places, and secured the abatement of many grievances, which more or less affected the welfare, and comfort of the pupils.

On November 4th, 1886, Vol. VI. of *The College Times*, made its presence known to the youthful constituency. The revived issue of 1886 was under the joint editorial care of Messrs. S. B. Leacock and F. J. Davidson, with B. M. Jones and H. G. Crocker, as sub-editors. A publishing committee aided in the work. It consisted of the editors, sub-editors and Messrs. D. J. Armour and O. P. Edgar. This series continued until the 9th June, of 1887. In October of 1888, Vol. VII., No. 1, was issued, with Messrs. G. F. Macdonnell and K. D. W. Macmillan as joint-editors, G. R. Geary, H. C, Small and W. P. Parker as sub-editors. Mr. C. J. Barr acted as secretary. Mr. W. C. C. Freeman as treasurer.

The Rev. T. Street Macklem, in writing of *The College Times*, recalls many pleasant and traditional associations connected with its publication. He states:

" In its columns may be found chronicled the *bon mots*, the nick-names, the escapades, the physical and mental exploits, the debates, the class-lists, the stories, the Munchausen-wise and otherwise, and many of the poetical and prose effusions of the boys and sometimes the masters. These date from those good old days when there were seven forms, and when boycotted victims were caned for being cornered on the shorts and longs. They read down to the present Utopian period, the modern outgrowth of young Canada's cosmopolitan civilization, when the power of love and the electric precocity of this generation are the pilots used to avoid the shoals of false quantities and false sentiments, and which render unnecessary the pickling of the budding rods.

" When one takes into consideration the youth and inexperience of the young editors, who from year to year, in shifting sanctums, with varying opportunities, with different inspirations and varied classes of readers, wielded quills of opinion and ventilated grievances of moment with frank, buoyancy and zeal and a realization of grave responsibility worthy of older heads and public journalists, one cannot but feel that there is no place like a public school for a boy of energy and character. Besides, if reading maketh the full man, speaking the ready man, and writing the exact man then, we may fairly maintain, that *The College Times* had been an educating and developing as well as pleasure-giving instrument in the hands of those who conducted it as a labour of love."

In reading over the names of the boys, who, for pure love of the work kept the editorial and news columns of the College up to the standard, the Rev. Mr. Macklem says:

"The remembrance of their association and the fellow-feeling of comradeship generated by their early literary ventures, both among those actively interested and among their readers, may be more enduring and more productive of good results than a closer application to other pursuits would have produced. Undoubtedly some things of questionable taste, some crude expressions, some rather personal but thoroughly good-natured remarks, and one or two spontaneous kicks against established authority might have been omitted without much loss to the Dominion. But we may say the same of every journal. As a surgeon wades through slaughter to a knowledge of practice so an editor must glide over some mistakes before reaching that mellow maturity of unimpassioned literature, the fit standard-bearer of the Fourth Estate. Besides what to many is reprehensible in style is to others mere spicy piquancy."

Of the value of College publications, Mr. Macklem also writes:

"As an adjunct to the Literary and Debating Societies, *The College Times* did its best work; it does it yet by showing how the literary products of pen and lips appear in public print and by teaching the practical lesson of writing and speaking most effectively so as to reach the public. It suggests the ideas of cohesion and responsibility and develops latent talent, But we must not under-estimate its value as a veracious reporting agency of games won and lost, of cricket and football matches played for the honour of the College, and of those numerous little incidents and honours of public school life, which, being printed in 'our own organ,' stimulate to further exertion and furnish an honourable and innocent reward for manly merit. With what pride does the boy who sees his name in print for the first time send his extra copies home, and how many notches higher does his flag float thereafter in his native place."

Since June of 1886, the traditional phœnix has had no occasion to arise in connection with the press of the old school, for *The College Times* is issued at regular intervals. Of the score of boys who trifled with the pen in these college days many are to the fore. The seed sown in 1857 has year after year returned a goodly harvest. Let us hope that the boys of the future will not let their love for the types fade away. The history of past efforts in the publishing line is ever before them. May they follow in the footsteps of the old boys, who, to-day, as they step past life's milestones, think of happy days spent in the old red pile. The boys of the College have made a record in every country, and in every clime. The honour rolls blaze with the names of those who in the halls of Parliament, on the bench, at the forum, or in the mercantile world have attained the highest positions. Others too have had renown, and in that thin red line or on the decks of old England's men-of-war, have registered their names on the tablets of fame, and laid down their lives amid the regret of all who honour their country and love the flag.

COLLEGE CRICKET.

BY G. G. S. LINDSEY.

IF IT be the public schools of England which have made her great it is the sports which, in turn have made the schools themselves famous. It is with cricket that the mind associates the names of Eton and Harrow, with football the name of Rugby. The academic halls have hardly exerted a larger or better influence in moulding the character of the schoolboy than has the playground; and what is true in this respect of English institutions is equally true of the Canadian public schools, foremost among which stands Upper Canada College. While she has been the *alma mater* of many of this country's greatest men, she too has been the mother and progenitor here of many of the manly sports, in which the landsmen of Ontario so freely and successfully engage. To the aborignee she yields the honour of his, the national game, indeed la crosse can hardly be said to have even taken hold until very recent years of the inclination of the college-boy; but to herself alone belongs the distinction of having introduced into the lake regions of Canada, cricket, football, and organized athletic games.

The regard in which cricket is held in Western Canada is largely due to the influence exerted in its favour by and through the two great public schools, Upper Canada College and Trinity College School, Port Hope. To Upper Canada College may be awarded the distinction of having consistently fostered the cricketing spirit since it opened its doors to pupils in January, 1830. As early as 1834 F. W. Barron, was appointed one of the classical masters, at which time George Anthony Barber, was College Collector, and John Kent, master of the boarding-house. These three gentlemen were enthusiastic cricketers, wielded the willow with great skill and at once made their favourite game the pastime of the pupils. Barber, Barron and Kent were the *triumviri* that posterity will remember as the fathers of Canadian cricket. Barber has been called *the* father of cricket in Canada, and perhaps justly so. He was absorbingly fond of all sports, a veritable encyclopædia of sporting history. The character of the man can be gleaned from his paper the *Herald*, which he published in the middle forties, and which is replete with sporting news. Principal Barron could not have been much less enthusiastic, nor could John Kent, and to these gentlemen, fortunately so placed, as to be able to exert a lasting influence upon their pupils, must be accorded the distinction of having introduced cricket permanently into Toronto. Barron and Barber are gone, but Kent, still an old bachelor, is living at Madeira, Spain where, until lately, he followed his calling as tutor, and among whose pupils was the Earl of Carnarvon, who died two years ago. In 1836 the College Eleven, which, on the 15th of July won from the Toronto Club, were : White, L. Robinson, A. Phillpots, J. Kent, A. Keefer, G. A. Barber, J. B. Robinson, F. W. Barron, Dyett, Hale and F. Keefer.

By the year 1847 so formidable had the cricketing strength of the College become that on the first day of September of that year eleven gentlemen of the College, past and present, defeated eleven gentlemen of the Province of Upper Canada. The *Herald* in reporting the match says, " We think it may justly be asserted that such another two-and-twenty could scarcely be brought together in Canada." The College eleven, without Heward and Helliwell, both crack players, were H. J. Ruttan, of Cobourg ; C. Sadlier and D. Crooks, of Hamilton ; Connolly, of Montreal ; F. W. Barron, A. Phillpots. G. A. Barber, B. Parsons, Muttlebury ; J. B. Robinson, and A. Patrick, of Toronto. The College scored 88 and 69, to which Phillpots contributed 19 and 5, Barron 6 and 22, Connolly 25 and 4, Barber 0 and 30, and for it the successful bowlers were Barron and Parsons. Parsons, better known as " Little Ben," had few equals as a bowler, and after leaving College probably took more wickets for the Toronto club than any man before or since. He was, as well, an excellent bat. Heward was a great run getter, as a few of his scores picked from the matches of the period will shew, 58, 56, 58, 39, 74, not out, 45, 67, not out and 58. Besides these he had highest scores in two International matches. J. O. Heward played longer for the Toronto club than any one else, his familiar figure being seen on the field until a very few years ago. His loss was a great one to the old club, by which he had stood for fifty years, doing yeoman service all the time. It was in the fifties, however, that he was in his prime and made his largest scores, although he had best average for his club in 1873. Phillpots was for many years the best wicket keeper in Canada ; those who remember him tell of wonderful feats performed by him behind the stumps. He was besides a reliable and successful bowler.

No more conspicuous figure than John Beverley Robinson appeared during these years upon the field. A tiptop bowler and dashing bat, his name figures in all the scores. In 1854 he won the ball for the highest score (54) in a college match. When he retired with well won laurels he was elected President of the Toronto club, and when later on he gave up this position, his friends gathered round and presented his estimable wife with a portrait of her husband.

This College and Province match to which allusion was made as having been begun in 1847 became at once an annual event, and was brought about by challenge and acceptance published in the press. In 1851 a clipping from one of the papers of the day announces that

"Eleven gentlemen of Upper Canada College will be happy to play the annual friendly game of cricket against eleven gentlemen of Upper Canada—to come off on the Toronto Club ground Thursday, July 24, 1851." On behalf of the College,

Toronto, June 28, 1851. JOHN BEVERLEY ROBINSON.

For six successive years the College defeated the Province, but in 1853 the tables turned and the Province won by 47 runs, due principally to the fine bowling of Napier. Up to this time there had been little change in the College team, except by the introduction of J. O. Howard and Helliwell who were consistently large scorers, and of G. Draper, C. Rykert and A. Hudspeth, from time to time valuable additions to the college strength. In 1850 the scoring was a little heavier than usual. Parsons made 7 and 35, Heward 22 and 14, J. B. Robinson 21 and 33, Barron 11 and 10, Cosens 5 and 36. The College totals were 82 and 164 for six wickets, those of the Province 172, to which Wilson, of Guelph, contributed 60 and 69.

In 1854 the Province again won; next year there was no game; in 1856 the College won by one run, and it is noticeable that in all these nine events there is not much change in the *personnel* of the College team. T. D. Phillips was a new and valuable addition to the later year elevens. This gentleman, afterwards the Rev. T. D. Phillips, made more runs than any player in the tournament held at Halifax in 1874 (197) though his average of 39.40 is second. He has always been a great run-getter and an enthusiastic cricketer and is now living in Chicago.

In 1859 the College won with the same old eleven by an innings and 35 runs. One of the papers of the day calls attention to the fact that "the College eleven, it should be understood, are not the present students of that College, but grown men who have been students of that institution and now comprising some of the best players in Canada." This view of the relations of the representative eleven to the College seems to have set people thinking, for in 1860 a complete change was made in the mode of choosing the College eleven, the players from this time, except G. A. Barber, being all young men, present or just graduated pupils; yet they won the annual match against the Province in 1860 by 9 wickets. J. and G. Brunel did the bowling, the former as well making top score, 25. E. W. Spragge got 17, Bogart 12 and 16. Next year the College again won, this time by 37 runs on the first innings; but it was the boys' unfinished second innings that is remarkable, they having amassed 158 runs for two wickets; of which memorable total E. W. Spragge got 22, G. Brunel 74, not out, Reginald Kennedy

24, and T. D. Phillips 19, not out. Brunel gave great promise at this time, and from that time on has been, till within a few years, a consistent scorer. His name appears in the scores against Daft's and Fitzgerald's eleven, as well as in those of several American international games, and he has always been a tower of strength to the Ottawa Club.

In 1861 G. R. R. Cockburn became Principal of the College, and at the same time a friend and ally of the game, and continued as such till he resigned ten years ago. In 1862, fortunately for the College, John Martland, an Oxford man, became second classical master, and was given charge of the Residence. Fresh from college, he brought with him the traditions of England's manly game and a love of it which time only served to increase. Elected president of the club in 1863, he continued in office until 1890, when amidst universal regrets he severed his connection with the old school. It is not probable that anyone has held a presidency so long as Mr. Martland. He at once took hold of the idea, then gaining ground, that the true secret of success lay in bringing the present pupils to the front, though not forgetting the claims of those who had left college to a share in her laurels. The policy initiated then has since prevailed. The matches of the College proper were played by the pupils of the day; the ex and present pupils meeting in friendly contest once a year. This annual event brought together those who had left the academic halls for more serious pursuits, and was the occasion of their renewing old friendships and meeting in the happiest way their successors on the eleven. During the afternoon of the match the garden party given by the Residence was ever in progress. Indeed, there must always be an inseparable connection in the players' minds between cricket and the social concomitants which were by no means the least enjoyable part of the day's proceedings or least responsible for the ever increasing popularity of the game. Is there an old boy who has ever played cricket at Upper Canada College who does not, when pondering over the matches on the College green, instantly associate with the pleasant memories of the match the hospitalities lavished in the rooms to the right of the Residence entrance, where the president, Mr. Martland, lived?

The Residence contributed more men on an average by one-half to the College eleven than the day boys. When then the graduating year said good-bye to college corridors and returned to their respective homes, the majority of them went forth into different quarters of the Province schooled in the game, trained to command, learned in the art of handling an eleven, and these are the men who, carrying away enthusiasm with them, founded the numerous clubs of Ontario, rekindled the smouldering embers of the game at home or strengthened their local club. During the ten years between 1860 and 1870, thanks to the kindness of the officers of the garrison, the soldiers were allowed to come to the school and coach the boys. The officers themselves, among them Captain Wallace, a former captain at Harrow, and Captain Northey, an old captain at Eton, were generous in their assistance, and, being well trained cricketers, by their contact in matches with the boys at the College, materially bettered the form of the youngsters. Two Americans, Ellard and Kemper, who had been trained by Wright at that time living in Cincinnati, but afterwards in New York, were a tower of strength to the eleven.

A perusal of the old scores between 1860 and 1870 will convince the reader that College cricket at that time was relatively much stronger than at any time since. In 1867 the College eleven won all its matches, defeating Toronto twice, Hamilton, the Royal Artillery and Hussars, the resident eleven of Trinity College and Trinity College and Trinity College School. The scores were large and the bowling effective. The names of those who distinguished themselves during those years are George Brunel, J. Brunel, E. W. Spragge, Bogart, T. D. Phillips, R. Æ. Kennedy, F. C. Perkins, Allan Anderson, a destructive bowler; R. K. Hope, a particularly fine and reliable bat, who played in admirable form and left on the pages of the College score books records which no successor will make; F. W. Hall, Robert Killaly, J. B. Laing, the best run getting bat the College ever turned out—he made 92 against Trinity College School in 1867; J. Brunel, a good bowler; W. J. Laing, G. Drummond, A. Laing, a fine bowler and scoring bat; F. Draper, J. Ellard, both a bat and destructive bowler; A. Hope, S. S. Kemper, A. M. Baines, good with bat and ball; J. R. Van Allan, W. Anderson and Curran Morrison, a destructive bowler.

The next decade produced some excellent men, individuals, among whom have been unexcelled, but whose achievements as a whole, contrasted with those of their predecessors, do not rank so high; possibly because they often had their predecessors for opponents. They were A. W. Spragge, E. C. Sills, W. B. Northrup, E. R. C. Proctor, R. R. Boulton, C. R. Atkinson, a destructive bowler and rapid scorer, J. Montgomery, J. C. Grace, D. Browning, F. L. Fellows, G. G. S. Lindsey, A. Gillespie, who never did much while at College, but who has since become Canada's best all round man, Hynes, the captain of the Irish Eleven of 1888, used to call him the "Canadian Bonner," E. E. Kittson, D. Armour, W. L. Connolly, W. W. Vickers and A. G. Brown. The brightest star, however, in all this constellation was E. R. Ogden, one of the best, if not the best bat, and one of the ablest bowlers and all-round men the college has ever produced. Later we find A. G. Smith, F. and C. Pardee, W. J. Fleury, and R. Montgomery doing good work. The Senklers, Harry and Ivan, Hal McGiverin, A. A. Macdonald, W. Marshell, and Fritz Martin are all fine cricketers, who will achieve greater things in the future and bring laurels to the old school. In 1889 Hugh Fleming, of Ottawa, and Fred. Langmuir put a very successful eleven in the field. J. M. Laing, now of Trinity University, and who played in the last International match, is the best of the latest men. At present L. and N. Cosby, J. Counsell, T. MacMaster, Mockridge and W. Moss and F. Waldie are maintaining the prestige of the old College.

What may be properly termed the First Canadian Eleven visiting the "old country," was organized by the writer in 1887. All who went were native Canadians, young men, the average age being less than twenty-three. Chosen from the Dominion at large they were a thoroughly representative eleven. The old College boys on the team were, A. Gillespie, W. J. Fleury, W. W. Jones, Dr. E. R. Ogden and G. G. S. Lindsey. C. N. Shanly went as umpire, R. C. Dickson as scorer and Lyon Lindsey as correspondent. The tour must be regarded in every way as a success. It had the sympathy and support of the whole people of Canada who have good reason to be satisfied with the results, which speak for themselves. One half the played out matches were won, and in most cases, the scores were large, much larger than the great majority of home scores. Ogden, had the best bowling analysis, and third average 23·37 for 701 runs. He also made 133 against Hampshire, and 99 against Northumberland. W. J. Fleury's average was 17·17 for 206 runs; W. W. Jones got a good many wickets and 234 runs, with an average of 9·36, and Gillespie put up 392 runs for an average of 13·07, and took more than his share of wickets. His best scores were 54 against Ireland, 45 against Hampshire and 44 against Northumberland.

The great match of the year since 1867 has been the one with the rival school, which was founded in that year at Weston, but which two years later moved to Port Hope. Fortune has favoured either side at different times, but at present Trinity College School is three wins ahead, having won thirteen matches as against ten, three games having been drawn. It has been usual hitherto to include in the list of intercollegiate matches those of 1874 and 1875 played between the Past and Present pupils, but they ought not to be so counted. The results of these two games were:

DATE.	PLACE.	SCORE.	RESULT.
July 17th, 1874..	Port Hope ..	T. C. S. .. 30 & 53 U. C. C... 74 & *10	Won by 9 wickets. (Past vs. Present.) *(1 wicket down.)
July 23rd, 1875..	Toronto	T. C. S. .. 97 & 57 U. C. C... 130 & *25	Won by 5 wickets. (Past vs. Present.) *(5 wickets down.)

A complete list of the games is given to 1892.

COLLEGE CRICKET.

Date.	Place.	Score.	Result.
June 25th, 1867..	Toronto	T. C. S. .. 14 & 10 U. C. C. .. 200	Won by an innings and 176 runs.
June 25th, 1868 .	Weston	T. C. S. .. 19 & 16 U. C. C. .. 33 & 103	Won by 101 runs.
June 15th, 1872..	Port Hope ..	T. C. S. .. 29 & 68 U. C. C. .. 50 & 107	Won by 60 runs.
Sept. 28th, 1872.	Toronto	T. C. S. .. 48 & 66 U. C. C. .. 98	Drawn.
June 14th, 1873 .	Port Hope ..	T. C. S. .. 44 & *34 U. C. C. .. 33 & 43	Lost by 7 wickets *(3 wickets down.)
June 26th, 1873..	Toronto	T. C. S. .. 37 & *29 U. C. C. .. 35 & 27	Lost by 4 wickets. *(6 wickets down.)
June 13th, 1874..	Port Hope ..	T. C. S. .. 46 & 86 U. C. C. .. 72 & *18	Drawn *(4 wickets down.)
June 27th, 1875..	Toronto	T. C. S. .. 37 & 29 U. C. C. .. 35 & 27	Lost by 4 runs.
June 26th, 1876..	Toronto	T. C. S. .. 55 & 81 U. C. C. .. 66 & 44	Lost by 26 runs.
Sept. 30th, 1876.	Port Hope	T. C. S. .. 82 & 57 U. C. C. .. 41 & 100	Won by 2 runs.
June 11th, 1877..	Toronto	T. C. S. .. 93 & 129 U. C. C. .. 96 & *32	Drawn *(3 wickets down.)
June 25th, 1878..	Port Hope ..	T. C. S. .. 35 & 32 U. C. C. .. 23 & 33	Lost by 11 runs.
June 25th, 1879..	Toronto	T. C. S. . 47 & 33 U. C. C. .. 98 & 50	Won by 68 runs.
June 26th, 1880..	Port Hope ..	T. C. S. .. 29 & 22 U. C. C. .. 56	Won by an innings and 5 runs.
June 11th, 1881..	Toronto	T. C. S. .. 45 & 50 U. C. C. .. 46 & 55	Won by 6 runs.
June 17th, 1882..	Port Hope ..	T. C. S. .. 62 & *26 U. C. C. .. 51 & 36	Lost by 8 wickets. *(2 wickets down.)
June 23rd, 1883..	Toronto	T. C. S. .. 28 & 68 U. C. C. .. 47 & 93	Won by 44 runs.
June 14th, 1884..	Port Hope ..	T. C. S. ..101 4 U. C. C. .. 19 & 57	Lost by an innings and 25 runs.
June 15th, 1885..	Toronto	T. C. S. .. 45 & *56 U. C. C. .. 56 & 44	Lost by 2 wickets. *(8 wickets down.)
June 12th, 1886..	Port Hope ..	T. C. S. ..138 & 63 U. C. C. .. 88 & 80	Lost by 33 runs.
June 25th, 1887..	Toronto	T. C. S. .. 85 & 60 U. C. C. .. 74 & 64	Lost by 7 runs.
June 25th, 1888.	Port Hope ..	T. C. S. .. 76 & 81 U. C. C. .. 65 & 45	Lost by 47 runs.
June 22nd, 1889..	Toronto	T. C. S. .. 26 & 64 U. C. C. .. 69 & *23	Won by 5 wickets. *(For 5 wickets.)
June 28th, 1890..	Port Hope ..	T. C. S. . 97 U. C. C. .. 31 & 44	Lost by an innings and 22 runs.
June 27th, 1891..	Toronto	T. C. S. .. 59 & 81 U. C. C. ..104 & *39	Won by 8 wickets. *(For 2 wickets.)

An effort has been made within the last two years to revive the old College and Province match, not however with very much success, still out of the effort has grown a desire on the part of many old members of college teams to play under the auspices of the old U. C. C. Association, a match between the old boys and an eleven of native Canadians, which shall take place on prize day, each July, on the new College grounds at Deer Park. Such a match ought to be the most interesting home game of the year.

For some years back professionals have had charge of the College eleven, and their work is beginning to bear fruit. At present cricket is strongly backed by Principal Dickson, who is having the elevens from the earliest time engraved on tablets to be put up in the entrance hall, and has a good friend in W. S. Jackson, while F. W. Terry, one of the new masters, a dashing bat and excellent wicket keeper, is sure to make his influence felt.

The records of the Upper Canada College clubs were not kept as well as they should have been. Score books and scores are missing. Every year at the close of the season a transcript of the scores should be made into a book kept for the purpose, and the averages and analyses appended for the year. As long ago as 1847 G. A. Barber preserved the balls used in the matches of the day, and had inscribed on them the records of the event in which they played so important a part. Some of them may be seen at the College to-day. Mr. J. C. Rykert, Q. C., who has the most complete book of cricket scores between 1847 and 1860, has kindly lent it to the writer, and from it many important facts and figures have been gleaned.

OTHER COLLEGE SPORTS.

BY A. A. MACDONALD.

THE Grand old English game of Rugby Foot-ball has only existed in Upper Canada College for a comparatively short time. Previous to 1876 the association game was played. In the latter year Mr. Edward Fürrer, then Modern Language Master, took a great interest in the game, and introduced some features of the English Rugby. In 1877 Mr. W. S. Jackson, present Dean of Residence, came to the School, and with his valuable experience gained at Rugby, became an inspiration to the players, who, under his instruction, completely adopted the English game. Mr. Jackson played on the forward line of the College team in 1877 and '78, and materially aided the boys in defeating Toronto University the first year and Trinity the second. Among the originators of the game were H. Woodruff, W. L. Conolly, C. Atkinson and Frank Keefer. The team was recognized as one of the "crack" aggregations of Toronto, and played matches successfully with all the senior clubs. Rugby foot-ball became the distinctive fall game of the school, and steadily gained in favour with the boys. The teams of 1885 and '86 were especially strong, largely owing to the efforts of Messrs. A. Y. Scott and G. Gordon. The former played forward, and was in himself a tower of strength. The latter played half-back, and by his consistently brilliant play, gained the reputation of being one of the best players in Canada. With him was associated Laurie Boyd, famous for four years in the same position at Varsity and now playing the same dashing game for Toronto. In latter years the great advance made in playing by senior clubs, largely owing to systematic organization and training, has made it a physical impossibility for the College team to compete with them on even terms. That they have been able to compete successfully with all the second fifteen of the best clubs has been clearly shown by the record of the last few years. In '88 "Pat" Ferguson captained a splendid team, which had an unbroken record of victory. In '90 and '91, T. F. Mill organized a fast and plucky team that in the former year defeated Trinity University, and in the latter year

Trinity School. Some years before there had been a regular annual football match with the Port Hope School. The revival of this will do much to stimulate the game in Canada. In '92, Port Hope visited Deer Park and again the blue and white was triumphant. Nothing is more significant of the grand work that Upper Canada College has done for foot-ball in this country than the great number of old boys who fill prominent places on the crack teams of Canada. And just as the College has been a nursery for the Dominion, so the junior teams of the School have produced the first fifteen that have won fame and honour by a victorious career. No better example of this can be found than Jack Counsell, the plucky and brilliant quarter-back of '92, who gained his experience by three years captaincy of the junior team. To the fact that boys learn the game as youngsters College owes her success. Brilliant as the last fifteen years have been in foot-ball fame, the prospects are now brighter than ever with the increased facilities and space for training, and the game will flourish at Deer Park as it did at the old King street grounds, and will continue to send out players to reflect credit on the good old School, in which they learned to "play the game."

There is no game in which Canada is so sadly behind the time as Lawn Tennis. We are children at the game in comparison with the Americans, who are again very inferior to the English players. The reason is manifest. The game is not properly played in the schools. Like all other games, it must be played from infancy. On the old college grounds lack of space prevented proper attention being given to the game. Now a new era is dawning, and the tennis enthusiasts are daily increasing. Three good courts are now available, and it is hoped that a large part of the central portion of the running track will be laid out in courts that will compete favourably with any in America, and under such circumstances, players worthy of the school will soon be developed.

Hockey, though only three years old in the School, has already made great strides, and has become firmly established as *the* winter sport. In 1888 an outside Hockey rink was made on the west side of the Gymnasium, and a Toboggan Slide was put up running into the grounds. No kind of exercise is better adapted for the winter months to keep the boys in the good condition to which they have attained by following out the excellent series of sports provided by the Hendrie Steeple-chase and Athletic Meeting in the Spring, cricket in the Summer, and Rugby football and the Macdonald Cross Country Race in the Fall; and nothing is more striking in College athletics than the fact that the best exponents of each of these branches are good, all-round athletes. As examples of this, we may mention F. H. C. Kelso, champion cross country runner, and a

THE PRINCIPAL'S PRIVATE ROOM, OLD COLLEGE.

brilliant hockey-player, and J. G. M. Burnside, winner of the Hendrie cup, and a sterling wing player in Rugby foot-ball. The first hockey team was formed at the old school in '90-'91, and was captained by J. B. McMurrich. Their record was excellent :—6 matches won, 2 lost and 2 drawn. In '91-'92, A. F. Barr was captain of a dashing team that defeated Varsity, Trinity and the New Fort, and only suffered defeat at the hands of the Granite Colts. In '92-'93 Fred McLennan led a brilliant seven to uninterrupted victory with the exception of one match lost to Peterborough. One of their signal victories was at Port Hope against the School. Their last and most famous win was against the Limestones of Kingston, champions of the Junior Ontario League. Already, old boys have come to the front in other clubs—Jack McMurrich on the New Fort team and the Gilmour brothers and Barr at Varsity. Fred McLennan will be eagerly watched when he leaves School, and the club that secures him will be fortunate. There are now two rinks, one outside and one covered, so that the game will be played with increased vigour and enthusiasm.

No athletic event at old Upper Canada College was more popular than the annual athletic sports. The day was always a time for renewal of recollections and old associations, and old boys never lost a chance of coming to see the youngsters striving for victory on the famous 220 yards track. The facilities for good running were necessarily limited by insufficient space. The track was simply roped round in the middle of the play ground, and its sharp turns made really fast time impossible. The 100 yards was fortunately a straight course, and many a good race was run over it. In '85 this race was won by H. Senkler, who afterwards won the all-round championship at Toronto University. In '86 the winner was Laurie Boyd, who was just a neck ahead of Ivan Senkler. In '90 W. Gilmour, now one of Varsity's best athletes won the race, and the following year W. Hargraft. Probably the best sprinter that the old School ever turned out was Telfer Arthurs, who, some years ago was the best short distance runner in Canada. One of the most interesting events was the ex-pupils' race, for which Mr. Martland always presented a beautiful cup. Winners of this have been : C. N. Shanley, G. H. Muntz, "Jud" Sewell, Telfer Arthurs, A. A. Macdonald, etc. The championship used to be decided by one race—namely, the quarter-mile. In latter years, it has been decided on the point system. In '90 the winner was W. Gilmour, and in '91 W. Hargraft and Pearson tied for it. The first sports in the new School were held in '92, on a track much the same as that at the old School. The next meeting will, it is hoped, take place on the new quarter-mile track, and then we may look for breaking of all the old records. There is excellent material among the present boys. There was never a better all-round runner in the School than W. A. Moore, who showed such good form in the sprints last spring, and who is hot favourite for the same races this year.

Old boys who come to visit the new School are greatly struck with the smart, business-like appearance of the Gymnasium, but they think with a feeling of fondness of the time-honoured, old building at King street, with its dirty sawdust, its draughts and its peculiar equipments. How the timid "new boy" used to stand by that door and watch the boys indulge in the forbidden excitement of "going off the beam!" And what a proud, yet anxious moment it was when some senior took him under his protection, and, carefully adjusting him to the trapeze, initiated him to this delight. Who will forget the drill that used to take the form of "tag," in which Sergeant Parr joined with the greatest zeal? But there were good gymnasts in those days. J. Chewett, now a graduate of the School of Science, and De Locke Brush were famous in their day. And then, the fights!

Fighting has now almost died out of existence. In the old days, it was a common occurrence. Sometimes there was a genuine cause. Often a fight was started to provide a little excitement. Recess was the popular time for such things, and, I imagine, many will remember the tall form of Mr. Cockburn appearing at the door and announcing to the throng of boys crowding on the floor and perched on beams and ladders, that they had better get a little fresh air outside. In 1887 the building was improved, an armory and a reading-room being added; the minstrels gave their performances on the floor of the gymnasium. The present rifle company in College has given a new interest to the once dreary drill, and every branch of gymnastics must flourish, with the grand opportunities that are now afforded.

UPPER CANADA COLLEGE CRICKET CLUB.

ORGANIZED 1836.

Contributed by
J. E. HALL.

HE first match played by the College eleven was with the Toronto Cricket Club, in July, 1836. The exact date was not given in the Toronto "Courier," the paper reporting the match. The game was won easily by the College eleven, with an innings to spare.

Cricket seems to have been played at Upper Canada College from the first year it was opened, but it was not until 1836 that the club was organized. The first officers were as follows:

OFFICERS:

Patron.
HIS EXCELLENCY SIR FRANCIS BOND HEAD.

President.
MR. JOHN KENT.

Vice-President.
MR. JAMES LUKIN ROBINSON.

Treasurer.
AUGUSTUS KEEFER.

Secretary.
LARRATT W. SMITH.

White, whose name appears on the College side, was a Sussex man, and did not belong to the College at all. The Toronto Club, in arranging the match, made the concession that White should be allowed to assist their opponents.

The members of the College eleven were as follows :—

1. White (a Sussex player).
2. L. Robinson.
3. Phillpots.
4. J. Kent.
5. A. Keefer.
6. G. A. Barber.
7. John Beverley Robinson.
8. F. W. Barron.
9. Walter Dyett.
10. F. Hall.
11. T. Keefer.

In August, 1836, another match was played, Sampson taking Phillpots' place on the team.

The following names of those playing for the College were copied from papers giving accounts of matches in the years noted in the margin.

1837.—F. W. Barron, G. A. Barber, L. Robinson, J. B. Robinson, J. P. Henderson, T. Keefer, R. Nichol, H. G. Stoughton, R. A. Connolly, S. Jarvis, G. Smith.

1843.—G. A. Barber, C. Glasgow, E. Patrick, J. Helliwell, Phillpots, W. T. Boyd, Cameron, G. McMicking, F. W. Barron, O. Gildersleeve, D. McLeod.

1844.—Boyd, Shaw, McLeod, Hudspeth, S. Cosens, A. Crooks, W. Cosens, C. Crooks, Anderson, Wallbridge, Ridley.

1845.—S. Cosens, Hudspeth, Crooks, Arnold, Weller, H. Draper, Stinson, Ridley, Wallbridge, W. Cosens, G. Rykert.

1846.—Cronyn, A. Crooks, Ridley, Stinson, Armour, Cary, Harris, Boyd, Elliot, C. Rykert, W. Cosens.

1849.—Heward, Parsons, Conolly, Phillpots, Robinson, Barber, Barron, Draper, Patrick, Hudspeth, *Muttlebury.*

1850.—Parsons, Heward, Helliwell, J. B. Robinson, Phillpots, Barron, G. Draper, Patrick, Hudspeth, W. Cosens, C. Rykert.

1852.—McLean, Kingsmill, O'Reilly, Gildersleeve, Vansittart, Hammond, Newbigging, Murray, Moss, Draper, Usher.

1853.—Kingsmill, A. E. Rykert, T. D. Phillips, Boyd, G. Rykert, C. Rykert, Powell, H. Phillips, Towers, Nichol, Conolly.

1854.—H. Phillips, Powell, T. D. Phillips, G. Rykert, C. Rykert, A. Rykert, Kingsmill, *Mittleberger,* Dickson, Heron, Benson.

1856.—T. D. Phillips, C. Rykert, H. Phillips, B. Parsons, J. O. Heward, J. Helliwell, R. Bayley, Phillpots, F. A. Barton, G. Draper, F. Draper.

1857.—H. Phillips, Heward, J. C. Rykert, Parsons, T. D. Phillips, Helliwell, R. Bayley, Draper, Robinson, Barron, Hutcheson.

1858.—*Past and Present.*—T. D. Phillips, D. F. Bogert, Parsons, Heward, Helliwell, Rykert, H. Phillips, F. A. Read, F. Taylor, Jessup, Gildersleeve.

1859.—*Present.*—Thomas, Rykert, Parsons, Heward, Draper, Read, Helliwell, Bayley, Draper, Barber, Wright.

1860.—*Past and Present.*—J. Kennedy, T. D. Phillips, H. Phillips, Benjamin, Bogert, C. Rykert, Spragge, T. Brunel, G. A. Barber, G. Brunel, McCaul.

1861.—*Past and Present.*—Phillips, Spragge, Read, Kennedy, Draper, Rykert, Heward, Brunel, Helliwell, Brown, Creighton.

1865.—P. Brunel, R. Hope, D. W. Shaw, F. Perkins, J. Laing, G. Drummond, T. H. Leggo, G. Lount, F. Bethune, W. Browne, R. Henderson.

1866.—J. Brunel, Hope, Lount, Shaw, J. Laing, Draper, VanAllen, McLean, A. Laing, Wright, Guest.

1867.—S. L. Kemper, D. G. Macdonell, J. R. VanAllen, R. K. Hope, J. Laing, H. Watson, W. J. Bickle, A. Laing, A. H. Hope, J. V. Ellard, R. J. Gill.

1868. J. V. Ellard, S. L. Kemper, A. H. Hope, A. Laing, R. Gill, Clump, Bickle, Crowe, Long.

1869.—J. H. Long, R. B. Barber, Crostlewaite, J. V. Ellard, A. H. Hope, A. M. Baines, J. L. Small, J. L. C. Cronyn, D. G. D. Clump, W. Anderson, J. Barber.

1870.—Sills, Anderson, A. Baines, Jarvis, A. Spragge, R. Gamble, Hector, G. Brunel, E. Spragge, C. Baines, Perkins.

1871.—Parsons, Hope, Cronyn, Barron, W. Hector, Spragge, R. Gamble, Sills.
" —*Past and Present*,—Parsons, J. Brunel, G. Brunel, R. Hope, R. Gamble, G. Drummond, Bolus, Barron, W. Hector, A. Baines, F. Draper.

1872.—E. R. C. Proctor, R. Boulton, R. Richardson, J. L. C. Cronyn, A. W. Spragge, M. B. Wood, W. B. Northrup, F. Case, G. L. Cope, *T. Witcher, Esq.*, E. B. Brown.

1873.—E. Proctor, S. Richards, F. Case, B. Northrup, G. L. Cope, G. Hatton, A. Spragge, E. Browne, H. Atkinson, Ashby.

1874.—E. R. C. Proctor, Montgomery, Prentice, R. R. Boulton, H. H. Atkinson, W. B. Northrup, Arthurs, Woods, J. J. Stuart, Smith, D. Hague.

1875.—Ogden, Smith, Hague, H. Atkinson, Boulton, VanAllen, Montgomery, Freeman, C. R. Atkinson, Seyler, Begg.

1876.—J. C. Grace, E. Kittson, D. Browning, G. Brooke, A. Harvey, C. R. Atkinson, F. Keefer, W. Thompson, C. Ford, J. W. Hendrie, A. B. Barber.

1877.—J. C. Grace, E. E. Kittson, A. Gillespie, H. T. Brock, D. Browning, C. R. Atkinson, F. N. Keefer, E. R. Ogden, W. Browning, G. G. S. Lindsey, D. Armour.

1878.—E. U. Sayers, H. T. Brock, E. R. Ogden, T. F. Coleman, W. L. Conolly, C. R. Atkinson, H. Woodruff, F. L. Fellowes, T. Benson, C. N. Shanly, Moore.

1879.—E. R. Ogden, A. B. Thompson, F. L. Fellowes, D. Peterson, W. L. Conolly, A. B. Cameron, T. F. Coleman, W. W. Vickers, M. Ferris, A. D. Langmuir, W. A. Richardson.

1880.—E. R. Ogden, A. B. Thompson, A. D. Langmuir, F. L. Fellowes, T. F. Coleman, W. W. Vickers, W. L. Conolly, A. G. Brown, J. Montgomery, A. G. Smith, E. Coleman.

1881.—A. G. Smith, E. C. Coleman, A. B. Thompson, W. Coldham, J. D. Montgomery, W. W. Vickers, I. Elliott, A. H. Scott, R. S. Martin, I. H. Vidal, G. R. Mickle.

1882.—A. G. Smith, R. Montgomery, E. Smith, A. D. Gordon, C. Worth, W. Coldham, A. H. Scott, A. Martin, H. P. Torrance, H. Vankoughnet, T. Esson.

1883.—E. S. Martin, A. H. Crerar, A. G. Smith, R. Montgomery, H. P. Goering, W. J. Fleury, J. D. Thorburn, E. C. Pardee, F. Field, T. Esson, H. MacLaren.

1884.—G. H. Muntz, H. Pardee, J. H. Senkler, H. Goering, F. Field, A. H. Crerar, C. Pardee, A. Wilgress, E. S. Martin, N. Smith, M. A. McFarlane.

1885.—A. Smart, J. D. McLean, E. C. Pardee, J. H. Senkler, I. Senkler, A. H. S. Marks, I. Harvey, H. S. Smith, G. Brown, G. Biggar, J. F. Snetsinger.

1886.—A. Hollis, J. D. MacLean, O. P. Edgar, E. C. Pardee, I. Senkler, W. A. Fleming, H. B. McGiverin, F. Martin, A. A. Roberts, A. A. Macdonald, A. Montgomery.

1887.—O. P. Edgar, H. Small, H. B. McGiverin, A. Hollis, J. B. Pardee, H. Crocker, A. Montgomery, H. C. Parsons, W. H. Bunting, W. R. Marshall, W. C. C. Freeman.

1888.—H. Crocker, H. Small, E. Brown, J. B. Pardee, H. C. Parsons, A. Montgomery, W. R. Marshall, W. H. Bunting, H. Fleming, H. G. Martin, F. Langmuir.

1889.—H. P. Fleming, C. Patterson, C. Stuart, W. C. C. Freeman, H. Small, F. Langmuir, A. F. Moren, H. C. Baird, H. Wood, C. K. Wilson, G. L. Smith.

1890.—A. F. Moren, M. A. Macfarlane, W. C. Laidlaw, G. H. Harris, J. L. Counsell, W. H. Montgomery, H. H. Wood, E. C. Wragge, W. M. Losh, W. A. Gilmour, R. W. White.

1891.—M. A. McFarlane, W. Montgomery, R. W. White, J. M. Laing, E. C. Pearman, J. L. Counsell, F. L. Cosby, C. H. Mockridge, F. N. Waldie, A. A. Small, H. Boultbee.

1892.—R. W. White, J. L. Counsell, F. L. Cosby, C. H. Mockridge, F. N. Waldie, H. Boultbee, T. H. Crerar, A. W. G. Hoskin, T. G. McMaster, N. W. Cosby, W. P. Moss.

APPENDIX I.

On the walls of the Public Hall of the College there were eight walnut tables containing the names of the boys who had distinguished themselves at Matriculation and other University Examinations. These tables were arranged along the west, north and east walls.

TABLE I.
UPPER CANADA COLLEGE.
HEAD BOYS.

Scadding, Henry......1830-33	O'Brien, Donough 1853	Biggar, W. H 1872
Ruttan, William 1834	Moss, Thomas 1854	Bowes, F. A 1873
Fitzgerald, William J....1835	Jones, William..........1855	Northrup, W. B 1874
Ewart, Thomas 1836	Bethune, Charles J. S....1856	Davis, A. G 1875
Hurd, Edward 1837	Henderson, Elmes 1857	Sutherland, A 1876
Ewart, John 1838	Loudon, James... 1858	Ponton, A. D.. 1877
Helliwell, John..........1839	Jessup, James G 1859	Davis, E. P 1878
Boulton, Henry John 1840	Tyner, Adam C 1860	Langton, H. H..........1879
Crookshank, George 1841	Paterson, John A........1861	McKenzie, W. P........1880
Bethune, Norman........1842	Bell, Charles W 1862	Walker, W. H..........1881
Wedd, William 1843	Cannon, Charles H 1863	Young, A. H...........1882
Cosens, Chas. Sidney .. .1844	Cassels, Alan 1864	Smith, A. G 1883
Hudspeth, Thomas 1845	Ryrie, Daniel 1865	Jones, J. E 1884
Crooks, Adam 1846	Armstrong, William 1866	Biggar, G. C...........1885
Palmer, George.........1847	Dale, William 1867	Macdonald, A. A........1886
Grier, James G.........1848	Fletcher, J 1868	Leacock, S. B.........1887
Huggard, John T........1849	Wallace, F. H 1869	Crocker, H. G 1888
Blake, Dominick E......1850	Bruce, J. } Æq....1870	Macdonnell, G. F........1889
Rykert, Alfred E.......1851	Cameron, J. C. }	Moss, C. A.............1890
Walker, Nathaniel 1852	Elliott, J. W..........1871	Hilliar, T. H...........1891

TABLE II.

UNIVERSITY, ETC., HONORS

OBTAINED BY PUPILS OF UPPER CANADA COLLEGE.

1845—KING'S COLLEGE, TORONTO.

Helliwell, J., B.A.	I. 1.	Classical Medals, English Poem.
McDonell, S. S., B.A.	I. 2.	
Wedd, W., B.A.	I. 3.	⎰ Latin Poem, Greek Iambics, Greek
Boulton, H. J., B.A.	I. 4.	⎱ Prose.
Crookshank, G., B.A.	II. 1.	
Draper, W. G., B.A.	IV. 1.	
Stennett, W., B.A.	.....	⎰ Metaphysics Medal, Biblical Literature
		⎱ Medal, Jameson Medal, Latin Poem.
Roaf, J.	.....	Natural Philosophy Medal.

1846—KING'S COLLEGE, TORONTO.

Jessopp, H. B., B.A.	I. 1.	*Classical Medal.*
Robinson, C., B.A.	.....	Jameson Medal.
Wedd, W., B.A.	.....	⎰ Hebrew Class I. 1, Greek Iambics,
		⎱ Latin Poem, English Poem.
Stennett, W., B.A.	.....	⎰ Divinity Class I., 1, Strachan Prize,
		⎱ Latin Poem, English Essay.
Crookshank, G., B.A.	.....	Greek Prose.
Wickson, A.	.....	Wellington Scholar.
Hudspeth, T.	.....	Greek Prose.

1847—WOOLWICH.

Elliott, H. Y				First place.

1847—KING'S COLLEGE, TORONTO.

	C.	M.	Scholarships.
Evans, G. M.	I. 3.	I. 1.	University, Mathematical.
Armour, J. D.	I. 1.		University, Classical.
Palmer, G.	I. 2.		Wellington District.
Barber, G. A.	I. 4.		Upper Canada College.
Hutton, Joseph	I. 5.		Victoria District.
Wickson, Arthur, B.A.	I. 2.		*Gold Medal, Classics.*
Stennett, Rev. W., B.A.			Divinity, 2nd Year I. 1.
Jessopp, H. B., B.A.			Divinity, 1st Year, 1, 1 Hebrew I. 1.
McDonell, S. S., B.A.			Law I. 1.
Roaf, J., B.A			Law I. 2.
Boulton, H. J., B.A			Law II. 1.
Crookshank, G., B.A.			Law II. 3.
Wedd, Wm., B.A			Greek Verse, English Poem.
Stennett, Rev. W., B.A.			Latin Verse.
Jessopp, H. B., B.A.			English Prose.
Hudspeth, Thos.			Greek Prose.
McKenzie, Rev. J. G. D			English Prose.
Hudspeth, Thos.			Wellington Scholar.

1848—KING'S COLLEGE, LONDON.

				Prizeman.
Boulton, W. S.				Surveying Workshop.

UNIVERSITY, ETC., HONORS. 281

TABLE II.—Continued.

UNIVERSITY, ETC., HONORS

OBTAINED BY PUPILS OF UPPER CANADA COLLEGE.—Continued.

1848—KING'S COLLEGE, TORONTO.

Wedd, W., B.A		Latin Prose, Greek Ode, English Verse, Latin Verse.
Jessopp, H. B., B.A		Divinity, 2nd Year, I. 1.
Wickson, A., B.A		Hebrew Prize.
Hudspeth, T., B.A		English Verse.
Crooks, A		Wellington Scholar.
Crooks, A		Classics, Metaphysics and Ethics, Rhetoric Prizes.
Stinson, E		Mathematics and Physics Prize.
Cronyn, T		Biblical Literature Prize.
Armour, J. D		Latin Ode, Greek Prose, Classics Prize.
Evans, G. M		Mathematics, Chemistry, Evidences, Biblical Literature Prizes.

1848—C. M. SCHOLARSHIP.

	C.	M.	Scholarships.
Grier, J. G	I. 1.	II. 2.	University, Classical.
Freer, Cdt	I. 5.	I. 2.	UPPER CANADA COLLEGE.
Tyner, R. J	I. 4.	II. 1.	Home District.
Clark, A. M	I. 2.	III. 2.	UPPER CANADA COLLEGE.
Eliot, C. F	I. 3.	III. 1.	Western District.

1844-5—GUY'S HOSPITAL, LONDON.

Richardson, J. H		Anatomy, 1st Prize.

1846-7—GUY'S HOSPITAL, LONDON.

Richardson, J. H		Free Dressership.

1849—KING'S COLLEGE, LONDON.

Ridout, Thos		Descriptive Geology, 1st Prize; Practical Geology, 1st Prize; Certificate of Approval Associate.
Boulton, W. S		Manufacturing Art and Machinery, 1st Prize; Workshop, 1st Prize; Geometry, Drawing, 2nd Prize; Certificate of Approval.

1849—KING'S COLLEGE, TORONTO.

Baldwin, Rev. E., B.A		Theology, 2nd Year, I. 1 Prize.
Wickson, A., B.A		Hebrew Prize.
Hudspeth, T. A., B.A		English Poem, Latin Poem, English Essay.
Crooks, Adam		English Essay, Latin Prose.
McKenzie, Rev. J. G. D		Greek Tragedy, Iambics.
Armour, J. D		Wellington Scholar, Greek Prose.
Tyner, R. J		English Poem.
Clark, A. M		Latin Poem.
Crooks, Adam, B.A	I. 1.	Litt., Human.
McKenzie, Rev. J. G. D., B.A	I. 2.	Litt., Human.
Kingsmill, J. J., B.A	I. 3.	Litt., Human.

36

TABLE III.
UNIVERSITY, ETC., HONORS.

1849—Crooks, Adam, B.A............	.....	....	Gold Medal, Classics ; Metaphysics Medal.	
McKenzie, Rev. J. G. D., B.A..	......	......	Evidences and Biblical Literature Medal.	
Stinson, Ebenezer, B.A........	......	....	Natural Philosophy Medal.	

C. M. SCHOLARSHIPS.

	C.	M.	Scholarships.
Huggard, J. T.................	I. 1.	I. 2.	University Classical.
1850—Keefer, T. C., (C.E.)	.....	.....	Elgin Prize Essay.

UNIVERSITY OF TORONTO.

Law.

1850—Stinson, E., B.A..................	.....	I. 1.	Prizeman.
Crooks, A., B.A................	.....	I. 2.	
Hudspeth, T. A., B.A...........	.....	.....	English Verse.
Crooks, A., B.A	.....	.....	English Prose.
		Clas'cs	
Armour, J. D., B.A	.....	I. 1.	University Class Medal.
Evans, G. M., B.A	.....	I. 2.	University Medal, Natural Philosophy, I. 1. University Medal, Metaphysics and Ethics, I. 1. University Medal, Evidences, I. 1.
Clark, A. M	.....	.....	Greek Verse, Latin Verse, English Prose.
Tyner, R. J	.....	.....	English Verse, English Prose.
Evans, G. M., B.A	.....	.....	Greek Verse.
Clark, A. M	.....	.....	Wellington Scholar.

C. M. SCHOLARSHIPS.

	C.	M.	Scholarships.
1850—Brown, James	I. 1.	I. 2.	University Classical.
Blake, D. E	I. 2.	III. 1.	Upper Canada College.
Freeland, W	III. 2.	I. 3.	Upper Canada College.
Marling, S. A	I. 3.	IV. 1.	Home District.
Campbell, T. C.............	I. 4.	.....	
Boulton, G. D	I. 6.	.....	

UNIVERSITY OF TORONTO.

1851—Stinson, E., B.A	....	......	Greek Verse, English Verse.
Crooks, A., B.A	....	......	English Essay.
		Law.	
Crooks, A., B.C.L	.....	I. 1.	Prize.
Stinson, E., B.C.L	.....	I. 2.	
Clark, A. M	.....	.....	Jameson Medal { Greek Verse. Latin Verse.
Freer, C.....................	.....	......	Latin Verse, Belles Lettres Prize.
		Clas'cs	
Clark, A. M., B.A	.....	I. 1.	University Gold Medal.
Freer, C., B.A	.....	I. 2.	
		Ethics	
Eliot, C. F., B.A.............	.....	I. 1.	University Medal.

UNIVERSITY, ETC., HONORS. 283

TABLE III.—*Continued.*

UNIVERSITY, ETC., HONORS.

1851—Marling S. A .... | .... | .... | English Verse.

C. M. Scholarships.

	C.	M.	Scholarships.
1851—Rykert, A. E.	I. 1.	I. 2.	University Classical.
Counsell, G. S	I. 3.	III. 1.	Upper Canada College.
Tyner, R. J., B.A			{ Chancellor's *Medal*, Evidences. { English Prose.

Cobourg Scholarships.

1849—Johnson, C. C			First Scholar.
1850—Barber, G. A			First Scholar.
1851—Thomson, Charles E			First Scholar.
Phillips, Thomas			Third Scholar.
Beaven, Edward			Fifth Scholar.

University of Toronto.

1852—Hutton, J	Law.		
Covernton, C. J	I. 1.		Practical Anatomy (I. 1), Chirurg (I. 3).
Huggard, J. T., B.A			{ University Gold *Medal*, *Classics*. { Litt. Human (I. 2.)
Peterson, H. W., B.A.		I. 1.	University Medal, Ethics.
Marling, S. A			Chancellor's Medal, Evidences.
Clark, A. M., B.A			English Prose.
Peterson, H. W., B.A			English Verse, English Prose.
Bull, S. J., B.A			English Verse.
Brown, J			Latin Prose.
Rykert, A. E.			Latin Verse.

C. M. Scholarships.

| Walker, N. O .... | I. 3. | I. 1. | First Mathematical Scholar. |
| Kingsmill, N .... | I. 1. | | First Classical Scholar. |

Trinity College Toronto.

1855—Thompson, C. E			English Verse.
Phillips, T. D			Latin Verse.
O'Reilly, J. E			Wellington Scholar.
1854—Cooper, W. E			Wellington Scholar.

University of Toronto.

| Francis, W .... | | | { Mathematics, 2nd Scholarship; Classics, 3rd Scholarship. |

TABLE IV.

UNIVERSITY, ETC., HONORS.

1854—Cambridge.

	M.	C.	
Whitt, J., B.A.	I. 1.	I. 1.	Seventh Wrangler.
Elliot, W., B.A.			Fellow Magdalene.

1853—University of Toronto.

	L. H.	M.	
Brown, J., B.A.	I. 1.	I. 1.	*University Gold Medal*, Mathematics. University Silver Medal, Ethics.
Marling, S. A., B.A.	I. 2.		*University Gold Medal*, Classics.
Blake, D. E., B.A.	I. 3.		
Jones, C., B.A.	II. 1.		

1854—Scholarships.

Blake, D. E., B.A.		I. 1.	Law.
Sanderson, J. E		I. 1.	Pol. Civ. and History.
Francis, W.		I. 1.	Medicine.
Moss, T		I. 1.	Classics.
		I. 1.	Mathematics.

1855—Scholarships.

Kingsmill, N., B.A.		I. 2.	*Class Silver Medal*.
		I. 2.	History, Latin Verse.
Walker, N. O., B.A		I. 1.	*Chemistry Gold Medal*.
		I. 1.	Natural History, Gold Medal.
Peterson, H. W., B.A.			English Prose.
Sanderson, J. E., B.A.			English Prose, English Verse.
Moss, T			Latin Prose.
Milroy, W			English Verse.
		I. 1.	Class Scholarship.
Sullivan, R.		I. 1.	English.
		I. 1.	French.
		I. 1.	History.

1856—Scholarships.

Hume, R.	I. 1.		Oriental Languages.
Moss, T			Latin Verse, Latin Prose, English Prose, French.

TABLE IV.—*Continued.*

UNIVERSITY, ETC., HONORS.

Sampson, D. A. .... { I. 1. Classics Scholarship.
1. 1. History.
I. 1. French.
I. 2. English.

Boyd, J. A. .... { I. 1. English Scholarship.
I. 2. French.

1855-6—TRINITY COLLEGE.

Jones, W. .... Wellington Scholar.
Badgley, C. H. .... Allan Scholar.

1855—UNIVERSITY OF TORONTO.

Fraser, J. T. .... { I. 3. Greek and Latin. }
I. 2. French.   } Scholar.
I. 2. History.   }

1857—UNIVERSITY OF TORONTO.

Ridout, J. G. .... Matriculation Class Scholarship.
Fraser, J. T. .... First Year Class. Scholarship.
Moss, T. .... Third Year Class. Scholarship.
Thom, J. .... Matriculation Mathematical Scholarship.
Moss, T. .... Third Year Mathematical Scholarship.
Boyd, J. A. .... { First Year Modern Language Scholarship.
Moss, T. .... { Third Year Modern Language Scholarship.
Sullivan, R. .... { Second Year Modern Language Scholarship.
                                        { Metaphysics and Ethics Scholarship.
Sampson, D. A. .... { First Year General Proficiency Scholarship.
Moss, T. .... { Greek Verse.
                                        { Greek Prose.
Boyd, J. A. .... English Verse.

1856-7—TRINITY COLLEGE.

Bethune, C. J. S. .... Wellington Scholar.
Cayley, E. .... Burnside Scholar.
Badgley, C. H. .... Second Year Classical Prize.
Beaven, E. W. .... Moral Science Prize.
Cooper, W. E. .... Kent Prize.
Benson, C. I. .... Latin Prose.
1853—Bethune, J. J. .... Divinity Scholar.
1854—O'Reilly, J. E. .... Law Scholar.
1855—Benson, C. I. .... Strachan Scholar.
1856—Bethune, C. J. S. .... Divinity Scholar.
Thomson, C. E. .... Divinity Prize.

TABLE V.

UNIVERSITY, ETC., HONORS

OBTAINED AT MATRICULATION BY UPPER CANADA COLLEGE.

1858.—London, J.	Classics.
Loudon, J.	Mathematics.
O'Brien, W. E.	Law.
Henderson, E.	Foundation, Trinity College.
Evans, L. H.	Cameron, Trinity College.
1859.—Lafferty, A. M.	Mathematics.
Thompson, W.	General Proficiency.
Read, F. A.	Law.
Baldwin, A. H.	Foundation, Trinity College.
Jones, W.	Foundation, St. John's College, Cambridge.
Jones, C.	9th Comparative R. M. Academy, Woolwich.
1860.—Snider, E. F.	General Proficiency.
Bogart, D. F.	Foundation, Trinity College.
Givens, C. S.	Cameron, Trinity College.
1861.—Kennedy, T. S.	Foundation, Trinity College.
Jessup, J. H.	Foundation, Trinity College.
Bethune, F.	Dickson, Trinity College.
Bethune, F.	Cameron, Trinity College.
Henderson, R.	Foundation, Trinity College.
1862.—Paterson, J. A.	Classics.
Paterson, J. A.	Mathematics.
Tyner, A. C.	Classics.
Bell, C. W.	General Proficiency.
Holmes, W. R.	General Proficiency.
Holmes, W. R.	Medicine.
Delamere, T. D.	General Proficiency.
Matheson, C. A.	Foundation, Trinity College.
1863.—Mewburn, J. H.	Mathematics.
Mewburn, J. H.	General Proficiency.
Connon, C. H.	General Proficiency.
Evans, T. F. L.	Foundation, Trinity College.
Ridout, J.	1st Comparative R. S. College, Sandhurst.
Robinson, C.	4th Comparative R. S. College, Sandhurst.
1864.—Cassels, A.	Classics.
Purdy, J.	General Proficiency.
Grover, T. M.	General Proficiency.
1865.—Ryrie, D.	1st Classics.
Ryrie, D.	1st Mathematics.
Ryrie, D.	1st General Proficiency.
Kingsford, R. E.	2nd Classics.
Graham, J. E.	Medicine.
Ford, O. P.	1st Foundation, Trinity College.
1866.—Gibson, G.	1st Classics.
Gibson, G.	1st General Proficiency.
Armstrong, W.	4th General Proficiency.
Robinson, H. G.	6th General Proficiency.
Wagner, W. J.	Medicine.

TABLE V.—*Continued.*

UNIVERSITY, ETC., HONORS

OBTAINED AT MATRICULATION BY UPPER CANADA COLLEGE.

1866.—	Ball, C. W.	2nd Foundation, Trinity College.
	Paterson, T. W.	4th Foundation, Trinity College.
1867.—	Dale, W.	1st Classics.
	Dale, W.	1st Mathematics.
	Dale, W.	1st General Proficiency.
	Fletcher, H.	2nd General Proficiency.
	Fotheringham, T. F.	4th General Proficiency.
	Kew, M.	5th General Proficiency.
	Harman, L. C.	2nd Foundation, Trinity College.
1868.—	Fletcher, J.	1st Classics.
	Fletcher, J.	1st General Proficiency.
	White, J.	2nd Classics.
	Crerar, J.	3rd Æq. General Proficiency.
	Clarkson, F. A.	3rd Æq. General Proficiency.
	Zimmerman, R.	Medicine.
	Matheson, A. F.	Dickson, Trinity College.
1869.—	Wallace, F. H.	1st Classics.
	Wallace, F. H.	1st General Proficiency.
	Long, J. H.	3rd General Proficiency.
	Small, J. T.	5th General Proficiency.
1870.—	Bruce, J.	2nd Classics.
	Bruce, J.	1st General Proficiency.
	Dawson, A.	1st Mathematics.
	Dawson, A.	2nd General Proficiency.
	Thompson, G. W.	7th General Proficiency.
	Cameron, D.	Medicine.
	Logan, C. J.	Foundation, Trinity College.
1871.—	Harstone, L.	2nd Æq. Classics.
	Harstone, L.	1st Mathematics.
	Harstone, L.	1st General Proficiency.
	Kerr, F. W.	2nd Æq. Classics.
	Mortimer, C. W.	Cooper Examiner, Trinity College.
	Sills, C. E.	Foundation Trinity College.
1872.—	McKeown, J. G.	1st Classics.
	McKeown, J. G.	3rd General Proficiency.
	Hodgins, F. E.	5th General Proficiency.
1873.—	Bowes, E. A.	1st Classics.
	Bowes, E. A.	1st Mathematics.
	Bowes, E. A.	1st General Proficiency.
	Ponton, W. N.	4th General Proficiency.
1874.—	Northrup, W. B.	1st Classics.
	Northrup, W. B.	1st English, French and History.
	Northrup, W. B.	1st General Proficiency.
	Smith, J. S.	2nd Mathematics.
	Keys, D. R.	2nd English, French and History.
	Nason, H.	6th General Proficiency.

TABLE V.—*Continued.*

UNIVERSITY, ETC., HONORS

OBTAINED AT MATRICULATION BY UPPER CANADA COLLEGE.

1875.	Elliott, J. W.	7th General Proficiency.
	McMichael, A. J. W.	3rd Foundation, Trinity College.
1876.	London, W. J.	2nd Classics.
	London, W. J.	1st General Proficiency.
	MacLean, W.	4th General Proficiency.
1877.	Cayley, H. St. Q.	English, French, German and History.
	Kerr, D. B.	1st General Proficiency.
	Milner, W. S.	2nd General Proficiency.
	Reid, J. W.	3rd General Proficiency.
	McKenzie, K.	McDonald Exhibition, McGill **University.**
1878.	Davis, E. P.	4th Æq. General Proficiency.
1879.	Laugton, H. H.	1st General Proficiency.
1880.	Bowes, J. H.	Modern Languages.
	McKenzie, W. P.	1st Bursary, Knox College.
1881.	Walker, W. H.	4th General Proficiency.
1882.	Young, A. H.	Modern Languages.
	Young, A. H.	**Prince of Wales.**
	Young, A. H.	3rd General Proficiency.
	Beck, C. B.	Bishop Strachan, Trinity **College.**
1883.	McArthur, R. A.	Prince of Wales.
	Smith, A. G.	4th General Proficiency.
1884.	Jones, J. E.	Prince of Wales.
1885.	Biggar, G. C.	3rd General Proficiency.
	Moss, J. H.	4th General Proficiency.
1886.	MacDonald, A. A.	Modern Languages.
	MacDonald, A. A.	Prince of Wales.
1887.	Leacock, S. B.	1st General Proficiency.
	Jones, B. M.	3rd General Proficiency.
1888.	Crocker, H. G.	Prince of Wales.
	Crocker, H. G.	1st Mathematics.
	Crocker, H. G.	Modern Languages.
	Crocker, H. G.	1st General Proficiency.
	Shiel, A. J.	2nd General Proficiency.
1889.	MacDonnell, G. F.	Prince of Wales' Scholarship.
	MacDonnell, G. F.	2nd in Classics.
	MacDonnell, G. F.	2nd in Mathematics.
	MacDonnell, G. F.	General Proficiency.
	Geary, G. R.	Modern Languages.
1890.	Moss, C. A.	2nd General Proficiency.
	Lash, W. M.	3rd General Proficiency.
1891.	Hapter, R. J. E.	1st Royal Military College.
	Frith G. R.	2nd Royal Military College.

TABLE VI.

J. HERBERT MASON MEDALS.

FOUNDED 1888.

Gold.		Silver.	
George Clayes	1888		
G. F. MacDonnell	1889	A. E. Hoskin	1889
H. P. Biggar	1890	E. C. P. Clark	1890
J. L. Counsell	1891	A. F. Barr	1891

THE SCHOOL STUDY.

THE OLD DINING HALL.

TABLE VII.
EXHIBITIONERS.

Charles Sidney Cosens		1842.
Arthur Wickson		"
Walter Arnold		1843.
Overton S. Gildersleeve		"
George Palmer	January,	1844.
Adam Crooks	"	"
John Whit	"	"
William Elliot	"	"
Thomas Cronyn	"	"
G. A. Barber	"	"
John J. Kingsmill	"	"
A. H. Wallbridge	"	"
George Mountain Evans	Septemb'r,	1844.
Ebenezer Stinson	"	"
Henry Thomas Ridley	"	"
William Ambrose	"	"
Courtlandt Freer		1845.
John Douglas Armour		"
Charles Edmund Goddard		"
Stuart Foster		"
Alister Clark		1846.
Charles F. Eliot		"
Richard Baley		"
C. P. Sampson		"
W. O'Brien		"
J. T. Huggard		1847.
W. C. Palmer		"
W. Meudill		"
W. Freeland		"
T. D. Phillips		"
V. McKenzie		1848.
A. E. Rykert		"
Richard L. J. O'Brien		"
W. C. Cosens		"
N. O. Walker		1849.
C. B. Jones		"
Nicol Kingsmill		"
F. Mackelcan		"
C. Gildersleeve		"
Donough L. A. O'Brien		1850.
William H. Radenhurst		"
W. Francis		"
G. T. Beard		"
Thomas Moss		1851.
F. C. Draper		"
J. W. Robarts		"
A. S. Kirkpatrick		"
D. A. Sampson		1852.
F. H. Stayner		"
William Jones		"
J. D. Birchall		"
William James Baines		"

APPENDIX II.

List of Exhibitioners taken from the Exhibition Book. After 1852 the names were not inscribed on the wall tables.

M. B. Overfield	1853.
C. H. Badgley	"
J. F. Frazer	"
T. L. Stayner	"
G. D. Mayer	"
H. Phillips	"
James D. Wells	"
G. B. Roberts	"
John G. Ridout	1854.
Cyril Archibald	"
E. Cayley	"
N. Maynard	"
C. Jones	"
A. Stuart	"
James McGlashan	1855.
John Thom	"
Thomas Grahame	"
G. Seymour	"
Joel Bradbury	"
F. A. Read	1856.
H. R. Robertson	"
Edward Webb	"
Alfred Lafferty	"
Andrew McGlashen	1857.
Thomas S. Reid	"
David Ford Bogert	"
James Lamon	"
A. C. Tyner	1858.
F. Montizambert	"
William H. vanderSmissen	"
James F. Dennistoun	"

J. W. Mitchell	Form IV	1859.
John F. Goodridge	"	"
L. N. Benjamin	"	"
F. M. Paterson	"	"
E. F. Snyder	Form V	"
A. C. Tyner	"	"
William H. vanderSmissen	"	"
C. W. Bell	Form IV	1860.
T. D. Hawley	"	"
R. Orr	"	"
T. D. Delamere	"	"
J. A. Paterson	Form V	"
W. J. Mitchell	"	"
C. Radenhurst	"	"
Charles Masterson	Form IV	1861.
C. H. Connon	"	"
Robert Mills	"	"
G. S. Filliter	"	"
C. W. Bell	Form V	"
T. D. Delamere	"	"
C. A. Mathewson	"	"

EXHIBITIONERS.

J. G. Hawley	Form IV	1862.
J. H. Mewburn	"	"
T. Langton	"	"
J. McDougall	"	"
C. H. Connon	Form V	1862.
R. S. Hudson	"	"
John White	"	"
Daniel Ryrie	Form IV	1863.
Goodwin Gibson	"	"
H. J. Muckle	"	"
R. E. Kingsford	"	"
J. McDougall	Form V	"
John Purdy	"	"
T. Langton	"	"
William Armstrong	Form IV	1864.
A. Richards	"	"
W. Moss	"	"
R. H. Bowes	"	"
Daniel Ryrie	Form V	"
Goodwin Gibson	"	"
Ogden P. Ford	"	"
W. J. Wagner	Form IV	1865.
T. F. Fotheringham	"	"
L. C. Harman	"	"
W. Armstrong	Form V	"
John M. Porter	"	"
William Moss	"	"
J. Fletcher	Form IV	1866.
T. J. W. Burgess	"	"
J. H. Proctor	"	"
F. A. Clarkson	"	"
W. Dale	Form V	"
L. C. Harman	"	"
W. J. Wagner	"	"
J. T. Small	Form IV	1867.
T. F. Clarke	"	"
John Craig	"	"
W. H. Flint	"	"
J. Fletcher	Form V	"
F. A. Clarkson	"	"
J. White	"	"
R. Zimmerman	"	"
F. Ballantyne	Form IV	1868.
Robert Gill	"	"
E. P. Clement	"	"
J. Cameron	"	"
F. H. Wallace	Form V	"
J. T. Small	"	"
T. H. Long	"	"
T. F. Clarke	"	"
C. C. Robinson	Form IV	1869.
Andrew Luke	"	"
G. Inglis	"	"
J. W. Beaty	"	"
John Bruce	Form V	"
J. C. Cameron	"	"
E. P. Clement	"	"

W. A. Langton .... Form IV .. 1870.
W. A. Fletcher ....   "   "
F. E. Hodgins ....   "   "
R. D. Richardson ....   "   "

J. W. Elliott .... Form V .. 1870.
Andrew Luke ....   "   "
L. Harstone ....   "   "

W. N. Ponton .... Form IV .. 1871.
Trevelyan Ridout ....   "   "
William Wedd ....   "   "
Richard E. Reynolds ....   "   "
J. G. McKeown .... Form V ..   "
W. H. Biggar ....   "   "
F. E. Hodgins ....   "   "
W. A. Langton ....   "   "

W. B. Northrup .... Form IV .. 1872.
P. F. J. Ridout ....   "   "
H. D. Hunter ....   "   "
D. R. Keyes ....   "   "
E. A. Bowes .... Form V ..   "
W. N. Ponton ....   "   "
Trevelyan Ridout ....   "   "
J. C. Harstone ....   "   "

W. J. Loudon .... Form IV .. 1873.
C. C. McCaul ....   "   "
J. P. McMurrich ....   "   "
W. B. Northrup .... Form V ..   "
H. D. Hunter ....   "   "
T. N. Clarke ....   "   "
D. R. Keys ....   "   "

W. S. Milner .... Form IV .. 1874.
D. Henderson ....   "   "
C. W. Thompson ....   "   "
D. Armour ....   "   "
W. J. Loudon .... Form V ..   "
J. McDougall ....   "   "
A. Davis ....   "   "
J. W. Elliott ....   "   "

F. J. Langstaff .... Form IV .. 1875.
D. B. Kerr ....   "   "
A. D. Ponton ....   "   "
E. Kittson ....   "   "
A. Sutherland .... Form V ..   "
W. J. James ....   "   "

E. P. Davis .... Form IV .. 1876.
H. W. Mickle ....   "   "
E. L. Simonds ....   "   "
D. M. Browning ....   "   "
A. D. Ponton .... Form V ..   "
F. F. Langstaff ....   "   "
J. A. McAndrew ....   "   "
D. B. Kerr ....   "   "

E. P. Davis .... Form IV .. 1877.
T. Parker ....   "   "
E. F. Gunther ....   "   "
G. S. Wilgress ....   "   "
H. H. Langton ....   "   "
J. Picken ....   "   "
C. P. Smith ....   "   "

EXHIBITIONERS. 293

A. C. Helliwell	Form IV.	1878.
R. Bain	"	"
J. H. Bowes	"	"
A. J. Boyd	"	"
H. H. Langton	Form V.	"
C. S. Wilgress	"	"
R. Balmer	"	"
C. P. Smith	"	"

W. H. Walker	Form IV.	1879.
S. George Gray	"	"
A. B. Thompson	"	"
W. P. McKenzie	Form V.	"
A. C. Helliwell	"	"
R. Bain	"	"
F. C. Powell	"	"

J. A. Sievert	Form IV.	1880.
C. B. Beck	"	"
A. D. Gordon	"	"
W. Copp	"	"
W. H. Walker	Form V.	"
W. W. Baldwin	"	"
G. R. Mickle	"	"
A. B. Thompson	"	"

J. E. Jones	Form IV.	1881.
A. G. Smith	"	"
E. F. Blake	"	"
J. F. Edgar	"	"
A. H. Young	Form V.	"
J. A. Sievert	"	"
C. B. Beck	"	"
Charles S. Slawson	"	"

John H. Moss	Form IV.	1882.
J. J. Ferguson	"	"
W. A. Leys	"	"
Fred. W. Jones	"	"
A. G. Smith	Form V.	"
R. McArthur	"	"
A. H. Morphy	"	"
A. B. Thompson	"	"

George C. Biggar	Proficiency, Mathematical, Modern Languages	Form IV.	1883.
Lionel B. Stephenson	Classical	"	"
A. A. Macdonald	Reversion of Modern Languages	"	"
J. D. Holmes	Reversion of Mathematical	"	"
J. E. Jones	Proficiency, Classical, Modern Languages	Form V.	"
E. F. Blake	Reversion of Reversion of Modern Languages	"	"
J. J. Ferguson	Mathematical	"	"
W. A. Leys	Reversion of Classical	"	"
F. W. Jones	Reversion of Modern Languages	"	"

E. R. Van Koughnet	General Proficiency Exhibition	Form IV.	1884.
J. Hewetson	Modern Languages	"	"
F. J. A. Davidson	Classical Exhibition	"	"
A. E. Hilker	Mathematical Exhibition	"	"
John H. Moss	General Proficiency and Mathematical	Form V.	"
George C. Biggar	Reversion in Mathematics	"	"
Fletcher C. Snider	Modern Languages	"	"

Stephen B. Leacock	General Proficiency, Classical, Modern Languages	Form IV.	1885.
Thomas D. Dockray	Mathematical	"	"
B. Morton Jones	Reversions, Modern Languages and Classics	"	"
L. E. Wedd	Reversion of Classical		
A. A. Macdonald	Classical, Mathematical, Modern Languages and General Proficiency	Form V.	"

UPPER CANADA COLLEGE MEMORIAL VOLUME.

H. G. Crocker	Modern Languages, General Proficiency	Form IV.	1886.
Harry M. Wood	Reversion in Modern Languages and Mathematics.	"	"
Henry de Stuler Miller	Half Reversion Mathematics, Classical, Mathematical	"	"
James Barber McLeod	Reversion Classical	"	"
Stephen B. Leacock	Classical, Mathematical, Modern Languages and General Proficiency	Form V.	"
Thomas D. Dockray	Reversion, Mathematics	"	"
B. Morton Jones	Half Reversion Classical	"	"
F. J. Davidson	Half Reversion Classical	"	"
D. J. Armour	Reversion, Modern Languages	"	"
G. F. Macdonell	Classical, Mathematical, Modern Languages and General Proficiency	Form IV.	1887.
Henry C. Small	Reversion	"	"
George Reginald Greary	Reversion	"	"
H. G. Crocker	Classical, Mathematical, Modern Languages and General Proficiency	Form V.	"
A. Shiel	Reversion of Classical	"	"
F. A. Kerns	Modern Languages, Reversion	"	"
Charles A. Moss	General Proficiency	Form IV.	1888.
Harold R. Kingsmill	Classical	"	"
W. M. Lash	Modern Languages	"	"
W. T. Parker	Mathematical Reversion	Form V.	"
G. F. Macdonnell	Classical, Mathematical and General Proficiency	"	"
R. G. Geary	Modern Languages, Reversion	"	"
K. D. McMillan	Classical Reversion	"	"
T. H. Hilliar	General Proficiency	Form IV.	1889.
B. H. Thomson	Modern Languages	"	"
J. L. Bryant	Mathematical, Reversion	"	"
E. C. P. Clark	Classical	"	"
C. A. Moss	Modern Languages, Mathematical and General Proficiency	Form V.	"
Harold R. Kingsmill (4)	The Classical	"	"
W. M. Lash	Modern Languages, Reversion	"	"
W. M. Boultbee	Mathematical, Reversion	"	"
W. W. Edgar	Modern Languages and General Proficiency	Form IV.	1890.
R. Franchot	Mathematical	"	"
R. W. White	Classical	"	"
A. C. Hardy	Modern Languages, Reversion	"	"
J. H. L. Patterson	Sciences	"	"
Thos. H. Hilliar	Classical, Modern Languages and General Proficiency	Form V.	"
J. L. Bryant	Mathematical	"	"
A. S. McKay	Classical, Reversion	"	"
Fred. Jas. H. McIntosh	Modern Languages, Reversion	"	"
R. K. Sandwell	Classical, Mathematical and General Proficiency	Form IV.	1891.
F. G. Leslie	Mathematical	"	"
F. C. Pearman	Modern Languages	"	"
R. C. Wilson	Modern Languages, Reversion	"	"
F. E. Miller	Science	"	"
W. W. Edgar	Classical	Form V.	"
T. H. Mullin	Mathematical	"	"
R. Franchot	Modern Languages and General Proficiency	"	"
H. A. Bruce	Modern Languages, Reversion	"	"

APPENDIX III.

THE U. C. C. ROLL, 1829-1892.

The names are taken from the Entry Books and from the General Register, and the dates are the years of entering the College.

1830.

Scadding, Henry.
Strachan, John.
Wells, George Dupont.
Givins, Adolphus.
McDonald, William.
Wells, Robert.
Strachan, Alexander.
McDonald, Charles.
McDonald, John.
Robinson, James Lukin.
Robinson, John Beverley.
Richardson, Hugh.
Richardson, Richard.
Turquand, John.
Duggan, Richard.
Givins, George.
Power, William Dummer.
Powell, Grant.
Phillips, Samuel.
Allan, William George.
Fitzgibbon, Charles.
Fitzgibbon, George.
Fitzgibbon, William.
Fitzgibbon James.
Fitzgerald, James William.
Sherwood, Samuel.
Jones, Hugh.
Heward, Peter.
Heward, John.
Radenhurst, Thomas.
Smith, Samuel.
Billings, George.
Billings, James.
Foster, Colley.
Denison, Richard.
Denison, George.
Hartney, Henry.
Brooke, George.
Fenton, James.
Dunn, John.
McNab, Robert Allan.
Jarvis, William.
Jarvis, Samuel.
Jarvis, George.
Ridout, Joseph.
Ridout Samuel.
Stanton, Henry William.
Latham, Henry.
Wells, Frederick.
Horne, John.
Horne, Charles.
Sherwood, Edward.
Richardson, Henry.

Powell, Henry.
Cameron, William.
Ewart, John.
Ewart, Thomas.
Scarlett, Edward.
Scarlett, Archibald.
Scarlett, St. George.
Moore, John.
Moore, Thomas.
Collins, Nicholas.
Ridout, Lionel.
Ridout, Septimus.
Heward, Francis.
Murchison, John.
Gray, Francis.
Parsons, John.
Beynon, William.
Rendall, George McCarthy.
Rendall, John.
Wilmot, Samuel Street.
Boulton, William.
Clench, Holcroft.
Weatherhead, William Henry.
Jones, David Ford.
Stevenson, Robert St. Patrick.
Stevenson, John Gustavus.
Connolly, Robert Addison.
Stephenson, James Halfhide Corbet.
McEwan, John.
MacNider, William.
Brooke, John Edmund.
Phillpots, George Alexander.
Phillpots, John.
Phillpots, Thomas Charles.
Thomson, George.
White, Andrew.
McDonald, Donald.
Small, John.
Covert, Henry.
Collombus, Isaac.
McDonell, Alexander.
McDonell, Samuel.
Nation, Edward.
Barnhart, John.
Barnhart, Noah.
Fairbanks, Silas Benjamin.
Roberts, Brownlow.
Roberts, Henry.
Roberts, Peregrine.
Throop, Robert.
Boswell, William.
Fowler, Harvey.
Collins, Francis.
Meagher, James.

Willard, Charles.
Deacon, John.
Briscoe, Henry.
Nelles, Robert Fanning.
McDonell, Angus Duncan.
Stanton, James.
Bartlett, John F.
Small, John Thomas.
Ruttan, William.
Covert, Frederick.
Keegan, Edmund.
O'Grady, William.
Ham, Norman.
McLean, Allan Neil.
Ketchum, Jesse.
Stuart, Charles.
Turpin, Wellington.
Hall, Francis.
Sullivan, Augustus.
Garrett, Henry.
Stennett, William.
Stennett, Walter.
Stennett, Alfred.
Hewson, Francis.

1831.

Parker, Aldis.
Denison, Robert.
Patton, James.
Patton, Andrew.
Wenham, John George.
Heward, William.
Morrison, Joseph.
Mount, Charles.
Wilmot, John.
Phillips, Thomas.
Phillips, Alfred.
Wallbridge, Lewis.
Wallbridge, William.
Meyers, Justus.
Meyers, William.
Keefer, Samuel.
Powell, John.
Wilkins, Charles.
Pyke, James.
Barwick, Hugh Crawford.
Barwick, John.
Barwick, James Stratton.
Cameron, John.
Cameron, Robert.
O'Grady, William.
Warren, Thomas.

Morgan, James.
Boulton, Henry.
Dixie, Wolstan.
Dixie, Beaumont.
Dixie, Richard.
Mack, Theophilus.
Davis, Edward.
Morgan, Thomas.
Thomas, George W.
Downs, William George Fallon.
O'Hara, Robert.
Reade, William.
Powell, Alexander.

1832.

Rubidge, Charles.
Colborne, James.
Pinkey, Horace.
Cameron, Duncan.
Hall, George Parker.
Latham, Thomas.
Fisher, Edwin.
Richardson, Charles.
Kennedy, John.
Meyers, John.
Armstrong, John.
Latham, John.
Colborne, Francis.
Hurd, Thomas.
Hurd, Edward.
Turner, Fitzherbert.
Adamson, James.
McDonald, Donald.
Cockburn, James.
Spilsbury, Henry Bailey.
Muttlebury, Frederick.
Muttlebury, Augustus.
Kennedy, Daniel.
Muttlebury, James.
Askin, James Hamilton.
Rapelje, Henry Van Allen.
Monk, Benning.
Wonham, William George.
Robinson, Arthur.
Keegan, George Whister.
Perry, Charles.
O'Neil, Edward.
Spencer, Richard.
Nichol, Robert.

1833.

Ruttan, Charles.
Dalton, Robert.
Muttlebury, John.
Hamilton, Johnson Quinton.
Strett, Richard Porter.
Street, Robert Henry.
Rutherford, James.
Barry, Edward.
Dyett, Mark.
Dyett, Walter.
Campbell, Stedman.

Roddy, John Robert.
Chafee, Isaac.
Crickmore, John.
Rogers, John Holbert.
Wilson, Francis.
Geale, John.
Hawke, Anthony Bawden.
Hawke, Edward Henry.
Kingsmill, Charles Edward.
Cooke, Ferdinand.
Maughan, Robert.
Breakenridge, John.
Colborne, Edmund.
Wells, Arthur.
Steele, Henry.
Ross, James Hamilton.
Sampson, Thomas.
Ridout, Thomas.
Ross, John.
Hopkins, Henry.
Wright, Malcolm.
Wright, Richard William.
Ingall, William.
Smith, William Larratt.
Smith, George.
Street, Warren.
Jones, Frederick.
Ottley, John.
Crawford, ——.
O'Grady, Cornelius.
Ruttan, Henry.
Colborne, Graham.
Stratford, George.
Crookshank, George.
Crookshank, John.
Crookshank, Robert.
Ritchey, William.
Keefer, Augustus.
Keefer, Thomas.
Keefer, James.
Cubitt, Frederick.
Bartley, John Cowell.
McDonald, Robert.
Smith, Richard.
Kavanagh, John.

1834.

Clemow, Francis.
Stow, Frederick.
Franks, James.
Townsend, Charles.
Townsend, Henry.
Baldwin, John.
Bell, William.
Bellingham, William.
Duncombe, Charles Henry.
Wilkes, George Samuel.
Botsford, John.
Denham, Benjamin Joseph Marshall.
Wright, George Rose.
Crawley, Henry.
Elliot, William.
Cahusac, William.

Cahusac, Edward.
Draper, William George.
Draper, Robert Henry.
McDonell, Hugh.
Thomson, Archibald Whitehead.
Jarvis, Stephen M.
Dawson, George.
Dawson, Julius.
Beswick, James Prestwick.
Arnold, John Thomas.
Arnold, William Rawson.
Vidal, William Penrose.
Vidal, Townsend George.
Whitney, Frederick Augustus.
Horne, James Macaulay.
Whitney, William John Gamble.
Lewis, Robert Frederick.
Lewis, Thomas.
Lewis, Richard.
Helliwell, John.
Brooke, Daniel.
Warren, William.
Lyons, William Markland.
Buchanan, William Oliver.
Leslie, George.
Cockburn, Richard.
Talbot, Alfred.
Talbot, Joseph Walter.
Bergin, Darby O'Flanagan.
Bell, James.
Perry, John.
Hagerman, James Talbot.

1835.

Currie, Alexander Charles.
Ravenhill, Lefroy.
Jarvis, Frederick W.
Grover, Peregrine Maitland.
Hawke, George Macauley.
Hale, Edward Dashwood.
Cumming, Robert.
Edwards, George.
Henriod, Napoleon.
Duggan, Edmund Cudmoze.
Higgins, Moore.
Daniell, James.
Swann, Matthew.
Crowther, James.
Robinson, Christopher.
Blevins, John.
Daniell, Dawson.
Willard, Charles.
Dixon, William.
Boulton, D'Arcy.
Romain, Charles Edward.
Silverthorn, Nathan.
Armstrong, James Rogers.
Reid, James Hales.
Reid, Blair Thomas.
Connolly, John Hamilton.
Irving, Æmilius Thomas.
McDowall, Daniell.
Ravenhill, William Courtenay.
O'Hara, Walter.

Weller, William Henry.
McVittie, Thomas Jones.
Kirkpatrick, John.
Baldwin, Edmund.
Henderson, James P.
Billings, John.
Macaulay, John J.
Hart, Benjamin.
Skinner, Henry.
Cameron, Hugh.
Cameron, Duncan.
Fraser, Thomas.

1836.

Breakenridge, William David.
Jarvis, Robinson.
Heron, Thomas William.
Richardson, John Beverley Robinson.
Hamilton, George.
Prince, William Stratton.
Prince, Albert.
Prince, Charles.
Bergin, John.
Dupuy, Glen.
Joseph, Gershom.
Merritt, William Hamilton.
Macaulay, George.
Nation, John.
Nation, James Cushing.
Houghton, George W.
Bailey, Moses Nathan.
DeBlaquiere, Henry.
McMicking, George Milmine.
Read, David Breakenridge.
Stoughton, Henry Gray.
Leonard, Charles Maitland.
Ruttan, Richard.
Walmsley, Alexander.

1837.

Mercer, Lawrence.
Andrews, William.
Grover, George Alexander.
Spalding, John.
Rutherford, Orlando.
Barber, George Anthony.
Keele, Ross.
Ryerson, Egerton.
Wade, Charles Cooper.
Coleman, Charles Lester.
Cathcart, Joseph Allan.
Shedden, William.
Shedden, John.
Hutcheson, John Howell.
Bate, Henry.
Chalmers, George Canning.
Ewart, George.
Atkinson, James.
Ingersoll, James Hamilton.
Merritt, Thomas Rodman.
McKenzie, John George Delhoste.

38

Dempsey, Richard.
McLeod, Daniel.
Muttlebury, Francis.
Willson, William.
Chewett, William Cameron.
Scott, William.
Henderson, James.
Kerby, James Robert Nichol.
Stayner, Francis Wilson.
Stayner, Thomas Sutherland.
Goslee, George.
Keeler, Joseph.
Woodruff, James Counter.
Connolly, George Stuart.
Watson, Robert George.
Sibbald, Hugh.
Sibbald, Francis Clunie.
Sibbald, Ogilvie Dashwood.
Ridout, Thomas.
Steers, James.
Roe, William.
Cockburn, Robert.
Cameron, Charles.
Thomson, Hugh.
Turquand, Bernard.
Thomson, Edmund T.
Thomson, John S.
Thomson, Andrew William.
Mitchell, David.
Hardison, David.
Thomson, William.
Chisholm, William McKenzie.
Macnider, George.
Logie, Alexander.
Kyte, John.
Ryerson, Joseph William.
Wedd, William.
McLean, Thomas Alexander.
Jessopp, Dudley Frederick.
Jessopp, Henry Bate.
Jones, Edward.
Jones, Francis.
Jones, Jonas.
Gallego, Peter.

1838.

Bettridge, William.
George, James.
Roaf, John.
Boulton, John.
Yarwood, Edmund.
Coppinger, John Bramley.
Baxter, Richard.
Baines, Egerton Robert.
McLeod, Neile.
Smart, Robert Wallace.
Patrick, William.
O'Higgins, Patrick Charles.
Cummings, Robert.
Vidal, William Penrose.
Secord, Cortland.
Maughan, Robert.
Neill, John William.
Heward, Augustine Nathan.

Heward, Stephen.
Cosens, Charles Sidney.
Hepburn, William Carr.
Napier, Josias Charles.
Williams, Cornelius.
Boyd, Walter.
Paget, Robert John.
Paget, Edward.
Price, Henry William.
Small, James.
Muttlebury, Francis.
Macaulay, George Hayter.
Brooke, Daniel.
Billings, William Henry.
Shuter, James.
Innes, John Frederick.
Cameron, Matthew Crooks.
MacDonell, Charles.
MacDonell, Duncan Cameron.
Kingsmill, Charles Edward.
Molson, Samuel Elsdale.
Thomson, Henry Ash.
Duggan, Edmund.
Atkinson, James.
Monro, John.
Monro, George.
Muttlebury, Henry.
Smith, Ferdinaud Francis.
Boulton, Henry John.
Boulton, Charles Knightley.
Wilkes, Charles Ranu.
Macallum, ——
Farley, George.
Oliver, Walter Telfer.
Baldwin, William
Hawke, George.
Duke, Jephson.
Auldjo, John.
Perkis, Josias.
Raines, Conrad.
Robinson, Frederick.
Sadlier, Charles.
Thomson, Charles Edward.
Thomson, James Doyle.
Tucker, Nathaniel.

1839.

Walton, George Fredder.
Barber, Edward Cawdell.
Knowles, Horatio.
Jarvis, Thomas.
Sharpe, Edmund.
Parsons, Benjamin.
Parsons, Charles.
MacDonald, Robert.
MacDonald, William.
Binley, Joseph Isaac.
Dixon, William.
Thomson, John S.
Laurie, Robert Brown.
Hamilton, George.
Rogers, Charles Van Coon.
Ross, George.
McBean, George.

MacBean, Forbes.
Radcliff, Thomas.
Wickson, Arthur.
Arthur, John.
Paterson, David.
Paterson, John.
Rennie, Alexander.
Roy, William.
Bostwick, Amos.
Taylor, Arthur J.
Taylor, Alexander G.
Crooks, Adam.
Crooks, David.
Hamilton, John.
Longley, William.
Longley, Cay.
Fisher, M.
Cathcart, Robert.
Dampier, John.
Dampier, William.
Kerby, Abraham.
Kerby, James.
Doyle, Michael.
Mone, John.
Mone, Charles.
Harvey, John.
Bampfield, William.
Crawford, Abraham.
Johns, Peter.
Corbett, Alexander.
Chewett, Alexander.
Chichester, Charles.
Jacob, George.
McLeod, James.
Mewburn, Thomas.
Murkisson, William.
Price, E.
Richardson, J. H.
Stewart, J. G.
Sharpe, Alfred.
Williamson, Thomas.
Wawanock, David.
Watkins, Thomas.
Peay, Joshua.
Powell, John.
Anderson, Gustavus.
Hall, Joseph.
McCutcheon, Peter.
McCutcheon, Henry.
Kirkpatrick, Richard.
Froite, Frederick.
Froite, Francis.
Nichol, Thomas.
Lyttle, John.
Molson, George D.
Molson, Joseph D.
Molson, Alexander.

1840.

Dee, Francis O.
McMiching, Peter.
Kingsmill, John.
Eilmore, John.
Wakefield, William.

Spalding, Thomas.
Ritchey, John.
Ritchey, James.
Ritchey, Richard.
Arnold, Walter.
Maule, Arthur.
Loder, James.
Loder, William.
Higgins, John.
Hamilton, J. R.
Gildersleeve, ———
Torrance, Robert.
Patrick, ———
Bethune, John George.
Bethune, Norman.
Bethune, James.
Bethune, Alexander.
Bethune, John Madden.
Thompson, Walter.
Stotsbury, ———
Dee, Thomas.
Grasett, Elliott.
Glasgow, George.
Boswell, Augustus.
Assiginack, Francis.
Clarke, O. M.
McFarland, J. C.

1841.

Barnum, James.
Hammond, Anselm.
Lewis, Oscar.
Watson, John.
Dampier, H.
O'Brien, Edward.
Doel, W. H.
Williams, Hodgins.
Mountcastle, Alfred.
Powell, John.
Powell, Charles Henry.
McKenzie, Matthew Bell.
McKenzie, Frederick William.
McKenzie, Kenneth.
Leaycraft, George.
Norwise, Joseph.
Jackes, Franklin.
Snider, Charles.
Jackes, William.
Cathcart, James.
O'Hara, Charles.
Lamb, John.
Boys, Thomas.
Henry, William.
McMurray, Lucan.
Cameron, Hugh.
Harvey, Edward.
Cornwall, Vincent.
Boyd, William Thomas.
Thompson, Peter Robinson.
Thorne, William Henry.
Wells, Clarence E.
Palmer, Fitzmaurice.
Overfield, Charles.
Daly, Thomas Mayne.

Petoskay, Francis.
Thompson, James Wilson.
Thompson, James Richard.
Syme, William.
Syme, Charles.
Jones, Charles Edward.

1842.

Arnold, Robert.
Crooks, Charles.
Clark, Thomas.
Mittleberger, Henry John.
Harris, Charles Le Burn.
Harris, William Robert.
Usher, Frederick Samuel.
Usher, John.
Usher, John Sennett.
Beatty, William Henry.
Cosens, William C.
Latham, James.
Moore, Charles.
Coates, John Denison.
Coates, Thomas.
Hudepeth, Thomas.
Musson, James W.
Richey, Matthew Henry.
Bloor, John.
Daniel, William.
Lamb, William.
Nickson, William.
Thompson, Octavius.
Carfrae, Hugh.
Fortye, Loen.
Molson, John Henry.
Anderson, Francis.
Helliwell, Thomas.
Wallbridge, Henry.
Harper, Richard.
Alma, John.
McMullen, William.
Jones, Clarkson.
Hamilton, William.
Usher, Henry.
Boyd, John.
McCormack, Samuel.
Campbell, Archibald Shaw John.
Hubertus, Julius.
Crysler, Manuel.
Johnson, Rawson.
Harris, Augustus B.
McIntosh, John.
Boulton, Alexander Gregg.
Boulton, James Foster.
Baker, Norman.
Goodwane, William Frederick.
Baldwin, Edward Haughton.
Baldwin, Robert.
Gordon, John Bell.
O'Brien, Richard Lucius J.
Elliott, William.
Gordon, James.
Elliott, Henry.
McDonald, Duncan.

Imray, David.
Willard, George.
Northcote, Henry.
Keefer, Charles Henry.
McCormick, George D.
Helliwell, Thomas.
Helliwell, John.
Clarke, James McNab.
Catton, Alfred.
Bell, John.
Kidd, Edward Flood.
Bell, James.
Sky, Charles.
Ching-wa Joseph.
Jarvis, Henry William.
Nelles, James Cummings.
Ridley, Charles Neville.
Ridley, Henry Thomas.
Beaty, Robert.

1843.

Wilkins, Charles.
Thorner, ——
Watkins, Charles.
Armour, John.
Watkins, John.
Baldwin, Morgan.
Wickson, Samuel.
Harris, John.
Boulton, Somerville.
Boulton, Henry.
Beck, Walton.
Boulton, Edward.
Bouter, John Cole.
Donnelly, Charles.
O'Brien, Donough.
Esten, Hutcheson.
Thomson, Jesse.
Ryan, James C.
Hart, Henry.
Watts, Alfred.
Carfrae, James.
Carfrae, Thomas.
Digby, Thomas.
Marling, Samuel.
Marling, Alexander.
Boulton, George D'Arcy.
Craig, John Lindsay.
McCallum, Arthur.
Beaver, John Froud.
Beaver, Edward William.
Harvey, G. R.
Young, Austin.
Birchall, Thomas Shivers.
Melville, Winniett.
Stinson, Ebenezer.
Jones, Charles Blackburn.
Evans, G. M.
Carr, ——
Douglas, ——
Syme, ——
Small, John.
Hawkins, W. C.
Anderson, Francis.

Bright, ——
Cathcart, Robert.
Cathcart, John.
Donnelly, G.
Loring, ——
Lawrason, William.
Rykert, George.
Tinning, N.
Abraham, Henry.
Carey, A.
Fraser, Colin.
Hayward, William Field.
Watson, ——
Crookshank, George.
Shaw, Samuel.
Williams, R.
Watkins, ——
Unwin, Charles.
Maule, Stephen.
Maule, Thomas.

1844.

Burn, William David.
Bonter, Abraham.
Bell, W. H.
Dixon, Fred Eldon.
Whitt, John.
Cronyn, Thomas.
Dixon, John.
McMahon, Edward Dudley.
Ridley, Alfred.
Stinson, John.
Tyner, Richard.
Newbigging, Robert.
Carfrae, John.
Draper, Frank.
Price, Edwin.
Fortye, Leon.
Kirkpatrick, R.
Robinson, Charles.
Sullivan, William.
Bailey, John.
Bell, James.
Beaver, Robert.
Bruce, Robert.
Keefer, Alexander.
Marsh, Henry William.
Clark, Charles John.
Clark, Allister McKenzie.
Freer, Courtlandt.
Seymour, Charles.
Ogilvie, ——
Preston, J. T.
Jack, Alexander.
Palmer, George.
Ambrose, ——
Bull, Henry.
Barclay, Adalbert.
Campbell, Thomas.
Crawford, John.
Dunn, Alexander.
Green, Columbus.
Hutton, Joseph.
Mackintosh, ——

O'Brien, William.
O'Brien, Richard Lucius.
O'Brien, Edward.
Small, James Charles.
Small, George Edward.
Thomas, Albert.
Thomas, Cyrus Pole.
Weller, Charles.
Wright, Joshua.
Freeland, William.
Freeland, Robert.
Wright, Alfred.
Ingersoll, Charles Henry.
Docker, Thomas Bower.
Ridout, Charles.
MacDonald, Douglas Charles.

1845.

Widmer, Christopher Rolph.
Baldwin, Morgan.
Small, Joseph.
Cooper, William England.
Radenhurst, John Charles.
Roy, Norman Watt.
Jarvis, Charles Frederick.
Stevenson, Edward Powel.
Campbell, William James A.
Campbell, Henry Jameson.
Crooks, Archibald.
Small, Charles Coxwell.
Terington, Henry Marvin.
Gilkison, William Sanders.
Bradley, Robert Cuff.
Jarvis, William Dummer.
McKeown, John.
Small, William Eines.
Small, Edward Goldsmith.
McKenzie, John Thomas.
Ross, Donald Proctor.
Powers, Charles James.
Partridge, Thomas.
Beckett, Alfred Richard.
Turner, Charles Frederick.
Turner, Henry Montresor.
Turner, Archibald Campbell.
Turner, William Loftus.
Daintry, John.
Nourse, Jacob William.
Simpson, Caleb P.
Grasett, Charles Barrett.
Grier, James.
Kingsmill, Nicol.
Helliwell, William.
Docker, Arthur.
Maddock, Dyer Henry.
Holwell, William James.
Knowlson, James Bancs.
Mack, Alexander Augustus.
Helliwell, Edward.
Wallbridge, Thos. C.
McLeod, Donald.
McLeod, Henry.
McLeod, Donald John T.
McLeod, James.

Barwick, Andrew.
Brewer, Richard Irvine.
Goddard, ——
King, Livius Sherwood.
King, John Lyons.
Corbett, Augustus Myers.
Price, George Joseph.
Keefer, Robert Grant.
Neil, George James.
Elliot, Charles.
Hawkins, Nicholas.
Read, Alfred.
Elmsley, Peter Sherwood.

1846.

McDonell, Charles John.
Denison, George T.
Barber, Frank William.
Cawthra, Henry.
McGill, James.
Bousfield, Thomas.
Clarke, James Fuller.
Clarke, Alexander.
McMaster, William J.
Phillips, Thomas Dowell.
Keiller, James.
Pritchard, Frederick.
Hamilton, Alexander.
Bilton, William.
Peterson, Henry William.
Sullivan, Robert Baldwin.
Keefer, William.
Walker, John Gardner.
Rowsell, Henry Samuel.
Stainsby, Thomas.
Harrison, Robert Alexander.
Nash, George Richard.
Thorne, Benjamin John.
Clarkson, John Brunskill.
Maddock, John Ford.
Marsh, Francis Smart.
Marsh, Edward Washington.
Barber, Frederick William.
Bray, James Edwin.
Clarke, Charles Anthony.
Bailey, Charles Frost.
Black, John Russell.
Webb, John Henry.
Heyden, Lawrence.
Hornby, Frederick William.
Hornby, Reginald George.
Joseph, Frank John.
Hastings, Edward.
Orton, Thomas Jerome.
Smith, David John.
Smith, Charles Frank.
Ridley, James McGill.
Wood, Douglas P.
Hawley, John.
Gildersleeve, Charles.
Murray, William.
Murray, Daniel.
Lampman, Archibald.
Blake, Dominick Edward.

Blake, Samuel H.
O'Carr, Peter.
White, Frederick.
Maynard, Newland E.
Baldwin, Morrice S.
Powell, Edwin.
Rykert, John Charles.
Townsend, Gilbert.
Thompson, Charles Edward.
Elmer, Andrew.
Baldwin, Robert.
Jones, Chilion.
Arthurs, George.
Townley, James A. L.
Roper, James West.
Phillips, Horace.
Patterson, Charles William.
McKenzie, Valentine.
Matheson, William N.
Harris, Henry J.
Harris, Robert F.
Grasett, Clement Darley.
Bethune, John James.
Bethune, Robert Henry.
Wickson, John Rushby.
Wallis, Brown.
Kersheval, Alexander W.
Doyle, James H.
Jones, William.
Met-twa-aush, Moses.
Cameron, Alexander.
Machin, Henry.
O'Higgins, Joseph Paschal.
Prince, Henry.

1847.

Shortt, Lawrence Hartshorne.
Thomson, George.
Backas, George.
McDonell, Alexander Winette.
McDonell, Samuel Smith.
Townsend, Frederick.
Beard, George.
Bull, Samuel.
Davey, Peter Robinson.
Keefor, Henry.
Holder, Edward Francis Troy.
Richardson, Frank Beverley.
Richardson, Arthur.
Butterfield, John Almus.
Woodcock, Henry.
Denison, John.
Baines, William James.
Bilton, George Usher.
Foster, John.
Johnson, Colin Campbell.
Spencer, James J.
Scott, John B.
Arthurs, William.
Arthurs, John.
Ross, John Le Breton.
Francis, William.
Marr, Graham.
Turner, Frank E. P.

Corbett, William Henry.
O'Dea, Martin John.
O'Dea, James.
Baines, Edward Charles.
Radenhurst, William.
Morgan, Charles George.
Baldwin, Thomas Henry.
Whitehead, Charles James.
Whitehead, William Henry.
Lloyd, Harry.
Atkin, William.
Kirkpatrick, Alexander Sutton.
Kirkpatrick, Thomas Frank S.
Brown, James.
McArthur, John Archibald.
Rykert, Alfred Edwin.
Hatt, Frederick Augustus.
Benson, Thomas.
Harris, Thomas W.
Bowlby, David.
Walker, Nathaniel.
Benjamin, Emmanuel Hyman.
Coleman, Everitt Hastings.
Flannagan, William.
Wetenhall, Rodney James.
Mack, George.
Shaw, Henry.
Jackes, Joseph.
Boyd, John Alexander.
Ridout, Joseph Bramley.
Smith, William.
Hayward, Henry F.
Birchall, John Dorset.
Williams, Arthur.
Richardson, Charles E.
Radenhurst, William H.
Aikman, Charles M.
Calcott, Henry.
Morris, James Henry.
McMillan, Alexander.
Keeler, William H.
Doyle, James.
Peterson, H. W.
Tyner, Richard.
Palmer, William.
Kerr, Joseph.
Holwell, William J. S.
Thompson, C. E.
Jones, William.
Thorne, William.
Nelles, Samuel.
Lewis, Charles D.
Murray, Hewson W.
Barwick, John.
Blakey, Robert.
Jones, Andrew.
Lindsey, Edward Templeman.
Veith, Christian John.

1848.

Stibbs, William John.
Oxenham, James.
White, David.
Merigold, Charles I.
Sisson, W. J. W.

THE U. C. C. ROLL, 1829-1892.   301

Campbell, John.
Harper, William John.
Harper, John.
Cooper, James.
Beamish, William Adely.
Cooper, George.
Kennedy, Michael.
Makefield, Richard P.
Street, Charles.
Field, John.
Fraser, James.
Nelson, John.
Bates, ——
Glasford, Edward Augustus.
McDonell, James F.
Jones, Charles.
Jefferies, John R.
Bethune, Angus R.
Van Ingen, William H.
Ridout, William.
Denison, Charles Leslie.
Orris, Francis Bond.
Nash, Charles Henry.
Nash, Frederick.
Gage, Marshall Spring Bidwell.
Baldwin, Augustus.
Morris, Edmund.
Denison, Richard L.
Lapenoliere, Frederick John.
Loscombe, Robert Russell.
Overfield, Marshall S. B.
Salt, William Henry.
Foster, Edward Charles Colley.
Foster, Charles Colley.
Scollie, George Jacob.
Covernton, Charles James.
Graham, Robert Nichol.
Maddock, George Shipster.
Mitchell, William Henry.
Wardell, William Henry.
Bowman, Charles.
Duggan, George Frederick.
Hume, Joseph Samuel.
Hume, Henry Harrington.
Harris, Edwin.
Hopkins, Alexander.
Hodder Ernest.
Taylor, George L. **L. M.**
Taylor, Arthur **D. H.**

1849.

Smyth, Thomas Sheppard.
Shortt, John William.
Helliwell, Charles **C.**
Lee, John Channon.
Ridout, John Gibbs.
Keeler, Thomas Charles.
Beard, George Edward.
Beard, Joshua George.
Turner, Robert C.
Attrill, Edward.
Ellis, John.
Armstrong, Arthur.
Conlin, John.

Andrews, James **Shade.**
Macdonald, William.
Conlin, Henry.
Robarts, John William.
Robarts, George Brereton.
Willoughby, John.
Smith, Joseph Shuter.
Clements, F. W. R.
Jackson, John Henry.
Peters, Paul.
Squire, William Wood.
Mayerhoffer, Julius Alexander.
Counsell, George S.
Marr, Joseph.
Powell, Berkeley.
Doran, James.
Crease, John.
Burns, Robert Taylor.
Burns, Thomas.
Crease, Charles.
Platt, Richard.
Maynard, Jonas Foster.
Campbell, Robert Dickson.
Campbell, Edward Clarke.
Lewis, George Watkins.
Fitzgerald, James.
Morphy, Thomas.
McDonnell, John G.
Heward, Francis Gordon.
Russell, James.
Wightman, Robert.
Wadsworth, Thomas R.
Wadsworth, Thomas Page.
Eastwood, Anthony.
Esten, Charles Philip.
McLean, Neil.
Taché, Eugene.
Hincks, Alexander Stewart.
McNab, John Maxwell.
Hincks, Thomas.
Mayer, Lehman.

1850.

McDonald, Donald M.
Richey, James Arminius.
Murray, William.
Wallis, George Hewitt.
Musson, Thomas Henry.
Sullivan, Robert.
Beard, Samuel William.
Robarts, Henry.
Robarts, James J.
Nation, George A.
Batt, Benjamin.
McLean, Duncan Cameron.
Dufort, Hector.
Robinson, James Edwin.
Norman, Thomas Edward.
Gooderham, Alfred.
Lister, Fred. A. W.
Atkinson, William K.
Atkinson, Henry M.
Atkinson, Thomas.
Powell, Thomas.

De Blaquiere, George.
Rogers, Alexander.
Stratford, Edmund.
Lindsay, Henry.
Veith, Christian **John.**
Lindsay, Arthur.
Mendell, George.
Lynn, James William.
Lynn, John G.
Harris, Thomas **W.**
Kirkpatrick, Francis **W.**
Ramsey, Samuel F.
Sanderson, Joseph E.
Sanderson, Isaac **H.**
Savage, William.
Savage, John.
Badgley, Charles.
Joseph, Frank.
Smith, James William.
Smith, Frederick J. D.
Jones, Edward Charles.
Mayer, Samuel David.
Hume, Robert.
Baldwin, Arthur Henry.
Baldwin, St. George.
Baldwin, James.
Hawke, John.
Smith, James.
Musson, George.
Freeland, R.
Barber, Albert G.
Robertson, John Ross.
Trotter, Henry.
Musson, Edward.
Wallis, Charles H.
McClelland, Robert.
O'Reilly, Edwin.
Nicol, William Boys.
Nicol, George Boys.
Neeve, John Bonnor.
Murray, Edmund H.
Cameron, John Buchanan.
Heward, Stephen Beverley.

1851.

Vansittart, Henry Christopher.
Vansittart John P.
Vansittart, James G.
Sproatt, Charles.
Moss, Thomas.
Miller, George.
Aylmer, Charles W. Brabazon.
Morgan, James Theodore.
Williams, George J. J.
Burns, Edward.
Gibson, George.
Bradley, A. John.
Stayner, Frank Henry.
Sampson, David R.
King, George C.
Hopwood, Thomas Henry.
Smith, Ephraim.
Smith Egbert.
Horwood, Charles George.

302 UPPER CANADA COLLEGE MEMORIAL VOLUME.

Horwood, Edward **Henry.**
Hector, Alfred.
Barrett, Clarence.
Hammond, Charles.
O'Reilly, Miles.
Baldwin, William A.
Rodd, John Edwin.
De La Haye. A. J. B.
O'Brien, Samuel L. G.
Buchan, James.
Buchan, Humphrey E.
Foster, Frederick.
Stayner, Lawrence.
McDonell, Alexander.
Stanton, Irvine.
McIntosh, James.
Robertson, Charles.
Robertson, Alexander.
Aikman, Hugh B. W.
Towers, Thos. H.
Helliwell, Gordon W.
Smith, James.
Lett, Francis R. **H.**
Forbes, Frank.
Burgess, William.
Archibald, Cyril.
Cowie, William.
Nash, Frank.
Buckland, Geo. **William.**
Brent, Charles **James.**
Evans, William **Berthomé.**
Graham, Oliver.
Platt, George A.
Haworth, William Henry.
Kirkpatrick, Alexander.
Kirkpatrick, Robert.
Coates, Aylmer.
Badenach, William.
Delmege, Edward.
Stanton, Francis R.
Murray, Tallamore **David.**
Kempshall, Francis.

1852.

Proudfoot, Frederick.
Graham, Samuel James.
Alma, Pedro.
Graham, James.
Graham, Thomas.
Graham, Richard.
Paterson, James Frederick.
Nation, Frederick.
Rolph, Thomas.
Scadding, William.
Webb, Edward.
Champion, Thomas Edward.
Woodruff, George.
Woodruff, William **W.**
Salmoni, Mark.
Wanzer, **George G.**
Perrin, **Alfred Poyntz.**
Foster, **William.**
Harman, **Samuel B.**
Dickson, **Walter Augustus.**
Parry, Reginald Coleridge.

Collier, Charles.
Mishaw, Thomas.
McGregor, Alexander.
Tullock, John H.
Cayley, John D'A.
Roberts, William P.
Baines, Christopher C.
Cayley, Edward.
Fraser, James.
Mendell, James.
Cayley, Frank.
Scadding, Edward.
Benson, Charles **J.**
Sherwood, George.
Sherwood, Donald B.
Brown, Henry John.
Wells, James D.
Bradbury, William A. **R.**
Bradbury, Joel L.
Dixon, William A.
Robertson, Hector S.
Robertson, Alexander J.
Leys, John.
Ridout, John.
Mead Robert.
Sandilands, Thomas.
Thompson, David.
vanderSmissen, William Henry
Jones, Charles Arthur.
Lett, Benjamin Henry.
Lett, Fred. Augustus.
Spragge, Edward William.
McKenzie, William.
Champion, John Henry
Thom, John.
Vale, Theodoric James.
McGlashon, James A.
McGlashon, Andrew.
McGlashon, Alexander.
Loughead, Joseph.
Grange, Frank.
Grange, George.
McKenzie, William.
McKenzie, George.
Garth, Richard.
Garth, Henry.
Hammond, Thomas.
Whitney, George.
Lindsay, Arthur.
Loring, Robert George **L.**
Thomas, Richard.

1853.

Kerby, Andrew.
Cerswell, John.
Seymour, Grant **T.**
Lafferty, Alfred.
Stewart, Albert H.
DeGrassi, George P.
Dowding, Frederick **C.**
Sherwood, Henry.
Joseph, George J.
Kennedy, John Edward.
McCaul, Lefroy G.

Mulholland, John Henry.
Newbery, Robert William.
Newbery, George Fraser.
Humphreys, James D.
Wilkins, Oscar F.
Henderson, Robert.
Bright, William Lewis.
Warren, Charles.
Proudfoot, William S.
Kennedy, T. S.
Wilder, Harvey.
Heron, Charles.
Magrath, James Frederick.
Harcourt, John.
Harrison, Richard A.
Taylor, John.
McIntosh, Charles.
Wilson, John.
Musson, Charles S.
Browne, William A.
Ellis, James E.
Wardell, George.
Walker, Joshua.
Smallwood, William Henry.
Goring, Harry Yelverton.
Rossin, Julius.
Milroy, William.
Goodenough, Rollin **A.**
Benson, James.
Machin, William **N.**
McConkey, George **S.**
McConkey, Charles **T.**
McConkey, Thomas.
Cassels, James M. N.
Peel, Jonathan.
Robertson, Helenus **R.**
Goode, Cephas.
Churchill, Thomas.
Musterson, Charles **M.**
Nicol, Henry B.
Baldwin, Robert Russell.
Small, Joseph Samuel.
Shaw, George Alexander.
Badgley, Fred. M.
Mayer, James C.
Birdsall, Richard.
Rogers, Edward O'B.
Harkness, Francis T.
Cameron, Hillyard H. **A.**
Maitland, James S.
Fowler, Jacob.
Ward, John.
Lewis, Lisbon.
Wright, Joseph.
Boswell, Arthur.
Boswell, Frederick.
Parke, Samuel.
Gamble, John H.

1854.

Duggan, Edmund Henry.
Hopkins, George.
Killip, John.
McMurray, Thomas W.

Piper, Henry L.
Newbery, Walter.
Meacham, George M.
Brunel, Troilus.
Brunel, Alfred.
Ellis, John E.
Peters, Horace.
Heakes, Frederick.
Hutty, Jos. William.
Davis, Joseph.
Warren, Robert.
Furniss, Bernard.
Boulton, Charles.
Boulton, George D'A.
Smith, Thomas.
Smith, Charles Edwin.
Whitmarsh, George Augustus.
MacDonald, Alfred Edward.
Romain, Charles Edward.
Thistle, William.
Workman, Frederick.
Workman, Joseph.
Noble, John.
Irving, Henry Irskine.
Verplanck, Abraham.
Murray, Robert Gillie.
Morgan, Charles.
Mulleney, James Beatty.
Shaw, James.
Upton, Walter.
Richardson, Frederick.
Carpenter, Thomas Talbot.
Wakefield, Alfred.
Scott, William.
McDonell, Duncan.
Dixon, Alexander.
Graham, Frederick.
Leslie, George.
Creighton, William.
Gildersleeve, James P.
Hallowell, James.
Bright, Thomas G.
Mack, Francis.
Jones, Strachan Graham
Jones, Charles Mercer.
Goring, Foster.
Blake, John N.
Crawford, John Sidney.
Crawford, Joseph Ury.
Harbeson, David.
Denison, William.
Harper, Geo. Robert.
Brown, Alfred.
Henderson, James.
Henderson, Elmes.
Henderson, Robert.
Proctor, James.
Gooderham Robert.
Gooderham, Horace.
Hainer, De Loss W.
Boyd, David.
Lovejoy, George.
Mills, Thomas A.
Rankin, George.
Campbell, Alexander.
Reid, Thomas.

Wells, Wilmer.
Grant, Colborne.
Webb, Harry.
Roy, Alexander K.
Edmand, William.
Anderson, Charles E.
Darling, William S.
Elliot, Christopher
Taylor, William H.
Clarkson, Robert.

1855.

Newbery, Cosmo.
Gibson, William.
Boyd, David.
Patterson, Fred. Mannsell.
Horwood, William.
Bethune, Charles J. S.
Stinson, Thomas B.
Sherwood, Livius P.
Pim, George.
Prince, Octavius.
Eberts, Joseph M.
Robertson, James.
Bacon, William N.
Bacon, Robert A.
Hall, Charles.
Tyner, Adam Clarke.
Williamson, Alexander Erskine
Scadding, Charles.
Hodgetts, James.
Clarkson, ——
Read, Frederick.
Howland, William H.
Howland, Oliver.
Thompson, William.
Buchanan, Peter, Toronto.
Shaw, John.
Nimmo, John Henry.
Ross, George Anthony.
Denison, George Shirley.
Coxwell, Edward Fall.
Casper, Albert Samuel.
Grand, Charles Frederick.
Crooks, Robert.
Elliot, Adam Theophilus.
Wilson, William.
Goldstone, Edmund A.
Auston, James.
Graveley, John Vance.
French, Richard.
Muttlebury, George Augustus.
Kennedy, John Edward.
Kennedy, Thomas Smith.
Dennistown, James F.
Irving, Edward Herbert.
Smith, Robert Walker.
Whitney, Fred. Benjamin.
Bogert, David Ford.
Harris, Rusk.
Macfarlane, Walter Henderson.
Dickinson, George.
Burnham, Laccheus.
Barber, Albert Granger.

Barber, Alfred Leopold.
Barber, William Boulton.
Hammond, James Henry.
Frenche, John.
Frenche, Isaac.
McMurrich, William B.
McMurrich, George.
McGlashan, Robert B.
Britton, Joseph.
Jones, Beverley.
Jarvis, Robert E. C.
Whan, James.
Rankin, Henry.
Moffatt, Henry.
Owen, Richard L.
Dukes, Rowland.
Russell, Alexander.
Lansing, Henry G.
Thomas, Charles.
Nicholls, Mark A.
Ferris, William B.
Spink, Frederick William.
Lamon, James.
Sladden, Percy.
Rubidge, Frederick.
Lee, William H.
Duffill, Albert.
Ross, David G. B.
Thibodeau, Urban.
Thibodeau, Joseph.
Head, John.
Muckle, Alexander M.
Muckle, Henry John.
Killaly, Thomas.
King, Frederick.
Finch, William D.
Berry, William.
Wicksteed, R. J.
Lett, Stephen.
Gilbert, James.
Ross, Allan.
Brooke, Lambert.

1856.

Grahame, John.
Harris, J. R.
Kent, R. A.
Flett, George.
Hector, Alfred.
Robarts, Alfred.
Robarts, Josiah.
Paterson, Thomas.
McKenzie, William.
McKenzie, Frederick.
Crombie, Charles Stewart.
Alexander, Richard Henry.
Alexander, Henry S.
Belyea, William Nelson.
Haworth, Robert.
Fuller, William.
Fuller, Velancy E.
Weller, Thomas M. T.
Piper, Edward.
Wright, George Henry.
Morgan, W. B.

UPPER CANADA COLLEGE MEMORIAL VOLUME.

Killaly, **Robert S.**
Morrison, Hugh.
Howell, Richard.
Collins, William E.
Collins, Charles W.
Bouchette, George.
Merigold, Francis W.
Taylor, Frederick.
Taylor, Albert.
Grainger, Albert P.
Flanagan, Peter.
Clark, Willoughby.
Haswell, William W.
Cobban, Matthew W
Hampton, William B.
Brown, John.
Strange, John M.
Twohy, Henry.
Twohy, William A.
Cruse, Oswald E.
Bostwick, George F.
Campbell, Paul.
Vale, Charles.
Alexander, Samuel John.
Lee, Charles R.
Steele, Charles Albert.
Raukin, Arthur.
McKenzie, Keith.
Beatty, Samuel.
Auston, John.
Mishaw, Robert.
Vale, William.
Smith, Simeon M.
Smith, James M.
Browne, Edward.
Holland, Ralph.
McBride, Archibald.
Lewis, Francis J.
Mair, Charles A.
Switzer, William F.
Switzer, Tobias Edward.
Carnegie, David.
Farr, Joseph.
Hamilton, Arthur.
Plunkett, Thomas.
Young, John.
Winstanley, Charles.
Campbell, Duncan.
Snider, C. R.
Grainger, William.
Dexter, George.
Campbell, Duncan.
Dorion, Charles Fred.
Givins, Charles Scott.
Givins, Henry Cecil.
Cameron, Kenneth.
Gage, Robert Russell.
Jones, William John.
Otter, William Dillon.
Lillie, James Cullen.
Tye, Luther.
Butters, Edward.
Tiffany, Edward Hibbert.
Helliwell, Clarence.
Riddell, Richmond.
Hoig, Anthony Ure.

Hoig, John Charles.
Crawford, Charles Henry
Kerr, Robert.
Jennings, Robert **C.**
Jennings, William **Tindal.**
Badenach, Alexander.
Bayley, Frederick.
Bethune, Fred. Alexander.
Henderson, John.
Henderson, William.
Mara, Thomas Albert.
Swann, E. Clifford.
Brent, J. Henry.
Whitney, William **Gamble.**
Tyner, Edward.
Rice, William Henry.
Blake, Warren.
Harris, Joseph.
McCallum, Robert.
Henderson, H. L.
Henderson, John.
Henderson, James.
Stonehouse, William.
Weatherley, James J.
Schuch, Edward W.
Ure, Nathaniel.
Perrin, James Henry **E.**
Baldwin, William A.
Gorrie, Joseph.
Baldwin, R. R.
Arnoldi, King McCord.
Brunel, Alfred.
Brunel, George.
Brunel, John.
Lawrence, C. P.
Perrin, W. L.
Baldwin, Æmilius.
Lee, Philip.
Lee, Joseph Robert.
Spence, Thomas.
Turquand, W. H.
Turquand, Charles R.
Steele, W. H.
Carpenter, T. T.
Clark, James.
Jessup, J. G.
Walker, John.
Montizambert, Chas. Edward.
Montizambert, Fred.
Heward, F. G.
Heward, S. B.
Heward, H. C.
Murray, R. G.
Hutty, J. W.
Hutty, Alfred.
Smith, R. W.
Davidson, **George.**
Davidson, **William.**
Lett, H.
Ross, Robert.
Hume, Skeffington.
Peck, George P.
Reed, Hayter.
Gage, Philip.
Bywater, Alfred.

1857.

Donelly, **Joseph.**
Vaux, Harry **Edward.**
Hobson, E. **Joseph.**
Garden, **Daniel.**
Topping, **John Coat.**
Loudon, **James.**
Lapenotiere, **W. H.**
Vallerand, Thomas.
MacPherson, Robt. Denniston.
Ryan, Patrick.
Dorothey, William.
Keefer, Geo. A.
Stuart, Arthur John.
Palmer, Corydon.
Auston, Henry.
Grant, J. A.
Oliver, T. D.
Helliwell, Albert.
Henderson, Robert.
Henderson, Andrew.
Foster, James Read.
Givins, Salten Everard.
Wetenhall, Gilbert James.
Graveley, James Vance.
Auston, James.
Auston, Francis.
Stuart, James.
Baines, Christopher.
Bramley, Sydney Charles.
Schroder, Arthur.
Givins, R. Cartwright.
Benjamin, Lewis Nathan.
Harris, Stuart.
McClure, Robert Steadman.
Graveley, Henry L.
Ballard, Henry **Allan.**
Rame, Eugene.
Hallowell, William Clark G.
Earl, Thomas Bowes.
Dobson, William E.
Furlong, Herbert James.
Skinner, Samuel.
Smith, Andrew George.
Ames, William L.
Batt, Edwin.
Bayley, Fred.
Broadgerst, John.
Price, Joseph.
Price, Charles T.
Steward, William.
Duggan, George.
Heward, Henry Charles.
Sutherland, James Henry.
Rattray, David.
Champion, Henry.
Casper, Samuel A.
O'Brien, Samuel **L.**
Snarr, William S.
Snarr, George Edmund.
Lillie, Henry **P. L.**
Roy, James Inglez.
Farmer, William.
McCallum, Robert.
Evans, Louis Hamilton.

THE OLD COLLEGE, LOOKING EAST FROM THE QUADRANGLE.

THE OLD COLLEGE, LOOKING WEST FROM "NO. 2."

THE U. C. C. ROLL, 1829-1892. 305

Potts, Robert.
Jones, Keasney L.
Wetenhall, Henry.
Preston, Arthur W.
Preston, Fred. Thomas.
Mercer, Robert.
Mercer, Henry.
Keele, Charles Conway.
Bernard, Joseph.
Thornton, Herman Charles.
Wightman, Edward.
Clark, James.
Nourse, William C.
Smith, Alfred Wightman.
Scadding, John.
Marshall, Kenric Countze.
Dunn, Samuel.
Waddell, Thomas R.
Farmer, George Arthur.
Hammond, Herbert C.
Tinney, Edmund Edward W.
Piper, Edward.
Ross, William Millmont.
Rubidge, Frederick K.
Scott, William Roaf.
McTavish, Donald Campbell.
Derislets, Moyer.
Dion, Louis.
McKellar, Peter D.
Corbett, Henry Thomas.
Corbett, Thomas Augustus.
Shaw, John.
Aiken Edward.
Hunter, James.
Leavitt, Francis Robert.
Leavitt, Henry A.
Lount, George Fenwick.
Crickmore, Snelling Roper.
Beatty, Joseph Walker.
Skelton, Leslie James Hamilton.
Radenhurst, Charles.
Cumming, James Cuthbert.
Ross, Alexander.
Hutty, Alfred.
Evans, John Dunlop.
Steward, Thomas William B.
Evans, William Barnard.
Arnold, Clarence.
Windeat, James David.
Windeat, Edmund Wm.
Nickinson, John.
Worthington, James.
Browne, John.
Richey, George.
Prittie, Henry.
Hutty, James Henry.
Smith, Larratt Alexander.
Smith, George Capel.

1858.

McKay, George.
Mitchell, W.
Mitchell, George.

Creighton, Walter.
Hawkins, William Fred.
McLeary, David.
Jackes, Charles B.
Bowes, John George.
Bowes, R. Heber.
Stent, Edward.
Stent, Alfred.
Lackie, David.
Steward, Arthur.
Ranney, Frederick.
Ryan, William Astle.
Hartney, Alfred Turner.
Hartney, Henry Jarvis.
Hartney, Arthur Marshall.
Wright, Arthur Wilcox.
Davis, Montague.
Beirfield, Samuel.
Jones, George Edwin.
Coulson, Henry.
Fenwick, John Fair.
Brown, William George.
Delamere, Thomas Dawson.
Barrett, Walter H.
Lesueur, Charles Philip.
Pearson, Arthur.
Jackes, Albert G.
Church, Clarence Ronald.
Gale, John.
Martin, William.
Martin, Robert.
Hunt, Thomas Knapp.
Hunt, Henry H.
Forneri, James Ford.
Simpson, James Henry.
Gibbons, George Christie.
Potter, Henry.
Armstrong, William T.
McArthur, John Campbell.
Crombie, Charles Stuart.
Foley, Henry John.
Foley, Bernard H.
Weir, Ralph.
Ruttan, William Elias.
Snider, Thomas A.
De Grassi, William.
Robinson, Elwood.
Wright, Wm. Robert.
Love, Robert Cook.
Parkinson, Robert W.
Ridout, Donald Campbell.
French, Richard.
French, William.
Gray, Alexander.
Griffith, Thomas.
Gibb, James.
Brodie, George Lawson.
Dolmage, Henry Wm.
Barwick, William.
Simpson, George Albert.
Maclagan, John W. H.
Maclagan, Henry.
McKnight, Charles Adam.
Snider, Martin Edward.
McLean, William Allan.
Fortune, Thomas Jenkins.

Gamble, Baptist.
Belden, Charles Henry.
Mead, Robert Joseph.
McPherson, Robert Walter.
Paterson, John Andrew.
Duncombe, David T.
Backas, Wm.
Cattley, R. J.
Dunsford, Maurice.
Dunsford, Charles R.
Morrison, Angus Gilmore.
Sheppard, George.
Tamblyn, John R.
Cumming, Thomas Wallace.
Heighton, John.
Biscoe, Vincent.
Biscoe, Frederick.
Langton, Thomas.
McCartney, George Fredk.
Drummond, George.
Bell, Charles Thomas.
Ritchie, Charles G.
Ritchie, Allen N. McN.
Nisbet, Thomas.
Munro, John H.
Hoyles, Newman Wright.
Goodridge, John Fred.
Milligan, John.
Conlin, Philip.
Mills, Robert.
Borland, John W.
Bain, Hugh.
Campbell, Josias Wilson.
Lister, James Hardman.
Bell, Charles W.
Robertson, Charles R.
Hawley, Thomas.
Snider, Franklin.
Wood, A. W.
Denison, Fred. Charles.
Denison, Henry Tyrrwhit.
Forlong, Arthur H.
Church, George Bernard.
Grahame, John.
Hargrave, Joseph.
Clinkunbroomer, Henry Clay.
Burnham, William L.
Miller, William.
Lillie, Frank Watts.
Worthington, George.
Belden Charles Henry.
Campbell, Thomas.
Hamilton, Baird Wm.
McKeggie, John Charles.
Connon, Charles Henry.
Dewar, Edward Charles.
Hastings, Eastwood.
Tinning, Richard.
Clark, Randolph.
Boswell, F. Edward.
McBride, William.
Shaw, William.
Mulholland, James.
Richardson, John.
Richardson, Samuel.
Shaw, Alexander Croft.

Jones, Alpheus.
MacDonald, Arthur Robert.
Willcock, Stephen.
Turner, George Richard.
Wallis, Henry Alexander.
Daly, John Corrie Wilson.
Fauquier, Arnold Edward.
Worthington, John.
Bruce, James.
Borst, Charles Martin.
Daintry, Charles George.
Irons, William.
Connon, John Middleton.
Crombie, Robert John.
Crombie, David Bradshaw.
Stibbard, John.
Braham, Jacob.
Bethune, George Strachan.
Smith, Henry Hall.
Bond, John Richard.
Courtney, Thomas.
Arnoldi, Frank.
Powell, William Dummer.
Powell, Edward Grant G.
Collins, William E.
Willis, Walter George.
Thorne, Charles Edward.
Thorne, Horace.
Thorne, Alfred.
Lawrence, Burns.
White, John Edward.
Muckle, Robert James.
Wilkinson, Henry Moore.
Sutherland, Stewart.
Momaker, George.
Reeve, Henry H.
Blachford, Charles Edward.
Robinson, Egerton Walker.
Langton, Henry Stephen.

1859.

Platt, Samuel.
Scott, Henry.
Davis, Thomas.
Reckenberg, Charles John G.
Carlisle, William Clark.
Lamble, William Henry.
Becher, Henry.
Harris, David M.
Williamson, Ashworth.
Lumley, Alexander.
Cottingham, William Henry.
Rogers, Robert Z.
Grange, Joseph Stuart.
Carter, Walter Michell.
Petry, George Edward.
Henderson, Basil.
Brooks, George Thomas.
Boyd, Gardiner.
Manson, Angus H.
Dick, William Carfrae.
Cotton, James W.
Fraser, William.
McLear, William Henry.

Jackson, Charles Alfred.
Baxter, James B.
Casper, Charles Arnold.
Gibson, John.
McCord, Andrew Taylor.
Thompson, Leonard.
Groat, George Whitfield.
Douglas, William.
Anderson, Headley Leaming.
Lay, Alexander Gregory.
Abbott, William H.
Topping, Herbert William.
Dack, William Benjamin.
Owen, William Waller.
Morgan, Thomas Porteous.
Sibbald, William Lee.
Cole, William Enfield.
Filliker, George Sipon.
Holden, Albert.
Sterling, Sidney.
Wightman, John Roaf.
Robinson, John Beverley.
Robinson, Strachan Napier.
Kennedy, William C.
Kingsford, Rupert Etheridge.
Jessup, John Hamilton.
Crawford, Patrick E.
Robinson, Henry Grasett.
Houghton, Edwin Bell.
Lyons, Barron B.
Levey, Samuel.
Heath, Charles D'Arcy.
Heath, Stuart Beverley.
Oates, Edward Fred.
Oates, William Henry.
Gordon, James Webster.
Shaw, Duncan William.
Beardmore, Walter Dowker.
Ridout, Samuel.
Ridout, Henry Joseph.
Simms, Henry Jordan.
Clift, John Shannon.
Sherwood, George Edward.
King, Alfred McPherson.
Darling, Frank.
Darling, Charles Burrows.
Flood, Ernest Augustus.
Biscoe, Henry Alexander.
Flood, Charles Henry.
Gamble, Francis Clarke.
Becker, Richard L.

1860.

Warren, William M. H.
Innes, John Laurie.
Squire, Henry G.
Rogers, Frank Daskan.
Reynolds, Thomas.
Gamble, Alleyne Woodbridge.
De Blaquiere, Peter Henry.
Matheson, Charles Albert.
Matheson, Arthur James.
Matheson, Alan Frederick.
Fanning, Hiram Wesley.

Benson, Martin.
Higgins, Edward Melville.
Huggins, Peter Thomas.
Harrison, John James.
Harrison, Edward.
Hamilton, David Drummond.
Carter, Henry A.
Loring, Robert G. L.
Hay, James.
McDonald, William.
Forlong, Charles Albert.
Devlin, William Bowman.
Levey, Joseph.
Shaw, David.
McMurrich, John Bryce.
Crickmore, Arthur John.
Smith, John Thomas.
Grange, Charles Edward.
Davis, Robert.
Holden, Henry E. E.
Holden, John Augustus.
Franch, Henry G. G.
Adam, Robert A.
McCrea, Samuel Starr.
Phipp, Henry C.
Eston, George Crawford.
Taylor, George Higley.
Hawley, John Gardner.
Rupell, Logan D. H.
Russell, Logan D H.
Crapper, George V.
Jackson, Charles A.
Carter, Fred. J. W.
Donor, William J.
Maulson, Fred. Howcutt.
James, Robert.
Denison, Alfred Ernest.
Buchan, Lawrence.
Buchan, Ewing.
Stinson, Robert C.
Appleton, David.
King, George.
Arnoldi, Fulford.
Forbes, John Charles.
Kilialy, Richard.
Morrison, Peter.
Rowe, William.
Corbett, James.
Corbett, William.

1861.

Bell, Charles W.
Delamere, Thomas D.
Matheson, Charles A.
Bowes, John G.
Holmes, William.
Filliter, George S.
Crawford, Patrick E. J.
Munson, Charles F.
Lee, Charles R.
Masterson, Charles.
Connor, Charles H.
Mills, Robert.
Becher, Henry.

Platt, Samuel.
Jackes, Albert George.
Denison, Shirley.
Brunel, John.
Matheson, James A.
Biscoe, Frederick.
Wallis, Henry Alexander.
Biscoe, Vincent R.
Brunel, George.
Steele, Charles A.
Holden, Albert.
Hudson, Rufus.
Ridout, J. Grant.
Burns, James H.
White, John.
Burns, Arthur N.
Stevenson, Robert A.
Denison, William George.
Hume, Skiffington.
Scadding, Charles.
Nimmo, John Henry.
Britton, Joseph.
Langton, Thomas.
McBride, William.
Miller, William H.
Adam, Robert Archibald.
Davies, Thomas.
McArthur, John C.
Arnoldi, Frank.
Worthington, James M.
Earle, Thomas.
Creighton, Walter L.
Crombie, R. J.
Killaly, Robert A.
Buchan, Lawrence.
Gibbs, Frank E.
Evans, Thomas F. L.
Hawley, John Gardiner.
Gowinlock, William.
Scott, William.
Lesslie, James Graham.
Muttlebury, George A.
Robinson, Samuel Skeff.
Wickson, Arthur.
Irons, William.
Strange, John.
Williams, Charles H. A.
McDougall, Joseph.
McIntyre, Neil.
Barrett, Walter H.
McDonald, William.
Warren, William.
Shaw, William.
Douglas, William.
Robinson, Henry.
Crickmore, R. Snelling.
Anderson, Hadley.
Denison, Frederick Charles.
Thorne, Alfred.
Worthington, George.
Mercer, Henry.
Carter, Walter M.
Rechenburg, Charles.
Dixon, Mark Anthony.
Portas, Henry Thomas.
Tempest, William.

Muckle, Henry J.
Gibbs, Frederick W.
Muckle, Alex.
Purdy, John.
Moffatt, Henry Lewis.
McLean, William.
Vidal, Richard A.
Gamble, Baptist.
Champion, Henry.
Kingsford, Rupert Etherege.
Shaw, Alexander Crawford.
Stinson, Robert C.
Hawkins, William F.
McCrea, Samuel Starr.
Phillips, Henry C.
Wilkinson, Henry.
Cottingham, William.
Thompson, William.
Houghton, Edward.
Bowes, Robert Heber.
Oates, Wm. Henry.
Gordon, James.
Easton, George Crawford.
Scadding John.
Cumming, Thomas W.
Sterling, Sidney.
Higgins, Edward M.
Wightman, John R.
Robinson, Strachan N.
Biscoe, Henry Alexander.
Denison, John.
Denison, Henry T.
Strange, George.
Heath, Charles.
Bain, Hugh.
Paterson, Thomas W.
Monkman, John.
Huggins, Peter T.
Christie Peter.
Oliver, John D.
Chapman, Gerard C.
Gibbs, Wm. H.
Glass, Douglas.
Gamble, Clark.
Furlong, Arthur H.
Gibbs, Charles.
Pentland, Alfred.
Glass, Henry.
Wilson, Robert Jordan.
Hector, John W.
Appleton, David.
Mulholland, Robert.
Jackson, Charles.
Richards, Albert E.
Boulton, Fitzroy.
Robinson, John Beverley.
Sherewood, George E.
Denison, Alfred.
Hector, George.
Smith, Larratt A.
Campbell, Wilson.
Common, John W.
Rogers, Frank D.
Gamble, Allayne W.
Cameron, Alan.
Heath, Stuart B.

Forlong, Charles.
McMurrich, John.
James, Robert.
Devlin, Bowman.
Crickmore, Arthur.
Barrett, Michael.
Moss, William.
Ketchem, Oliver W.
Campbell, Loran.
Orr, John.
Glass, Arthur.
Arnoldi, Fulford.
Crooks, Robert P.
Crombie, David B.
Killaly, Richard.
Fitzgibbon, James.
White, John B.
McCallum, Frederick.
Muckle, Robert.
Shaw, Duncan W.
Holden, Charles A.
Fortye, Wm.
Dixon, Hillyard C.
Smith, Henry.
Cayley, Wm.
Perkins, C. Frederick.
Perkins, George.
Harman, Lloyd.
Clark, Alfred.
Clark, Maurice C.
Elliott, J. L. G.

1862.

Carney, Richard.
Mortimer, George B.
Mortimer, Arthur L.
Helliwell, Alexander James.
Kerster, Clarence E. W.
Smith, Wm.
Crapper, George B.
Walton, Robert F.
Delamere, Joseph M.
Hamilton, Arthur.
Robinson, Alfred.
Lowell, Herbert.
Cowdry, Edmund.
Cowdry, Nathaniel.
Sullivan, John D.
Barber, Wm. Franklin.
Austin, Frederick Wm.
Drummond, G.
Wilson, Rhodolphus.
Hardy, Frederick.
Kidner, Reuben.
Patterson, Kenneth.
Cassels, Allan.
Grover, Thomas M.
Grover, George A.
Mewburn, Herrmann J.
Gibson, Goodwin.
Forlong, Herbert James.
Blackwood, Donald N.
Coulson, Henry.

Harman, **Davidson**.
Daly, John.
Herchmer, George.
Ransom, William W.
Filliter, Clavell.
Boulton, Milford.
Denison, Clarence.
Denison, John.
Heath, Beverley.
Cayley, Beverley H.
Jackes, Price.
Jackes, Baldwin.
Earle, Theophilus.
Beanes, Edward.
Howland, Oliver.
Posey, Robert.
Posey, Robert D.
Lambert, Richard.
Slaughter, Robert.
Glass, Wynn.
Posey, William.
Mulholland, Henry.
Harman, William.
O'Hara, Jeoffrey.
Perkins, Edward John.
Robinson, Christopher C.
Heath, D'Arcy Boulton.
Gordon, C. Bullitt.
Gordon, John L.
Reed, Wm. D.
Reed, Solomon S.
McDougall, Wm.
Harman, Huson.
McDougall, Alfred.
Forlong, George Frederick.
Sholl, George.

1863.

Hunter, John Alexander.
Dunseith, David.
McNish, John.
McNab, James D.
Dougall, Charles.
Holden, Edward H. E.
Daly, Thomas Mayne.
Berckley, Theophilus Francis.
Hill, George Hollister.
Banthron, Christopher C.
Banthorn, Robert.
Yates, Frederick.
Siddons, Edgar.
Sutherland, John.
Sutherland, Frederick **Vivian**.
Stotesbury, Robert Cooper.
Paterson, John Henry.
Prince, Thomas.
McKay, John.
Gamble, Rainold **D'Arcy**.
Cayley, Claude.
Hunter, King Barton.
Hunter, Robert James.
Delmage, Anthony A.
O'Malley, Charles **A**.
Arnold, Robert Meredith.

Ault, Edwin.
Ryrie, Daniel.
Robertson, Frederick C.
Ford, Ogden P.
Carruthers, George F.
Bull, Clarence W.
McClelland, Thomas J.
Richards, William.
Anderson, Allan.
Willing, Robert Burns.
Fuller, Valancey E.
Martin, Robert.
Fotheringham, Thomas F.
Dennistoun, Robert H.
McClelland, Alexander M.
Davis, Wm. G.
Flitcher, Hugh.
Barber, James.
Plummer, James H.
Richards, Butler J.
Lount, George F
Proudfoot, Thomas.
Burgess, Thomas J. W.
Ball, Winniette.
Mitchell, Charles Alexander.
Snider, John Elgin.
McKinlay, Archibald **Reid**.
Arnoldi, Fulford.
Piper, George William.
Boak, William F.
Jarvis, Thomas S.
Boomer, Henry G. C.
Cox, Henry James.
Fletcher, John.
Noverre, Philip E.
Cochrane, Augustus.
Mowatt, Frederick.
Strange, Charles O.
Fuller, Shelton B.
Rattray, Alfred.
Best, Thomas J.
Crickmore, E.
Mortimer, Charles White.
Mortimer, John Strachan.
Spragge, Albert W
Killaly, Henry.
Jackes, George W.
Smith, Edwin A.
Burke, Edmund.
McMaster, Charles A.
Daly, Charles J.
Coulson, Robert B.
Wilkes, Frederick T.
Whiteland, John M.
Cricklow, Charles Lynde.
Hope, George.
Porter, John M.
Grahame, James E.
Breakey, George.
Armstrong, William.
Brough, Redmand.
Brough, Allan.
Aumond, George Thomas.
Mitchell, Alexander.
Cosford, John H.
Cosford, Joseph C.

Ryerson, Charles E.
Murray, Edward.
Murray, James H.
Lillie, Frank W.
Paterson, Donald.
Henderson, William.
Chichester, Frederick A.
Chichester, Charles E. J.
Rossin, Louis.
Rossin, Morris.
Griffiths, Charles D. R.
Morgan, Porteus.
Morgan, Peter.
Hodder, Mellow.
Killmaster, John.
Lovell, James.
Ermatinger, Frank.
Corbould, Gordon E.
McDonald, James Alexander
Buchan, Ewing.
Ewart, John S.
Workman, Thomas.
Hall, **Oscar**.
Rose, Wm. McMaster.
Beardmore, **George W**.
Hind, Thomas F. N.
Taylor, George B.
Chesnut, George D.
Hutty, Charles P.
McDonald, Robert.
Beaumont, Herbert.
Stone, James Walker.
Vance, Robert.
Vance, Hopefield.
Kempt, Charles.

1864.

Wilson, Ernest M.
Hope, Robert Knight.
McDougall, Samuel.
Lord, Robert Frederick.
Ware, Henry A.
Simms, Thomas J.
McNiven, Joseph.
Barrett, Frederick.
Miller, Robert Horatio.
Benson, Frederick.
Fishleigh, W. H.
Lockington, George **W**.
Hardy, John William.
Smith, Ebenezer.
Clay, John.
Clay, Henry.
Beardman, Walter D.
Hall, Frederick W.
Jamieson, Charles.
Patrick, Allan P.
Lewis, Albert R.
Gambel, Henry D.
Gingras, Antoine.
Edwards, John C.
McGuire, W. J.
Mara, Henry S.
Hardy, Robert Henry.

Clay, Thomas I.
Ingersoll, James B.
Kay, James.
Hunter, Alexander.
Clarkson, Edward R.
Lister, Evans W.
Peete, William J.
Peete, Edward D.
Stewart, George M.
Davy, Edward W.
McDonald H.
Leggo, Thomas William.
Gemmell, John.
Dillon, John G. B.
McQuesten, Isaac B.
Patterson, Andrew D.
Chafee, Alexander B.
Boomer, Joseph B.
Cheevers, John.
Phipps, W. A.
Rogers, Christopher.
Hague, George E.
Shand, John D.
Richards, B. W.
Nash, Edward.
Nash, Loving.
Small, John T.
Small, A. H.
Fiskin, John.
Reford, John.
Lesslie, Rolph.
Lesslie, Joseph W.
Gartshore, John J.
Newcomb, Hermann.
Robinson, Frederick A.
Whightman, Albert R.
Wagner, W. J.
Dingle, Samuel.
Le Parr, Henry.
McNab, J. F.
Lawrence, Henry P.
Cosford, Samuel.
Barber, Robert.
Plummer, T.
Laing, Wm.
Laing, James.
Nordheimer, Isaac.
Nordheimer, Alfred.
Davidson, Wm.
Black, F. S. P.
Stayner, T. A.
Bennetts, Frank.
Rapelje, George J.
Kinkead, G. B.
Kinkead, R. S.
Worthington, J. N.
Denison, Edwin.
Clark, Thomas F.
Brown, Joseph.
Crawford, Henry D.
Heward, Edward H. T.

1865.

Strathy, Frederick R. L.
Foster, James.

Allen, Henry W.
Merrick, Edward A.
McCormack, H. J.
Clark, Arthur D.
Moffatt, Frederick C.
Burnham, John W.
Perry, Robert P.
Laing, Andrew.
Smyth, Edmund.
Henderson, Alex.
Henderson, James.
Mulanney, John M.
Wilson, Malcolm.
Watson, Henry.
Smith, James S.
Farquhar, Charles **A. J.**
McLean, Henry.
Macfie, Robert C.
Robinson, Charles E.
Jones, Edward C.
Ellis, Henry.
Austin, James H.
Cassels, John T.
Lake, Alba C.
Trow, Thomas.
Trow, James.
Campbell, Alexander.
Sadlier, Henry H.
Rees, Frederick Mussen.
Ball, Alfred Servos.
Harris, George F. R.
Van Allen, John R.
Craig, Joseph W.
Wright, Frederick Henry.
Hay, Robert.
Ridout, George L.
Langton, Henry S.
McCaul, John Alex.
Michie, John.
Shack, Julius.
Meux, Joseph P.
White, James.
Hyland, W. W.
Atkins, John S.
Warren, Frank.
Hewitt, Joseph R.
Ford, John G.
McColl, Wm. R.
Alston, Philip.
Mackenzie, Francis A.
Clark, F.
Darling, H.
Lindsay, C.
Cooper, Wm. Baines.
Robinson, Charles E.
Shack, Ferdinand.
Williams, Edmund.
Brown, Edward B.
Darling, Walter.
Ridout, Trevelyan.
Beswick, Edward James.
Connon, Stanley F.
Cameron, Irving Heward.
Wedd, Wm.
Hewitt, Wm.
Fuller, Henry Herbert.

Harrington, **Joseph.**
Murray, John W.
Gooderham, Wm. **George.**
Daly, Peter F.
Finch, Samuel W.
Stevenson, John.
Tucker, John R.
Tucker, Charles **E.**
Quarles, G.
Worts, James **G.**
Barber, Robert.

1866.

Rowat, Andrew.
Barron, John A.
Guest, Thomas F.
Servos, Francis.
Servos, John.
Nicholson, Henry A.
Richardson, Wm.
Smith, Sidney.
Smith, John D.
Thomson, John.
Rennie, James.
Gill, Robert.
Baker, Thomas.
Clark, Frederick.
Davies, Robert.
Dick, Arthur.
Laing, Reginald.
Giddings, Harry.
Crysler, Wm. H.
Proctor, James A.
Todd, Albert.
McPherson, Donald A.
Beatty, John W.
Kew, Michael.
Sibbald, Wm. M.
Lount, J. E.
Carruthers, F. H.
Perry, John O.
McDougall, Frank.
Lyall, Joseph Charles.
Powell, George A.
Ogilvie, Robert.
Kirkpatrick, John.
Kirkpatrick, W. E.
Egerton, H.
Egerton, P.
Bacon, Alfred H.
Dale, Wm.
Traver, Elliot.
Clarkson, Fredk. Archibald.
White, James.
Manley, John G.
Bickle, Wm. J.
Zimmerman Richard.
Mann, James.
Craig, John.
Leonhard, Edwin E.
Flint, Wm. H.
Crerar, John.
Kirkland, August M.
Lewis, Levi.

Clement, Edwin R.
Foster, Allen.
Gibson, John.
Hope, Adam H.
McDonnell, D. G.
Ellard, John V.
Mulholland, W. H.
Hassard, Henry S.
Smith, John A.
Plummer, Henry.
Hill, John C.
Alexander, A. M.
Reiman, Wm.
Dahlgren, J. A.
Flint, George H.
McKenzie, Henry G.
Morrison, Curran.
Snider, David.
Abraham, Robert H.
McVittie, Thomas.
Helm, Charles.
Hamilton, Chester.
McPhail, Richard.
Kingsmill, Charles E.
Morrison, Robert.
Wright, Wm. A.
Aikens, Wm. H.
Vickers, John.
Austin, Albert W.
Cayley, Francis D.
Worthington, John.
Worthington, Edward.
Nash, Harry.
Bowes, Edward.
Scales, Charles H.
McIntyre, Duncan.
Violet, Robert.
Horgan, Wm. C.
Miller, D.
Clump, Guildford.
Lake, Daniel W.

1867.

Hamilton, Alexander.
McGregor, Duncan.
Bethune, Francis.
Gowinlock, George.
Keeler, Thomas P.
Hague, Dyson.
Baker, Edmund.
Wyllie, John.
Perry, Charles.
Perry, George.
Thompson, Frederick Wm.
Luton, George.
Bourchier, Wm. J. O.
Ballantyne, Frank.
Platt, John.
Montgomery, Henry.
Kemper, Samuel L.
Kemper, James E.
Cowdry, John.
Stinson, Edwin, L. M.
Drouillard, Felix I.

Arthurs, Telfer.
Dick, Walter.
Roe, George H.
Cronyn, John L. C.
Griffith, John.
Griffith, Frederick D.
Griffith, Wm.
Hill, Daniel O.
Crocker, Wm.
Belcher, E. B.
Weizel, Paul.
Ford, Wm.
Scholefield George.
Trent, Henry E.
Clarkson, George H.
Thompson, C. W.
Thompson, F. W.
Thompson, H. P.
Thompson, P.
Snider, M.
Wilby, A. W.
Aikins, H. W.
Crowther J.
Thompson, Boyce.
Phipps, F. H.
Campbell T.
Patterson, D. S.
Carbert, J. A.
Inglis, G.
Anderson, R.
Anderson, W.
Miller, K.
Lewin, R.
Lloyd, Wellington.
Hartman, L.
Wickson, J. E.
Thompson, G.
Morphy, H.
Rose, S.
Sholl, G.
Fletcher, W.
Brooke, G.
Knowlys, T. F. C. E.
Holden, J.
Wallace, Francis Huston.
Long, John Henry.
Cronyn, James.
Baines, A. M.
Jones, G.
Northrup, J.
Northwood, W.
Hamilton, J.
Johnson, D. C.
Cameron, D.
Mainwaring, R. A.
Howard A.
Rogers, W.
Whiteley, E. W.

1868.

Wilson, J. E.
Reynolds, J.
Cumming, C. S.
Cumming, R. A.

Morrisey, R.
Mortimer, G. C.
Kimball, L. A.
McDougall, D. C.
McFadyen, H.
Cleary, W.
Kay, John.
Kingston, C. A.
Pernet, F. W.
Morse, G.
Stark, G. A.
Dyke, S. A.
Howard, A.
Black, F. S. P.
Noble, F.
Reynolds, George.
Crocker, H.
Crocker, S. M.
Anderson, Robert.
Thompson, J. H.
McVittie, A.
Crocker, P.
Tait, W. M.
Crowe, A. J.
Langton, Wm. A.
Perkins, H.
Kersteman, H.
Reiman, W. M.
Smith, G.
Beardmore, A.
McMurrich, J.
Freeland, F.
Buchan, J. H.
Cayley, H.
Cayley, A.
Mason, P.
Ridout, W.
Holmes, S.
Brown, C. J.
Clark, A.
Crouther, W.
Damer, G.
Brown, W.
Brown, P.
George, H. McI.
Fitch, W. C.
Boulton, B.
Howard, J. S.
Connon, H.
McCaul, C. C.
Thomas, G.
Boyd, G.
Holmes, M.
Adae, F.
Adae, H.
Strathy, C.
Bacon, A. H.
Mason, H.
Ridout, P. F. J.
Hay, John.
Campbell, A.
Boulton, H.
Fortier, C. B.
Howard, C. A.
Mortimer, T.
Keith, P. R.

THE U. C. C. ROLL, 1829-1892.   311

Otter, H.
Patterson, D.
Hickson, R. C.
Stewart, J.
Powell, F.
Graham, G.
Treadwell, F.
Johnson, J.
Keith, D. M.
McKenney, G.
Inglis, R. M.
Morrison, E. B.
Richardson, R. E.
Stanley, P. E.
Hodgins, F.
Biggar, W. H.
Gill, W.
Dack, R.
Edgar, J.
Kay, J.
Luke, A.
Carmichael, W. R.
Skinner, R. B.
Kerr, F. W.
Cameron, J. C.
Roger, R.
Gluck, J. F.
Fletcher, Colin.
Sutherland, Wm. M.
James, A.
Alexander, G. T.
Cassels, W. A.
Cassels, L.
Boeckh, E.
Keys, David Reade.
Masales, G. W.
Holcomb, J.
Lumsden, W. J.
Lumsden, H.
Barber, J.
Brown, C. P.
Ross, A.

1869.

Reeve, J.
Newman, C. U.
James, Charles.
James, Wm.
Campbell, W.
English, E.
Hunton, H.
Richards, S. O.
Atkinson, R.
Bruce, John.
Cox, C. T.
Carruthers, F. H.
Rochester, J.
Platt, J. T.
Stollery, U.
Gibson, G. S.
Lee, G. M.
Draper, W. H.
Byam, W. J.

Taylor, J. H.
Taylor, T.
Grahame, H. H.
Carruthers, John.
McKee, John.
Lauder, Waugh.
Sheard, C.
McKenzie, R. C.
Boulton, C. R.
Edwards, J.
Rogers, C.
Dick, A.
Youmans, J. A.
Dunbar, F. J.
Doering, Frank.
Ingersoll, John.
Joseph, R. F.
Mason, G. J.
Dewson, G. D.
Denison, H. F.
Denison, A. R.
Thyne, R.
Wedd, J. C.
Hilton, E.
Hilton, F.
Rutherford, E. C.
Nanton, H. W.
Aikins, James A.
Blackstock, T. A.
Rogers, Joseph.
Le Pan, J.
Stewart, J.
Newman, W. E.
Gamble, A. G.
Delaporte, A. V.
Dunspaugh, J.
Smith, George.
Winstanly, A.
Logan, C. J.
Wellbanks, C.
Byers, A. E.
Richardson, H.
Leonard, E. W.
Mutch, P.
McLellan, James.
Kirkwood, J. B.
Weller, H. B.
Ewing, James.
McGiverin, J. C.
Irving, A. M.
Dickinson, W.
Frazer, J. H.
Elliott, Wm.
Dawson, Alexander.
Thompson, G.
Allan, G. W.
Fee, George W.
Wood, M. B.
Wood, E.
McKay, B.
McKay, W.
Scatcherd, E.
Colwell, W. W.
Bullock, ——
Ewart, John H.
Carter, John.

Snider, A. F.
Snider, George.
English, W.
Cricknore, E.
Curry, W. H. S.
Miller, C. B.
McTaggart, A.
Small, A. H.
Moffatt, F. C.
Barber, C.
Jarvis, G. H.
Prentice, William.
McFayden, D.
Ryley, G. W.
Sprunt, J. D.
Sprunt, Alexander.
Frazer, J. W.
Denison, H.
Watt, D. M.
Lawrence, J. W.
Bacon, James.
Spragge, A. W.
Gemmell, J. E.
Harstone, L.
Dick, A. C.
Griffith, J. A.
Deveril, H.
Piper, H.
Kingstone, George.
Skelton, G. L.
Soreley, James.
Soreley, W. F.
Reynolds, R. E.
Williams, A.
Thompson, B.
Kingstone, George.
Rowand, J. A.
Hunter, E.
Hunter, K.
Hunter, F.
Langtry, Ernest.
Rathborne, R.
Hector, R.
Hector, Alexander.
Waddell, John.
James, W.
Geikie, William.
Rogers, C. H.
Jeffrey, W.
Rathborne, W.
McIntyre, C. C.
Littlejohn, J.
Littlejohn, W. A.
James, P. L.
McKay, E.
McNairy, N.
Violett, R. E.
Stuart, W.
Harris, W. T.
Wright, A.
Wilson, A.
Craig, J.
Cruikshank, E. A.
McKay, D.
Warwick, W.
Warwick, Guy.

1870.

Adae, L. W.
Adae, William.
Adae, Frank.
Maclean, A.
Clements, W.
Williams, R.
Fleming, J. B.
Dickson, F.
Hardy, H.
Skead, E. S.
McGillivray, A. J.
Bethune, A.
Bethune, M.
Hall, W. N.
Atkinson, W. H.
Low, Wm.
Downey, D.
Ross, D.
Evans, George.
Denison, S.
Merritt, W. H.
Morrison, A.
Hall, C. R.
White, S. M.
Crawford, A.
Crawford, E. S.
Whitney, A. H.
Mowatt, W. G.
Yorston, A.
Shanley, F. J.
Shanley, C. W.
Park, James.
Read, E.
Boomer, H.
Sills, E. C.
Conolly, R.
Clare, I. J.
Farquhar, C. A. J.
Kerr, A.
Kennedy, F.
Sutherland, Alexander.
Moncktou, A.
Brown, J. F.
Burns, L.
Campbell, A. T.
Kirkland, J. B.
Kirkland, R.
May, M. S.
McDonald, E. C.
Ponton, W. M.
Shepherd, B.
Tempest, G.
Read, W. J.
Apperson, M.
Coate, C. B.
Coate, H. J.
Dunning, H.
McGregor, W.
Ryley, J. E.
Walker, G. H.
Ross, J.
Ross, A. G.
Anderson, H. P.
*Hale, C. W.

Holden, A.
Robbins, H. A. R.
Garner, W.
Garner, G.
Holwell, Percy.
Virtue, G.
Virtue, H.
Capreol, C. F.
Day, C.
Esten, J. P.
Fraser, J. H.
Hague, L.
Morrison, S.
Strathey, G. H.
Sanson, J.
Winans, F.
Wedd, G.
Freeland, E. B.
Brooke, D. O.
Hall, John.
McMichael, John.
Winter, M.
Cross, G. H.
Rochester, J. E.
Thompson, Wm.
Day, W. H.
McDougall, F.
Rykert, W. A. P.
Patterson, J. A.
Henwood, A. J.
Moore, J. F.
Robinson, F.
Smith, D. L.
Bethune, A.
Williams, John.
Williams, M. T.
Armstrong, J.
Pares, E.
Russell, A.
McKeown, J. G.
Kennedy, R.
Perram, H.
Sharp, T. H.
Groundwater, H.
Plummer, F.
Plummer, A. E.

1871.

Picken, James.
Lalley, C.
McCrea, Walter.
Irwin, C.
McAndrew, D.
McAndrew, J.
Mills, James McV
Measam, F.
Moore, E.
Mackay, J.
Mahaffy, Wm.
Birtch, J.
Winter, G. H.
Wright, James.
Palmer, S. P.
Cumming, R.
Donaldson, E.

Griffiths, W. A.
Dunspaugh, C.
Angell, C.
Denison, E. E. A.
Robinson, W.
Anderson, Charles.
Anderson, W.
Cox, F. W.
Moore, C.
Baldwin, H. Y.
Reed, F. E.
Robbius, F. C.
Nation, W.
Cleland, H.
Cleland, G.
McKenzie, W.
Knowleys, T. F. C. E
Macdonald, G.
Denny, James.
Brock, H. T.
Sheppard, N.
Sheppard, S.
Sheppard, M.
Blake, E. W. H.
Montgomery, T.
Shaw, N. D.
Smith, W.
Aikins, F. T.
Kerr, D. B.
Stokes, S. P.
Barnum, E. S.
Wilkinson, G.
Halden, E. B.
Mills, J. M.
Platt, J. T.
Trowern, E.
Corby, C.
Bell, A. M.
Simpson, D. B.
Henwood, R. D.
Northrup, W. B.
Procter, E. R. C.
Bonter, H. R.
Blackstock, George T
Gordon, R.
Kreuson, W.
Allen, W. A.
Holt, J. A.
Harcourt, F. W.
Mills, J. B.
Pollard, R. D.
Ross, J. C.
Mussen, H.
Boulton, R. R.
Lester, T. W.
Strathy, A. J.
Barrett, R. G.
Bethune, M. N.
Freeman, W. F.
Carruthers, R. S.
Galbraith, J.
Tarbutt, J. A.
Damoreau, L.
Hope, A.
Lindsay, G. G. S.
Read, J. C.

Lewis, J.
Way, W. J.
Palmer, T. M.
Cartwright, W. C.
Leggatt, J.
Allen, E. H.
Boyd, F.
Boyd, E. W.
Carruthers, E.
Chafee, C. W.
Fraser, A. G.
Hodgins, J. P.
Hodgins, A. E.
Hodgins, C. R.
Howard, James A.
Howitt, John.
Johnson, H.
Kerr, J. B.
Love, S.
McBride, J. W.
Murray, B.
Parsons, W. H.
Connon, H. E.
Denison, A. E.
Halse, G.
Cooper, H.
Cooper, John.
Carey, R. D.
McDonagh, G.
Ridout, H. R.
Cope, George.
Armour, D.
Hague, H. J.
Hague, F.
Wells, A. C.
Ford, A.
Beer, L.
Jones, L.
Hunter, H.
Goering, Wm.
Gray, R.
Campbell, L.
Ruffner, A.
Gray, C. W.
Lawson, J.
Morphy, H. O.
Morphy, Arnold.
Uhlhorn, R.
Cathron, R.
Watson, W. E.
Grundy, W.
Topping, J. B.
Kennedy S.
Julian, H. G.
Jenkins, J. F.
Gibson, G. S.
Bryce, Peter H.
Downey, D. J.
Devlin, C.
Davidson, A.
Hall, W.
McKenzie, T. C.
McKenzie, K. A. J.
Myers, R. D.
Matheson, J.
Trow, C.
40

1872.

Gamsby, G.
Meneilly, W. T.
Helliwell, S.
Bell, R. J.
McCann, G. A.
LePan, F.
Campbell, F. S.
Barber, H.
Hespeler, C.
Henderson, W.
Coleman, H.
Shibley, T. G.
Stupart, R. F
Sparham, B.
Harstone, J. C.
Watson, J. H.
Bedingfield G.
Wilson, H. B.
Smith, G. H.
Ross, W. S.
Conolly, C. A.
Evans, A. T. K.
Gooch, F. H.
Freeman, W.
Sayers, Charles.
Taylor, J. W.
Smith, Charles P.
Kennedy, Robert.
McGill, S. G.
Simmers, A.
Simmers, H.
Colwell, A. H.
Barrett, J. M.
Barrett, R. A.
Spooner, W.
Parmenter, W. W.
Smith, E. A. C.
Baines, W. B.
Wallbridge, F.
Ross, A. N.
McKay, W.
Griffith, G.
Griffith, Thomas.
Kolfage, S. C.
Howard, H. L.
Cronyn, B. B.
Ford, Charles.
Lewis, F. E.
Holman, J. J.
Jarvis, S.
Vickers, Wm. W.
Barritt, E. M.
Jollett, St. G.
Manning, T. A.
Case, Fred.
McTavish, A.
Davis, A. G.
Best, W. H.
Kirkpatrick, K. J.
Fromberz, F.
Law, C. F.
Rennie, A. H.
Clark, A. W.
Clark, E. M.

Henderson, A.
Richey, J. F.
Currie, E.
Scott, F. W.
Davis, H. H.
Cockburn, C.
Walker, A.
Watkins, J.
Ross, E. W.
Aikins, W. H.
Howland, A. P.
Musson, W. J.
Callender, F.
Clench, T. R.
Rogers, M. M.
Millen, L. R.
Robarts, H.
Macklin, E.
Macklin, W.
Elliott, J. W.
Firman, E. H.
Smith, J. G.
Proctor, W. F.
Biggar, J. L.
Ross, J. W.
Hendrie, J. S.
Borradaile, F.
McDougall, J.
Orr, R. M.
Tucker, T. F.
Holmes, J.
VanNorman, J.
Tharp, W. H.
Gustin, G.
Lassen, Alexander.
Prince, John.
Simpson, C. W.
Geikie, A.
Stanton, O.
Brown, A. C.
Reid, J. P.
Seyler, W. H.
Ashby, T. H.
Duggan, G. H.
Laidlaw, G. E.
Laidlaw, J. W.
Montgomery, W. A. D.

1873.

Beaty, P. J.
Kolfage, W.
Wyatt, H.
Simpson, E.
Simpson, R.
Smith, J. A.
Gunn, W.
Gunn, R.
Molesworth, W.
London, W. J.
Campbell, A. McF.
Smith, J. S.
Baird, Andrew.
Knox, W. T.
Knox, A.

Hatton, G. W.
Wood, F. H.
Kertland, McL.
Bradshaw, W.
Brown, R. S.
Cole, H.
Sadlier, Charles.
McQuarrie, ——
Jones, G.
Parsons, Wm.
Dwight, H.
McCulloch, H.
McKechnie, W.
Tandy, George.
Pringle, A.
Hostetter, J. B.
Atkinson, C. R.
Atkinson, H. H.
Kauffmann, Wm.
Woods, John G.
Wilstead, F. W.
Wilstead, B. A.
Stuart, John J.
Stuart, James C. K.
Clay, E. W
Davies, James.
Greig, George.
Hunt, M. V.
Montgomery, D. W.
Playfair, James.
Symons, J. T.
Symons, D. T.
Scholefield, W. F.
Denison, E. E.
Booth, W. E.
Bowes, J. H.
Browett, J. W.
Coate, F. S.
Geddes, A.
Jackes, E. H.
Langton, H. H.
Malcouronne, H. E.
Montgomery, T. B.
Orr, W. R.
Park, F.
Sanson, R. D.
Stephens, H. N.
Taylor, W. J. D.
Thompson, J. P.
Watson, E. P.
Watson, W. J.
McNab, A.
Blake, W. H.
Jackson, James.
Machell, A. G.
Stephens, M. N.
Stephens, J. D.
Patterson, T. H.
Proudfoot, H. B.
Smith, T. R. B.
Molesworth, A.
Mills, J. McV.
Greene, H. V.
Boyd, J. B.
Gillespie, G. H.
Gillespie, A.

Clarkson, A. M.
Willoughby, H.
McDougall, G. D.
Barber, A. E.
Begg, G. O.
Bryan, W. R.
Corby, E.
Davies, William.
Hendric, J. W.
Langmuire, J. A.
McEachren, F.
Muntz, H.
Reid, J. W.
Blethen, F. A.
Mahony, R. J.
Beale, James.
Holmes, W. J.
Peterkin, W. M.
Eddis, F. A.
Gibbs, H. C.
McAndrew, J. A.
Hunton, W. E.
Alexander, G. T.
Sinclair, A. J.
Sinclair, H. D.
Hilliard, G. G.
Dymond, A. H.
Dymond, A. M.
Derrom, J. A.
Derrom, A.
Baldwin, J. M.
Baldwin, R.
Jarvis, C. T.
Jarvis, William.
Hatton, E.
Henderson, D.
McCrimmon, John.
VanAllen, Edward.
Mackenzie, Alexander.
Clark, T. N.
Scott, J. J.
McLaren, D.
McKay, George.
Harris, A. V.
Bloodgood, H.
Downie, T.
Jones, W. W
Gunther, E.
Pearson, A. G.
Pearson, A. W.
Arnold, J. R.
Fisher, Thompson.
Knill, F.
Milner, Wm. S.
Ludgate, T.
Little, N.

1874.

Miller, A. C.
Cleverdon, W.
Carrie, J.
Quimby, H.
McLachlan, W.
Broden, E.
Day, Charles.

Lee, A.
Lee, S. H.
Lee, T. B.
Mackenzie, Robert.
Irving, W. H.
Fraser, W.
Wallace, Charles.
Wallace, J. Henry.
Parker, Thomas.
Nason, H.
Tyrrell, J.
Keefer, F.
Dunsford, J L.
Tanner, W R.
Pollock, J E.
McKellar, John A.
Ferguson, T. A.
Horseman, Wm.
Stewart, Wm.
Thompson, Wm.
Sayers, Edward.
Sayers, George.
Pringle, Robert A.
Turver, Charles.
Burch, Charles.
Chisholm, V.
Cameron, John.
Cavan, John.
Kittson, Ernest E.
McKenzie, K.
Ponton, A. D.
Saunders, John.
Woodruff, H. K.
Canniff, W. H.
Davis, Thomas E.
Howland, E.
Elgie, Thomas.
Freeman, J. F.
Gray, R. T.
Haight, W. L.
Balmer, R.
Scott, R.
Stark, F. J.
Thurston, Wm.
Whittier, J. C.
Shanklin, E. A.
Shanklin, C. S.
Dickson, R. C.
Mason, F. W.
Howland, F.
Howland, C.
Hooper, E. B.
Pyfrom, R. F.
Stapleton, H. C.
Green, J. A.
Gemmell, J. E.
Belt, R. W.
Willoughby, C. H.
Nelmes, E. M.
Hodgins, G.
Baldwin, A. Y.
Saunders, John.
Simonds, E. L.
Esten, J. P.
Esten, G. H.
Esten, H. L.

THE U. C. C. ROLL, 1829–1892. 315

Eyre, W. J.
Sweetnam, L. M.
Hooper, H. C. L.
Baldwin, W. W.
Burns, J.
Drummond, A. P.
Helliwell, A. C.
Hodgins, F. B.
Howard, W. J.
Lambe, G. A.
McDougall, L. V.
Newton, J.
Ogden, E. R.
Palmer, E.
Purvis, G. E.
Smith, E.
Smith, C.
Smith, L. J.
Wardell, A.
Woodruff, W.
Booth, G.
Mortimer, H.
Leadley, E.
Buchan, D.
Ogden, C. P.
Harvey, Alex.
Gardner, G. C.
Agur, R. H.
Baldwin, R.
Browning, D.
Browning, L.
Browning, W.
Duggan, G. H.
Cockburn, M. J.
Greene, C. W.
Mitchell, J.
Plummer, C. V.
Brock, W. L.
Dick, W.
Taylor, W. F.
Ball, R. S.
Ingersoll, J. H.
Killmaster, C. H.
Stewart, R. A.
Arnold, H.
Slemen, W. J.
Thompson, A. B.
Thompson, H. W.
Macdonald, A. H.
Campbell, A. J.
Scholes, H. M.
Lailey, Charles.
Garrard, F. C.
Prior, B.
Middleton, W. E.
McLaren, J.
Watherston, P.
Macklem, T. C. S.
Baldwin, F. M.
Benson, T.
Rattray, Robert.

1875.

Thompson, Herbert.
Rothwell, Wm.

Barker, H. C.
Murray, C. B.
Sherwood, W. J.
Waters, B.
Clark, Thomas.
Parsons, Charles.
Jarvis, A. E.
Gwynne, W.
Grace, J. C.
Warren, F. W.
Langstaff, E. F.
Grierson, D. A.
Saunders, M. Richard.
Mickle, H.
Holtermann, R.
McGiverin, Thomas.
Boyd, A. J.
Boyd, J. L.
Tucker W. H.
McDonald, Wm.
Kelley, John.
Cochrane, W. T.
Fielding, Edward.
Field, Henry.
Farmer, A.
Gillespie, G.
McLachlin, D.
McLachlin, H. W.
Prior, B.
Agnew, J. H.
Vernal, G. W.
Powell, W. F.
Powell, F. C.
Montgomery, J. D.
Wright, E. E.
McLaren, A.
Quimby, A. B.
Wilson, H. C.
Rogers, E. O.
Robertson, H. H.
Brooke, G. C.
Shanley, C. N.
Day, G. F.
Day, E. J.
Campbell, F. J.
Purvis, W. T.
Langmuir, A. D.
Langmuir, W.
Haight, C. E.
Thomson, W. C.
Thomson, G. S.
Jarvis, T.
Lindsey, W. L. M.
Elliot, J. J. H.
Elliot, W. L. G.
Peniston, C. W.
Laird, R.
Thorburn, J. D.
Thompson, M. C.
Moss, R. S.
Porteous, R. A.
Woodruff, E. A.
Stanton, F. J.
Cameron, A. B.
Glassford, W. J.
Smith, H. H.

Capreol, A. R.
Ross, J. L.
Fairfield, C. J.
Canniff, J. F.
Hume, H.
Castle, A.
Mickle, H. W.
McLay, John.
Lynch-Staunton, G. S.
Wilgress, G. S.
Maclean, W. F.
Drew, L.
Jarvis, G. H.
McDougall, W. K.
Lauder, W. W.
Wilson, A. Y.
Burns, W. H.
Dawson, W.
Macrae, H. H.
Milloy, C. C.
Macdonald, J. Kidston.
Gillespie, J. C.
Boyd, J. T.
Smith, A. C.
Fellows, F. L.
Plummer, F.
McMillan, A. G.
Roe, C.
Davidson, John.
Pomeroy, R.
Wardrop, Thomas W.
Wardrop, John.
Cayley, H.
Quay, F.
Gunther, E. R.
Brown, C. J.
Conolly, W. L.
Pearson, H. E.
Morrison, R.
Green, M. E.

1876.

Nicholson, J. A.
Moffatt, K.
Thurston, H. S.
Miller, J. B.
Brennan, Edward.
Brennan, Hugh.
Edgar, J. F.
Beatty, H. W.
Gray, St. George.
Fleury, H. W.
Clark, W.
Hoskins, F. H.
Mitchell, Alexander.
Duffield, W. S.
Tuckett, George.
Meredith, L.
Harvey, J. S.
Eddis, E. W.
Briant, W. H.
Ball, R. L.
Bilton, H.
Gilmour, C. W.

Kirkpatrick, R. C.
Duffield, J. C.
Duffield, W. A.
Campbell, H. D.
Warwick, George R.
Kirkpatrick, R. K.
Small, P. S.
Lindsay, J. M. P.
Boyd, G.
Kennelly, A. J.
Thompson, Robert.
Thompson, Richard.
Stark, H. L.
Stark, C. T.
Davies, O.
Smith, E.
Routh, P. G.
Bryce, John W.
Bryce, Wm. J.
Gooch, W. M.
Richardson, W. A.
Littlejohn, J. E. B.
Richardson, C. S.
Gillespie, F. G.
Macdonald, G. A.
Thompson, C. A.
Thompson, David.
Black, C.
Orr, W R.
McLimont, W.
Boice, C. J.
Stapleton, C. S.
Markle, A.
Prockter, W. H.
Watson, A.
Duggan, G. H.
Sievert, L. F.
Patterson, C. J.
Stikeman, A.
Walker, W. H.
Scott, A. H.
Pepler, W. H.
Pepler, T. S. G.
Macdonald, R.
Langstaff, H.
Speake, S. M.
Ewing, J.
Higgs, S. J.
Ritchie, William.
Patterson, J. B.
Waddle, Frank.
Cochrane, M. S.
Pellatt, H. A.
Gormley, T. J.
Moore, W. H. C.
Moore, F.
McGee, William F.
McGee, F. X.
Walls, T.
Archibald, A.
Duckworth, J.
Badenach, E. A.
Muntz, R.
Burgess, A.
Torrington, H.
Stevenson, G.

McMahon, J.
Greig, E. R.
Jarvis, F C.
Thomas, G. F.
Gillespie, F. G.
Lobb, A. F.
Bilton, F. V.
Maughan, H. J
Pratt, W L.
Thompson, W. E.
Cameron, J. W.
Redden, F. A. C.
Wolff, E.
Boulton, C. R.
Davis, E. P.
Nanton, H.
Barrett, E. M.
Grier, E. W
Grier, L. R. J.
Grier, A. M.
Winer, J. K.
Eyre, W. J.
Holton, L.
Thomson, George M.

1877.

Torrance, W. P.
Leman, G. H.
Monteith, F. W.
Burton, George.
Mackay, E.
Cameron, E. D.
Copp, Wm.
Gillespie, Walter.
Atkinson, F. Wm.
Kinahan, Robert.
Bruce, L.
Boulton, R. R.
Macdonnell, Alexander.
Lyman, A.
Turner, P. E.
Macdonnell, Ambrose.
Hayes, Daniel.
Spratt, Wm.
Toothe, R. M.
Boyd, W. T. C.
Richardson, G. H.
Sewell, H. E.
Shaw, H. L.
Staunton, T. A.
Tempest, J. A.
Thomson, A. M.
Thomson, W. P.
Galbraith, G.
Gordon, A. D.
Harrington, W.
McKeown, P. W.
Rich, A. R.
Rich, S. F.
Ross, H. W.
Spencer, H. A.
Sievert, J. A.
Van Allen, W.
Wagner, C. F.

Wagner, D. C.
Wilcocks, H. S.
Winter, P. C.
Gooderham, A. E.
Coleman, E. C.
Coleman, T. F.
Gillespie, F. A.
Hughes, P. D.
Mickle, C. R.
Smith, J. A.
Cawthra, H. V. H.
Torrance, A.
Torrance, W.
Wedd, M. D.
Aikins, H. A.
Boulton, A. H.
Badenach, C. H.
Baldwin, R. W. Y.
Fellows, E. L.
Morphy, E. W.
Morphy, A. H.
Mortimer, E.
Sharpe, G. H.
Scatcherd, J. A. D.
Thomson, T. K.
Henry, W. G.
Chisholm, R. W.
Chisholm, H. L.
Brown, G. S.
Finlayson, D. N.
Thompson, A. S.
Cooper, D. D. E.
Cooper, C. H.
Cameron, K.
Arthurs, W. F.
Booth, G. W.
Boulton, G. D.
Brunel, F. G.
Cattle, G. R.
Cawthra, J. E.
Cawthra, W. H.
Cockburn, H. Z. C.
Cooke, W. A.
Fry, S. G.
Greene, P. T.
Hughes, J. J.
Lewis, W. M.
Macdonald, J. F.
McLaren, C. C.
Bristol, E. J.
Gemmel, W. M.
Hammond, C.
Van Norman, J. C.
Rattray, F. A.
Bagshaw, F.
Carter, J.
Mortimer, A. E.
Phipps, C.
Hendrie, George.
Hendrie, William.
Cox, W. H.
Grahame, L. H.
Moss, J. H.
Gimson, T. F.
Gough, A.
Bain, William.

Bain, Robert.
Murray, S. B.
Stewart, F. J.
Allen, C. G.
Verral, C.
Strathy, A.
Jones, J. E.

1878.

Pears, G.
Fraser, John.
Kay, F.
Pott, C. E.
MacAdam, P.
Romaine, F. N.
Robertson, Charles S.
Campbell, W. M.
Wickson, A. F.
McLeod, R.
Rolph, F. W.
Beaver, Charles.
Kelly, H.
Lasher, E. A.
Brown, C. S. M.
Cassels, R. S.
Dusty, J.
Farmer, D. McL.
Kerr, F. O. M.
Hagaman, B.
Peterson, D.
Peterson, W. T.
Gay, R.
Horgan, Charles.
Gough, Charles.
Blake, E. F.
Dinnis, A.
Somers, J. W.
Ferguson, J. J.
McLaren, H.
Tolmie, R. A.
Andrews, W. H.
Rogers, F.
Denison, F. N.
Craigie, J. R.
Clark, C. H.
Scott, J.
Moore, C. J.
Nation, J.
Dickey, A. H.
Stewart, W. H.
Hunter, H.
Wilson, C. R. L.
Clarke, G.
Wilgress, A. T.
Alexander, R. H.
Aikins, B. M.
Boyd, H. G. H.
Boyd, W. T. H.
Boyd, J. R. S.
Leys, W. A.
Fraser, D. L.
Boulton, A. H.
Baldwin, D. C.

Boyd, L.
Blake, S. V.
Snider, F.
Petersen, W. E.
Denny, A.
Langmuir, A. D.
Ferris, M. J.
Hyde, G. R.
Fisher, F. T.
Montgomery, J. D.
Hyndman, H. K.
Dawson, J.
Elliott, J.
Lemeux, F. F.
Cassidy, W. E.
Woodruff, T. A.
Drayner, F.
McArthur, W. J.
McArthur, R. A.
Jarvis, H.
Rogers, H.
Burns, R. A. E.
McArthur, C.
Hop, J. H.
Wharin, W. J.
Ferguson, T. R.
Ferguson, G.
Armour, S.
Beck, C. B.
Birney, W. C.
Frost, J. E.
Martin, R. S.
Riordon, J. C.
Brown, J. F.
Jones, G. R.
Mackenzie, W. P.
Lewis, W.
Curry, B. H.
Brown, A. H.
Aldwell, T. T.
Brown, G. M.
Neelon, G. M.
Thompson, J. M.
Ginson, T. F.
Young, A. H.

1879.

Smith, T. E.
Pigott, R. S.
Samuel, S.
Carmichael, T.
Davis, James.
Farrall, J.
Urquhart, Robert.
Dunlop, John.
Dawson, M.
Wright, E.
Watson, H. J.
Breden, H.
Vidal, C. E. K.
Silverthorn, G.
Saunders, F. J. S.
Laidlaw, J. H.

Tilson, George.
Jarvis, P.
Hallamore, J. C.
Haldan, B.
Garden, F. M.
Mulholland, A. A.
Sankey, G. L.
Shutt, C. H.
Kirkpatrick, A. M. N.
Eddis, E. W.
Lough, T. S.
Maddison, E. W. R.
Kilbourn, F. H.
Wedd, L. E.
Smith, H. S.
Booth, C. S.
Macdonald, Alexander A
Thorner, T.
Clark, J. W. S.
Warwick, C. E.
Brayley, R. G.
Edgar, O. Pelham.
Brown, E. R.
Jarvis, E. B.
Jarvis, Harold H.
Pardee, E. C.
Blake, S. V.
Marks, S. A.
Layton, J. R.
Willson, William.
Jarvis, E. B.
Dalton, R. G.
Morton, E. L.
Nairn, John.
McIntosh, R. L.
Ross, J. R.
Benson, R. L.
Draper, H.
Brown, G. McL.
Moss, F. H.
Vickers, V. G. R.
Symington, G.
Robertson, W.
Pardee, F. F.
Montgomery, R.
Platt, N. L.
McLaren, J. B.
Haldan, W. J.
Cassels, R.
Kennelly, R.
Emigh, G. T.
Howell, R.
Milligan, W. J. L.
DuVernet, E. E.
McLean, J. D.
Taylor, G. A. C.
Tupper, W.
Wylie, J. W.
Carmichael, J. S.
Haldane, H. C.
Doyle, J. H.
Chewitt, H. J.
Hime, A. G.
Rathburn, E. W.
Coatsworth, C.
Coate, P. S.

1880.

Silverthorn, G.
Lawrence, L. T.
Stinson, C. A.
Powell, W. B.
Heward, C. E.
Copp, A.
Burrell, E.
Reford, R. W.
Reford, William R.
Reford, T. M.
Purdy, F.
Marsh, W.
Lightbourn, D.
Carden, G. F. L.
Chute, C.
McConnell, F.
Totten, H. B.
McLay, James.
Gordon, C. R.
Kilvert, F. E.
Bireley, E. L.
Haskins, G. M.
Crerar, A. H.
Kenrick, W. B.
Kenrick, E. B.
Kenrick, R. B.
Smith, H. P.
Battle, James.
McGill, W. R.
Kelly, J. A. A.
Thomas, H. F.
Proctor, G.
Muldrew, W. H.
Nicholson, G.
Hyland, C. D. H.
Drynan, J.
Wiley, A. M.
Galt, H.
Thompson, J. J.
Gooch, W. M.
Wood, J. S.
Sullivan, S. H.
Hope, W. B.
Rathbun, W. C. B.
Corsan, G. H.
McMurray, L. S.
Cowan, F. P.
Cowan, R. L.
Gemmell, H. J.
Hillary, R.
Drake, W. A.
Fraser, W. A.
Parsons, F. E.
Parsons, H. C.
Brush, De Locke.
Macfarlane, J. M.
McMurray, L. S.
Hagarty, G. V.
Brock, R. A.
Douglas, F.
Muntz, G. H.
Barnhart, F. K.
Barnhart, N. C.
Gates, H. G.

Denison, G. T.
Godson, F. W.
Jones, F. W.
Vankoughnet, A. H. S.
Vankoughnet, E. R.
Marling, J. H. O.
Coldham, W. W.
Burns, S.
Slawson, C. S.
Reynolds, H. M.
Major, V. E.
Biggar, G. C.
Cloyes, F. E.
Postlethwaite, C.
Guest, J. S.
Guest, S. W.
Thacker, N. G.
Thacker, C. F.
Ramsey, W.
Snowball, William.
Landsberg, F. W.
Howard, H. R.
Gow, J.

1881.

Kirkpatrick, R. C.
Campbell, E. A.
Loudon, A.
Routh, S. H. R.
Howell, H. B.
Forbes, W. N.
Murray, A. H.
Chadwick, H. C. V.
Lingham, W. A.
York, J.
Moodie, J. W. D.
McMaster, A.
Vidal, J. H.
Vidal, H. P.
Bowell, C. J.
Lamont, J.
Worth, C.
Brayley, C. H.
Gale, J. W.
Appleton, L. G.
Davidson, F.
Temple, C. A. D.
Scarth, W. H.
Scarth, M. B.
Notman, C. R.
Ruttan, R. R.
Kirkpatrick, George.
Gibson, Joseph.
Donaldson, G.
Denison, H. P. B.
Kennedy, F. W.
Green, S.
Smart, J. A.
Eddis, H. C.
Rae, W.
Towner, G. H.
Herod, W.
McCollum, J. H. K.
Evans, D. J.

Snetzinger, J. F.
Snowball, M. D.
Field, G. W.
Field, A. G.
Hendrie, S.
Hall, J. P. M.
Cook, G. C.
Thorp, H.
Culverwell, J. A.
Baird, G.
Boas, A. B.
McGill, G. W.
Notman, C. R.
Palmer, T.
Thompson, F. B.
Pain, G. H.
Montgomery, A.
Mulock, William M.
Beardmore, F. N.
Thompson, F. C.
Dalton, E. H.
Baxter, D. W.
Vickers, A. A.
Dixon, T. F. D.
Haskins, T. F.
Campbell, M.
Power, W. G.
Fisher, W. M.
McDougald, A. W.
Darrell, C.
Smith, S. W.
Jones, H. T.
MacAdam, P. E. W.
Kingsmill, G. R.
Noxon, J.
Noxon, W. C.
Davidson, J. F.
Hamilton, J. D.
Thompson, A.
Douglas, W.
Douglas, J. S.
Grant, A. D. C.
Hitt, S. E.
Risch, H. F.
Risch, E. W.
Owen, L. C.
Buchan, J. L. S.
McGill, W. H.
Keown, R. J.
Leacock, T. J.
Leacock, A. M.
Esson, W. K.
Douglas, F.
Esson, F. G.
Morton, Wm. L.
Lyon, E.
Stovel, C. J.
Stovel, R. D.

1882.

Lingham, W. A.
Dockray, T. D.
Bunting, W. H.
Bunting, G. A.

Burns, W.
Armstrong, R. T.
Gemmel, W. L.
Ballard, J. A.
Barnhart, R.
Shaw, C. E.
Comstock, E. P.
Woodworth, P. C.
Leacock, S. B.
Jones, D. F. S.
Tushingham, F.
McMichael, A. F.
Hewetson, John.
Proctor, J. C.
McGiverin, H. G. B.
Shields, J. D.
Sayer, J.
Martin, S.
McMaster, F.
Holmes, W.
Binnings, C. E.
Bradley, H. S.
Leggatt, J.
Goering, H. P.
Cory, J. W.
Sandham, A. S.
Laury, T. H.
Baxter, R. J.
Mackenzie, W. A.
Brown, G.
Bethune, C. J. R.
Harvard, W. A.
Grantham, A. M.
Laidlaw, C. S. R.
Thompson, J. T.
Ward, E.
Patterson, W.
Fish, R. B.
Armour, G. W.
Armour, D. J.
Cruso, J.
Archibald, F. B.
Eyre, G. F. C.
Stevenson, E. V.
Macdonald, A. P.
Pardee, J. B.
Lamb, P. R.
Bachly, C. E.
Holmes, H.
Rae, H.
Ramsey, J. F.
Ditmer, G. A.
Doull, A. J.
Massie, J. A.
Wyndham, E. A.
Kirkpatrick, W. R.
Donaldson, J. C.
McColl, A. W.
McPherson, J.
Gildersleeve, A. M.
Gildersleeve, E. C.
Leggatt, M. H.
Denison, S.
Appleton, A.
Sparks, C.
Gale, C. E.

Cotter, G. S.
Cotter, W. M. O.
Chadwick, E. A. E.
Elliot, F.
Gault, H. F.
Swallow, J. C.
Watts, A. G.
Colquhoun, W. E.
Fleury, W. T.
Shaw, W. E.
Willson, H.
Esson, A.
Holderness, W.
Field, P.
Field, F.
Hamilton, W.
Smart, W. C.
McClung, A. T.
Morris, E. M.
Walden, C. W.
Miles, E. W.
Watson, H. J.
Cook, G. W.
Gamsby, Larratt.
Dodds, A. K. R.
Sutherland, H. L.
Fish, J. A.
Mackay, A. S.

1883.

McMichael, F. N.
Close, T. W.
Barnard, A. W.
Watson, H. H.
Sproat, A. B.
Davis, M. H.
Montgomery, R.
Oxley, C.
Oxley, G.
Troup, G.
Munro, G.
McRae, D.
Faughner, W. A.
Davis, C. H.
Brown, E. V.
Mackenzie, Norman.
Clark, P. B.
Armstrong, B.
Burgess, R.
Kerr, F. M.
McMaster, B. B.
Macdonnell, G. F.
Irving, W.
Hillary, N. T. M.
Turner, J. A.
Dennis, J. B.
Jaffray, W. G.
Oliver, F. P.
Barnhart, R.
Mathews, E.
Scatchard, A. T.
Gustin, A. M.
Page, B. B.
Duncan, H.

Ballantyne, A.
Fairbairn, R. D.
Farmer, W. McL.
Paton, P.
Davidson, J. A.
Haldane, W. R.
Scanlon, A. C.
Smith, J. E.
Russell, J. P.
Thacker, N. C.
Morgan, St. G. V. F.
Roberts, A. A.
Whitehead, J. A.
Maclaren, D.
McMaster, L.
Turner, Campbell.
Willson, C. R.
Frost, Fred. A.
Jarvis, E.
Langmuir, Fred.
Wadsworth, A. R.
Kirkpatrick, G. S.
Smith, G. L.
McKay, W. C.
Ferguson, W. N.
Berry, J. C.
Macfarlane, H. K.
Yeomans, A. A.
McCrancy, G. E.
Smith, S. B.
Bonnell, W. H. M.
Elliot, W. C. S.
Badgerow, G. A.
Mattice, C. E. S.
Bethune, A.
Martin, P. W.
Harvey, James.
Hanmer, L. E.
Martin, F. R.
Farmer, W.
Robertson, F. M.
Morrow, W. S.
Gregory, A. E.
Kingsmill, H. R.
Boyd, G.
Suardon, R.
Tilt, F.
Pears, E. W.
Buckley, W. P.
Buckley, A. P.
Kirkwood, T.
Hilker, A. E.
Nash, F. M.
Strathy, H. E.
Clark, D. E.
Buckingham, N. P.
Currey, E. H.
Rogerson, E. J.
Boultbee, A.

1884.

Gillies, J. B.
May, F. J.
Paterson, William Walter.

Ferrie, Robert Russell.
Bendy, Charles Arthur.
Shiel, Advid John.
Jordan, Walter.
Curran, Reginald Somerset M.
Gillies, David Strathern.
Laidlaw, James T
Hamilton, Frederick J.
Senkler William Ivan.
McMullen, Albert J.
Martin, George Ellsworth.
Martin, Edgar Philip.
Bidgood, Henry Raby.
Cross, William
Barlee, George Toker.
Fairbairn, James Frederick.
Mackenzie, William Innis.
Counsell, Charles.
Jebb, Thomas Arnold.
Jebb, Charles Francis.
Nason, Russell Fortescue.
Mackenzie, Hope Fleming.
Mackenzie, John.
Mackenzie, Alexander Houston.
Ferguson, William Robinson.
Jackson, George Edmund.
Marks, Arthur Selwyn.
Wallbridge, Campbell Miller.
Biggar, Henry Percival.
Mattice, William Arthur.
Hannaford, Edmund Phillips.
Snetzinger, James Arthur.
Phillips, George Leamington.
Hume, Francis Edward.
Galbraith, James Richardson.
Mitchell, Francis.
Gosling, Charles.
Wallbridge, Francis George.
Attrill, Edward Chancy.
Gartshore Alexander L.
Gibb, Arthur Norman.
Joy, Bertram Henry.
Thorne, Richard Edgar.
Chandler, Walter Heward.
Russell, George Emery.
Miller, Henry De.
Knowles, James.
Boyd, Lawrence.
Boyd, David Griffith.
McMurrich, John Dewar.
Reid, George Butt.
Reid, John Young.
Clayes, George.
Ponton, William Hamilton Hanwell.
Morton, William Lyall.
Jones, Benjamin Morton.
Small, Henry Campbell.
McMahon, D'Arcy H. K.
Freeman, William Charles.
West, Francis James.
Badgerow, George W.
Spence, James Edward.
Drew, John Jacob.
Smith, Frederick.
Brown, John Alexander.

Adam, Herbert Stevenson.
McGaw, Thomas Dick.
Cole, William John.
Hardy, Joseph Curran Morrison.
Smith, James Edward.
McArthur, Angus Douglas.
McKeand, James William.
Baxter, Robert Jacob.
McLaren, Albert.
Wodsworth, Charles.
Kilbourn, George Stirke.
Kilbourn, John Macready.
Fleming, Walter Arthur.
Fleming, Hugh Percy.
Calcutt, Clare Fester.
Harvey, George.
Wilson, Frederick William.
Purves, James George Harrison
Cowan, Herbert Street.
Millechamp, Reuben Wm.
Elliot, Heward.
Watts, Wm. Arthur.
Simpson, Wm. Gordon.
Lough, James Perrot.
Campbell, Walter Scott.
Dixon, Harold Wm. Alexander.
Swan, James Henry.
Paton, Robert F T.
Paton, James Frederick.
Paton, Wm. Angus.
McMaster, Clarence Wilkes.
Hagarty, Arthur Edward.
Hagarty, Henry John.
Boutbee, Wm. Mulock.
Esten, Charles Hamilton.
Edgar, Wm. Wilkie.
Laidlaw, Wm. Charles.
Denison, Oliver Macklem.
Wilson, Louis Arthur.
Ireland, Percy Wilson.
May, Henry Stafford.
Brown, John Alexander.
Leacock, Charles John.
Lee, William Joseph.
Watson, Herbert James.
Horn, Luther.
Maule, Percy Sidney.
Cunningham, Alured Alex.
McKibbin, Herbert Albert.
Balmer, George Francis.
Sisley, Opie.
Thomas, Frederick Milton.
Buchan, Humphrey Ewing.
McGuire, Wm. Henry.
Blackwood, Charles Keith.
Campbell, Wm. Macpherson.
Myers, Walter Herbert.
Wilson, David Hunter
Farrer, Henry.
Cheape, John Albert.
Cheape, Henry Windsor.
Scadding, Walter Reginald.
McGregor, Henry Mortimer.
Clark, George S. W.
Thacker, Herbert Cyril.

McCraken, Thomas Ernest.
Jameson, James Alexander.

1885.

McLeod, James Barber.
Barber, Francis James.
Wallbridge, Gavin.
Kenrick, Francis Matthews.
Clark, Robert Irving.
Dawson, George.
Dawson, John.
Waldie, John Edward.
Mason, Homer.
Eager, Archibald Allen.
Henderson, John Alexander.
Robeson, Wm. Rollo.
Wood, Enoch Irving.
Strickland, Henry Fred. S.
Parsons, Harold Campbell.
Houghan, Robert Wesley.
Petersen, Walter Stewart.
Dixon, Thomas Fraser Homer.
Orton, Henry George.
Briggs, John Naylor
Skae, Edward Askin.
Kenrick, Cranmer Edward.
Lingham, George Nelson.
Bailey, Eugene Tryon.
Brown, Rodman Merritt.
Harrison, Earl Stanley.
Lee, Percy.
Ridout, N. S.
Ridout, D. C.
Malloch, Stewart Ernest.
Baker, Hugh.
Temple, Cuthbert Knapton Winslow.
Anderson, Frank.
Thompson, Charles A.
Wood, W. T.
Rykert, Arthur Fred.
Grumbacker, Isaac.
Wood, William F.
Kirkpatrick, Arthur J. E.
Buell, William Senkler.
Swett, Samuel.
Kilvert, R. Y.
Thompson, Andrew T.
Mason, Frank.
Cartwright, James S.
Crocker, Henry C.
Clelan, James Hamilton.
Wallbridge, F. G.
Bunting, George Elwood.
Findlay, Walter Alexander
Sampson, Arthur R.
Dixon, Thomas.
Moss, Walter Philip.
Cameron, Allan.
Dyment, Albert Edward.
Roberts, Albert W. S.
Moberly, Halford, K.
Noble, R. K.
Martin, C. E.
Hendershot*, Wm. A.

ENTRANCE HALL, PRINCIPAL'S HOUSE.

PRINCIPAL'S GARDEN.

Hendershott, Charles W.
Ballard, George.
Oldright, H. H.
Denison, H. P. B.
Cole, G. C.
Evans, C. F. E.
Bently, Charles W.
Fleming, James Henry.
Moss, Charles.
Kingstone, A. E.
McMurrich, J. B.
Gale, G. C.
Watson, H. J.
Gillespie, F. L.
Lash, W. M.
Hime, W. L.
Smith, Fred. B.
Barber, Vincent.
Sweatman, Arthur.
Drayton, Charles Robt. Lumley
Goode, E. W.
Fulton, J. R.
Burgess, Arthur Charles.
Hillbur, Thomas H.
Macdonald, Arthur Nimmo.
Macdonald, Duncan N.
Oliver, Frederick Percy.
Kerns, Frederick Arthur.
Hamilton, Charles G.
Ellis, H. E.
Verral, E. J.
Cleghorn, A. T.
Cartwright, J. S.
Manning, Percy.
Freeman, W. C.
Freeman, J. H.
Gianelli, Lewis Francis.
Gianelli, Victor E.
Horrocks, Trevre.
McKeown, Benjamin.
Mayo, Henry.
Mayo, Joseph.
Merritt, Prescott.
Dallas, Thomas.
Keith, Wilfred.
Merritt, Prescott.
Dallas, Thomas.
Keith, William.
Burnham, James Gilchrist.
Duffus, Henry.
Duffus, Arthur.
Parsons, Harold C.
Winder, George.
Hollis, Austin W.
Dowding, Henry.
Ghent, James Albert.
Fraser, James Gordon.
Mitchell, George Mackenzie.
Roberts, Thomas L.
Mill, Thomas John.
Stokes, William.
Rimer, George W.
Cunningham, A.
McGaw, James D.
Moody, Thomas.
McIntosh, F. J.

1886.

Temple, Charles A.
Michael, Frank M.
Hamilton, Charles G.
Smith, Walter.
Baird, H. M.
Leys, F. D. T.
Thompson, H. P.
Osler, Featherstone Britton.
Oldwright, Percy.
O'Mara, Fred C.
Irish, Mark H.
Martin, Frank S.
Wade, Frank.
Crawford, Dixon.
Thompson, W. J.
Carvell, Arthur.
Brown, Joseph.
Wilkie, Charles Stuart.
Quay, Donald D.
Dawson, William N.
Moren, Arthur F. S.
Fraser, E. A.
Fraser, Herald Wm.
Gibson, David S.
Warren, Charles Hubert.
Law, William John.
Tremayne, Ernest.
Pickard, Charles Edward.
Geary, George Reginald.
Vivian, Reginald Percy.
Richardson, C. H. R.
Laidlaw, Walter.
Lount, Fred. Alexander.
Lenigan, J. F.
McDougall, Douglass Howard.
McClure, Charles W.
McNider, James.
Matthews, Harold Alfred.
Godson, Arthur Ferguson.
Eakin, Nelson D. R.
Pardee, Henry.
Rice, Charles Bishop.
Rice, Carydon V.
Lash, Norwood Maxwell.
Vernon, Frank Lawson.
Vernon, Albert Crawford.
Westerman, Charles Everett.
Berry, Herbert.
Cameron, Robert George.
Chittenden, Frank.
Andros, Ralf Craven.
Love, Henry G.
Montgomery, William Henry.
Barr, Charles James.
Watt, Herbert Lorne.
Hayne, Charles Cochrane.
Hayne, George Osborn.
Brough, Richard William.
Patterson, John Henry L.
Bruce, Walter Hamilton.
McCully, Ralph.
Kemp, Thomas Campbell.
Kemp, David Campbell.
Crawford, James Malcolm

Allen, William Lyall.
Wood, Herbert H.
Hamilton, Harry Ross.
Moran, William James.
O'Mera, William Henry Frank.
Dockray, Adam.
Dockray, Herbert.
Willis, Harvey A.
Hastings, George.
VanWormer, Park James.
Battle, Martin.
Arnold, R. C.
Wilby, Roger.
Almon, E. P.
Score, R. J.
Clathe, Charles.
Henry, G. S.
Niehaus, F. W.
Woods, S. B.
Hipkins, R. H.
Small, A.
Lapsley, F. W.
Boultbee, Horace.
Abrey, G. A.
Fensom, W. E.
Wadsworth, W.
Meek, C. S.
Shepherd, H.
Bright, W. M.
Burrell, Harry Stephen.
Counsell, Norman William.
Douglass, William J.
Hyde James.
Matthews, Harold.
Bunting, Christopher.
Coulson, Frank Lees.
Brown, Richard Charles.
Lockhart, Gilbert Arthur.
Carscallen, Oswald Gurney.
Carscallen, Charles Gurney.
Ballantyne, Adam William.
Morrison, Robert Arthur.
Baldwin, Norman McLeod.
Garratt, Alexander.
Carrall, Robert William.
Spence, Frederick Charles.
Belden, Edgar.
Spink, Eugene.
Wilson, Philip Clarence.
Robb, Charles C.
Pyke, George Alfred.
Peck, William Wallace.
Echlin, Samuel A.
Middleton O. J.
O'Dell, Harry Day.
Davies, Joseph Edgar.
Sproat, John.
Thomson, Bernard.
Mussen, Thomas Charles.
Moore, Charles Thomas.
Huff, Montgomery.
Barnhisel, John Collins.
Adair, John.
Norton-Taylor, Alfred.
Matthews, George.
Webb, Albert Edward.

UPPER CANADA COLLEGE MEMORIAL VOLUME.

Kemp, Herbert.
Johnson, Percy **Hall.**
Allan, Stewart.
Allan, Rutherford.

1887.

McMichael, Allan R.
Holt, Herbert Richard.
McGill, Frederick Walter.
Lough, John.
Burns, Frank.
Burns, John.
Mackenzie, Gerald.
Ross, Garibaldi.
Furness, David Robert.
Marshall, William R.
Robinson, Charles.
Stubbs, Henry G.
Parke, Edward D.
Barrick, Sidney J.
Macdonald, John J.
Idington, Peter S.
Mathews, Albert A.
Ardagh, John C.
Wedd, Edward, K. **M.**
Hyslop, William.
Kingsford, George E.
Beatty, Adam.
Woods, Fred. Joseph.
Kiely, William Edwards.
Kiely, George.
Dineen, William.
Wyllie, Alexander **Clark.**
Quay, Ralph I. D.
Massey, Arthur.
McKeown, Aloyise.
Boyd, George H.
Hunter, James A.
Gardner, Matthew S.
Keefer, Harry M.
Richardson, Fred. H.
Rolls, John.
Sweetman, John **William.**
Duncan, Gordon.
Innis, William L.
Harnden, Luther.
Nicholson, James.
Rowe, Valentine Edward **S.**
Barton, Arthur William.
Smith, Charles William.
Dwight, Charles P.
Wragge, Edmund C.
Bucke, Edward P.
Bucke, Ernest.
Beck, Jacob Fred.
Clark, James C.
Steed, Robert William.
Weld, Corbin.
McDonnell, Richard.
Ryan, Roderick.
Bannerman, David.
Jamieson, Hugh.
Stovel, Fred. B.
Potter, Charles H.

Sutton, William Hubert.
Taylor, Richard N.
Archibald, William.
Watlington, Frank William.
Nason, Frank.
Campbell, Arthur **H.**
Gosling, Henry H.
Gosling, Edgar H.
Musson, George.
Walker, Augustus H.
Anderson, Wm. Ingles.
Gurd, Norman.
McMurrich, G. T.
Devlin, Ernest W.
Thacker, Percy N.
Payne, John W.
Noble, Stafford.
Jackson, Maunsell B.
Clark, Edward C.
Mackenzie, Wm.
Morgan, Arthur.
Tench, John E.
Poussett, Henry R.
Caldwell, Alexander **Clyde.**
Heartz, Frank R.
Wesley, John A.
Wesley, Frank J.
Kingsmill, Wm.
Taber, T. C.
Wood, Robert.
Wood, T.
Somerville, C. **T.**
Somerville, R. **A.**
Mabee, O. H.
Pyke, H. T.
Hutchins, Charles H.
Denison, H. E.
Bell, A. J.
Macmillan, **K. D.**
Eby, W. P.
Eby, H. D.
Strickland, R. C.
McMurray, F.
Bruce, H. A.
Silverthorn, C.
McKibbon, J. E.
Burnfield, J. C.
Tremaine, Morris S.
Clark, Joseph A.
Gillard, James T.
Farmer, Thomas W.
Robinson, Burnside.
Cosby, Fred. L.
Cosby, Norman **W.**
Murdock, Alexander **W.**
Beatty, Henry A.
Beatty, Edward W.
Werden, Edward.
Sinclair, Charles A.
Cranston, James G.
Kirkpatrick, Charles **S.**
McWilliams, R. A.
Taylor, E.
Denison, Garnet **Wolsey.**
Staunton, E. G.
Greenfield, James.

Darrell, H.
Boddy, C. A. S.
Smith, H. E.
Meek, E. J.
Gibson, R. L.
Gibson, T. E.
Kennedy, F. J.
Macdonald, **Oscar O.**
Wickins, A.
Bain, J. W.
Temple, R. **H.**
How, J. A.
Barnhart, **F.**
Martin, H. **J.**
Elliot, W.
Wilkie, A. B.
Parker, W. R.
Thompson, B. A.
Douglass, J. S.
Farr, H. J.
Burton, A.
Quinn, E.
Creelman, **A.**
Günther, E. **H.**
Fleming, A.
Gray, A. **L.**
McLaren, **D.**
Oliver, Frank Reginald.
Bain, John F. L.
Blackley, J. M.
Thomson, David.
Badenach, Ernest Stuart.
Urquhart, Wm. Morris.
Boyd, Philip Ewing.
Boyd, Walter H.
Malloch, Harold A. S.
Counsell, John **Leith.**
Tate, E. F R.
Sears, George **M.**
Jones Simeon.
Sutherland, **J. A.**
Hoskins, A. **E.**
Doty, E. F.
Burns, A. H.
Canniff, A. Q.
McLean, D.
McLeod, G. **S.**
Kingsmill, Harold B.
Clark, Gordon Mortimer.
Lawson, William.
Mitchell, G. E.
Chandler, W. M.
Kincaid, K. G.
Wells, J. D.
Titus, F. J.
Townsend, F.
Lobb, J. N.
Griffin, V. **T.**

1888.

Gibson, R. **L.**
Burr, H. R.
Smith, F. E.
Band, C. W P.

Gordon, H. D. L.
Linton, F. D.
Cameron, C. S.
Gilray, H. B.
Lefevre, A. G. T.
Smith, H. G.
Pearson, H. C.
Holcombe, R. C.
Macdonald, Albert A.
Hagarty, D. G.
Armstrong, A.
Mulvey, C.
Bedson, E. N.
Pease, H. D.
Doty, F. D.
Robinson, E. L.
Bell, J. D.
Metcalf, U. A.
Parker, W. E.
Bond, A. A.
Doble, J. R.
Gooch, G. E.
Pilkey, R. P.
Taylor, G. E.
Fearman, Edward M.
Outerbridge, S. N.
Proudfoot, H. W.
Macklem, J. J. T.
Coulter, L. M.
Poussett, W. C.
Bertram R. N.
Moore, H. T.
Sanders, J. A.
Davis, H. S.
Scilly, A. G.
Wilcox, D. U.
McNairn, William Harvey.
Fowler, Henry Ades.
Holcroft, Austin.
Harvey, Harry Burton.
Burns, Cecil Hamilton.
Hendrie, Murray.
Toller, Guy Northcote.
Gurney, William Cromwell.
Townsend, Harry Hillyard.
Patterson, Christopher Stuart.
Patterson, Francis Denison.
Gooderham, Henry Holwell.
White, William Rushman.
Gregg, James William.
Burbidge, Harry.
Strathey, Allan Dundas.
Pearman, Eugene.
Eager, Archibald.
Lockie, Everard James.
Stovel, Russell Wellesly.
Darrell, Ernest Hill.
Eaton, William Fletcher.
Eaton, John Craig.
Leslie, Charles Wilby Parke.
Bertram, John Alexander.
Spears, Norman Norris.
McNee, Arthur Finlay.
Gilmour, John Wardrop.
Gilmour, William Alexander.
Hargraft, William Hewson.

Franchot, Richard.
Stewart, Charles James Townsend.
Hardy, Arthur Curran W.
Cotter, Stuart.
Boré, Henry Peter.
Anderson, Clarence James.
Palmer, John Christie.
Vooght, Reginald.
Ballantyne, Walter.
Wilson, William Ernest.
Lepper, David.
Holcroft, Herbert Spencer.
Hayter, Ross J. T.
Hayter, Herbert Roche.
Kirkpatrick, William Macpherson.
Kirkpatrick, Guy Hamilton.
Cross, Charles Wilson.
Bryant, John Leslie.
Huntington, Erastus Samuel.
Buck, Harry Stanley.
Harmer, John.
Stewart, Sherley.
Michie, Henry Stuart.
Garrett, John Elmer.
Biglow, Nelson Calvin.
Lister, Frederick Alexander.
Isbister, John.
Upper, Frank Joseph.
Robertson, Andrew Russell.
Ellis, Charles Mark.
Ellis, Edwin Harding.
Jones, Ralph Taylor.
MacKenzie, Charles.
MacKenzie, Roderick John.
Southam, Harry Stevenson.
Crerar, Thomas Halford.
Mallon, Edward Henry.
Flintoft, James Herbert.
McDonald, John Herbert.
Leckie, William Henry.
Mullin, James Heurner.
White, Robert Warren.
Storey, Duncan Stewart.
Bellsmith, Eustace John.
Rice, William Hercules.
Lailey, Frederick Thomas.
Burns, Alexander F.
Morrice, George.
Morrice, Arthur.
Jackson, W. T.
Gilmour, Robert Hugh Lovett.
Bond, Aubrey Clifford.
Lefroy, Augustus George.
Armstrong, Karl Gooderham.
Graham, Sharon.
Hime, Morris Wm.
Biggar, James Lyons.
Biggar, Oliver Mowat.
Henry, Wm. Percival.
McConnell, John Herbert Frederick.
Bunting, John.
Bailey, Eugene Taylor.
Godson, Walter Pollard.

Mackintosh, Harold.
Connor, Robert Nicholas.
Boddy, Austin.
Bain, Louis Rutherford.
Staunton, Victor Charles.
Haldane, Peter Caldwell.
Shields, Francis Alexander.
Smith, James F.
Snell, Edgar Milton.
Miller, Frank Edgar.
Creighton, Charles Dickens.
Watts, Ernest.
Braun, Lewis.
Carscallen, Henry Gurney.
Frith, Gilbert Roberts.
Verner, James Frederick.
Gellespie, Clarence Alexander.
Ridout, Douglas Kay.
Woods, Thomas Ambrose.
Ridgley, Ernest Harcourt.
Smith, William Harrison.
Morrice, George.
Flett, Harry Ridley.
Noble, James Burrows.
Black, Oliver Steele.
Russell, Arthur Dickson.
Bridges, Chas. Sidney Whitla.
Robertson, Douglas Sinclair.
Miller, Wm. Thomas.
Strickland, Cecil Hamilton.
Johnston, Henry.
Lee, Wm. Charles Crabb.
Smith, Frederick Byers.
Leslie, Francis Guy.
Leslie, George L.
Sparling, Chris. P.

1889.

Armstrong, Bartle Mahon.
Bird, Henry J.
Corey, Bloss Parson.
Watson, John William.
Harder, William Worthington.
Johnston, Harvey.
Buschlen, Arthur.
Barwick, Shabbham Guy.
Scott, Victor Lewis Mitchell.
Walsh, William Crogin.
Bull, Bartholemew Frank.
Sims, Henry Augustus.
Wilson, Reginald Clarence.
Orton, William Carlax.
Hally, James.
Duggan, Henry Van Norman.
Ross, Donald Aynsley.
Ross, John Hugo.
Cluthe, Frederick William.
Bell-Smith, Frederick Martell.
Morton, Ernest.
Brown, George Benson.
Brown, Gordon Arthur.
Armstrong, Arthur Dawson.
Halliday, William Henry.
McBean, Wm. Elvins.
Goodman, Leon.

Dixon, Henry Eugene.
McLennan, Frederick John.
McLennan, Francis William.
MacIntyre, Edwin John.
Sandwell, Bernard Keble.
Holwell, Richard Percy Haywood.
Hannington, **Charles Stanley**.
MacFarlane, **Malcolm Arthur**.
Gibbs, Frank **S**.
Walmsley, **Charles Thomas** Franklin.
Harris, George W. Henry.
Biggar, Arthur Pettit.
Burk, John Alexander.
Bendelari, Frederick Napoli.
Bathgate, James Alexander.
Barnard, Harold Robert.
Burk, John Edmund Warner.
Burk, Clarence Baldwin.
Costè Maurice Rèuè Gabriel.
Doward, Norman Redgrave.
Muir, James G.
Martin, Robert **Oliver**.
Patterson, John.
Pardee, Timothy **Blair**.
Primrose, John.
Porter, Walter Ferguson.
Taylor, Joseph Egbert **Paul**.
Upper, Lachlin William.
White, Alfred Cawley.
Milburn, Thomas Edward.
Wilson, Theophile James Herbert.
Putnam, Harry.
Shotbolt, Herbert Thomas.
Jaffray, Robert Alexander.
Street, Edmund Rochford.
Laycock, James L.
McGregor, George.
Draper, Alfred.
Struthers, Edward R. G.
Struthers, Harry H.
Boucher, George Burnham.
Smith, Frank Austin.
Morton, Walter Dean.
Mallon, Michael Patrick.
McMaster, John Alexander.
McMaster, Thomas Greer Carson
McMaster, Edward Blake.
Kellogg, William.
Noblet, Russell.
Braide, Claude.
Edgar, David Keith.
Willoughby, Arthur Gordon.
Webster, Wm. J. P.
Wellington, Earle Stanley.
Cartwright, Robert John.
Cameron, Matthew Crooks.
Singer, Moses M.
Henry, John S.
McMurrich, Arthur Redpath.
Hackett, John.
Scott, Fred. W.
Hesson, Sidney Ernest.
Gillespie, Henry Howland.

Birney, George.
Suter, Fred. A.
Carson, Robert Stevenson.
Hyde, Walter Hubert.
McIntosh, Donald J.
Braun, Wm.
Dougherty, James **Ernest**.
Price, Fred, Courtenay.
Price, Llewellyn.
Marsden, Frank Victor.
Labatt, Chas. Robert.
Bryant, James Fraser.
Waldie, Fred. Norval.
Yeamans, Clinton C.
Field, Edward James.
Lepper, Henry H.
Drancy, Charles Robert.
Draney, James Herbert.
Todd, Arthur L.
Blong, George.
Davidson, Edward **G**.
Baby, Raymond Francis.
Hamilton, George P.
Macdonald, Henry Blong.
Wallbridge, Arthur Robert.

1890.

Heasen, W. J.
Macdonnell, James Smellie.
Stovel, Herbert Roy.
Todd, John Launcelot.
Todd, Albert Edward.
Getchell, John E.
Newsome, F. W.
Oldbury, Wm.
Sutherland, Wm.
Roos, Irving K.
Beck, Charles M.
Watson, George Ruston.
Handy, Edward F. T.
Mockridge, John C. H.
Wickson, Walter.
Robb, James A.
McLaughlin, Leonard.
Thomson, Burns K.
Dowding, John P.
Moores, Ernest Joseph.
Ryerson, George Egerton.
Goold, Albert Septimus.
Lount, Norman Mulock.
Armour, **Eric**.
Snetzinger, **Harold Wylie**.
Hayter, F. **W**.
Sachs, Michael.
Whitney, Richard Albert.
Lewis, Charles Austin.
Scott, Walter Lyall.
Burnham, C. Hurd.
Bolton, Samuel Edward.
Burton, Harry P.
Burton, George H.
Kerns, William Charles.

Henderson, Velyien **Ewart**.
Armstrong, John M.
Westwood, Frank Benjamin.
Hunter, Fraser Frederick.
Hunter, Harry Alexander.
Wanless, Robert Douglas.
Barr, Adam Fordyce.
McKibben, John Edward.
Richardson, Max Avery.
Campbell, Archibald B.
West, William Needham.
Mackenzie, Charles.
Heathorn, Herbert Warner.
Shortreed, William John.
Maclean, John Carruthers.
Taylor, John Eban Buffon.
Winchester, Gordon Hossack.
Waldie, Robert Stanley.
Miller, Clarence John.
Harrington, Edward Ries.
Brereton, Clondesley Herbert.
Saunders, Thomas Malcolm Macpherson.
Masson, George.
Crawford, Andrew Gordon.
Watson, William Ogilvie.
Edgar, Robert McBeth.
Thompson, Edwin Barritt.
Mitchell, Edward Hamilton.
Saunders, **Arthur** Bennett.
Earle, Walter Allan.
Macdonald, William Randolph.
Millburn, John Albert.
Burns, Edward.
McArthur, Clarence.
Cramer, Donald A.
Evans, Verner Sims.
Verner, James Frederick.
Robinson, George.
Boddy, Arthur Percival.
Kingsford, William Rupert.
Mockridge, William Horace Montague.
Dineen, Frank.
Townley, Frank Watt.
Cameron, Arthur Russell.
Thomas, Jacque J.
Walker, James.
Jones, Alan Macdougall.
Bearman, James.
Stuart, David Worts.
Smith, Frank Edgar Wolsey.
Broad, Thomas.
Dickson, Clarence.
Glass, William D.
Robertson, Hector Harry.
Meredith, John Redmond Walsingham.
Swinford, Arthur Sidney.
Martin, E. C.
Backe, S. Pardee.
Robertson, Lee C.
Barnet, Alexander Black.
McKinnon, Neil C.
Cooey, Arthur Joseph.

THE OLD COLLEGE BELL.

1891.

Snyder, Alfred Hartman.
Fairchild, H. R.
Routh, Albert.
Kerr, William Allan.
Ridout, Walter.
Brown, William Henry
Lennox, Richard Allan.
Braithwaite, Robert William.
Alma, William Edward Lee.
Laing, John M.
Wood, Arthur Robert Ogden.
Haas, Charles Otis.
McDonell, James Joseph.
Moncrieff, George Glenn.
Philbrick, Frank Spencer.
Lamb, Charles Melbourn.
Bird, Robert Oliver.
Harvey, Charles Hamilton.
Denison, Edgar Street.
Denison, Walter Walbridge.
Wright, David Ernest.
Flack, Albert W. J.
MacKenzie, Harold.
MacDougall, Glenholm.
Hoskin, Wm. Arthur Gordon.
Jackes, Horace.
Darrell, Chapman Hill.
Rodgers, Robert.
Whitney, Garnet Milford.
Ross, George William.
Rayside, David John.
Ryerson, Edward Stanley.
Cooper, Hugh Gamble.
Croft, John.
Gooderham, James Horace.
Gooderham, Henry Folwell.
Stevenson, James Corliss.
Page, Charles Alexander.
Noble, Ernest Annesley.
Tiffany, George Sistcoster.
Bradford, Edward Elliot.
Reid, Frank Aspinall.
Hett, Sibbald.
Hett, Francis Paget.
Falconer, James Roderick.
Steele, Walter Dickson.
Steele, Robert Clarke.
Wilson, Norman Frank.
Lash, Zebulon, G.
Hees, Harris Lincoln.
Leslie, E. V.

Lumbers, Walter Glen.
Furness, Clarence Sydenham.
Meighn, William Arthur
McCracken, Thomas Ernest.
Dixon, Frank Irving.
Kelso, Henry Frederick Charles
Corson, William D.
Bradburn, Charles Herbert.
Mallock, Stuart.
Caldwell, James Boyd.
Frankland, Arthur Hope.
Lauder, William John.
Leslie, Ernest J.
Crerar, Thomas Halford.
Gilmour, R.
McKay, Gifford Brown.
Draper, Selby.
Winch, Herbert A.
Heintzman, Adolph U. A.
Burden, Edgar Livingston.
Spink, Wilbur Lewis.
Wood, Lewis Percival.
Smith, Elmer Harvey.
Moss, Glenholme Falconbridge
Caldwell, Boyd Alexander Cunningham.
Brown, Horiotto Gordon.
Wells, John Alfred.
Turner, Robert F.
Spink, Debir Major.
Boon, Charles Amiel.
Hayne, George Osborne.
Moore, William Addison.
Moore, John Carlyle.
Atkinson, Edmund Percy.
Bricker, Albert Edward.
McMillan, George Paton.
Bunting, John.
Haskell, Charles Thomson.
Richardson, Norman McDougall.
Kay, William S.
McMaster, Alexander.
Chewett, Albert Ramsey.
Cawthra, John Joseph.
Armstrong, Fred. Alvin.
Boultbee, Percy Roxburgh.
Doherty, Manning W.
Selby, Benjamin F.
Burnside, Anson Jones.
Carruthers, John Calvert
McKinlay, Archibald Thayer.
McKinlay, Fred. Reid.

McKinlay, William Waldemar.
Kerswell, William Leopold.
Stonge, Harry Elmer.
Barrick, James Sidney.
Macdonnell, Logie Milnes.
Cossitt, Leonard R.
Montizambert, Norman Hamilton.
Badgerow, F.
Darrell, Nathan. B.
Jackson, Mannsell Bowers.
Phillips, Heber John Bacon.
McCallum, Duncan George.
Hayne, F. C.
Orr, George.
Piper, Arthur G.
Thomson, James.
Jones, Ralph Egerton.
Gillespie, George Edward.
Gillespie, Albert Courtney.
Hyman, Walton John.
Nisbet, Walter Alexander.
Blackstock, William Gooderham.
Burnside, John Thrift.
Hutchins, John Willard.
Lauder, Andrew.
Robb, Charles Carmichael.
Hammell, Frederick Stratford.
James, Alfred Sidney.
McKibbon, Walter E.
McKibbon, Robert Arthur.
Hewitson, John Sproat.
Hutchison, Henry Seaton.
Hudson, Harry Lyn.
Dill, Albert James.
Christie, James McAdam.
Tassie, William Olive.
Roche, Thomas Joseph.
Watkins, Reginald.
Sproat, Alexander Douglas.
McCallum, Duncan Alexander.
Tyner, Ernest Lawrence.
Ivey, Arnold Muchmore.
Rogers, Alfred Selby.
McNabb, Frederick G. G.
Clark, William Charles.
King, John William DeCourcy.
Beers, Philip Grover MacLean.
Weir, Edmund George.
Greig, W. C.

APPENDIX IV.
UPPER CANADA COLLEGE REPORT.

PART II.—ON THE AFFAIRS OF UPPER CANADA COLLEGE.

Upper Canada College, or the Royal Grammar School, was founded in the year 1829, by an order of the Provincial Government, vesting the government of the institution in a Board of Managers, designated the President, Directors and Trustees of Upper Canada College.

The endowment bestowed upon this institution consisted of the following lands, viz. :—

1st. Block A, known as Russell square, and containing nine acres, constituting the present site and grounds of the College,

2nd.	20,000	acres of land, granted	Dec. 16, 1832.
3rd.	1,080	do	do	July 4, 1834.
4th.	42,188	do	do	May 16, 1835.
	63,268 acres.			

5th. Part of Block D, Town of York, (now City of Toronto,) east of Church street and north of Newgate street, containing 5¼ acres, divided into Town-lots, 28th November, 1834.

The above total of 63,268 acres has, by exchanges of lands and resurveys, been increased to 63,994½ acres. These lands were situate in various parts of Upper Canada ; in some townships the quantity appears to have been large.

The grant of 20,000 acres, in 1832, consisted of lands situate in three townships, as follows :—

In Mossa	3,046 acres.
Ekfrid	12,501 do
Seymour	4,453 do
Total,	20,000 do

The grant of 1,080 acres, in 1834, was all in the township of York.

THE U. C. C. REPORT.

The grant of 42,188 acres, comprised the lands situate as follows :—

In Hawkesbury	600 acres.
Mountain	700 do
Wolford	965 do
Bastard	1,600 do
Thurlow	776 do
Ameliasburgh, (Huff's Island)	900 do
Seymour	17,358 do
York	558 do
Walsingham	2,000 do
Windham	600 do
Blenheim	700 do
Zorra	868 do
Carradoc	2,840 do
Woodhouse	539 do
Blandford	5,340 do
	36,340 acres.

The remaining portion of this grant, say 5,844 acres, was distributed over the following townships, in quantities varying from 400 to 100 acres in each, viz :—

Cambridge,	Leeds,	Cramahe,	Beverley,
Cornwall,	Yonge,	Markham,	Nelson,
Edwardsburgh,	Wolfe Island,	Gwillimsbury, E.	Townsend,
South Gower,	Hamilton,	Reach,	Oxford, N.
Oxford, E.	Haldimand,	Scarborough,	Dorchester,
Montague,	Murray,	Toronto,	Tilbury, E.

The lands were generally in a wild or unoccupied state ; some, however, were under cultivation, having been either leased by the Crown or sold prior to being granted to the College.

[Extract from the "Final Report of Commissioners of Enquiry into the affairs of King's College and Upper Canada College. Printed by order of the Legislative Assembly, 1852."]

www.ingramcontent.com/pod-product-compliance
Lightning Source LLC
Chambersburg PA
CBHW020258240426
43673CB00039B/637